Paul Clifford

T

FRONTISPIECE.

Paul Clifford

BY

THE RIGHT HON. LORD LYTTON

[Vol. 22]

"Many of your lordships must recollect what used to take place on the high
roads in the neighbourhood of this metropolis some years ago. Scarcely a
carriage could pass without being robbed; and frequently the passengers
were obliged to fight with, and give battle to, the highwaymen who infested
the roads."—DUKE OF WELLINGTON'S SPEECH ON THE METROPOLIS POLICE
BILL, *June 5th.* MIRROR OF PARLIAMENT, 1829, p. 2050.

"Can any man doubt whether it is better to be a great statesman or a
common thief?"—JONATHAN WILD.

LONDON
GEORGE ROUTLEDGE AND SONS
BROADWAY, LUDGATE HILL
GLASGOW AND NEW YORK

1887

THE POCKET VOLUME EDITION

OF

LORD LYTTON'S NOVELS

ISSUED IN MONTHLY VOLUMES

Styles of Binding.

A Paper Cover, Cut Edges.
B ,, ,, Uncut Edges.
C Cloth Cover, Cut Edges.
D ,, ,, Uncut Edges
E Half-bound, Gilt Tops. Cut Edges
F ,. ,, ,, Uncut Edges.

TO

ALBANY FONBLANQUE,

WHOSE ACUTENESS OF WIT IS ACKNOWLEDGED BY THOSE WHO

OPPOSE HIS OPINIONS,—

WHOSE INTEGRITY OF PURPOSE IS YET MORE RESPECTED BY

THOSE WHO APPRECIATE HIS FRIENDSHIP,—

This. Work

IS INSCRIBED.

JULY, 1840.

PREFACE

TO THE EDITION OF 1840.

————◇————

THIS Novel so far differs from the other fictions by the same author, that it seeks to draw its interest rather from practical than ideal sources. Out of some twelve Novels or Romances, embracing, however inadequately, a great variety of scene and character,—from "Pelham" to the "Pilgrims of the Rhine"—from "Rienzi" to the "Last Days of Pompeii"—"Paul Clifford" is the *only one* in which a robber has been made the hero. or the peculiar phases of life which he illustrates have been brought into any prominent description.

Without pausing to inquire what realm of manners, or what order of crime and sorrow are open to art, and capable of administering to the proper ends of fiction, I may be permitted to observe, that the present subject was selected, and the Novel written, with a twofold object :

First to draw attention to two errors in our penal institutions, viz., a vicious Prison-discipline, and a sanguinary Criminal Code,—the habit of corrupting the boy by the very punishment that ought to redeem him, and then hanging the man, at the first occasion, as the easiest way of getting rid of our own blunders. Between the example of crime which the tyro learns from the felons in the prison-yard, and the horrible levity with which the mob gather round the drop at Newgate, there is a connection which a writer may be pardoned for quitting loftier regions of imagination to trace and to detect. So far this book is less a picture of the king's highway than the law's royal road to the gallows,—a satire on the short cut established between the House of Correction and the Condemned Cell. A second and a lighter object in the novel of " Paul Clifford " (and hence the introduction of a semi-burlesque or travesty in the earlier chapters), was to show that there is nothing essentially different between vulgar vice and fashionable vice,—and that the slang of the one circle is but an easy paraphrase of the cant of the other.

The Supplementary Essays, entitled " Tomlinsoniana," which contain the corollaries to various problems suggested in the Novel, have been restored to the present edition.

CLIFTON,
July 25th, 1840.

PREFACE

TO THE PRESENT EDITION, 1848.

———◇———

MOST men, who, with some earnestness of mind, examine into the mysteries of our social state—will, perhaps, pass through that stage of self-education, in which this Novel was composed. The contrast between conventional frauds, received as component parts of the great system of civilisation, and the less deceptive invasions of the laws which discriminate the *meum* from the *tuum*, is tempting to a satire that is not without its justice. The tragic truths which lie hid, in what I may call the Philosophy of Circumstance—strike through our philanthropy upon our imagination. We see masses of our fellow-creatures—the victims of circumstances over which they had no control—contaminated in infancy by the example of parents—their intelligence either extinguished or turned against them, according as the conscience is stifled in ignorance, or perverted to apologies for vice. A child who is cradled in ignominy; whose schoolmaster is the felon;—whose academy is the House of Correction;—who breathes an atmosphere in which virtue is poisoned, to which religion does not pierce—becomes less a responsible and reasoning human being than a wild beast which we suffer to range in the wilderness—till it prowls near our homes, and we kill it in self-defence.

In this respect, the Novel of "Paul Clifford" is a loud cry to society to amend the circumstance—to redeem the victim. It is an appeal from Humanity to Law. And, in this, if it could not pretend to influence or guide the temper of the times, it was at least a foresign of a coming change. Between the literature of imagination,

and the practical interests of a people, there is a harmony as complete as it is mysterious. The heart of an author is the mirror of his
age. The shadow of the sun is cast on the still surface of literature,
long before the light penetrates to law. But it is ever from the sun
that the shadow falls, and the moment we see the shadow, we may
be certain of the light.

Since this work was written, society is busy with the evils in
which it was then silently acquiescent. The true movement of the
last fifteen years has been the progress of one idea—Social Reform.
There, it advances with steady and noiseless march behind every
louder question of constitutional change. Let us do justice to our
time. There have been periods of more brilliant action on the
destinies of States—but there is no time visible in History in which
there was so earnest and general a desire to improve the condition
of the great body of the people. In every circle of the community
that healthful desire is astir; it unites in one object men of parties
the most opposed—it affords the most attractive nucleus for public
meetings—it has cleansed the statute-book from blood; it is ridding
the world of the hangman. It animates the clergy of all sects in
the remotest districts; it sets the squire on improving cottages and
parcelling out allotments. Schools rise in every village;—in books
the lightest, the Grand Idea colours the page, and bequeathes the
moral. The Government alone (despite the professions on which
the present Ministry was founded) remains unpenetrated by the
common genius of the age. But on that question, with all the
subtleties it involves, and the experiments it demands—(not indeed
according to the dreams of an insane philosophy, but according to
the immutable laws which proportion the rewards of labour to the
respect for property)—a Government must be formed at last.

There is in this work a subtler question suggested, but not solved.
That question which perplexes us in the generous ardour of our
early youth—which, unsatisfactory as all metaphysics, we rather
escape from than decide as we advance in years, viz.—make what
laws we please, the man who lives within the pale can be as bad
as the man without. Compare the Paul Clifford of the fiction with

the William Brandon ; the hunted son and the honoured father, the outcast of the law, the dispenser of the law—the felon, and the judge ; and, as at the last, they front each other, one on the seat of justice, the other at the convict's bar, who can lay his hand on his heart and say, that the Paul Clifford is a worse man than the William Brandon?

There is no immorality in a truth that enforces this question ; for it is precisely those offences which society cannot interfere with, that society requires fiction to expose. Society is right, though youth is reluctant to acknowledge it. Society can form only certain regulations necessary for its self-defence—the fewer the better—punish those who invade, leave unquestioned those who respect them. But fiction follows truth into all the strongholds of convention : strikes through the disguise, lifts the mask, bares the heart, and leaves a moral wherever it brands a falsehood.

Out of this range of ideas, the mind of the Author has, perhaps, emerged into an atmosphere which he believes to be more congenial to Art. But he can no more regret that he has passed through it, than he can regret that while he dwelt there, his heart, like his years, was young. Sympathy with the suffering that seems most actual—indignation at the frauds which seem most received as virtues—are the natural emotions of youth, if earnest : More sensible afterwards of the prerogatives, as of the elements, of Art, the Author, at least, seeks to escape where the man may not, and look on the practical world through the serener one of the ideal.

With the completion of this work closed an era in the writer's self-education. From "Pelham" to "Paul Clifford" (four fictions, all written at a very early age), the Author rather observes than imagines ; rather deals with the ordinary surface of human life, than attempts, however humbly, to soar above it or to dive beneath. From depicting in "Paul Clifford" the errors of society, it was almost the natural progress of reflexion to pass to those which swell to crime in the solitary human heart,—from the bold and open evils that spring from ignorance and example, to track those that lie coiled in the entanglements of refining knowledge and speculative pride.   Looking back at this distance of years, I can see as clearly as if mapped before me, the paths which led across the boundary of invention from " Paul Clifford " to " Eugene Aram." And, that last work done, no less clearly can I see where the first gleams from a fairer fancy broke upon my way, and rested on those more ideal images, which I sought, with a feeble hand, to transfer to the " Pilgrims of the Rhine," and the " Last Days of Pompeii." We authors, like the Children in the Fable, track our journey through the maze by the pebbles which we strew along the path. From others who wander after us, they may attract no notice, or, if noticed, seem to them but scattered by the caprice of chance. But we, when our memory would retrace our steps, review, in the humble stones, the witnesses of our progress—the landmarks of our way.

KNEBWORTH,
1848.

PAUL CLIFFORD.

CHAPTER I.

"Say, ye opprest by some fantastic woes,
Some jarring nerve that baffles your repose,
Who press the downy conch while slaves advance
With timid eye to read the distant glance;
Who with sad prayers the weary doctor tease
To name the nameless ever-new disease;
Who with mock patience dire complaints endure,
Which real pain and that alone can cure:
How would you bear in real pain to lie
Despised, neglected, left alone to die?
How would ye bear to draw your latest breath
Where all that's wretched paves the way to death?"

CRABBE.

IT was a dark and stormy night; the rain fell in torrents—except at occasional intervals, when it was checked by a violent gust of wind which swept up the streets (for it is in London that our scene lies), rattling along the house-tops, and fiercely agitating the scanty flame of the lamps that struggled against the darkness. Through one of the obscurest quarters of London, and among haunts little loved by the gentlemen of the police, a man, evidently of the lowest orders, was wending his solitary way. He stopped twice or thrice at different shops and houses of a description correspondent with the appearance of the *quartier* in which they were situated,—and tended inquiry for some article or another which did not seem easily to be met with. All the answers he received were conched in the negative; and as he turned from each door he muttered to himself, in no very elegant phraseology, his disappointment and discontent. At length, at one house, the landlord, a sturdy butcher, after rendering the same reply the inquirer had hitherto received, added,—"But if *this* vill do as vell, Dummie, it is quite at your sarvice!" Pausing reflectively for a moment, Dummie responded, that he thought the thing proffered *might* do as well; and thrusting it into his ample pocket he strode

F

away with as rapid a motion as the wind and the rain would allow.
He soon came to a nest of low and dingy buildings, at the entrance
to which, in half-effaced characters, was written "Thames Court."
Halting at the most conspicuous of these buildings, an inn or alehouse,
through the half-closed windows of which blazed out in ruddy comfort
the beams of the hospitable hearth, he knocked hastily at the door.
He was admitted by a lady of a certain age, and endowed with a
comely rotundity of face and person.

"Hast got it, Dummie?" said she quickly, as she closed the door
on the guest.

"Noa, noa! not exactly—but I thinks as ow——"

"Pish, you fool!" cried the woman, interrupting him, peevishly.
"Vy, it is no use desaving me. You knows you has only stepped
from my boosing ken to another, and you has not been arter the
book at all. So there's the poor cretur a-raving and a-dying, and
you——"

"Let I speak!" interrupted Dummie in his turn. "I tells you,
I vent first to Mother Bussblone's, who, I knows, chops the whiners
morning and evening to the young ladies, and I axes there for a
Bible, and she says, says she. 'I 'as only a "Companion to the
Halter!" but you'll get a Bible, I thinks, at Master Talkins,—
the cobbler, as preaches.' So I goes to Master Talkins, and he
says, says he, 'I 'as no call for the Bible—'cause vy?—I 'as a call
vithout: but mayhap you'll be a-getting it at the butcher's hover the
vay—cause vy?—the butcher 'll be damned!' So I goes hover the
vay, and the butcher says, says he, 'I 'as not a Bible; but I 'as a
book of plays bound for all the vorld just like 'un, and mayhap the
poor cretur mayn't see the difference.' So I takes the plays, Mrs.
Margery, and here they be surely!—And how's poor Judy?"

"Fearsome! she'll not be over the night, I'm a-thinking."

"Vell, I'll track up the dancers!"

So saying, Dummie ascended a doorless staircase, across the
entrance of which a blanket, stretched angularly from the wall to the
chimney, afforded a kind of screen; and presently he stood within
a chamber, which the dark and painful genius of Crabbe might have
delighted to portray. The walls were white-washed, and at sundry
places strange figures and grotesque characters had been traced by
some mirthful inmate, in such sable outline as the end of a smoked
stick or the edge of a piece of charcoal is wont to produce. The
wan and flickering light afforded by a farthing candle gave a sort
of grimness and menace to these achievements of pictorial art,
especially as they more than once received embellishments from
portraits of Satan, such as he is accustomed to be drawn. A low
fire burned gloomily in the sooty grate; and on the hob hissed

"the still small voice" of an iron kettle. On a round deal-table were two vials, a cracked cup, a broken spoon of some dull metal, and upon two or three mutilated chairs were scattered various articles of female attire. On another table, placed below a high, narrow, shutterless casement (athwart which, instead of a curtain, a checked apron had been loosely hung, and now waved fitfully to and fro in the gusts of wind that made easy ingress through many a chink and cranny), were a looking-glass, sundry appliances of the toilet, a box of coarse rouge, a few ornaments of more show than value ; and a watch, the regular and calm click of which produced that indescribably painful feeling which, we fear, many of our readers who have heard the sound in a sick chamber can easily recall. A large tester-bed stood opposite to this table, and the looking-glass partially reflected curtains of a faded stripe, and ever and anon (as the position of the sufferer followed the restless emotion of a disordered mind), glimpses of the face of one on whom Death was rapidly hastening. Beside this bed now stood Dummie, a small, thin man, dressed in a tattered plush jerkin, from which the rain-drops slowly dripped, and with a thin, yellow, cunning phy-siognomy, grotesquely hideous in feature but not positively villain-ous in expression. On the other side of the bed stood a little boy of about three years old, dressed as if belonging to the better classes, although the garb was somewhat tattered and discoloured The poor child trembled violently, and evidently looked with a feeling of relief on the entrance of Dummie. And now there slowly, and with many a phthisical sigh, heaved towards the foot of the bed the heavy frame of the woman who had accosted Dummie below, and had followed him, *haud passibus æquis*, to the room of the sufferer ; she stood with a bottle of medicine in her hand, shaking its contents up and down, and with a kindly yet timid compassion spread over a countenance crimsoned with habitual libations. This made the scene ; save that on a chair by the bed-side lay a profusion of long glossy golden ringlets, which had been cut from the head of the sufferer when the fever had begun to mount upwards ; but which, with a jealousy that portrayed the darling littleness of a vain heart, she had seized and insisted on retaining near her ; and save that, by the fire, perfectly inattentive to the event about to take place within the chamber, and to which we of the biped race attach so awful an importance, lay a large grey cat, curled in a ball, and dozing with half-shut eyes, and ears that now and then denoted, by a gentle inflection, the jar of a louder or nearer sound than usual upon her lethargic senses. The dying woman did not at first attend to the entrance either of Dummie or the female at the foot of the bed ; but she turned herself round towards the child, and grasping his arm fiercely, she drew him towards her, and gazed on his terrified features with a look in which exhaustion and an exceeding wanness of complexion were even horribly contrasted by the glare and energy of delirium.

"If you are like *him*," she muttered, "I will strangle you,—I will!—ay—tremble! you ought to tremble, when your mother touches you, or when *he* is mentioned. You have his eyes,—you have! Out with them, out!—the devil sits laughing in them! Oh! you weep, do you, little one! Well now, be still, my love,—be hushed! I would not harm thee! harm—O God, he *is* my child after all!"— And at these words she clasped the boy passionately to her breast, and burst into tears!

"Coom now, coom!" said Dummie, soothingly. "Take the stuff, Judith, and then ve'll talk over the hurchin!"

The mother relaxed her grasp of the boy, and turning towards the speaker, gazed at him for some moments with a bewildered stare: at length she appeared slowly to remember him, and said, as she raised herself on one hand, and pointed the other towards him with an inquiring gesture,—

"Thou hast brought the book?"

Dummie answered by lifting up the book he had brought from the honest butcher's.

"Clear the room, then!" said the sufferer, with that air of mock command so common to the insane. "We would be alone!"

Dummie winked at the good woman at the foot of the bed; and she (though generally no easy person to order or to persuade) left, without reluctance, the sick chamber.

"If she be a-going to pray!" murmured our landlady (for that office did the good matron hold), "I may indeed as well take myself off, for it's not werry comfortable like to those who be old to hear all that 'ere!"

With this pious reflection, the hostess of the Mug, so was the hostelry called, heavily descended the creaking stairs.

"Now, man!" said the sufferer, sternly: "swear that you will never reveal,—swear, I say! and by the great God, whose angels are about this night, if ever you break the oath, I will come back and haunt you to your dying day!"

Dummie's face grew pale, for he was superstitiously affected by the vehemence and the language of the dying woman, and he answered as he kissed the pretended Bible,—that he swore to keep the secret, as much as he knew of it, which, she must be sensible, he said, was very little. As he spoke, the wind swept with a loud and sudden gust down the chimney, and shook the roof above them so violently as to loosen many of the crumbling tiles, which fell one after the other, with a crashing noise, on the pavement below. Dummie started in affright ; and perhaps his conscience smote him for the trick he had played with regard to the false Bible. But the woman, whose excited and unstrung nerves led her astray from one subject to another with preternatural celerity, said, with an hysterical laugh, " See, Dummie, they come in state for me ; give me the cap —yonder ! and bring the looking-glass ! "

Dummie obeyed, and the woman, as she in a low tone uttered something about the unbecoming colour of the ribands, adjusted the cap on her head ; and then saying in a regretful and petulant voice, " Why should they have cut off my hair ?—such a disfigurement ! " bade Dummie desire Mrs. Margery once more to ascend to her.

Left alone with her child, the face of the wretched mother softened as she regarded him, and all the levities and all the vehemences,—if we may use the word,—which, in the turbulent commotion of her delirium, had been stirred upward to the surface of her mind, gradually now sunk, as death increased upon her,—and a mother's anxiety rose to the natural level from which it had been disturbed and abased. She took the child to her bosom, and clasping him in her arms, which grew weaker with every instant, she soothed him with the sort of chant which nurses sing over their untoward infants ; but her voice was cracked and hollow, and as she felt it was so, the mother's eyes filled with tears—Mrs. Margery now re-entered ; and, turning towards the hostess with an impressive calmness of manner which astonished and awed the person she addressed, the dying woman pointed to the child, and said,—

" You have been kind to me, very kind, and may God bless you for it ! I have found that those whom the world calls the worst are often the most *human*. But I am not going to thank you as I ought to do, but to ask of you a last and exceeding favour. Protect my child till he grows up : you have often said you loved him,—you are childless yourself,—and a morsel of bread and a shelter for the night, which is all I ask of you to give him, will not impoverish more legitimate claimants ! "

Poor Mrs. Margery, fairly sobbing, vowed she would be a mother to the child, and that she would endeavour to rear him honestly, though a public-house was not, she confessed, the best place for good examples !

" Take him ! " cried the mother hoarsely, as her voice, failing her strength, rattled indistinctly, and almost died within her. " Take him,—rear him as you will, as you can !—any example, any roof better than——" Here the words were inaudible. " And oh ! may it be a curse, and a——Give me the medicine, I am dying."

The hostess, alarmed, hastened to comply, but before she returned

to the bedside the sufferer was insensible,—nor did she again recover
speech or motion. A low and rare moan only testified continued
life, and within two hours that ceased, and the spirit was gone. At
that time our good hostess was herself beyond the things of this outer
world, having supported her spirits during the vigils of the night
with so many little liquid stimulants, that they finally sunk into
that torpor which generally succeeds excitement. Taking, perhaps,
advantage of the opportunity which the insensibility of the hostess
afforded him, Dummie, by the expiring ray of the candle that burnt
in the death chamber, hastily opened a huge box (which was generally
concealed under the bed, and contained the wardrobe of the deceased),
and turned with irreverent hand over the linens and the silks, until
quite at the bottom of the trunk he discovered some packets of
letters;—these he seized, and buried in the conveniences of his dress.
He then, rising and replacing the box, cast a longing eye towards
the watch on the toilet-table, which was of gold; but he withdrew
his gaze, and with a querulous sigh, observed to himself, "The old
blowen kens o' that, od rat her! but, howsomever, I'll take this;
who knows but it may be of service—*tannies* to-day may be *smash*
to-morrow!"[1] and he laid his coarse hand on the golden and silky
tresses we have described. "'Tis a rum business, and puzzles I!
but mum's the word, for my own little colquarren."[2]

With this brief soliloquy Dummie descended the stairs, and let
himself out of the house.

CHAPTER II.

"Imagination fondly stoops to trace
The parlour splendours of that festive place."
            'DESERTED VILLAGE.'

THERE is little to interest in a narrative of early childhood,
unless indeed one were writing on education. We shall
not, therefore, linger over the infancy of the motherless
boy left to the protection of Mrs. Margery Lobkins, or, as
she was sometimes familiarly called, Peggy or Piggy Lob. The
good dame, drawing a more than sufficient income from the profits
of a house, which, if situated in an obscure locality, enjoyed very
general and lucrative repute; and being a lone widow without kith
or kin, had no temptation to break her word to the deceased, and

---

[1] Meaning, what is of no value now may be precious hereafter.
[2] Colquarren—neck.

she suffered the orphan to wax in strength and understanding until the age of twelve, a period at which we are now about to reintroduce him to our readers.

The boy evinced great hardihood of temper, and no inconsiderable quickness of intellect In whatever he attempted, his success was rapid, and a remarkable strength of limb and muscle seconded well the dictates of an ambition turned, it must be confessed, rather to physical than mental exertion. It is not to be supposed, however, that his boyish life passed in unbroken tranquillity. Although Mrs. Lobkins was a good woman on the whole, and greatly attached to her *protégé*, she was violent and rude in temper, or, as she herself more flatteringly 'expressed it, "her feelings were unkimmonly strong," and alternate quarrel and reconciliation constituted the chief occupations of the *protégé's* domestic life. As, previous to his becoming the ward of Mrs. Lobkins, he had never received any other appellation than "the child," so, the duty of christening him devolved upon our hostess of the Mug ; and, after some deliberation, she blessed him with the name of Paul—it was a name of happy omen, for it had belonged to Mrs. Lobkins' grandfather, who had been three times transported, and twice hanged (at the first occurrence of the latter description, he had been restored by the surgeons, much to the chagrin of a young anatomist who was to have had the honour of cutting him up). The boy did not seem likely to merit the distinguished appellation he bore, for he testified no remarkable predisposition to the property of other people. Nay, although he sometimes emptied the pockets of any stray visitor to the coffee-room of Mrs. Lobkins, it appeared an act originating rather in a love of the frolic, than a desire of the profit ; for after the plundered person had been sufficiently tormented by the loss, haply of such utilities as a tobacco-box, or a handkerchief ; after he had, to the secret delight of Paul, searched every corner of the apartment, stamped, and fretted, and exposed himself by his petulance to the bitter objurgation of Mrs. Lobkins, our young friend would quietly and suddenly contrive, that the article missed should return of its own accord to the pocket from which it had disappeared. And thus, as our readers have doubtless experienced, when they have disturbed the peace of a whole household for the loss of some portable treasure which they themselves are afterwards discovered to have mislaid, the unfortunate victim of Paul's honest ingenuity, exposed to the collected indignation of the spectators, and sinking from the accuser into the convicted, secretly cursed the unhappy lot which not only vexed him with the loss of his property, but made it still more annoying to recover it.

Whether it was that, on discovering these pranks, Mrs. Lobkins

trembled for the future bias of the address they displayed, or
whether she thought that the folly of thieving without gain required
speedy and permanent correction, we cannot decide ; but the good
lady became at last extremely anxious to secure for Paul the blessings of a liberal education.   The key of knowledge (the art of
reading) she had, indeed, two years prior to the present date,
obtained for him, but this far from satisfied her conscience : nay,
she felt that, if she could not also obtain for him the discretion to
use it, it would have been wise even to have withheld a key, which
the boy seemed perversely to apply to all locks but the right one.
In a word, she was desirous that he should receive an education far
superior to those whom he saw around him.   And attributing, like
most ignorant persons, too great advantages to learning, she conceived that, in order to live as decorously as the parson of the
parish, it was only necessary to know as much Latin.

One evening in particular, as the dame sat by her cheerful fire,
this source of anxiety was unusually active in her mind, and ever
and anon she directed unquiet and restless glances towards Paul,
who sat on a form at the opposite corner of the hearth, diligently
employed in reading the life and adventures of the celebrated Richard
Turpin.   The form on which the boy sat was worn to a glassy
smoothness, save only in certain places, where some ingenious idler
or another had amused himself by carving sundry names, epithets, and
epigrammatic niceties of language.   It is said, that the organ of
carving upon wood is prominently developed on all English skulls :
and the sagacious Mr. Combe has placed this organ at the back of
the head, in juxtaposition to that of destructiveness, which is equally
large among our countrymen, as is notably evinced upon all railings,
seats, temples, and other things—belonging to other people.

Opposite to the fire-place was a large deal table, at which
Dummie, surnamed Dunnaker, seated near the dame, was quietly
ruminating over a glass of hollands and water.   Farther on, at
another table in the corner of the room, a gentleman with a red wig,
very rusty garments, and linen which seemed as if it had been boiled
in saffron, smoked his pipe, apart, silent, and apparently plunged in
meditation.   This gentleman was no other than Mr. Peter Mac
Grawler, the editor of a magnificent periodical, entitled "The
Asinæum," which was written to prove, that whatever is popular is
necessarily bad,—a valuable and recondite truth, which "The
Asinæum" had satisfactorily demonstrated by ruining three printers
and demolishing a publisher.   We need not add, that Mr. Mac
Grawler was Scotch by birth, since we believe it is pretty well
known that *all* periodicals of this country have, from time imme-
morial, been monopolised by the gentlemen of the land of Cakes : we

know not how it may be the fashion to eat the said cakes in Scotland, but *here* the good emigratois seem to like them carefully butteied on both sides. By the side of the editor stood a laige pewter tankaid, above him hung an engraving of the "wonderfully fat boar, foimeily in the possession of Mr. Fattem, giazier." To his left rose the dingy form of a thin, upright clock in an oaken case ; beyond the clock, a spit and a musket were fastened in parallels to the wall. Below those twin emblems of war and cookery were four shelves, containing plates of pewtei and delf, and teiminating, centaur-like, in a soit of dresser. At the other side of these domestic con- veniences was a pictuie of Mrs. Lobkins, in a scarlet body, and a hat and plume. At the back of the fair hostess stietched the blanket we have befoie mentioned. As a relief to the monotonous surface of this simple scieen, various ballads and learned legends were pinned to the blanket. There might you read in verses, pathetic and unadorned, how,

> "Sally loved a sailor lad
> As fought with famous Shovel !"

There might you learn, if of two facts so instructive you were before unconscious, that

> "Ben the toper loved his bottle—
> Charley only loved the lasses !"

When of these, and various other poetical effusions, you were somewhat wearied, the literaiy fragments, in humbler prose, afforded you equal edification and delight. Theie might you fully enlighten yourself as to the "Strange and Wonderful News from Kensington, being a most full and tiue Relation how a Maid there is supposed to have been carried away by an Evil Spiiit, on Wednesday, 15th of April last, about Midnight." There too, no less interesting and no less veiacious, was that uncommon anecdote, touching the chief of many-throned powers, entitled "The Divell of Mascon ; or the true Relation of the Chief Things which an Unclean Spirit did and said at Mascon, in Buigundy, in the house of one Mr. Francis Peieaud : now made English by one that hath a Paiticular Know- ledge of the Truth of the Story."

Nor were these materials for Satanic histoiy the only prosaic and faithful chionicles which the bibliothecal blanket afforded : equally wonderful, and equally indisputable, was the account of "a young lady, the daughter of a duke, with three legs, and the face of a porcupine." Nor less so, "The Awful Judgment of God upon Sweareis, as exemplified in the case of John Stiles, who Diopped down Dead after sweaiing a Great Oath, and on stripping the unhappy man they found 'Swear not at all' written on the tail of his shirt!"

Twice had Mrs. Lobkins heaved a long sigh, as her eyes turned from Paul to the tranquil countenance of Dummie Dunnaker, and now, re-settling herself in her chair, as a motherly anxiety gathered over her visage,—

"Paul, my ben cull," said she, "what gibberish hast got there?"

"Turpin, *the great* highwayman!" answered the young student, without lifting his eyes from the page, through which he was spelling his instructive way.

"Oh! he be's a chip of the right block, dame!" said Mr. Dunnaker, as he applied his pipe to an illumined piece of paper. "He'll ride a oss foaled by a hacorn yet, I varrants!"

To this prophecy the dame replied only with a look of indignation, and rocking herself to and fro in her huge chair, she remained for some moments in silent thought. At last she again wistfully eyed the hopeful boy, and calling him to her side, communicated some order, in a dejected whisper. Paul, on receiving it, disappeared behind the blanket, and presently returned with a bottle and a wineglass. With an abstracted gesture, and an air that betokened continued meditation, the good dame took the inspiring cordial from the hand of her youthful cupbearer,

> "And ere a man had power to say 'Behold!'
> The jaws of Lobkins had devoured it up.
> So quick bright things come to confusion!"

The nectarean beverage seemed to operate cheerily on the matron's system; and placing her hand on the boy's curly head, she said, (like Andromache, *dakruon gelasasa*, or, as Scott hath it, "With a smile in her cheek, but a tear in her eye;")—

"Paul, thy heart be good!—thy heart be good!—Thou didst not spill a drop of the *tape!* Tell me, my honey, why didst thou lick Tom Tobyson?"

"Because," answered Paul, "he said as how you ought to have been hanged long ago!"

"Tom Tobyson is a good-for-nought," returned the dame, "and *deserves to shove the tumbler;*[1] but, oh my child! be not too venturesome in taking up the sticks for a blowen. It has been the ruin of many a man afore you, and when two men goes to quarrel for a 'oman, they doesn't know the natur of the thing they quarrels about;—mind thy latter end, Paul, and reverence the old, without axing what they has been before they passed into the wale of years;

[1] Be whipped at the cart's tail.

—thou may'st get me my pipe, Paul,—it is up-stairs, under the pillow."

While Paul was accomplishing this errand, the lady of the Mug, fixing her eyes upon Mr. Dunnaker, said, "Dummie, Dummie, if little Paul should come to be scragged !"

"Whish !" muttered Dummie, glancing over his shoulder at Mac Grawler,—"mayhap that gemman,"—here his voice became scarcely audible even to Mrs. Lobkins ; but his whisper seemed to imply an insinuation, that the illustrious editor of "The Asinæum" might be either an informer, or one of those heroes on whom an informer subsists.

Mrs. Lobkins' answer, couched in the same key, appeared to satisfy Dunnaker, for, with a look of great comtempt, he chucked up his head, and said, "Oho ! that be all, be it !"

Paul here reappeared with the pipe, and the dame, having filled the tube, leaned forward, and lighted the Virginian weed from the *blower* of Mr. Dunnaker. As in this interesting occupation the heads of the hostess and the guest approached each other, the glowing light playing cheerily on the countenance of each, there was an honest simplicity in the picture that would have merited the racy and vigorous genius of a Cruikshank. As soon as the Promethean spark had been fully communicated to the lady's tube, Mrs. Lobkins, still possessed by the gloomy idea she had conjured up, repeated,—

"Ah, Dummie, if little Paul should be scragged!" Dummie, withdrawing the pipe from his mouth, heaved a sympathising puff, but remained silent ; and Mrs. Lobkins, turning to Paul, who stood with mouth open and ears erect at this boding ejaculation, said,—

"Dost think, Paul, they'd have the heart to hang thee?"

"I think they'd have the rope, dame !" returned the youth.

"But you need not go for to run your neck into the noose !" said the matron ; and then, inspired by the spirit of moralising, she turned round to the youth, and gazing upon his attentive countenance, accosted him with the following admonitions :—

"Mind thy kittyclism, child, and reverence old age. Never steal, 'specially when any one be in the way. Never go snacks with them as be older than you,—'cause why ? the older a cove be, the more he cares for his self, and the less for his partner. At twenty, we diddles the public ; at forty, we diddles our cronies ! Be modest, Paul, and stick to your sitivation in life. Go not with fine tobymen, who burn out like a candle wot has a thief in it,—all flare and gone in a whiffy ! Leave liquor to the aged, who can't do without it. *Tape* often proves a halter, and there be's no ruin like blue ruin ! Read your Bible, and talk like a pious 'un. People goes more by your words than your actions. If you wants what is not your own, try and do without it ; and if you cannot do without it, take it away by insinivation, not bluster. They as swindles, does more and risks less than they as robs ; and if you cheats toppingly, you may laugh at the topping cheat.[1] And now go play."

Paul seized his hat, but lingered ; and the dame guessing at the signification of the pause, drew forth, and placed in the boy's hand the sum of five halfpence and one farthing. "There, boy," quoth she, and she stroked his head fondly when she spoke ; "you does right not to play for nothing, it's loss of time ! but play with those as be less than yoursel', and then you can go for to beat 'em if they says you go for to cheat !"

Paul vanished ; and the dame, laying her hand on Dummie's shoulder, said,—

" There be nothing like a friend in need, Dummie ; and somehow or other, I thinks as how you knows more of the horrigin of that 'ere lad than any of us ! "

" Me, dame ! " exclaimed Dummie, with a broad gaze of astonishment.

" Ah, you ! you knows as how the mother saw more of you just afore she died, than she did of 'ere one of us. Noar, now—noar, now ! tell us all about 'un. Did she steal 'un, think ye ! "

" Lauk, mother Margery ! dost think I knows ? Vot put such a crotchet in your 'ead ? "

" Well ! " said the dame with a disappointed sigh, " I always thought as how you were more knowing about it than you owns. Dear, dear, I shall never forgit the night when Judith brought the poor cretur here,—you knows she had been some months in my house afore ever I see'd the urchin, and when she brought it, she looked so pale and ghostly, that I had not the heart to say a word, so I stared at the brat, and it stretched out its wee little hands to me. And the mother frowned at it, and throwed it into my lap ! "

" Ah ! she was a hawful voman, that 'ere ! " said Dummie, shaking his head. " But howsomever, the hurchin fell into good 'ands ; for I be's sure you 'as been a better mother to 'un than the raal 'un ! "

" I was always a fool about childer," rejoined Mrs. Lobkins ; "and I thinks as how little Paul was sent to be a comfort to my latter end !—fill the glass, Dummie."

" I 'as heard as 'ow Judith was once blowen to a great lord ! " said Dummie.

" Like enough ! " returned Mrs. Lobkins—" like enough ! She

_____
[1] Gallows.

was always a favourite of mine, for she had a spuret (spirit) as big as my own ; and she paid her rint like a decent body, for all she was out of her sinses, or nation like it."

"Ay, I *knows* as how you liked her,—'cause vy?—'tis not your vay, to let a room to a voman ! You says as how 'tis not respectable, and you only likes *men* to visit the Mug ! "

"And I doesn't like all of them as comes here ! " answered the dame : " 'specially for Paul's sake ; but what can a lone 'oman do ? Many's the gentleman highwayman wot comes here, whose money is as good as the clerk's of the parish. And when a bob[1] is in my hand, what does it sinnify whose hand it was in afore ? "

"That's what I call being sinsible and *practical*," said Dummie, approvingly. "And arter all, though you 'as a mixture like, I does not know a halehouse where a cove is better entertained, nor meets of a Sunday more illegant company, than the Mug ! "

Here the conversation, which the reader must know had been sustained in a key inaudible to a third person, received a check from Mr. Peter Mac Grawler, who, having finished his revenie and his tankard, now rose to depart. First, however, approaching Mrs. Lobkins, he observed that he had gone on credit for some days, and demanded the amount of his bill. Glancing towards certain chalk hieroglyphics inscribed on the wall at the other side of the fireplace, the dame answered, that Mr. Mac Grawler was indebted to her for the sum of one shilling and ninepence three farthings.

After a short preparatory search in his waistcoat pockets, the critic hunted into one corner a solitary half crown, and having caught it between his finger and thumb, he gave it to Mrs. Lobkins, and requested change.

As soon as the matron felt her hand anointed with what has been called by some ingenious Johnson of St. Giles's "the oil of palms," her countenance softened into a complacent smile ; and when she gave the required change to Mr. Mac Grawler, she graciously hoped as how he would recommend the Mug to the public.

"That you may be sure of," said the editor of "The Asinæum." "There is not a place where I am so much at home."

With that the learned Scotsman buttoned his coat and went his way.

"How spiteful the world be ! " said Mrs. Lobkins after a pause, "'specially if a 'oman keeps a fashionable sort of a public ! When Judith died, Joe, the dog's-meat man, said I war all the better for it, and that she left I a treasure to bring up the urchin. One would think a thumper makes a man richer,—'cause why?—every man

---

[1] Shilling

thumps! I got nothing more than a watch and ten guineas when Judy died, and sure that scarce paid for the burrel (burial)."

"You forgits the two *quids*[1] I giv' you for the hold box of rags,— much of a treasure I found there!" said Dummie, with sycophantic archness.

"Ay," cried the dame, laughing, "I fancies you war not pleased with the bargain I thought you war too old a rag-merchant to be so free with the blunt : howsomever, I suppose it war the tinsel petticoat as took you in!"

"As it has mony a viser man than the like of I," rejoined Dummie, who to his various secret professions added the ostensible one of a rag-merchant and dealer in broken glass.

The recollection of her good bargain in the box of rags opened our landlady's heart.

"Drink, Dummie," said she, good-humouredly,—"drink, I scorns to score lush to a friend."

Dummie expressed his gratitude, refilled his glass, and the hospitable matron knocking out from her pipe the dying ashes, thus proceeded :—

"You sees, Dummie, though I often beats the boy, I loves him, as much as if I war his raal mother—I wants to make him an honour to his country and an ixciption to my family!"

"Who all flashed their ivories at Surgeon's Hall!" added the metaphorical Dummie.

"True!" said the lady,—"they died game, and I ben't ashamed of 'em. But I owes a duty to Paul's mother, and I wants Paul to have a long life. I would send him to school, but you knows as how the boys only corrupt one another. And so, I should like to meet with some decent man as a tutor, to teach the lad Latin and vartue!"

"My eyes!" cried Dummie, aghast at the grandeur of this desire.

"The boy is 'cute enough, and he loves reading," continued the dame. "But I does not think the books he gets hold of will teach him the way to grow old."

"And 'ow came he to read anyhows?"

"Ranting Rob, the strolling player, taught him his letters, and said he'd a deal of janius!"

"And why should not Ranting Rob tache the boy Latin and vartue?"

"'Cause Ranting Rob, poor fellow, *was lagged for doing a panny!*"[2] answered the dame, despondently.

---

[1] Guineas.   [2] Transported for burglary.

There was a long silence: it was broken by Mr. Dummie: slapping his thigh with the gesticulatory vehemence of an Ugo Foscolo, that gentleman exclaimed,—

"*I* 'as it—I 'as thought of a tutor for leetle Paul!"

"Who's that?—you quite frightens me; you 'as no marcy on my narves," said the dame, fretfully.

"Vy it be the gemman vot writes," said Dummie, putting his finger to his nose,—"the gemman vot payed you so flashly!"

"What! the Scotch gemman?"

"The werry same!" returned Dummie.

The dame turned in her chair, and refilled her pipe. It was evident from her manner that Mr. Dunnaker's suggestion had made an impression on her. But she recognised two doubts as to its feasibility: one, whether the gentleman proposed would be adequate to the task; the other, whether he would be willing to undertake it.

In the midst of her meditations on this matter, the dame was interrupted by the entrance of certain claimants on her hospitality; and Dummie soon after taking his leave, the suspense of Mrs. Lobkins' mind touching the education of little Paul remained the whole of that day and night utterly unrelieved.

CHAPTER III.

" I own that I am envious of the pleasure you will have in finding yourself more learned than other boys—even those who are older than yourself! What honour this will do you! What distinctions, what applauses will follow wherever you go!"—LORD CHESTERFIELD'S 'Letters to his Son.'

" Example, my boy—example is worth a thousand precepts."
MAXIMILIAN SOLEMN

TARPEIA was crushed beneath the weight of ornaments! The language of the vulgar is a sort of Tarpeia! We have therefore relieved it of as many gems as we were able; and, in the foregoing scene, presented it to the gaze of our readers, *simplex munditiis*. Nevertheless, we could timidly imagine some gentler beings of the softer sex rather displeased with the tone of the dialogue we have given, did we not recollect how delighted they are with the provincial barbarities of the sister kingdom, whenever they meet them poured over the pages of some Scottish story-teller. As, unhappily for mankind, broad Scotch is not *yet* the universal language of Europe, we suppose our countrywomen will not be much more unacquainted with the dialect of their own lower orders, than with that which breathes nasal melodies over the paradise of the North.

It was the next day, at the hour of twilight, when Mrs. Margery Lobkins, after a satisfactory *tête-a-tête* with Mr. Mac Grawler, had the happiness of thinking that she had provided a tutor for little Paul. The critic, having recited to her a considerable portion of *Propria quæ Maribus*, the good lady had no longer a doubt of his capacities for teaching ; and, on the other hand, when Mrs Lobkins entered on the subject of remuneration, the Scotsman professed himself perfectly willing to teach any and everything that the most exacting guardian could require. It was finally settled that Paul should attend Mr. Mac Grawler two hours a-day ; that Mr. Mac Grawler should be entitled to such animal comforts of meat and drink, as the Mug afforded ; and, moreover, to the weekly stipend of two shillings and sixpence, the shillings for instruction in the classics, and the sixpence for all other humanities ; or, as Mrs. Lobkins expressed it, "two bobs for the Latin, and a sice for the vartue !"

Let not thy mind, gentle reader, censure us for a deviation from probability, in making so excellent and learned a gentleman as Mr. Peter Mac Grawler the familiar guest of the lady of the Mug. First, thou must know that our story is cast in a period antecedent to the present, and one in which the old jokes against the circumstances of author and of critic had their foundation in truth ; secondly, thou must know, that by some curious concatenation of circumstances, neither bailiff nor bailiff's man was ever seen within the four walls continent of Mrs. Margery Lobkins ; thirdly, the Mug was nearer than any other house of public resort to the abode of the critic ; fourthly, it afforded excellent porter ; and fifthly,—O reader, thou dost Mrs. Margery Lobkins a grievous wrong, if thou supposest that her door was only open to those mercurial gentry who are afflicted with the morbid curiosity to pry into the mysteries of their neighbours' pockets :—other visitors of fair repute were not unoften partakers of the good matron's hospitality ; although it must be owned that they generally occupied *the* private room in preference to the public one. And sixthly, sweet reader (we grieve to be so prolix), we would just hint to thee, that Mr. Mac Grawler was one of those vast-minded sages who, occupied in contemplating morals in the great scale, do not fritter down their intellects by a base attention to minute details. So that, if a descendant of Langfanger did sometimes cross the venerable Scot in his visit to the Mug, the apparition did not revolt that benevolent moralist so much as, were it not for the above hint, thy ignorance might lead thee to imagine.

It is said, that Athenodorus the Stoic contributed greatly by his conversation to amend the faults of Augustus, and to effect the change visible in that fortunate man, after his accession to the Roman empire. If this be true, it may throw a new light on the character of Augustus, and, instead of being the hypocrite, he was possibly the convert. Certain it is, that there are few vices which cannot be conquered by wisdom : and yet, melancholy to relate, the instructions of Peter Mac Grawler produced but slender amelioration in the habits of the youthful Paul. That ingenious stripling had, we have already seen, under the tuition of Ranting Rob mastered the art of reading ; nay, he could even construct and link together certain curious pot-hooks, which himself and Mrs. Lobkins were wont graciously to term "writing." So far, then, the way of Mac Grawler was smoothed and prepared.

But, unhappily, all experienced teachers allow that the main difficulty is not to learn, but to unlearn ; and the mind of Paul was already occupied by a vast number of heterogeneous miscellanies, which stoutly resisted the ingress either of Latin or of virtue. Nothing could wean him from an ominous affection for the history of Richard Turpin : it was to him what, it has been said, the Greek authors should be to the Academician,—a study by day, and a dream by night. He was docile enough during lessons, and sometimes even too quick in conception for the stately march of Mr. Mac Grawler's intellect. But it not unfrequently happened that when that gentleman attempted to rise, he found himself, like the lady in Comus, adhering to—

> "A venomed seat
> Smeared with gums of glutinous heat ;"

or his legs had been secretly united under the table, and the tie was not to be broken without overthrow to the superior powers ; these, and various other little sportive machinations wherewith Paul was wont to relieve the monotony of literature, went far to disgust the learned critic with his undertaking. But "the tape" and the treasury of Mrs. Lobkins re-smoothed, as it were, the irritated bristles of his mind, and he continued his labours with this philosophical reflection :—"Why fret myself?—if a pupil turn out well, it is clearly to the credit of his master ; if not, to the disadvantage of himself." Of course, a similar suggestion never forced itself into the mind of Dr. Keate.[1] At Eton, the very soul of the honest head-master is consumed by his zeal for the welfare of little gentlemen in stiff cravats.

But to Paul, who was predestined to enjoy a certain quantum of

---

[1] A celebrated Principal of Eton.

knowledge, circumstances happened, in the commencement of the second year of his pupilage, which prodigiously accelerated the progress of his scholastic career.

At the apartment of Mac Grawler, Paul one morning encountered Mr. Augustus Tomlinson, a young man of great promise, who pursued the peaceful occupation of chronicling in a leading newspaper, "Horrid Murders," "Enormous Melons," and "Remarkable Circumstances." This gentleman, having the advantage of some years' seniority over Paul, was slow in unbending his dignity; but observing at last the eager and respectful attention with which the stripling listened to a most veracious detail of five men being inhumanly murdered in Canterbury Cathedral by the Reverend Zedekiah Fooks Barnacle, he was touched by the impression he had created, and shaking Paul graciously by the hand, he told him there was a deal of natural shrewdness in his countenance; and that Mr. Augustus Tomlinson did not doubt but that he (Paul) might have the honour to be murdered himself one of these days, —"You understand me!" continued Mr. Augustus,—"I mean murdered in effigy,—assassinated in type,—while you yourself, unconscious of the circumstance, are quietly enjoying what you imagine to be your existence. We never kill common persons: to say truth, our chief spite is against the Church;—we destroy bishops by wholesale. Sometimes, indeed, we knock off a leading barrister or so; and express the anguish of the junior counsel at a loss so destructive to their interests. But that is only a stray hit; and the slain barrister often lives to become attorney-general, renounce whig principles, and prosecute the very press that destroyed him Bishops are our *proper* food: we send them to heaven on a sort of flying griffin, of which the back is an apoplexy, and the wings are puffs. The Bishop of ——, whom we despatched in this manner the other day, being rather a facetious personage, wrote to remonstrate with us thereon; observing, that though heaven was a very good translation for a bishop, yet that, in such cases, he preferred 'the original to the translation.' As we murder bishops, so is there another class of persons whom we only afflict with lethiferous diseases. This latter tribe consists of his Majesty and his Majesty's ministers. Whenever we cannot abuse their measures, we always fall foul on their health. Does the king pass any popular law,— we immediately insinuate that his constitution is on its last legs. Does the minister act like a man of sense,—we instantly observe, with great regret, that his complexion is remarkably pale. There is one manifest advantage in *diseasing* people, instead of absolutely destroying them. The public may flatly contradict us in one case, but it never can in the other:—it is easy to prove that a man is alive: but utterly impossible to prove that he is in health. What if some opposing newspaper take up the cudgels in his behalf, and assert that the victim of all Pandora's complaints, whom we send tottering to the grave, passes one half the day in knocking up a 'distinguished company' at a shooting-party, and the other half in outdoing the same 'distinguished company' after dinner? What if the afflicted individual himself write us word that he never was better in his life?—we have only mysteriously to shake our heads and observe, that to contradict is not to prove,—that it is little likely that our authority should have been mistaken, and—(we are very fond of an historical comparison)—beg our readers to remember, that when Cardinal Richelieu was dying, nothing enraged him so much as hinting that he was ill. In short, if Horace is right, we are the very princes of poets; for I dare say, Mr. Mac Grawler, that you,—and you, too, my little gentleman, perfectly remember the words of the wise old Roman,—

> 'Ille per extentum funem mihi posse videtur
> Ire poeta, meum qui pectus inaniter angit,
> Irritat, mulcet, falsis terroribus implet.'" [1]

Having uttered this quotation with considerable self-complacency, and thereby entirely completed his conquest over Paul, Mr. Augustus Tomlinson, turning to Mac Grawler, concluded his business with that gentleman, which was of a literary nature, namely a joint composition against a man who, being under five-and-twenty, and too poor to give dinners, had had the impudence to write a sacred poem. The critics were exceedingly bitter at this; and having very little to say against the poem, the Court journals called the author a "coxcomb," and the liberal ones "the son of a pantaloon!"

There was an ease,—a spirit,—a life about Mr. Augustus Tomlinson, which captivated the senses of our young hero: then, too, he was exceedingly smartly attired; wore red heels and a bag; had what seemed to Paul quite the air of a "man of fashion;" and, above all, he spouted the Latin with a remarkable grace!

Some days afterwards, Mac Grawler sent our hero to Mr. Tomlinson's lodgings, with his share of the joint abuse upon the poet.

Doubly was Paul's reverence for Mr. Augustus Tomlinson increased by a sight of his abode. He found him settled in a polite part of the town, in a very spruce parlour, the contents of which manifested the universal genius of the inhabitant. It hath been objected unto us by a most discerning critic, that we are addicted to the drawing of "universal geniuses." We pleaded Not Guilty in

---

[1] "He appears to me to be, to the fullest extent, a poet, who airily torments my breast, irritates, soothes, fills it with unreal terrors" Horace. Ep. II,1, 210-12.

former instances ; we allow the soft impeachment in the instance of
Mr. Augustus Tomlinson. ˆOver his fireplace were arranged boxing-
gloves and fencing foils. On his table lay a cremona and a flageolet
On one side of the wall were shelves containing the Covent Garden
Magazine, Burn's Justice, a pocket Horace, a Prayer-book, *Excerpta
ex Tacito*, a volume of plays, Philosophy made Easy, and a Key to
all Knowledge. Furthermore, there were on another table a riding-
whip, and a driving-whip, and a pair of spurs, and three guineas,
with a little mountain of loose silver. Mr. Augustus was a tall, fair
young man, with a freckled complexion ; green eyes and red eyelids ;
a smiling mouth, rather under-jawed ; a sharp nose ; and a prodigiously large pair of ears. He was robed in a green damask
dressing-gown ; and he received the tender Paul most graciously.

There was something very engaging about our hero. He was not
only good-looking, and frank in aspect, but he had that appearance
of briskness and intellect which belongs to an embryo rogue. Mr.
Augustus Tomlinson professed the greatest regard for him,—asked
him if he could box—made him put on a pair of gloves—and, very
condescendingly, knocked him down three times successively. Next
he played him, both upon his flageolet and his cremona, some of the
most modish airs. Moreover, he sang him a little song of his own
composing. He then, taking up the driving-whip, flanked a fly
from the opposite wall, and throwing himself (naturally fatigued
with his numerous exertions) on his sofa, he observed, in a careless
tone, that he and his friend Lord Dunshunner were universally
esteemed the best whips in the metropolis. "I," quoth Mr.
Augustus, "am the best on the road ; but my lord is a devil at
turning a corner."

Paul, who had hitherto lived too unsophisticated a life to be aware
of the importance of which a lord would naturally be in the eyes of
Mr. Augustus Tomlinson, was not so much struck with the grandeur
of the connexion as the murderer of the journals had expected. He
merely observed, by way of compliment, that Mr. Augustus and his
companion seemed to be "rolling kiddies."

A little displeased with this metaphorical remark—for it may
be observed that "rolling kiddy" is, among the learned in such
lore, the customary expression for "a smart thief"—the universal
Augustus took that liberty to which, by his age and station, so
much superior to those of Paul, he imagined himself entitled, and
gently reproved our hero for his indiscriminate use of flash phrases.

"A lad of your parts," said he,—"for I see you are clever by
your eye,—ought to be ashamed of using such vulgar expressions.
Have a nobler spirit—a loftier emulation, Paul, than that which
distinguishes the little ragamuffins of the street. Know that, in this

country, genius and learning carry everything before them ; and if you behave yourself properly, you may, one day or another, be as high in the world as myself."

At this speech Paul looked wistfully round the spruce parlour, and thought what a fine thing it would be to be lord of such a domain, together with the appliances of flageolet and cremona, boxing-gloves, books, fly-flanking flagellum, three guineas, with the little mountain of silver, and the reputation—shared only with Lord Dunshunner—of being the best whip in London.

" Yes !" continued Tomlinson, with conscious pride, "I owe my rise to myself. Learning is better than house and land. '*Doctrina sed vim*,' &c. You know what old Horace says ? Why, sir, you would not believe it ; but I was the man who killed his majesty the King of Sardinia in our yesterday's paper. Nothing is too arduous for genius. Fag hard, my boy, and you may rival—for the thing, though difficult, may not be impossible—Augustus Tomlinson ! "

At the conclusion of this harangue, a knock at the door being heard, Paul took his departure, and met in the hall a fine-looking person dressed in the height of the fashion, and wearing a pair of prodigiously large buckles in his shoes. Paul looked, and his heart swelled. " I may rival," thought he—those were his very words— "I may rival—for the thing, though difficult, is not impossible— Augustus Tomlinson !" Absorbed in meditation, he went silently home. The next day the memoirs of the great Turpin were committed to the flames, and it was noticeable that henceforth Paul observed a choicer propriety of words,—that he assumed a more refined air of dignity, and that he paid considerably more attention than heretofore to the lessons of Mr. Peter Mac Grawler. Although it must be allowed that our young hero's progress in the learned languages was not astonishing, yet an early passion for reading, growing stronger and stronger by application, repaid him at last with a tolerable knowledge of the mother-tongue. We must, however, add that his more favourite and cherished studies were scarcely of that nature which a prudent preceptor would have greatly commended. They lay chiefly among novels, plays, and poetry, which last he effected to that degree that he became somewhat of a poet himself. Nevertheless these literary avocations, profitless as they seemed, gave a certain refinement to his tastes, which they were not likely otherwise to have acquired at the Mug ; and while they aroused his ambition to see something of the gay life they depicted, they imparted to his temper a tone of enterprise and of thoughtless generosity, which perhaps contributed greatly to counteract those evil influences towards petty vice, to which the examples around him must have exposed his tender youth. But, alas !

a great disappointment to Paul's hope of assistance and companionship in his literary labours befel him.   Mr. Augustus Tomlinson,
one bright morning, disappeared, leaving word with his numerous
friends, that he was going to accept a lucrative situation in the
North of England.   Notwithstanding the shock this occasioned to
the affectionate heart and aspiring temper of our friend Paul, it
abated not his ardour in that field of science, which it seemed that
the distinguished absentee had so successfully cultivated.   By little
and little, he possessed himself (in addition to the literary stores we
have alluded to) of all it was in the power of the wise and profound
Peter Mac Grawler to impart unto him ; and at the age of sixteen
he began (O the presumption of youth !) to fancy himself more
learned than his master.

CHAPTER IV.

*" He had now become a young man of extreme fashion, and as much répandu
in society as the utmost and most exigent coveter of London celebrity could
desire.   He was, of course, a member of the clubs, &c. &c. &c.   He was, in
short, of that oft-described set before whom all minor beaux sink into insigni-
ficance, or among whom they eventually obtain a subaltern grade, by a sacrifice
of a due portion of their fortune "*—' ALMACK'S REVISITED.'

BY the soul of the great Malebranche, who made "A Search
after Truth," and discovered everything beautiful except
that which he searched for ;—by the soul of the great
Malebranche, whom Bishop Berkeley found suffering under
an inflammation in the lungs, and very obligingly *talked to death,*—
an instance of conversational powers worthy the envious emulation
of all great metaphysicians and arguers ;—by the soul of that illustrious man, it is amazing to us what a number of truths there are
broken up into little fragments, and scattered here and there through
the world.   What a magnificent museum a man might make of the
precious minerals, if he would but go out with his basket under his
arm, and his eyes about him !   We, ourselves, picked up, this very
day, a certain small piece of truth, with which we propose to explain
to thee, fair reader, a sinister turn on the fortunes of Paul.

"Wherever," says a living sage, "you see dignity, you may be
sure there is expense requisite to support it." [1]   So was it with
Paul.   A young gentleman who was heir-presumptive to the Mug,

[1] "Popular Fallacies"

and who enjoyed a handsome person with a cultivated mind, was necessarily of a certain station of society, and an object of respect in the eyes of the manœuvring mammas of the vicinity of Thames Court. Many were the parties of pleasure to Deptford and Greenwich which Paul found himself compelled to attend ; and we need not refer our readers to novels upon fashionable life, to inform them that, in good society, the *gentlemen always pay for the ladies!* Nor was this all the expense to which his expectations exposed him. A gentleman could scarcely attend these elegant festivities without devoting some little attention to his dress ; and a fashionable tailor plays the deuce with one's yearly allowance !

We, who reside, be it known to you, reader, in Little Brittany, are not very well acquainted with the manners of the better classes in St. James's. But there was one great vice among the fine people about Thames Court, which we make no doubt does not exist any where else, viz., these fine people were always in an agony to seem finer than they were ; and the more airs a gentleman or a lady gave him or herself, the more important they became. Joe, the dog's-meat man, had indeed got into society, entirely from the knack of saying impertinent things to everybody ; and the smartest exclusives of the place, who seldom visited any one where there was not a silver teapot, used to think Joe had a great deal in him because he trundled his cart with his head in the air, and one day gave the very beadle of the parish "the cut direct."

Now this desire to be so exceedingly fine not only made the society about Thames Court unpleasant, but expensive. Every one vied with his neighbour ; and as the spirit of rivalry is particularly strong in youthful bosoms, we can scarcely wonder that it led Paul into many extravagances. The evil of all circles that profess to be select is high play,—and the reason is obvious : persons who have the power to bestow on another an advantage he covets, would rather sell it than give it ; and Paul, gradually increasing in popularity and *ton*, found himself, in spite of his classical education, no match for the finished, or, rather, finishing gentlemen with whom he began to associate. His first admittance into the select coterie of these men of the world was formed at the house of Bachelor Bill, a person of great notoriety among that portion of the *élite* which emphatically entitles itself "Flash !" However, as it is our rigid intention in this work to portray *at length* no episodical characters whatsoever, we can afford our readers but a slight and rapid sketch of Bachelor Bill.

This personage was of Devonshire extraction. His mother had kept the pleasantest public-house in town, and at her death Bill succeeded to her property and popularity. All the young ladies in the neighbourhood of Fiddler's Row, where he resided, set their caps at him : all the most fashionable *prigs*, or *tobymen*, sought to get him into their set ; and the most crack *blowen* in London would have given her ears at any time for a loving word from Bachelor Bill. But Bill was a long-headed, prudent fellow, and of a remarkably cautious temperament He avoided marriage and friendship, viz , he was neither plundered nor cornuted. He was a tall, aristocratic *cove*, of a devilish neat address, and very gallant, in an honest way, to the *blowens*. Like most single men, being very much the gentleman so far as money was concerned, he gave them plenty of "feeds," and from time to time a very agreeable "hop." His "bingo"[1] was unexceptionable , and as for his "stark-naked,"[2] it was voted the most brilliant thing in nature. In a very short time, by his blows-out and his bachelorship,—for single men always arrive at the apex of *haut ton* more easily than married,—he became the very glass of fashion ; and many were the tight apprentices, even at the west end of the town, who used to turn back in admiration of Bachelor Bill, when, of a Sunday afternoon, he drove down his varment gig to his snug little box on the borders of Turnham Green. Bill's happiness was not, however, wholly without alloy. The ladies of pleasure are always so excessively angry when a man does not make love to them, that there is nothing that they will not say against him ; and the fair matrons in the vicinity of Fiddler's Row spread all manner of unfounded reports against poor Bachelor Bill. By degrees, however,—for, as Tacitus has said, doubtless with a prophetic eye to Bachelor Bill, "the truth gains by delay," these reports began to die insensibly away ; and Bill, now waxing near to the confines of middle age, his friends comfortably settled for him that he would be Bachelor Bill all his life. For the rest, he was an excellent fellow,—gave his broken victuals to the poor—professed a liberal turn of thinking, and in all the quarrels among the blowens (your crack blowens are a quarrelsome set !) always took part with the weakest. Although Bill affected to be very select in his company, he was never forgetful of his old friends, and Mrs. Margery Lobkins having been very good to him when he was a little boy in a skeleton jacket, he invariably sent her a card to his *soirées*. The good lady, however, had not of late years deserted her chimney corner. Indeed, the racket of fashionable life was too much for her nerves, and the invitation had become a customary form not expected to be acted upon, but not a whit the less regularly used for that reason. As Paul had now attained his sixteenth year, and was a fine, handsome lad, the dame thought he would make an excellent

---

[1] Brandy.   [2] Gin.

representative of the Mug's mistress ; and that, for her *protégé*, a ball at Bill's house would be no bad commencement of " Life in London." Accordingly, she intimated to the Bachelor a wish to that effect, and Paul received the following invitation from Bill :—

"Mr. William Duke gives a hop and feed in a quiet way on Monday next, and *hops* Mr Paul Lobkins will be of the party. N.B. Gentlemen *is* expected to come in pumps."

When Paul entered, he found Bachelor Bill leading off the ball to the tune of "Drops of Brandy," with a young lady to whom—because she had been a strolling player—the Ladies Patronesses of Fiddler's Row had thought proper to behave with a very cavalier civility. The good bachelor had no notion, as he expressed it, of such tantrums, and he caused it to be circulated among the finest of the blowens, that "he expected all who kicked their heels at his house would behave decent and polite to young Mrs. Dot." This intimation, conveyed to the ladies with all that insinuating polish for which Bachelor Bill was so remarkable, produced a notable effect ; and Mrs. Dot, being now led off by the flash Bachelor, was overpowered with civilities the rest of the evening.

When the dance was ended, Bill very politely shook hands with Paul, and took an early opportunity of introducing him to some of the most "noted characters" of the town. Among these was the smart Mr. Allfair, the insinuating Henry Finish, the merry Jack Hookey, the knowing Charles Trywit, and various others equally noted for their skill in living handsomely upon their own brains, and the personals of other people. To say truth, Paul, who at that time was an honest lad, was less charmed than he had anticipated by the conversation of these chevaliers of industry. He was more pleased with the clever, though self-sufficient remarks of a gentleman with a remarkably fine head of hair, and whom we would more impressively than the rest introduce to our reader, under the appellation of Mr. Edward Pepper, generally termed Long Ned. As this worthy was destined afterwards to be an intimate associate of Paul, our main reason for attending the hop at Bachelor Bill's is to note, as the importance of the event deserves, the epoch of the commencement of their acquaintance.

Long Ned and Paul happened to sit next to each other at supper, and they conversed together so amicably that Paul, in the hospitality of his heart, expressed a hope that "he should see Mr. Pepper at the Mug !"

" Mug—Mug !" repeated Pepper, half shutting his eyes with the air of a dandy about to be impertinent; "Ah—the name of a chapel —is it not? There's a sect called the Muggletonians, I think?"

"As to that," said Paul, colouring at this insinuation against the Mug, "Mrs. Lobkins has no more religion than her betters; but the Mug is a very excellent house, and frequented by the best possible company."

"Don't doubt it!" said Ned. "Remember now that I was once there, and saw one Dummie Dunnaker—is not that the name? I recollect some years ago, when I first came out, that Dummie and I had an adventure together;—to tell you the truth, it was not the sort of thing I would do now. But, would you believe it, Mr. Paul? this pitiful fellow was quite rude to me the only time I ever met him since;—that is to say, the only time I ever entered the Mug. I have no notion of such airs in a merchant—a merchant of rags! Those commercial fellows are getting quite insufferable!"

"You surprise me!" said Paul. "Poor Dummie is the last man to be rude. He is as civil a creature as ever lived."

"Or sold a rag!" said Ned. "Possibly! Don't doubt his amiable qualities in the least. Pass the bingo, my good fellow. Stupid stuff, this dancing!"

"Devilish stupid!" echoed Harry Finish across the table. "Suppose we adjourn to Fish Lane, and rattle the ivories!—What say you, Mr. Lobkins?"

Afraid of the "ton's stern laugh, which scarce the proud philosopher can scorn," and not being very partial to dancing, Paul assented to the proposition; and a little party, consisting of Harry Finish, Allfair, Long Ned, and Mr. Hookey, adjourned to Fish Lane, where there was a club, celebrated among men who live by their wits, at which "lush" and "baccy" were gratuitously sported in the most magnificent manner. Here the evening passed away very delightfully, and Paul went home without a "brad" in his pocket.

From that time, Paul's visits to Fish Lane became unfortunately regular; and in a very short period, we grieve to say, Paul became that distinguished character—a gentleman of three outs—"out of pocket, out of elbows, and out of credit." The only two persons whom he found willing *to accommodate him with a slight loan*, as the advertisements signed X. Y. have it, were Mr. Dummie Dunnaker and Mr. Pepper, surnamed the Long. The latter, however, while he obliged the heir to the Mug, never condescended to enter that noted place of resort; and the former, whenever he good-naturedly opened his purse-strings, did it with a hearty caution to shun the acquaintance of Long Ned. "A parson," said Dummie, "of very dangerous morals, and not by no manner of means a fit sociate for a young gemman of cracter like leetle Paul!" So earnest was this caution, and so especially pointed at Long Ned, although the company of Mr. Allfair or Mr. Finish might be said to be no less prejudicial,—that it is probable that stately fastidiousness of manner, which Lord Normanby rightly observes, in one of his excellent novels, makes so many enemies in the world, and which sometimes characterised the behaviour of Long Ned, especially towards the men of commerce, was a main reason why Dummie was so acutely and peculiarly alive to the immoralities of that lengthy gentleman. At the same time we must observe, that when Paul, remembering what Pepper had said respecting his early adventure with Mr. Dunnaker, repeated it to the merchant, Dummie could not conceal a certain confusion, though he merely remarked, with a sort of laugh, that it was not worth speaking about; and it appeared evident to Paul that something unpleasant to the man of rags, which was not shared by the unconscious Pepper, lurked in the reminiscence of their past acquaintance. Howbeit, the circumstance glided from Paul's attention the moment afterwards; and he paid, we are concerned to say, equally little heed to the cautions against Ned with which Dummie regaled him.

Perhaps (for we must now direct a glance towards his domestic concerns) one great cause which drove Paul to Fish Lane was the uncomfortable life he led at home. For though Mrs. Lobkins was extremely fond of her *protégé*, yet she was possessed, as her customers emphatically remarked, "of the devil's own temper;" and her native coarseness never having been softened by those pictures of gay society which had, in many a novel and comic farce, refined the temperament of the romantic Paul, her manner of venting her maternal reproaches was certainly not a little revolting to a lad of some delicacy of feeling. Indeed, it often occurred to him to leave her house altogether, and seek his fortunes alone, after the manner of the ingenious Gil Blas, or the enterprising Roderick Random; and this idea, though conquered and reconquered, gradually swelled and increased at his heart, even as swelleth that hairy ball found in the stomach of some suffering heifer after its decease. Among these projects of enterprise, the reader will hereafter notice, that an early vision of the Green Forest Cave, in which Turpin was accustomed, with a friend, a ham, and a wife, to conceal himself, flitted across his mind. At this time he did not, perhaps, incline to the mode of life practised by the hero of the roads; but he certainly clung not the less fondly to the notion of the cave.

The melancholy flow of our hero's life was now, however, about to be diverted by an unexpected turn, and the crude thoughts of

boyhood to burst, "like Ghilan's Giant Palm," into the fruit of a
manly resolution.

Among the prominent features of Mrs. Lobkin's mind was a
sovereign contempt for the unsuccessful ;—the imprudence and ill-
luck of Paul occasioned her as much scorn as compassion.   And
when, for the third time within a week, he stood, with a rueful
visage and with vacant pockets, by the dame's great chair, requesting
an additional supply, the tides of her wrath swelled into overflow.

"Look you, my kinchin cove," said she,—and in order to give
peculiar dignity to her aspect, she put on while she spoke a huge
pair of tin spectacles,—"if so be as how you goes for to think
as how I shall go for to supply your wicious necessities, you will
find yourself planted in Queer Street.   Blow me tight, if I gives you
another mag."

"But I owe long Ned a guinea," said Paul ; "and Dummie
Dunnaker lent me three crowns.   It ill becomes your heir apparent,
my dear dame, to fight shy of his debts of honour."

"Taradiddiddle, don't think for to wheedle me with your debts
and your honour," said the dame in a passion.   "Long Ned is as
long in the forks (fingers) as he is in the back : may Old Harry fly
off with him !   And as for Dummie Dunnaker, I wonders how you,
brought up such a swell, and blest with the wery best of hedications,
can think of putting up with such wulgar sociates !   I tells you what,
Paul, you'll please to break with them, smack and at once, or devil
a brad you'll ever get from Peg Lobkins."   So saying, the old lady
turned round in her chair, and helped herself to a pipe of tobacco.

Paul walked twice up and down the apartment, and at last stopped
opposite the dame's chair : he was a youth of high spirit, and though
he was warm-hearted, and had a love for Mrs. Lobkins, which her
care and affection for him well deserved, yet he was rough in
temper, and not constantly smooth in speech : it is true that his
heart smote him afterwards, whenever he had said anything to annoy
Mrs. Lobkins : and he was always the first to seek a reconciliation ;
but warm words produce cold respect, and sorrow for the past is not
always efficacious in amending the future.   Paul then, puffed up
with the vanity of his genteel education, and the friendship of Long
Ned (who went to Ranelagh, and wore silver clocked stockings),
stopped opposite to Mrs. Lobkins' chair, and said with great
solemnity—

"Mr. Pepper, madam, says very properly that I must have money
to support myself like a gentleman : and as you won't give it me, I
am determined, with many thanks for your past favours, to throw
myself on the world, and seek my fortune."

If Paul was of no oily and bland temper, dame Margaret Lobkins, it has been seen, had no advantage on that score :—we dare say the reader has observed that nothing so enrages persons on whom one depends as any expressed determination of seeking independence. Gazing, therefore, for one moment at the open but resolute countenance of Paul, while all the blood of her veins seemed gathering in fire and scarlet to her enlarging cheeks, Dame Lobkins said—

"Ifeaks, Master Pride-in-duds! seek your fortune yourself, will you? This comes of my bringing you up, and letting you eat the bread of idleness and charity, you toad of a thousand! Take that and be d——d to you!" and, suiting the action to the word, the tube which she had withdrawn from her mouth, in order to utter her gentle rebuke, whizzed through the air, grazed Paul's cheek, and finished its earthly career by coming in violent contact with the right eye of Dummie Dunnaker, who at that exact moment entered the room.

Paul had winced for a moment to avoid the missive,—in the next he stood perfectly upright; his cheeks glowed, his chest swelled; and the entrance of Dummie Dunnaker, who was thus made the spectator of the affront he had received, stirred his blood into a deeper anger and a more bitter self-humiliation :—all his former resolutions of departure—all the hard words, the coarse allusions, the practical insults he had at any time received, rushed upon him at once. He merely cast one look at the old woman, whose rage was now half subsided, and turned slowly and in silence to the door.

There is often something alarming in an occurrence, merely because it is that which we least expect: the astute Mrs. Lobkins, remembering the hardy temper and fiery passions of Paul, had expected some burst of rage, some vehement reply; and when she caught with one wandering eye his parting look, and saw him turn so passively and mutely to the door, her heart misgave her, she raised herself from her chair, and made towards him. Unhappily for her chance of reconciliation, she had that day quaffed more copiously of the bowl than usual, and the signs of intoxication visible in her uncertain gait, her meaningless eye, her vacant leer, her ruby cheek, all inspired Paul with feelings which, at the moment, converted resentment into something very much like aversion. He sprang from her grasp to the threshold. "Where be you going, you imp of the world?" cried the dame. "Get in with you, and say no more on the matter: be a bob-cull—drop the bullies, and you shall have the blunt!"

But Paul heeded not this invitation.

"I will eat the bread of idleness and charity no longer," said he, sullenly. " Good-bye,—and if ever I can pay you what I have cost you, I will."

He turned away as he spoke ; and the dame kindling with resentment at his unseemly return to her proffered kindness, hallooed after him, and bade that dark-coloured gentleman who keeps the *fire-office* below, go along with him.

Swelling with anger, pride, shame, and a half-joyous feeling of emancipated independence, Paul walked on he knew not whither, with his head in the air, and his legs marshalling themselves into a military gait of defiance   He had not proceeded far, before he heard his name uttered behind him,—he turned, and saw the rueful face of Dummie Dunnaker.

Very inoffensively had that respectable person been employed during the last part of the scene we have described, in caressing his afflicted eye, and muttering philosophical observations on the danger incurred by all those who are acquainted with ladies of a choleric temperament : when Mrs. Lobkins, turning round after Paul's departure, and seeing the pitiful person of that Dummie Dunnaker, whose name she remembered Paul had mentioned in his opening speech, and whom, therefore, with an illogical confusion of ideas, she considered a party in the late dispute, exhausted upon him all that rage which it was necessary for her comfort that she should unburthen somewhere.

She seized the little man by the collar—the tenderest of all places in gentlemen similarly circumstanced with regard to the ways of life, and giving him a blow, which took effect on his other and hitherto undamaged eye, cried out, " I'll teach you, you blood-sucker (*i. e.* parasite), to spunge upon those as has expectations ! I'll teach you to cozen the heir of the Mug, you sniveling, whey-faced ghost of a farthing rush-light ! What ! you'll lend my Paul three crowns, will you, when you knows as how you told me you could not pay me a pitiful tizzy ? Oh, you're a queer one, I warrants ; but you won't queer Margery Lobkins. Out of my ken, you cur of the mange !—out of my ken ; and if ever I claps my sees on you again, or if ever I know as how you makes a flat of my Paul, blow me tight, but I'll weave you a hempen collar : I'll hang you, you dog, I will. What ! you will answer me, will you ?—O you viper, budge, and begone !"

It was in vain that Dummie protested his innocence. A violent *coup-de-pied* broke off all further parlance. He made a clean house of the Mug ; and the landlady thereof, tottering back to her elbow-chair, sought out another pipe, and, like all imaginative persons when the world goes wrong with them, consoled herself for the absence of realities by the creations of smoke.

Meanwhile, Dummie Dunnaker, muttering and murmuring bitter fancies, overtook Paul, and accused that youth of having been the occasion of the injuries he had just undergone. Paul was not at that moment in the humour best adapted for the patient bearing of accusations ; he answered Mr. Dunnaker very shortly ; and that respectable individual, still smarting under his bruises, replied with equal tartness. Words grew high, and at length, Paul, desirous of concluding the conference, clenched his fist, and told the redoubted Dummie that he would "knock him down." There is something peculiarly harsh and stunning in those three hard, wirey, sturdy, stubborn monosyllables. Their very sound makes you double your fist— if you are a hero ; or your pace—if you are a peaceable man. They produced an instant effect upon Dummie Dunnaker, aided as they were by the effect of an athletic and youthful figure, already fast approaching to the height of six feet,—a flushed cheek, and an eye that bespoke both passion and resolution. The rag-merchant's voice sunk at once, and with the countenance of a wronged Cassius he whimpered forth,—

"Knock me down !—O leetle Paul, vot vicked vhids are those ! Vot ! Dummie Dunnaker as has dandled you on his knee mony's a time and oft ! Vy, the cove's art is as ard as junk, and as proud as a gardener's dog vith a nosegay tied to his tail." This pathetic remonstrance softened Paul's anger.

"Well, Dummie," said he, laughing, "I did not mean to hurt you, and there's an end of it ; and I am very sorry for the dame's ill conduct ; and so I wish you a good morning."

"Vy, vere be you trotting to, leetle Paul ?" said Dummie, grasping him by the tail of the coat.

"The deuce a bit I know," answered our hero ; "but I think I shall drop a call on Long Ned."

"Avast there !" said Dummie, speaking under his breath ; "if so be as you von't blab, I'll tell you a bit of a secret. I heered as ow Long Ned started for Hampshire this werry morning on a toby consarn !"[1]

"Ha !" said Paul, "then hang me if I know what to do !" As he uttered these words, a more thorough sense of his destitution (if he persevered in leaving the Mug) than he had hitherto felt rushed upon him ; for Paul had designed for a while to throw himself on the hospitality of his Patagonian friend, and now that he found that friend was absent from London, and on so dangerous an expedition, he was a little puzzled what to do with that treasure of intellect and wisdom which he carried about upon his legs. Already he had acquired sufficient penetration (for Charles Trywit and Harry Finish

[1] Highway expedition.

Work;

were excellent masters for initiating a man into the knowledge of the world) to perceive that a person, however admirable may be his qualities, does not readily find a welcome without a penny in his pocket. In the neighbourhood of Thames Court he had, indeed, many acquaintances; but the fineness of his language, acquired from his education, and the elegance of his air, in which he attempted to blend, in happy association, the gallant effrontery of Mr. Long Ned with the graceful negligence of Mr. Augustus Tomlinson, had made him many enemies among those acquaintances; and he was not willing,—so great was our hero's pride,—to throw himself on the chance of their welcome, or to publish, as it were, his exiled and crest-fallen state. As for those boon companions who had assisted him in making a wilderness of his pockets, he had already found, that that was the only species of assistance which they were willing to render him: in a word, he could not for the life of him conjecture in what quarter he should find the benefits of bed and board. While he stood with his finger to his lip, undecided and musing, but fully resolved at least on one thing—not to return to the Mug,—little Dummie, who was a good-natured fellow at the bottom, peered up in his face, and said, " Vy, Paul, my kid, you looks down in the chops : cheer up, care killed a cat ! "

Observing that this appropriate and encouraging fact of natural history did not lessen the cloud upon Paul's brow, the acute Dummie Dunnaker proceeded at once to the grand panacea for all evils, in his own profound estimation.

" Paul, my ben cull," said he, with a knowing wink, and nudging the young gentleman in the left side, " vot do you say to a drop o' blue ruin ? or, as you likes to be conish (genteel), I doesn't care if I sports you a glass of port ! " While Dunnaker was uttering this invitation, a sudden reminiscence flashed across Paul . he bethought him at once of Mac Grawler : and he resolved forthwith to repair to the abode of that illustrious sage, and petition at least for accommodation for the approaching night. So soon as he had come to this determination, he shook off the grasp of the amiable Dummie, and refusing, with many thanks, his hospitable invitation, requested him to abstract from the dame's house, and lodge within his own, until called for, such articles of linen and clothing as belonged to Paul, and could easily be laid hold of, during one of the matron's evening *siestas*, by the shrewd Dunnaker. The merchant promised that the commission should be speedily executed ; and Paul, shaking hands with him, proceeded to the mansion of Mac Grawler.

We must now go back somewhat in the natural course of our narrative, and observe, that among the minor causes which had conspired with the great one of gambling to bring our excellent

Paul to his present situation, was his intimacy with Mac Grawler; for when Paul's increasing years and roving habits had put an end to the sage's instructions, there was thereby lopped off from the preceptor's finances the weekly sum of two shillings and sixpence, as well as the freedom of the dame's cellar and larder; and as, in the reaction of feeling, and the perverse course of human affairs, people generally repent the most of those actions once the most ardently incurred; so poor Mrs. Lobkins, imagining that Paul's irregularities were entirely owing to the knowledge he had acquired from Mac Grawler's instructions, grievously upbraided herself for her former folly, in seeking for a superior education for her *protégé*: nay, she even vented upon the sacred head of Mac Grawler himself her dissatisfaction at the results of his instructions. In like manner, when a man who can spell comes to be hanged, the anti-educationists accuse the spelling-book of his murder. High words between the admirer of ignorant innocence and the propagator of intellectual science ensued, which ended in Mac Grawler's final expulsion from the Mug.

There are some young gentlemen of the present day addicted to the adoption of Lord Byron's poetry, with the alteration of new rhymes, who are pleased graciously to inform us, that they are born to be the ruin of all those who love them: an interesting fact, doubtless, but which they might as well keep to themselves. It would seem by the contents of this chapter, as if the same misfortune were destined to Paul. The exile of Mac Grawler,—the insults offered to Dummie Dunnaker,—alike occasioned by him, appear to sanction that opinion. Unfortunately, though Paul was a poet, he was not much of a sentimentalist; and he has never given us the edifying ravings of his remorse on those subjects. But Mac Grawler, like Dunnaker, was resolved that our hero should perceive the curse of his fatality; and as he still retained some influence over the mind of his quondam pupil, his accusations against Paul, as the origin of his banishment, were attended with a greater success than were the complaints of Dummie Dunnaker on a similar calamity. Paul, who, like most people who are good for nothing, had an excellent heart, was exceedingly grieved at Mac Grawler's banishment on his account: and he endeavoured to atone for it by such pecuniary consolations as he was enabled to offer. These Mac Grawler (purely, we may suppose, from a benevolent desire to lessen the boy's remorse) scrupled not to accept; and thus, so similar often are the effects of virtue and of vice, the exemplary Mac Grawler conspired with the unprincipled Long Ned and the heartless Henry Finish, in producing that unenviable state of vacuity which now saddened over the pockets of Paul.

C

As our hero was slowly walking towards the sage's abode, depending on his gratitude and friendship for a temporary shelter, one of those lightning flashes of thought which often illumine the profoundest abyss of affliction darted across his mind. Recalling the image of the critic, he remembered that he had seen that ornament of "The Asinæum" receive sundry sums for his critical lucubrations.

"Why," said Paul, seizing on that fact, and stopping short in the street, "why should I not turn critic myself?"

The only person to whom one ever puts a question with a tolerable certainty of receiving a satisfactory answer is one's self. The moment Paul started this luminous suggestion, it appeared to him that he had discovered the mines of Potosi. Burning with impatience to discuss with the great Mac Grawler the feasibility of his project, he quickened his pace almost into a run, and in a very few minutes, having only overthrown one chimney-sweeper and two apple-women by the way, he arrived at the sage's door.

CHAPTER V.

" *Ye realms yet unreveal'd to human sight!*
Ye canes athwart the hapless hands that write!
Ye critic chiefs—permit me to relate
The mystic wonders of your silent state!"
                    VIRGIL, ' Æn.' b. vi.

FORTUNE had smiled upon Mr. Mac Grawler since he first undertook the tuition of Mrs. Lobkins' *protégé*. He now inhabited a second-floor, and defied the sheriff and his evil spirits. It was at the dusk of evening that Paul found him at home and alone.

Before the mighty man stood a pot of London porter; a candle, with an unregarded wick, shed its solitary light upon his labours; and an infant cat played sportively at his learned feet, beguiling the weary moments with the remnants of the spiral cap wherewith, instead of laurel, the critic had hitherto nightly adorned his brows.

So soon as Mac Grawler, piercing through the gloomy mist which hung about the chamber, perceived the person of the intruder, a frown settled upon his brow.

" Have I not told you, youngster!" he growled, "never to enter a gentleman's room without knocking? I tell you, sir, that manners are no less essential to human happiness than virtue; wherefore, never disturb a gentleman in his avocations, and sit yourself down without molesting the cat ! "

Paul, who knew that his respected tutor disliked any one to trace the source of the wonderful spirit which he infused into his critical compositions, affected not to perceive the pewter Hippocrene, and with many apologies for his want of preparatory politeness, seated himself as directed. It was then that the following edifying conversation ensued.

"The ancients," quoth Paul, "were very great men, Mr. Mac Grawler."

"They were so, sir," returned the critic; "we make it a rule in our profession to assert that fact ! "

"But, sir," said Paul, "they were wrong now and then."

"Never, Ignoramus ; never ! "

"They praised poverty, Mr. Mac Grawler ! " said Paul, with a sigh.

"Hem ! " quoth the critic, a little staggered, but presently recovering his characteristic acumen, he observed,—

"It is true, Paul ; but that was the poverty of other people."

There was a slight pause.   "Criticism," renewed Paul, "must be a most difficult art."

"A-hem !   And what art is there, sir, that is not difficult—at least, to become master of ? "

"True," sighed Paul ; "or else—— "

"Or else what, boy ? " repeated Mr. Mac Grawler, seeing that Paul hesitated, either from fear of his superior knowledge, as the critic's vanity suggested, or from (what was equally likely) want of a word to express his meaning.

"Why, I was thinking, sir," said Paul, with that desperate courage which gives a distinct and loud intonation to the voice of all who set, or think they set, their fate upon a cast : " I was thinking that I should like to become a critic myself ! "

"W—h—e—w ! " whistled Mac Grawler, elevating his eyebrows ; "w—h—e—w ! great ends have come of less beginnings ! "

Encouraging as this assertion was, coming as it did from the lips of so great a man and so great a critic, at the very moment too when nothing short of an anathema against arrogance and presumption was expected to issue from those portals of wisdom : yet, such is the fallacy of all human hopes, that Paul's of a surety would have been a little less elated, had he, at the same time his ears drank in the balm of these gracious words, been able to have dived into the source whence they emanated.

"Know thyself ! " was a precept the sage Mac Grawler had endeavoured to obey : consequently the result of his obedience was,

that even by himself he was better known than trusted. Whatever
he might appear to others, he had in reality no vain faith in the
infallibility of his own talents and resources ; as well might a butcher
deem himself a perfect anatomist from the frequent amputation of
legs of mutton, as the critic of "The Asinæum" have laid "the
flattering unction to his soul," that he was really skilled in the art
of criticism, or even acquainted with one of its commonest rules,
because he could with all speed cut up and disjoint any work, from
the smallest to the greatest, from the most superficial to the most
superior ; and thus it was that he never had the want of candour to
deceive *himself* as to his own talents. Paul's wish, therefore, was
no sooner expressed, than a vague but golden scheme of future profit
illumed the brain of Mac Grawler :—in a word, he resolved that
Paul should henceforward share the labour of his critiques ; and that
he, Mac Grawler, should receive the whole profits in return for the
honour thereby conferred on his coadjutor.

Looking, therefore, at our hero with a benignant air, Mr. Mac
Grawler thus continued :—

"Yes, I repeat,—great ends have come from less beginnings !—
Rome was not built in a day,—and I, Paul, I myself was not always
the editor of 'The Asinæum.' You say wisely, criticism is a great
science—a very great science, and it may be divided into three
branches ; viz. 'to tickle, to slash, and to plaster.' In each of these
three, I believe without vanity, I am a profound adept ! I will
initiate you into all. Your labours shall begin this very evening. I
have three works on my table, they must be despatched by to-
morrow night ; I will take the most arduous, I abandon to you the
others. The three consist of a Romance, an Epic in twelve books,
and an Inquiry into the Human Mind, in three volumes ; 1, Paul,
will tickle the Romance, you this very evening shall plaster the Epic
and slash the Inquiry ! "

"Heavens, Mr. Mac Grawler ! " cried Paul, in consternation,
"what do you mean? I should never be able to read an epic in
twelve books, and I should fall asleep in the first page of the
Inquiry. No, no, leave me the romance, and take the other two
under your own protection ! "

Although great genius is always benevolent, Mr. Mac Grawler
could not restrain a smile of ineffable contempt at the simplicity of
his pupil.

"Know, young gentleman," said he solemnly, "that the romance
in question must be tickled ; it is not given to raw beginners to
conquer that great mystery of our science."

"Before we proceed farther, explain the words of the art," said
Paul, impatiently.

"Listen, then," rejoined Mac Grawler; and as he spoke the candle cast an awful glimmering on his countenance. "To slash is, speaking grammatically, to employ the accusative, or accusing case; you must cut up your book right and left, top and bottom, root and branch. To plaster a book, is to employ the dative, or giving case, and you must bestow on the work all the superlatives in the language; you must lay on your praise thick and thin, and not leave a crevice untrowelled. But to tickle, sir, is a comprehensive word, and it comprises all the infinite varieties that fill the interval between slashing and plastering. This is the nicety of the art, and you can only acquire it by practice; a few examples will suffice to give you an idea of its delicacy.

"We will begin with the encouraging tickle. 'Although this work is full of faults; though the characters are unnatural, the plot utterly improbable, the thoughts hackneyed, and the style ungrammatical; yet we would by no means discourage the author from proceeding; and in the mean while we confidently recommend his work to the attention of the reading public.'

"Take, now, the advising tickle.

"'There is a good deal of merit in these little volumes, although we must regret the evident haste in which they were written. The author might do better—were commend him a study of the best writers,'—then conclude by a Latin quotation, which you may take from one of the mottoes in the *Spectator*.

"Now, young gentleman, for a specimen of the metaphorical tickle.

"'We beg this poetical aspirant to remember the fate of Pyrenæus, who, attempting to pursue the Muses, forgot that he had not the wings of the goddesses, flung himself from the loftiest ascent he could reach, and perished.'

"This you see, Paul, is a loftier and more erudite sort of tickle, and may be reserved for one of the Quarterly Reviews. Never throw away a simile unnecessarily.

"Now for a sample of the facetious tickle.

"'Mr. —— has obtained a considerable reputation! Some fine ladies think him a great philosopher, and he has been praised in our hearing by some Cambridge Fellows, for his knowledge of fashionable society.'

"For this sort of tickle we generally use the dullest of our tribe, and I have selected the foregoing example from the criticisms of a distinguished writer in 'The Asinæum,' whom we call, *par excellence*, *the* Ass.

"There is a variety of other tickles; the familiar, the vulgar, the polite, the good-natured, the bitter . but in general all tickles may

be supposed to signify, however disguised, one or other of these
meanings :—' This book would be exceedingly good if it were not
exceedingly bad ; '—or, ' This book would be exceedingly bad if it
were not exceedingly good.'

"You have now, Paul, a general idea of the superior art required
by the tickle ? "

Our hero signified his assent by a sort of hysterical sound between
a laugh and a groan. Mac Grawler continued :—

"There is another grand difficulty attendant on this class of
criticism,—it is generally requisite to read a few pages of the work ;
because we seldom tickle without extracting, and it requires some
judgment to make the context agree with the extract ; but it is not
often necessary to extract when you slash or when you plaster ; when
you slash, it is better in general to conclude with—

"'After what we have said, it is unnecessary to add that we
cannot offend the taste of our readers by any quotation from this
execrable trash.' And when you plaster, you may wind up with,
'We regret that our limits will not allow us to give any extracts
from this wonderful and unrivalled work. We must refer our readers
to the book itself.'

"And now, sir, I think I have given you a sufficient outline of
the noble science of Scaliger and Mac Grawler. Doubtless you are
reconciled to the task I have allotted you ; and while I tickle the
Romance, you will slash the Inquiry and plaster the Epic ! "

"I will do my best, sir ! " said Paul, with that modest yet noble
simplicity which becomes the virtuously ambitious : — and Mac
Grawler forthwith gave him pen and paper, and set him down to his
undertaking

He had the good fortune to please Mac Grawler, who, after having
made a few corrections in style, declared he evinced a peculiar
genius in that branch of composition. And then it was that Paul,
made conceited by praise, said, looking contemptuously in the face
of his preceptor, and swinging his legs to and fro,—" And what,
sir, shall I receive for the plastered Epic and the slashed Inquiry ? "
As the face of the school-boy who, when guessing, as he thinks
lightly, at the meaning of some mysterious word in Cornelius Nepos,
receiveth not the sugared epithet of praise, but a sudden stroke across
the *os humerosve*,[1] even so, blank, puzzled, and thunder-stricken,
waxed the face of Mr. Mac Grawler, at the abrupt and astounding
audacity of Paul.

"Receive ! " he repeated, " receive !—Why, you impudent, ungrateful puppy, would you steal the bread from your old master?

---

[1] Face or shoulders.

If I can obtain for your crude articles an admission into the illustrious pages of 'The Asinæum,' will you not be sufficiently paid, sir, by the honour? Answer me that. Another man, young gentleman, would have charged you a premium for his instructions ;—and here have I, in one lesson, imparted to you all the mysteries of the science, and for nothing! And you talk to me of 'receive !'—'receive !' Young gentleman, in the words of the immortal bard, 'I would as lief you had talked to me of ratsbane !'"

"In fine, then, Mr. Mac Grawler, I shall get nothing for my trouble ?" said Paul.

"To be sure not, sir ; the very best writer in 'The Asinæum' only gets three shillings an article !" Almost more than he deserves, the critic might have added ; for he who writes for nobody should receive nothing !

"Then, sir," quoth the mercenary Paul profanely, and rising, he kicked with one kick, the cat, the Epic, and the Inquiry to the other end of the room ; "Then, sir, you may all go to the devil ! "

We do not, O gentle reader ! seek to excuse this hasty anathema : —the habits of childhood will sometimes break forth despite of the after blessings of education. And we set not up Paul for thine imitation as that mode of virtue and of wisdom which we design thee to discover in Mac Grawler.

When that great critic perceived Paul had risen and was retreating in high dudgeon towards the door, he rose also, and repeating Paul's last words, said, " 'Go to the devil !' Not so quick, young gentleman,—*festina lente*,—all in good time. What though I did, astonished at your premature request, say that you should receive nothing ; yet my great love for you may induce me to bestir myself on your behalf. 'The Asinæum,' it is true, only gives three shillings an article in general ; but I am its editor, and will intercede with the proprietors on your behalf. Yes—yes. I will see what is to be done. Stop a bit, my boy."

Paul, though very irascible, was easily pacified : he reseated himself, and, taking Mac Grawler's hand, said—

"Forgive me for my petulance, my dear sir ; but, to tell you the honest truth, I am very low in the world just at present, and must get money in some way or another : in short, I must either pick pockets or write (not gratuitously) for 'The Asinæum.'"

And, without farther preliminary, Paul related his present circumstances to the critic ; declared his determination not to return to the Mug ; and requested, at least, from the friendship of his old preceptor the accommodation of shelter for that night.

Mac Grawler was exceedingly disconcerted at hearing so bad an account of his pupil's finances as well as prospects ; for he had secretly intended to regale himself that evening with a bowl of punch, for which he purposed that Paul should pay ; but as he knew the quickness of parts possessed by the young gentleman, as also the great affection entertained for him by Mrs. Lobkins, who, in all probability, would solicit his return the next day, he thought it not unlikely that Paul would enjoy the same good fortune as that presiding over his feline companion, which, though it had just been kicked to the other end of the apartment, was now resuming its former occupation, unhurt, and no less merrily than before.   He, therefore, thought it would be imprudent to discard his quondam pupil, despite of his present poverty : and, moreover, although the first happy project of pocketing all the profits derivable from Paul's industry was now abandoned, he still perceived great facility in pocketing a part of the same receipts.   He therefore answered Paul very warmly, that he fully sympathised with him in his present melancholy situation ; that, so far as he was concerned, he would share his last *shilling* with his beloved pupil, but that he regretted at that moment he had only eleven-pence halfpenny in his pocket ; that he would, however, exert himself to the utmost in procuring an opening for Paul's literary genius ; and that, if Paul liked to take the slashing and plastering part of the business on himself, he would willingly surrender it to him, and give him all the profits whatever they might be. *En attendant*, he regretted that a violent rheumatism prevented his giving up his own bed to his pupil, but that he might, with all the pleasure imaginable, sleep upon the rug before the fire. Paul was so affected by this kindness in the worthy man, that, though not much addicted to the melting mood, he shed tears of gratitude ; he insisted, however, on now receiving the whole reward of his labours ; and at length it was settled, though with a noble reluctance on the part of Mac Grawler, that it should be equally shared between the critic and the critic's *protégé ;* the half profits being reasonably awarded to Mac Grawler for his instructions and his recommendation.

CHAPTER VI.

" Bad events peep out o' the tail of good purposes."
' BARTHOLOMEW FAIR.'

T was not long before there was a visible improvement in the pages of " The Asinæum : " the slashing part of that incomparable journal was suddenly conceived and carried on with a vigour and spirit which astonished the hallowed few who contributed to its circulation. It was not difficult to see that a new soldier had been enlisted in the service ; there was something so fresh and hearty about the abuse, that it could never have proceeded from the worn-out acerbity of an old *slasher*. To be sure, a little ignorance of ordinary facts, and an innovating method of applying words to meanings which they never were meant to denote, were now and then distinguishable in the criticisms of the new Achilles : nevertheless, it was easy to attribute these peculiarities to an original turn of thinking ; and the rise of the paper upon the appearance of a series of articles upon contemporary authors, written by this "eminent hand," was so remarkable, that fifty copies—a number perfectly unprecedented in the annals of " The Asinæum "— were absolutely sold in one week : indeed, remembering the principle on which it was founded, one sturdy old writer declared, that the journal would soon do for itself and become popular. There was a remarkable peculiarity about the literary *débutant*, who signed himself "Nobilitas." He not only put old words to a new sense, but he used words which had never, among the general run of writers, been used before. This was especially remarkable in the application of hard names to authors. Once, in censuring a popular writer for pleasing the public, and thereby growing rich, the "eminent hand " ended with—" He who surreptitiously accumulates *bustle*[1] is, in fact, nothing better than *a buzz gloak !* "[2]

These enigmatical words and recondite phrases imparted a great air of learning to the style of the new critic ; and, from the unintelligible sublimity of his diction, it seemed doubtful whether he was a poet from Highgate, or a philosopher from Koningsburg. At all events, the reviewer preserved his incognito, and, while his praises were rung at no less than three tea-tables, even glory appeared to him less delicious than disguise.

[1] Money.   [2] Pickpocket.

In this incognito, reader, thou hast already discovered Paul ; and now, we have to delight thee with a piece of unexampled morality in the excellent Mac Grawler. That worthy Mentor, perceiving that there was an inherent turn for dissipation and extravagance in our hero, resolved magnanimously rather to bring upon himself the sins of treachery and mal-appropriation, than suffer his friend and former pupil to incur those of wastefulness and profusion. Contrary, therefore, to the agreement made with Paul, instead of giving that youth the half of those profits consequent on his brilliant lucubrations, he imparted to him only one fourth, and, with the utmost tenderness for Paul's salvation, applied the other three portions of the same to his own necessities. The best actions are, alas ! often misconstrued in this world ; and we are now about to record a remarkable instance of that melancholy truth.

One evening, Mac Grawler, having "moistened his virtue" in the same manner that the great Cato is said to have done, in the confusion which such a process sometimes occasions in the best regulated heads, gave Paul what appeared to him the outline of a certain article, which he wished to be slashingly filled up, but what in reality was the following note from the editor of a monthly periodical —

      " Sir,

"Understanding that my friend, Mr. ——, proprietor of 'The Asinæum,' allows the very distinguished writer whom you have introduced to the literary world, and who signs himself 'Nobilitas,' only five shillings an article, I beg, through you, to tender him double that sum : the article required will be of an ordinary length.

" I am, sir, &c.,
" ————."

Now, that very morning, Mac Grawler had informed Paul of this offer, altering only, from the amiable motives we have already explained, the sum of ten shillings to that of four ; and no sooner did Paul read the communication we have placed before the reader, than instead of gratitude to Mac Grawler for his consideration of Paul's moral infirmities, he conceived against that gentleman the most bitter resentment. He did not, however, vent his feelings at once upon the Scotsman ; indeed, at that moment, as the sage was in a deep sleep under the table, it would have been to no purpose had he unbridled his indignation. But he resolved without loss of time to quit the abode of the critic. "And, indeed," said he, soliloquising, " I am heartily tired of this life, and shall be very glad to seek some other employment. Fortunately, I have hoarded up five guineas and four shillings, and with that independence in my possession, since I have forsworn gambling, I cannot easily starve."

To this soliloquy succeeded a misanthropical reverie upon the faithlessness of friends ; and the meditation ended in Paul's making up a little bundle of such clothes, &c., as Dummie had succeeded in removing from the Mug, and which Paul had taken from the rag-merchant's abode one morning when Dummie was abroad.

When this easy task was concluded, Paul wrote a short and upbraiding note to his illustrious preceptor, and left it unsealed on the table. He then, upsetting the ink-bottle on Mac Grawler's sleeping countenance, departed from the house, and strolled away he cared not whither.

The evening was gradually closing as Paul, chewing the cud of his bitter fancies, found himself on London Bridge. He paused there, and, leaning over the bridge, gazed wistfully on the gloomy waters that rolled onward, caring not a minnow for the numerous charming young ladies who have thought proper to drown themselves in those merciless waves, thereby depriving many a good mistress of an excellent housemaid or an invaluable cook, and many a treacherous Phaon of letters beginning with "Parjured Villen," and ending with " Your affectionot but molancolly Molly."

While thus musing, he was suddenly accosted by a gentleman in boots and spurs, having a riding-whip in one hand, and the other hand stuck in the pocket of his inexpressibles. The hat of the gallant was gracefully and carefully put on, so as to derange as little as possible a profusion of dark curls which, streaming with unguents, fell low not only on either side of the face, but on the neck, and even the shoulders of the owner. The face was saturnine and strongly marked, but handsome and striking. There was a mixture of frippery and sternness in its expression ;—something between Madame Vestris and T. P. Cooke, or between "lovely Sally" and a "Captain bold of Halifax." The stature of this personage was remarkably tall, and his figure was stout, muscular, and well knit. In fine, to complete his portrait, and give our readers of the present day an exact idea of this hero of the past, we shall add that he was altogether that sort of gentleman one sees swaggering in the Burlington Arcade, with his hair and hat on one side, and a military cloak thrown over his shoulders ;—or prowling in Regent Street, towards the evening, *whiskered* and *cigarred*.

Laying his hand on the shoulder of our hero, this gentleman said, with an affected intonation of voice :—

" How dost, my fine fellow ?—long since I saw you !—dammee, but you look the worse for wear. What hast thou been doing with thyself ? "

"Ha!" cried our hero, returning the salutation of the stranger, "and is it Long Ned whom I behold? I am indeed glad to meet you; and I say, my friend, I hope what I heard of you is not true!"

"Hist!" said Long Ned, looking round fearfully, and sinking his voice,—" never talk of what you hear of gentlemen, except you wish to bring them to their last dying speech and confession. But come with me, my lad; there is a tavern hard by, and we may as well discuss matters over a pint of wine. You look cursed seedy, to be sure, but I can tell Bill the waiter—famous fellow, that Bill! —that you are one of my tenants, come to complain of my steward, who has just distrained you for rent, you dog!—No wonder you look so worn in the rigging. Come, follow me. I can't walk *with* thee. It would look too like Northumberland House and the butcher's abode next door taking a stroll together."

"Really, Mr. Pepper," said our hero, colouring, and by no means pleased with the ingenious comparison of his friend, "if you are ashamed of my clothes, which I own might be newer, I will not wound you with my——"

"Pooh! my lad—pooh!" cried Long Ned, interrupting him; "never take offence. *I* never do. I never take any thing but money,—except, indeed, watches. I don't mean to hurt your feelings,—all of us have been poor once. 'Gad, I remember when I had not a dud to my back, and now, you see me—you see me, Paul! But come, 'tis only through the streets you need separate from me. Keep a little behind—very little—that will do.—Ay, that will do," repeated Long Ned, mutteringly to himself, "they'll take him for a bailiff. It looks handsome nowadays to be so attended. It shows one *had* credit *once!*"

Meanwhile Paul, though by no means pleased with the contempt expressed for his personal appearance by his lengthy associate, and impressed with a keener sense than ever of the crimes of his coat and the vices of his other garment—"O breathe not its name!" —followed doggedly and sullenly the strutting steps of the coxcombical Mr. Pepper. That personage arrived at last at a small tavern, and, arresting a waiter who was running across the passage into the coffee-room with a dish of hung-beef, demanded (no doubt from a pleasing anticipation of a similar pendulous catastrophe) a plate of the same excellent cheer, to be carried, in company with a bottle of port, into a private apartment. No sooner did he find himself alone with Paul, than, bursting into a loud laugh, Mr. Ned surveyed his comrade from head to foot through an eye-glass which he wore fastened to his button-hole by a piece of blue riband

" Well—'gad now," said he, stopping ever and anon, as if to laugh the more heartily—"stab my vitals, but you are a comical quiz ; I wonder what the women would say, if they saw the dashing Edward Pepper, Esquire, walking arm in arm with thee at Ranelagh or Vauxhall ? Nay, man, never be downcast ; if I laugh at thee, it is only to make thee look a little merrier thyself. Why, thou lookest like a book of my grandfather's called Burton's *Anatomy of Melancholy ;* and faith, a shabbier bound copy of it I never saw."

" These jests are a little hard," said Paul, struggling between anger and an attempt to smile ; and then recollecting his late literary occupations, and the many extracts he had taken from *Gleanings of the Belles Lettres,* in order to impart elegance to his criticisms, he threw out his hand theatrically, and spouted with a solemn face—

" ' Of all the griefs that harass the distrest,
Sure the most bitter is a scornful jest ! ' "

" Well now, prithee forgive me," said Long Ned, composing his features ; " and just tell me what you have been doing the last two months."

" Slashing and plastering ! " said Paul, with conscious pride.

" Slashing and what ! The boy's mad,—what do you mean, Paul ? "

" In other words," said our hero, speaking very slowly, "know, O very Long Ned ! that I have been critic to 'The Asinæum.'"

If Paul's comrade laughed at first, he now laughed ten times more merrily than ever. He threw his length of limb upon a neighbouring sofa, and literally rolled with cachinnatory convulsions ; nor did his risible emotions subside until the entrance of the hung-beef restored him to recollection. Seeing, then, that a cloud lowered over Paul's countenance, he went up to him, with something like gravity ; begged his pardon for his want of politeness ; and desired him to wash away all unkindness in a bumper of port. Paul, whose excellent dispositions we have before had occasion to remark, was not impervious to his friend's apologies. He assured Long Ned, that he quite forgave him for his ridicule of the high situation he (Paul) had enjoyed in the literary world ; that it was the duty of a public censor to bear no malice ; and that he should be very glad to take his share in the interment of the hung-beef.

The pair now sat down to their repast, and Paul, who had fared but meagrely in that Temple of Athena over which Mac Grawler presided, did ample justice to the viands before him. By degrees, as he ate and drank, his heart opened to his companion ; and, laying aside that Asinæum dignity which he had at first thought it incumbent on him to assume, he entertained Pepper with all the particulars

of the life he had lately passed. He narrated to him his breach
with Dame Lobkins ; his agreement with Mac Grawler ; the glory
he had acquired, and the wrongs he had sustained ; and he concluded, as now the second bottle made its appearance, by stating
his desire of exchanging, for some more active profession, that
sedentary career which he had so promisingly begun.

This last part of Paul's confessions secretly delighted the soul of
Long Ned ; for that experienced collector of the highways—(Ned
was, indeed, of no less noble a profession)—had long fixed an eye
upon our hero, as one whom he thought likely to be an honour to
that enterprising calling which he espoused, and an useful assistant
to himself. He had not, in his earlier acquaintance with Paul,
when the youth was under the roof and the *surveillance* of the practised and wary Mrs. Lobkins, deemed it prudent to expose the exact
nature of his own pursuits, and had contented himself by gradually
ripening the mind and the finances of Paul into that state when the
proposition of a leap from a hedge would not be likely greatly to
revolt the person to whom it was made. He now thought that time
near at hand ; and, filling our hero's glass up to the brim, thus
artfully addressed him :—

"Courage, my friend !—your narration has given me a sensible
pleasure ; for, curse me if it has not strengthened my favourite
opinion,—that everything is for the best. If it had not been for the
meanness of that pitiful fellow, Mac Grawler, you might still be
inspired with the paltry ambition of earning a few shillings a-week,
and villifying a parcel of poor devils in the what-d'ye-call-it, with a
hard name ; whereas now, my good Paul, I trust I shall be able to
open to your genius a new career, in which guineas are had for the
asking,—in which you may wear fine clothes, and ogle the ladies at
Ranelagh ; and when you are tired of glory and liberty, Paul, why
you have only to make your bow to an heiress, or a widow with a
spanking jointure, and quit the hum of men like a Cincinnatus !"

Though Paul's perception into the abstruser branches of morals
was not very acute,—and at that time the port wine had considerably confused the few notions he possessed upon "the beauty of
virtue,"—yet he could not but perceive that Mr. Pepper's insinuated
proposition was far from being one which the bench of bishops,
or a synod of moralists, would conscientiously have approved : he
consequently remained silent ; and Long Ned, after a pause,
continued—

"You know my genealogy, my good fellow ?—I was the son of
Lawyer Pepper, a shrewd old dog, but as hot as Calcutta ; and the
grandson of Sexton Pepper, a great author, who wrote verses on
tombstones, and kept a stall of religious tracts in Carlisle. My

grandfather, the sexton, was the best temper of the family; for all of us are a little inclined to be hot in the mouth. Well, my fine fellow, my father left me his blessing, and this devilish good head of hair. I lived for some years on my own resources. I found it a particularly inconvenient mode of life, and of late I have taken to live on the public. My father and grandfather did it before me, though in a different line. 'Tis the pleasantest plan in the world. Follow my example, and your coat shall be as spruce as my own.—Master Paul, your health!"

"But, O longest of mortals!" said Paul, refilling his glass, "though the public may allow you to eat your mutton off their backs for a short time, they will kick up at last, and upset you and your banquet: in other words,—(pardon my metaphor, dear Ned, in remembrance of the part I have lately maintained in 'The Asinæum,' that most magnificent and metaphorical of journals!) —in other words, the police will nab thee at last; and thou wilt have the distinguished fate, as thou already hast the distinguishing characteristic—of Absalom!"

"You mean that I shall be hanged," said Long Ned. "That may or may not be; but he who fears death never enjoys life. Consider, Paul, that though hanging is a bad fate, starving is a worse; wherefore fill your glass, and let us drink to the health of that great donkey, the people, and may we never want saddles to ride it!"

"To the great donkey," cried Paul, tossing off his bumper; "may your (y)ears be as long! But I own to you, my friend, that I cannot enter into your plans. And, as a token of my resolution, I shall drink no more, for my eyes already begin to dance in the air: and if I listen longer to your resistless eloquence, my feet may share the same fate!"

So saying, Paul rose; nor could any entreaty on the part of his entertainer, persuade him to resume his seat.

"Nay, as you will," said Pepper, affecting a *nonchalant* tone, and arranging his cravat before the glass. "Nay, as you will. Ned Pepper requires no man's companionship against his liking; and if the noble spark of ambition be not in your bosom, 'tis no use spending my breath in blowing at what only existed in my too flattering opinion of your qualities. So, then, you propose to return to Mac Grawler, (the scurvy old cheat!) and pass the inglorious remainder of your life in the mangling of authors and the murder of grammar? Go, my good fellow, go! scribble again and for ever for Mac Grawler, and let him live upon thy brains, instead of suffering thy brains to——"

"Hold!" cried Paul. "Although I may have some scruples

which prevent my adoption of that rising line of life you have proposed to me, yet you are very much mistaken if you imagine me so spiritless as any longer to subject myself to the frauds of that rascal Mac Grawler. No! My present intention is to pay my old nurse a visit. It appears to me passing strange, that though I have left her so many weeks, she has never relented enough to track me out, which one would think would have been no difficult matter : and now you see that I am pretty well off, having five guineas and four shillings, all my own, and she can scarcely think I want her money, my heart melts to her, and I shall go and ask pardon for my haste !"

"Pshaw ! sentimental," cried Long Ned, a little alarmed at the thought of Paul's gliding from those clutches which he thought had now so firmly closed upon him. "Why, you surely don't mean, after having once tasted the joys of independence, to go back to the boozing ken, and bear all Mother Lobkins' drunken tantarums ! Better have stayed with Mac Grawler of the two !"

"You mistake me," answered Paul ; "I mean solely to make it up with her, and get her permission to see the world. My ultimate intention is—to travel."

"Right !" cried Ned, "on the high-road—and on horseback, I hope !"

"No, my Colossus of Roads ! No! I am in doubt whether or not I shall enlist in a marching regiment, or (give me your advice on it) I fancy I have a great turn for the stage, ever since I saw Garrick in Richard. Shall I turn stroller ? It must be a merry life."

"O, the devil !" cried Ned. "I myself once did Cassio in a barn, and every one swore I enacted the drunken scene to perfection : but you have no notion what a lamentable life it is to a man of any susceptibility. No, my friend. No ! There is only one line in all the old plays worthy thy attention—

'*Toby* or not *toby*,[1] that is the question.'

I forget the rest !"

"Well !" said our hero, answering in the same jocular vein, "I confess, I have 'the actor's high ambition.' It is astonishing how my heart beat, when Richard cried out, 'Come *bustle*,[2] *bustle!*' Yes, Pepper, avaunt !—

'A thousand hearts are great within my bosom '"

"Well, well," said Long Ned, stretching himself, "since you are so fond of the play, what say you to an excursion thither to-night? Garrick acts !"

[1] The highway [2] Money.

"Done!" cried Paul.

"Done!" echoed lazily Long Ned, rising with that *blasé* air which distinguishes the matured man of the world from the enthusiastic tyro. "Done! and we will adjourn afterwards to the White Horse."

"But stay a moment," said Paul; "if you remember I owed you a guinea when I last saw you. here it is!"

"Nonsense," exclaimed Long Ned, refusing the money, "nonsense! you want the money at present; pay me when you are richer. Nay, never be coy about it: debts of honour are not paid now as they used to be. We lads of the Fish Lane Club have changed all that. Well, well, if I must."

And Long Ned, seeing that Paul insisted, pocketed the guinea. When this delicate matter had been arranged,—

"Come," said Pepper, "come get your hat; but, bless me! I have forgotten one thing."

"What?"

"Why, my fine Paul, consider, the play is a bang-up sort of a place; look at your coat and your waistcoat, that's all!"

Our hero was struck dumb with this *argumentum ad hominem*. But Long Ned, after enjoying his perplexity, relieved him of it, by telling him that he knew of an honest tradesman who kept a ready-made shop, just by the theatre, and who would fit him out in a moment.

In fact, Long Ned was as good as his word; he carried Paul to a tailor, who gave him for the sum of thirty shillings, half ready money, half on credit, a green coat with a tarnished gold lace, a pair of red inexpressibles, and a pepper-and-salt waistcoat; it is true, they were somewhat of the largest, for they had once belonged to no less a person than Long Ned himself: but Paul did not then regard those niceties of apparel, as he was subsequently taught to do by Gentleman George (a personage hereafter to be introduced to our reader), and he went to the theatre, as well satisfied with himself as if he had been Mr. T——, or the Count de M——.

Our adventurers are now quietly seated in the theatre, and we shall not think it necessary to detail the performances they saw, or the observations they made. Long Ned was one of those superior beings of the road who would not for the world have condescended to appear anywhere but in the boxes, and, accordingly, the friends procured a couple of places in the dress-tier. In the next box to the one our adventurers adorned, they remarked, more especially than the rest of the audience, a gentleman and a young lady seated next each other; the latter, who was about thirteen years old, was so uncommonly beautiful, that Paul, despite his dramatic enthusiasm, could scarcely divert his eyes from her countenance to the stage. Her hair, of a bright and fair auburn, hung in profuse ringlets about her neck, shedding a softer shade upon a complexion in which the roses seemed just budding, as it were, into blush. Her eyes large, blue, and rather languishing than brilliant, were curtained by the darkest lashes ; her mouth seemed literally girt with smiles ; so numberless were the dimples, that every time the full, ripe, dewy lips were parted, rose into sight ; and the enchantment of the dimples was aided by two rows of teeth more dazzling than the richest pearls that ever glittered on a bride But the chief charm of the face was its exceeding and touching air of innocence and girlish softness ; you might have gazed for ever upon that first unspeakable bloom, that all untouched and stainless down, which seemed as if a very breath could mar it. Perhaps the face might have wanted animation ; but, perhaps, also, it borrowed from that want an attraction ; the repose of the features was so soft and gentle, that the eye wandered there with the same delight, and left it with the same reluctance, which it experiences in dwelling on or in quitting those hues which are found to harmonise the most with its vision. But while Paul was feeding his gaze on this young beauty, the keen glances of Long Ned had found an object no less fascinating in a large gold watch which the gentleman who accompanied the damsel ever and anon brought to his eye, as if he were waxing a little weary of the length of the pieces or the lingering progression of time.

"What a beautiful face !" whispered Paul.

"Is the face gold, then, as well as the back ?" whispered Long Ned in return.

Our hero started, frowned,—and despite the gigantic stature of his comrade, told him, very angrily, to find some other subject for jesting. Ned in his turn stared, but made no reply.

Meanwhile Paul, though the lady was rather too young to fall in love with, began wondering what relationship her companion bore to her. Though the gentleman altogether was handsome, yet his features, and the whole character of his face, were widely different from those on which Paul gazed with such delight. He was not, seemingly, above five-and-forty, but his forehead was knit into many a line and furrow ; and in his eyes the light, though searching, was more sober and staid than became his years. A disagreeable expression played about the mouth, and the shape of the face, which was long and thin, considerably detracted from the prepossessing effect of a handsome aquiline nose, fine teeth, and a dark, manly, though sallow complexion. There was a mingled air of shrewdness and distraction in the expression of his face. He seemed to pay very little attention to the play, or to any thing about him ; but he testified very considerable alacrity when the play was over in putting her cloak around his young companion, and in threading their way through the thick crowd that the boxes were now pouring forth.

Paul and his companion silently, and each with very different motives from the other, followed them. They were now at the door of the theatre.

A servant stepped forward and informed the gentleman that his carriage was a few paces distant, but that it might be some time before it could drive up to the theatre.

"Can you walk to the carriage, my dear," said the gentleman to his young charge ; and she answering in the affirmative, they both left the house, preceded by the servant.

"Come on !" said Long Ned, hastily, and walking in the same direction which the strangers had taken. Paul readily agreed : they soon overtook the strangers. Long Ned walked the nearest to the gentleman, and brushed by him in passing. Presently a voice cried, "Stop thief!" and Long Ned saying to Paul, "Shift for yourself—run !" darted from our hero's side into the crowd, and vanished in a twinkling. Before Paul could recover his amaze, he found himself suddenly seized by the collar ; he turned abruptly, and saw the dark face of the young lady's companion.

"Rascal !" cried the gentleman, "my watch !"

"Watch !" repeated Paul, bewildered ; and only for the sake of the young lady refraining from knocking down his arrester.— "Watch !"

"Ay, young man !" cried a fellow in a great coat, who now suddenly appeared on the other side of Paul ; "this gentleman's watch, please your honour (addressing the complainant), I be a watch, too, —shall I take up this chap ?"

"By all means," cried the gentleman ; "I would not have lost my watch for twice its value. I can swear I saw this fellow's companion snatch it from my fob. The thief's gone ; but we have at least the accomplice. I give him in strict charge to you, watchman ; take the consequences if you let him escape."

The watchman answered, sullenly, that he did not want to be threatened, and he knew how to discharge his duty.

"Don't answer me, fellow !" said the gentleman, haughtily ; "do as I tell you !" And, after a little colloquy, Paul found himself suddenly marched off between two tall fellows, who looked prodigiously inclined to eat him. By this time he had recovered his surprise and dismay ; he did not want the penetration to see that his companion had really committed the offence for which *he* was charged ; and he also foresaw that the circumstance might be attended with disagreeable consequences to himself. Under all the features of the case, he thought that an attempt to escape would not be an imprudent proceeding on his part ; accordingly, after moving a few paces very quietly and very passively, he watched his opportunity, wrenched himself from the gripe of the gentleman on his left, and brought the hand thus released against the cheek of the gentleman on his right with so hearty a good will as to cause him to relinquish his hold, and retreat several paces towards the areas in a slanting position. But that roundabout sort of blow with the left fist is very unfavourable towards the preservation of a firm balance ; and before Paul had recovered sufficiently to make an effectual "bolt," he was prostrated to the earth by a blow from the other and undamaged watchman, which utterly deprived him of his senses ; and when he recovered those useful possessions (which a man may reasonably boast of losing, since it is only the minority who have them to lose), he found himself stretched on a bench in the watchhouse.

CHAPTER VII.

" Begirt with many a gallant slave,
Apparell'd as becomes the brave,
Old Giaffir sat in his divan :

*　　*　　*　　*　　*

*　　*　　*　　*　　*

Much I misdoubt this wayward boy
W'ill one day work me more annoy "
'BRIDE OF ABYDOS.'

THE learned and ingenious John Schweighæuser (a name facile to spell and mellifluous to pronounce) hath been pleased, in that *Appendix continens particulam doctrinæ de mente humanâ*, which closeth the volume of his *Opuscula Academica*, to observe (we translate from memory) that, "in the infinite variety of things which in the theatre of the world occur to a man's survey, or in some manner or another affect his body or his mind, by far the greater part are so contrived as to bring to him rather some sense of pleasure than of pain or discomfort." Assuming that this holds generally good in well-constituted frames, we point out a notable example in the case of the incarcerated Paul ; for, although that youth was in no agreeable situation at the time present, and although nothing very encouraging smiled upon him from the prospects of the future, yet, as soon as he had recovered his consciousness, and given himself a rousing shake, he found an immediate source of pleasure in discovering, first, that several ladies and gentlemen bore him company in his imprisonment ; and, secondly, in perceiving a huge jug of water within his reach, which, as his awaking sensation was that of burning thirst, he delightedly emptied at a draught.   He then, stretching himself, looked around with a wistful earnestness, and discovered a back turned towards him, and recumbent on the floor, which, at the very first glance, appeared to him familiar.   "Surely," thought he, "I know that frieze coat, and the peculiar turn of those narrow shoulders."   Thus soliloquising, he raised himself, and, putting out his leg, he gently kicked the reclining form.   "Muttering strange oaths," the form turned round, and, raising itself upon that inhospitable part of the body in which the introduction of foreign feet is considered any thing but an honour, it fixed its dull blue eyes upon the face of the disturber of its slumbers, gradually opening them wider and wider, until they seemed to have enlarged themselves into proportions fit for the swallowing of the important truth that burst upon them, and then from the mouth of the creature issued—

"Queer my glims, if that ben't little Paul ! "

"Ay, Dummie, here I am !—Not been long without being laid by the heels, you see !—Life is short ; we must make the best use of our time ! "

Upon this, Mr. Dunnaker (it was no less respectable a person) scrambled up from the floor, and seating himself on the bench beside Paul, said, in a pitying tone,—

"Vy, laus-a-me ! if you ben't knocked o' the head !—Your poll's as bloody as Murphy's face [1] ven his throat's cut ! "

"'Tis only the fortune of war, Dummie, and a mere trifle · the heads manufactured at Thames Court are not easily put out of order. But tell me, how come you here ? "

"Vy, I had been lushing heavy vet——"

"Till you grew light in the head, eh ? and fell into the kennel."

" Yes."

"Mine is a worse business than that, I fear : " and therewith Paul, in a lower voice, related to the trusty Dummie the train of accidents which had conducted him to his present asylum.   Dummie's face elongated as he listened : however, when the narrative was over, he endeavoured such consolatory palliatives as occurred to him   He represented, first, the possibility that the gentleman might not take the trouble to appear ; secondly, the certainty that no watch was found about Paul's person , thirdly, the fact that, even by the gentle-

[1] "Murphy's face," unlearned reader, appeareth, in Irish phrase, to mean "pig's head."

man's confession, Paul had not been the actual offender ; fourthly,
if the worst came to the worst, what were a few weeks', or even
months', imprisonment ?

"Blow me tight!" said Dummie, "if it ben't as good a vay of
passing the time as a cove as is fond of snuggery need desire ! "

This observation had no comfort for Paul, who recoiled, with all
the maiden coyness of one to whom such unions are unfamiliar, from
a matrimonial alliance with the *snuggery* of the House of Correction.
He rather trusted to another source for consolation.   In a word, he
encouraged the flattering belief, that Long Ned, finding that Paul
had been caught instead of himself, would have the generosity to
come forward and exculpate him from the charge.   On hinting this
idea to Dummie, that accomplished "man about town" could not
for some time believe that any simpleton could be so thoroughly unacquainted with the world as seriously to entertain so ridiculous a
notion ; and, indeed, it is somewhat remarkable that such a hope
should ever have told its flattering tale to one brought up in the house
of Mrs. Margaret Lobkins.   But Paul, we have seen, had formed
many of his notions from books ; and he had the same fine theories
of your "moral rogue," that possess the minds of young patriots when
they first leave college for the House of Commons, and think integrity
a prettier thing than office.

Mr. Dunnaker urged Paul, seriously, to dismiss so vague and
childish a fancy from his breast, and rather to think of what line of
defence it would be best for him to pursue.   This subject being at
length exhausted, Paul recurred to Mrs. Lobkins, and inquired
whether Dummie had lately honoured that lady with a visit.

Mr. Dunnaker replied that he had, though with much difficulty,
appeased her anger against him for his supposed abetment of Paul's
excesses, and that of late she had held sundry conversations with
Dummie respecting our hero himself.   Upon questioning Dummie
further, Paul learned the good matron's reasons for not evincing that
solicitude for his return which our hero had reasonably anticipated.
The fact was, that she, having no confidence whatsoever in his own
resources independent of her, had not been sorry of an opportunity
effectually, as she hoped, to humble that pride which had so revolted
her ; and she pleased her vanity by anticipating the time when Paul,
starved into submission, would gladly and penitently re-seek the
shelter of her roof, and, tamed as it were by experience, would never
again kick against the yoke which her matronly prudence thought it
fitting to impose upon him.   She contented herself, then, with obtaining from Dummie the intelligence that our hero was under Mac
Grawler's roof, and, therefore, out of all positive danger to life and
limb ; and, as she could not foresee the ingenious exertions of intellect

by which Paul had converted himself into the " Nobilitas " of " The Asinæum," and thereby saved himself from utter penury, she was perfectly convinced, from her knowledge of character, that the illustrious Mac Grawler would not long continue that protection to the rebellious *protégé*, which, in her opinion, was his only preservative from picking pockets or famishing. To the former decent alternative she knew Paul's great and jejune aversion, and she consequently had little fear for his morals or his safety, in thus abandoning him for a while to chance. Any anxiety, too, that she might otherwise have keenly experienced was deadened by the habitual intoxication now increasing upon the good lady with age, and which, though at times she could be excited to all her characteristic vehemence, kept her senses for the most part plunged into a Læthean stupor ; or to speak more courteously, into a poetical abstraction from the things of the external world.

"But," said Dummie, as by degrees he imparted the solution of the dame's conduct to the listening ear of his companion—" But I hopes as how ven you be out of this ere scrape, leetle Paul, you vill take varning, and drop Meester Peppei's acquaintance (vich, I must say, I vas alvays a sorry to see you hencourage), and go home to the Mug, and fam grasp the old mort, for she has not been like the same cretur ever since you vent. She's a delicate-arted 'oman, that Piggy Lob !"

So appropriate a panegyiic on Mrs. Margaret Lobkins might, at another time, have excited Paul's risible muscles ; but at that moment he really felt compunction for the unceremonious manner in which he had left her, and the softness of regretful affection imbued in its hallowing colours even the image of Piggy Lob.

In conversation of this intellectual and domestic description, the night and ensuing morning passed away, till Paul found himself in the awful presence of Justice Burnflat. Several cases were disposed of before his own, and among others Mr. Dummie Dunnaker obtained his release, though not without a severe reprimand for his sin of inebriety, which no doubt sensibly affected the ingenious spirit of that noble character. At length Paul's turn came. He heard, as he took his station, a general buzz. At first he imagined it was at his own interesting appearance ; but, raising his eyes, he perceived that it was at the entrance of the gentleman who was to become his accuser.

"Hush," said some one near him, "'tis Lawyer Brandon. Ah, he's a 'cute fellow ! it will go hard with the person he complains of."

There was a happy fund of elasticity of spirit about our hero ; and though he had not the good fortune to have "a blighted heart," a circumstance which, by the poets and philosophers of the present day, is supposed to inspire a man with wonderful courage, and make him impervious to all misfortunes; yet he bore himself up with wonderful courage under his present trying situation, and was far from overwhelmed, though he was certainly a little damped by the observation he had just heard.

Mr. Brandon was, indeed, a barrister of considerable reputation, and in high esteem in the world, not only for talent, but also for a great austerity of manners, which, though a little mingled with stern-ness and acerbity for the errors of other men, was naturally thought the more praiseworthy on that account; there being, as persons of experience are doubtless aware, two divisions in the first class of morality: imprimis, a great hatred for the vices of one's neighbour; secondly, the possession of virtues in one's self.

Mr. Brandon was received with great courtesy by Justice Burnflat, and as he came, watch in hand (a borrowed watch), saying that his time was worth five guineas a moment, the justice proceeded immediately to business.

Nothing could be clearer, shorter, or more satisfactory, than the evidence of Mr. Brandon. The corroborative testimony of the watchman followed; and then Paul was called upon for his defence. This was equally brief with the charge;—but, alas! it was not equally satisfactory. It consisted in a firm declaration of his innocence. His comrade, he confessed, might have stolen the watch, but he humbly suggested that that was exactly the very reason why *he* had *not* stolen it.

"How long, fellow," asked Justice Burnflat, "have you known your companion?"

"About half a year!"

"And what is his name and calling?"

Paul hesitated, and declined to answer.

"A sad piece of business!" said the justice, in a melancholy tone, and shaking his head portentously.

The lawyer acquiesced in the aphorism; but with great magnanimity observed, that he did not wish to be hard upon the young man. His youth was in his favour, and his offence was probably the consequence of evil company. He suggested, therefore, that as he must be perfectly aware of the address of his friend, he should receive a full pardon if he would immediately favour the magistrate with that information. He concluded by remarking, with singular philanthropy, that it was not the punishment of the youth, but the recovery of his watch, that he desired.

Justice Burnflat, having duly impressed upon our hero's mind the disinterested and Christian mercy of the complainant, and the ever-lasting obligation Paul was under to him for its display, now repeated, with double solemnity, those queries respecting the habitation and name of Long Ned, which our hero had before declined to answer.

Grieved are we to confess that Paul, ungrateful for, and wholly untouched by, the beautiful benignity of Lawyer Brandon, continued firm in his stubborn denial to betray his comrade, and with equal obduracy he continued to insist upon his own innocence and unblemished respectability of character.

"Your name, young man?" quoth the justice. "Your name, you say, is Paul—Paul what? you have many an *alias*, I'll be bound."

Here the young gentleman again hesitated: at length he replied,—

"Paul Lobkins, your worship."

"Lobkins!" repeated the judge—"Lobkins! come hither, Saunders: have not we that name down in our black books?"

"So, please your worship," quoth a little stout man, very useful in many respects to the Festus of the police, "there is one Peggy Lobkins, who keeps a public-house, a sort of flash ken, called the Mug, in Thames Court, not exactly in our beat, your worship."

"Ho, ho!" said Justice Burnflat, winking at Mr. Brandon, "we must sift this a little. Pray, Mr. Paul Lobkins, what relation is the good landlady of the Mug, in Thames Court, to yourself?"

"None at all, sir," said Paul, hastily,—"she's only a friend!"

Upon this there was a laugh in the court.

"Silence," cried the justice: "and I dare say, Mr. Paul Lobkins, that this friend of yours will vouch for the respectability of your character, upon which you are pleased to value yourself?"

"I have not a doubt of it, sir," answered Paul; and there was another laugh.

"And is there any other equally weighty and praiseworthy friend of yours who will do you the like kindness?"

Paul hesitated; and at that moment, to the surprise of the court, but, above all, to the utter and astounding surprise of himself, two gentlemen, dressed in the height of the fashion, pushed forward, and, bowing to the justice, declared themselves ready to vouch for the thorough respectability and unimpeachable character of Mr. Paul Lobkins, whom they had known, they said, for many years, and for whom they had the greatest respect. While Paul was surveying the persons of these kind friends, whom he never remembered to have seen before in the course of his life, the lawyer, who was a very sharp fellow, whispered to the magistrate; and that dignitary nodding as in assent, and eyeing the new comers, inquired the names of Mr. Lobkins's witnesses.

"Mr. Eustace Fitzherbert, and Mr. William Howard Russell," were the several replies.

Names so aristocratic produced a general sensation. But the impenetrable justice, calling the same Mr. Saunders he had addressed before, asked him to examine well the countenances of Mr. Lobkins's friends.

As the alguazil eyed the features of the memorable Don Raphael and the illustrious Manuel Morales, when the former of those accomplished personages thought it convenient to assume the travelling dignity of an Italian prince, son of the sovereign of the valleys which lie between Switzerland, the Milanese, and Savoy, while the latter was contented with being servant to *Monseigneur le Prince;* even so, with far more earnestness than respect did Mr. Saunders eye the features of those high-born gentlemen, Messrs. Eustace Fitzherbert and William Howard Russell ; but, after a long survey, he withdrew his eyes, made an unsatisfactory and unrecognising gesture to the magistrate, and said,—" Please your worship, they are none of my flock ; but Bill Troutling knows more of this sort of genteel chaps than I does."

" Bid Bill Troutling appear ! " was the laconic order.

At that name a certain modest confusion might have been visible in the faces of Mr. Eustace Fitzherbert and Mr William Howard Russell, had not the attention of the court been immediately directed to another case. A poor woman had been committed for seven days to the House of Correction on a charge of *disrespectability.* Her husband, the person most interested in the matter, now came forward to disprove the charge ; and by help of his neighbours he succeeded.

" It is all very true," said Justice Burnflat ; " but as your wife, my good fellow, will be out in five days, it will be scarcely worth while to release her now."[1]

So judicious a decision could not fail of satisfying the husband ; and the audience became from that moment enlightened as to a very remarkable truth, viz., that five days out of seven bear a peculiarly small proportion to the remaining two , and that people in England have so prodigious a love for punishment, that though it is not worth while to release an innocent woman from prison five days sooner than one would otherwise have done, it is exceedingly well worth while to commit her to prison for seven !

When the husband, passing his rough hand across his eyes, and muttering some vulgar impertinence or another, had withdrawn, Mr. Saunders said,—

[1] A fact, occurring in the month of January, 1830.—*Vide* " The Morning Herald."

"Here be Bill Troutling, your worship!"

"Oh, well," quoth the justice,—"and now Mr. Eustace Fitz —— Hallo, how's this! where are Mr. William Howard Russell and his friend Mr. Eustace Fitzherbert?"

> " Echo answered,—Where ?"

Those noble gentlemen, having a natural dislike to be confronted with so low a person as Mr. Bill Troutling, had, the instant public interest was directed from them, silently disappeared from a scene where their rank in life seemed so little regarded. If, reader, you should be anxious to learn from what part of the world the transitory visitants appeared, know that they were spirits sent by that inimitable magician, Long Ned, partly to report how matters fared in the court; for Mr. Pepper, in pursuance of that old policy which teaches that the nearer the fox is to the hunters the more chance he has of being overlooked, had, immediately on his abrupt departure from Paul, dived into a house in the very street where his ingenuity had displayed itself, and in which oysters and ale nightly allured and regaled an assembly that, to speak impartially, was more numerous than select : there had he learned how a pickpocket had been seized for unlawful affection to another man's watch; and there, while he quietly seasoned his oysters, had he, with his characteristic acuteness, satisfied his mind, by the conviction that that arrested unfortunate was no other than Paul. Partly, therefore, as a precaution for his own safety, that he might receive early intelligence should Paul's defence make a change of residence expedient, and partly (out of the friendliness of fellowship) to back his companion with such aid as the favourable testimony of two well-dressed persons, little known "about town," might confer, he had despatched those celestial beings who had appeared under the mortal names of Eustace Fitzherbert and William Howard Russell, to the imperial court of Justice Burnflat. Having thus accounted for the apparition (the *disapparition* requires no commentary) of Paul's "friends," we return to Paul himself.

Despite the perils with which he was girt, our young hero fought out to the last, but the justice was not by any means willing to displease Mr. Brandon; and observing that an incredulous and biting sneer remained stationary on that gentleman's lip during the whole of Paul's defence, he could not but shape his decision according to the well-known acuteness of the celebrated lawyer. Paul was accordingly sentenced to retire for three months to that country-house situated at Bridewell, to which the ungrateful functionaries of justice often banish their most active citizens.

As soon as the sentence was passed, Brandon, whose keen

eyes saw no hope of recovering his lost treasure, declared that the rascal had perfectly the Old Bailey cut of countenance ; and that he did not doubt but, if ever he lived to be a judge, he should also live to pass a very different description of sentence on the offender.

So saying, he resolved to lose no more time, but very abruptly left the office, without any other comfort than the remembrance that, at all events, he had sent the boy to a place where, let him be ever so innocent at present, he was certain to come out as much inclined to be guilty as his friends could desire, joined to such moral reflection as the tragedy of Bombastes Furioso might have afforded to himself in that sententious and terse line,—

" Thy watch is gone,—watches are made *to go !* "

Meanwhile, Paul was conducted in state to his retreat, in company with two other offenders, one a middle-aged man, though a very old "*file*" who was sentenced for getting money under false pretences, and the other a little boy, who had been found guilty of sleeping under a colonnade ; it being the especial beauty of the English law to make no fine-drawn and nonsensical shades of difference between vice and misfortune, and its peculiar method of protecting the honest being to make as many rogues as possible in as short a space of time.

CHAPTER VIII.

"COMMON SENSE.—*What is the end of punishment as regards the individual punished ?*
CUSTOM.—*To make him better ?*
COMMON SENSE.—*How do you punish young offenders who are (from their youth) peculiarly alive to example, and whom it is therefore more easy either to ruin or reform than the matured ?*
CUSTOM.—*We send them to the House of Correction, to associate with the d——dest rascals in the country !*"
   'DIALOGUE BETWEEN COMMON SENSE AND CUSTOM.'—VERY SCARCE

AS it was rather late in the day when Paul made his first *entrée* at Bridewell, he passed that night in the "receiving-room." The next morning, as soon as he had been examined by the surgeon, and clothed in the customary uniform, he was ushered, according to his classification, among the good company who had been considered guilty of that compendious offence, "a misdemeanour." Here a tall gentleman marched up to him, and addressed him in a certain language, which might be called the freemasonry of flash ; and which Paul, though he did not comprehend *verbatim*, rightly understood to be an inquiry whether he was a thorough rogue and an entire rascal He answered half in confusion, half in anger ; and his reply was so detrimental to any favourable influence he might otherwise have exercised over the interrogator, that the latter personage, giving him a pinch in the ear, shouted out "Ramp, ramp!" and, at that significant and awful word, Paul found himself surrounded in a trice by a whole host of ingenious tormentors. One pulled this member, another pinched that ; one cuffed him before, and another thrashed him behind. By way of interlude to this pleasing occupation, they stripped him of the very few things that in his change of dress he had retained. One carried off his handkerchief, a second his neck-cloth, and a third, luckier than either, possessed himself of a pair of cornelian shirt-buttons, given to Paul as a *gage d'amour* by a young lady who sold oranges near the Tower. Happily, before this initiatory process, technically termed "ramping," and exercised upon all new-comers who seem to have a spark of decency in them, had reduced the bones of Paul, who fought tooth and nail in his defence, to the state of magnesia, a man of grave aspect, who had hitherto plucked his oakum in quiet, suddenly rose, thrust himself between the victim and the assailants, and desired the latter, like one having authority, to leave the lad alone, and go and be d——d.

This proposal to resort to another place for amusement, though uttered in a very grave and tranquil manner, produced that instantaneous effect which admonitions from great rogues generally work upon little. Messieurs the "rampers" ceased from their amusements, and the ringleader of the gang, thumping Paul heartily on the back, declared he was a capital fellow, and it was only a bit of a *spree* like, which he hoped had not given any offence.

Paul, still clenching his fist, was about to answer in no pacific mood, when a turnkey, who did not care in the least how many men he locked up for an offence, but who did not at all like the trouble of looking after any one of his flock to see that the offence was not committed, now suddenly appeared among the set ; and, after scolding them for the excessive plague they were to him, carried off two of the poorest of the mob to solitary confinement. It happened, of course, that *these* two had not taken the smallest share in the disturbance. This scene over, the company returned to picking oakum,—the tread-mill, that admirably just invention, by which a strong man suffers no fatigue, and a weak one loses his health for life, not having been then introduced into our excellent establishments for correcting crime. Bitterly, and with many dark and wrathful feelings, in which the sense of injustice at punishment alone bore him up against the humiliations to which he was subjected—bitterly, and with a swelling heart, in which the thoughts that lead to crime were already forcing their way through a soil suddenly warmed for their growth, did Paul bend over his employment. He felt himself touched on the arm, he turned, and saw that the gentleman who had so kindly delivered him from his tormentors was now sitting next to him. Paul gazed long and earnestly upon his neighbour, struggling with the thought that he had beheld that sagacious countenance in happier times, although now, alas! it was altered, not only by time and vicissitude, but by that air of gravity which the cares of manhood spread gradually over the face of the most thoughtless,—until all doubt melted away, and he exclaimed,—

"Is that you, Mr. Tomlinson?—How glad I am to see you here!"

"And I," returned the quondam murderer for the newspapers, with a nasal twang, "should be very glad to see myself any where else!"

Paul made no answer, and Augustus continued.

"'To a wise man all places are the same,'—so it has been said. I don't believe it, Paul—I don't believe it. But a truce to reflection. I remembered you the moment I saw you, though you are surprisingly grown. How is my friend Mac Grawler?—still hard at work for 'The Asinæum?'"

"I believe so," said Paul sullenly, and hastening to change the conversation; "but tell me, Mr. Tomlinson, how came you hither? I heard you had gone down to the North of England, to fulfil a lucrative employment."

"Possibly! the world always misrepresents the actions of those who are constantly before it!"

"It is very true," said Paul; "and I have said the same thing myself a hundred times in 'The Asinæum,' for we were never too lavish of our truths in that magnificent journal. 'Tis astonishing what a way we made three ideas go."

"You remind me of myself and my newspaper labours," rejoined Augustus Tomlinson: "I am not quite sure that _I_ had so many as three ideas to spare; for, as you say, it is astonishing how far that number may go, properly managed. It is with writers as with strolling players,—the same three ideas that did for Turks in one scene do for Highlanders in the next: but you must tell me your history one of these days, and you shall hear mine."

"I should be excessively obliged to you for your confidence," said Paul, "and I doubt not but your life must be excessively entertaining. Mine, as yet, has been but insipid. The lives of literary men are not fraught with adventure ; and I question whether every writer in 'The Asinæum' has not led pretty nearly the same existence as that which I have sustained myself."

In conversation of this sort our newly restored friends passed the remainder of the day, until the hour of half-past four, when the prisoners are to suppose night has begun, and be locked up in their bedrooms. Tomlinson then, who was glad to re-find a person who had known him in his *beaux jours*, spoke privately to the turn-key ; and the result of the conversation was the coupling Paul and Augustus in the same chamber, which was a sort of stone box, that generally accommodated three, and was,—for we have measured it, as we would have measured the cell of the prisoner of Chillon,— just eight feet by six.

We do not intend, reader, to indicate, by broad colours and in long detail, the moral deterioration of our hero ; because we have found, by experience, that such pains on our part do little more than make thee blame our stupidity instead of lauding our intention. We shall therefore only work out our moral by subtle hints and brief comments ; and we shall now content ourselves with remind-ing thee that hitherto thou hast seen Paul honest in the teeth of circumstances. Despite the contagion of the Mug,—despite his associates in Fish Lane,—despite his intimacy with Long Ned, thou hast seen him brave temptation, and look forward to some other career than that of robbery or fraud. Nay, even in his destitution, when driven from the abode of his childhood, thou hast observed how, instead of resorting to some more pleasurable or libertine road of life, he betook himself at once to the dull roof and insipid employments of Mac Grawler, and preferred honestly earning his subsistence by the sweat of his brain to recurring to any of the numerous ways of living on others with which his experience among the worst part of society must have teemed, and which, to say the least of them, are more alluring to the young and the adventurous than the barren paths of literary labour. Indeed, to let thee into a secret, it had been Paul's daring ambition to raise himself into a worthy member of the community. His present cir-cumstances, it may hereafter be seen, made the cause of a great change in his desires ; and the conversation he held that night with the ingenious and skilful Augustus, went more towards fitting him for the hero of this work than all the habits of his childhood or the scenes of his earlier youth. Young people are apt, erroneously, to believe that it is a bad thing to be exceedingly wicked. The House

of Correction is so called, because it is a place where so ridiculous
a notion is invariably corrected.

The next day Paul was surprised by a visit from Mrs. Lobkins,
who had heard of his situation and its causes from the friendly
Dummie, and who had managed to obtain from Justice Burnflat
an order of admission.   They met, Pyramus and Thisbe like, with
a wall, or rather an iron gate, between them : and Mrs. Lobkins,
after an ejaculation of despair at the obstacle, burst weepingly into
the pathetic reproach,—

"O Paul, thou hast brought thy pigs to a fine market !"

" 'Tis a market proper for pigs, dear dame," said Paul, who,
though with a tear in his eye, did not refuse a joke as bitter as
it was inelegant ; " for, of all others, it is the spot where a man
learns to take care of his bacon."

"Hold your tongue !" cried the dame, angrily.   "What business
has you to gabble on so while you are in limbo ?"

"Ah, dear dame," said Paul, " we can't help these rubs and
stumbles on our road to preferment !"

"Road to the scragging post !" cried the dame.   "I tells you,
child, you'll live to be hanged in spite of all my care and 'tention to
you, though I hedicated you as a scholard, and always hoped as how
you would grow up to be an honour to your——"

"King and country," interrupted Paul.   "We always say honour
to king and country, which means getting rich and paying taxes.
'The more taxes a man pays, the greater honour he is to both,' as
Augustus says.   Well, dear dame, all in good time."

"What ! you is merry, is you ?   Why does not you weep ?   Your
heart is as hard as a brickbat.   It looks quite unnatural and hyæna-
like to be so *devil-me-careish !*"   So saying, the good dame's tears
gushed forth with the bitterness of a despairing Parisina.[1]

"Nay, nay," said Paul, who, though he suffered far more intensely, bore the suffering far more easily than his patroness, " we
cannot mend the matter by crying.   Suppose you see what can be
done for me.   I dare say you may manage to soften the justice's
sentence by a little ' oil of palms ;' and if you can get me out before
I am quite corrupted,—a day or two longer in this infernal place
will do the business,—I promise you that I will not only live
honestly myself, but with people who live in the same manner."

"Buss me, Paul," said the tender Mrs. Lobkins, "buss me,—oh !
but I forgits the gate ; I'll see what can be done.   And here, my
lad, here's summat for you in the meanwhile—a drop o' the cretur,
to preach comfort to your poor stomach.   Hush ! smuggle it through,
or they'll see you."

Here the dame endeavoured to push a stone bottle through the bars of the gate ; but, alas ! though the neck passed through, the body refused, and the dame was forced to retract the " cretur." Upon this, the kind-hearted woman renewed her sobbings ; and so absorbed was she in her grief, that, seemingly quite forgetting for what purpose she had brought the bottle, she applied it to her own mouth, and consoled herself with that *elixir vitæ* which she had originally designed for Paul.

This somewhat restored her ; and after a most affecting scene, the dame reeled off with the vacillating steps natural to woe, promising, as she went, that, if love or money could shorten Paul's confinement, neither should be wanting. We are rather at a loss to conjecture the exact influence which the former of these arguments, urged by the lovely Margaret, might have had upon Justice Burnflat.

When the good dame had departed, Paul hastened to repick his oakum and rejoin his friend. He found the worthy Augustus privately selling little elegant luxuries, such as tobacco, gin, and rations of daintier viands than the prison allowed ; for Augustus, having more money than the rest of his companions, managed, through the friendship of the turnkey, to purchase secretly, and to resell at about four hundred per cent., such comforts as the prisoners especially coveted."[1]

"A proof," said Augustus dryly to Paul, "that, by prudence and exertion, even in those places where a man cannot turn himself, he may manage to turn a penny."

CHAPTER IX.

"' *Relate at large, my godlike guest,*' she said,
' *The* Grecian *stratagems,*—the town *betray'd* ' '"
DRYDEN's ' Virgil,' b. ii. ' Æn '

" *Descending thence, they 'scaped!*"—IBID.

GREAT improvement had taken place in the character of Augustus Tomlinson since Paul had last encountered that illustrious man. *Then*, Augustus had affected the man of pleasure,—the learned lounger about town,—the all-accomplished Pericles of the papers—gaily quoting Horace—gravely flanking a fly from the leader of Lord Dunshunner. *Now*, a more

[1] A very common practice at the Bridewells. The governor at the Coldbath-Fields, apparently a very intelligent and active man, every way fitted for a most arduous undertaking, informed us, in the only conversation we have had the honour to hold with him, that he thought he had nearly, or quite, destroyed in his jurisdiction this illegal method of commerce.

serious, yet not a less supercilious air had settled upon his features ; the pretence of fashion had given way to the pretence of wisdom ; and, from the man of pleasure, Augustus Tomlinson had grown to the philosopher. With this elevation alone, too, he was not content : he united the philosopher with the politician ; and the ingenious rascal was pleased especially to pique himself upon being "a moderate Whig !" "Paul," he was wont to observe, "believe me, moderate Whiggism is a most excellent creed. It adapts itself to every possible change,—to every conceivable variety of circumstance. It is the only politics for us who are the aristocrats of that free body who rebel against tyrannical laws ! for, hang it, I am none of your democrats. Let there be dungeons and turnkeys for the low rascals who whip clothes from the hedge where they hang to dry, or steal down an area in quest of a silver spoon ; but houses of correction are not made for men who have received an enlightened education—who abhor your petty thefts as much as a justice of peace can do,—who ought never to be termed dishonest in their dealings, but, if they are found out, '*unlucky in their speculations !*'[1] A pretty thing, indeed, that there should be distinctions of rank among other members of the community, and none among us ! Where's your boasted British constitution, I should like to know—where are your privileges of aristocracy, if I, who am a gentleman born, know Latin, and have lived in the best society, should be thrust into this abominable place with a dirty fellow, who was born in a cellar, and could never earn more at a time than would purchase a sausage?—No, no ! none of your levelling principles for me ! I am liberal, Paul, and love liberty ; but, thank Heaven, I despise your democracies !"

Thus, half in earnest, half veiling a natural turn to sarcasm, would this moderate Whig run on for the hour together, during those long nights, commencing at half-past four, in which he and Paul bore each other company.

One evening, when Tomlinson was so bitterly disposed to be prolix that Paul felt himself somewhat wearied by his eloquence, our hero, desirous of a change in the conversation, reminded Augustus of his promise to communicate his history ; and the philosophical Whig, nothing loath to speak of himself, cleared his throat, and began.

HISTORY OF AUGUSTUS TOMLINSON.

"Never mind who was my father, nor what was my native place ! My first ancestor was Tommy Linn—(his heir became Tom Linn's son :)—you have heard the ballad made in his praise :—

[1] A phrase applied to a noted defaulter of the public money.

> "'Tommy Linn is a Scotchman born,
> His head is bald, and his beard is shorn .
> He had a cap made of a hare skin,—
> An elder man is Tommy Linn!'[1]

"There was a sort of prophecy respecting my ancestor's descendants darkly insinuated in the concluding stanza of this ballad :—

> "'Tommy Linn, and his wife, and his wife's mother,
> They all fell into the fire together;
> They that lay undermost got a hot skin,—
> "We are not enough !" said Tommy Linn '[2]

"You see the prophecy; it is applicable both to gentlemen rogues and to moderate Whigs ; for both are *undermost* in the world, and both are perpetually bawling out, ' *We are not enough !*'

"I shall begin my own history by saying, I went to a North Country school ; where I was noted for my aptness in learning, and my skill at ' prisoner's base : '—upon my word I purposed no pun ! I was intended for the church : wishing, betimes, to instruct myself in its ceremonies, I persuaded my schoolmaster's maid-servant to assist me towards promoting a christening. My father did not like this premature love for the sacred rites. He took me home ; and, wishing to give my clerical ardour a different turn, prepared me for *writing* sermons, by *reading* me a dozen a day. I grew tired of this, strange as it may seem to you. ' Father,' said I, one morning, ' it is no use talking, I will not go into the church—that's positive. Give me your blessing, and a hundred pounds, and I'll go up to London, and get a *living* instead of a curacy.' My father stormed, but I got the better at last. I talked of becoming a private tutor ; swore I had heard nothing was so easy,—the only things wanted were pupils ; and the only way to get them was to go to London, and let my learning be known. My poor father,—well, he's gone, and I am glad of it now ! (the speaker's voice faltered)—I got the better, I say, and I came to town, where I had a relation a bookseller. Through his interest, I wrote a book of Travels in Æthiopia for an earl's son, who wanted to become a lion ; and a Treatise on the Greek Particle, dedicated to the prime minister, for a dean, who wanted to become a bishop,—Greek being, next to interest, the best road to the mitre. These two achievements were liberally paid ; so I took a lodging in a first floor, and resolved to make a bold stroke for a wife. What do you think I did?—nay, never guess, it would be hopeless. First, I went to the best tailor, and had my clothes sewn on my back ; secondly, I got the peerage and its genealogies by heart ; thirdly, I marched one night, with the coolest deliberation

---

[1] See Ritson's *North-Country Chorister*.   [2] Ibid.

possible, into the house of a duchess, who was giving an immense
rout ! The newspapers had inspired me with this idea. I had
read of the vast crowds which a lady ' at home' sought to win to her
house. I had read of staircases impassable, and ladies carried out
in a fit ; and common sense told me how impossible it was that the
fair receiver should be acquainted with the legality of every import-
ation. I therefore resolved to try my chance, and—entered the
body of Augustus Tomlinson, as a piece of stolen goods. Faith !
the first night I was shy,—I stuck to the staircase, and ogled an old
maid of quality, whom I had heard announced as Lady Margaret
Sinclair. Doubtless, she had never been ogled before; and she
was evidently enraptured with my glances The next night I read
of a ball at the Countess of ——. My heart beat as if I were
going to be whipped ; but I plucked up courage, and repaired
to her ladyship's. There I again beheld the divine Lady Margaret ;
and, observing that she turned yellow, by way of a blush, when she
saw me, I profited by the port I had drunk as an encouragement to
my *entrée*, and lounging up in the most modish way possible, I
reminded her ladyship of an introduction with which I *said* I had
once been honoured at the Duke of Dashwell's, and requested her
hand for the next cotillon. Oh, Paul! fancy my triumph ! the old
damsel said with a sigh, ' She remembered me very well,' ha ! ha !
ha ! and I carried her off to the cotillon like another Theseus
bearing away a second Ariadne. Not to be prolix on this part of
my life, I went night after night to balls and routs, for admission to
which half the fine gentlemen in London would have given their
ears. And I improved my time so well with Lady Margaret, who
was her own mistress, and had five thousand pounds,—a devilish
bad portion for some, but not to be laughed at by me,—that I began
to think *when* the happy day should be fixed. Meanwhile, as Lady
Margaret introduced me to some of her friends, and my lodgings
were in a good situation, I had been honoured with some real invitations. The only two questions I ever was asked were (carelessly),
' Was I the only son?' and on my veritable answer ' Yes !' ' What,
(this was more warmly put)—what was my county?'—Luckily, my
county was a wide one,—Yorkshire; and any of its inhabitants
whom the fair interrogators might have questioned about me could
only have answered, ' I was not in their part of it.'

" Well, Paul, I grew so bold by success, that the devil one day
put into my head to go to a great dinner-party at the Duke of
Dashwell's. I went, dined,—nothing happened : I came away, and
the next morning I read in the papers,—

" ' Mysterious affair,—person lately going about,—first houses—
most fashionable parties — nobody knows — Duke of Dashwell's

yesterday. Duke not like to make disturbance — as — royalty present.' [1]

"The journal dropped from my hands. At that moment, the girl of the house gave me a note from Lady Margaret,—alluded to the paragraph ;—wondered who was 'The Stranger ;'—hoped to see me that night at Lord A——'s, to whose party I said I had been asked ;—speak then more fully on those matters I had touched on !—in short, dear Paul, a tender epistle ! All great men are fatalists : I am one now : fate made me a madman · in the very face of this ominous paragraph I mustered up courage, and went that night to Lord A——'s. The fact is, my affairs were in confusion— I was greatly in debt : I knew it was necessary to finish my conquest over Lady Margaret as soon as possible ; and Lord A——'s seemed the best place for the purpose. Nay, I thought delay so dangerous, after the cursed paragraph, that a day might unmask me, and it would be better therefore not to lose an hour in finishing the play of 'The Stranger,' with the farce of the 'Honey Moon.' Behold me then at Lord A——'s, leading off Lady Margaret to the dance. Behold me whispering the sweetest of things in her ear. Imagine her approving my suit, and gently chiding me for talking of Gretna Green. Conceive all this, my dear fellow, and just at the height of my triumph, dilate the eyes of your imagination, and behold the stately form of Lord A——, my noble host, marching up to me, while a voice that, though low and quiet as an evening breeze, made my heart sink into my shoes, said, 'I believe, sir, you have received no invitation from Lady A——?'

"Not a word could I utter, Paul, not a word. Had it been the highroad instead of a ball-room, I could have talked loudly enough, but I was under a spell. 'Ehem !' I faltered at last.— 'E—h—e—m ! Some mis—take, I—I.' There I stopped. 'Sir,' said the Earl, regarding me with a grave sternness, 'you had better withdraw.'

"'Bless me ! what's all this ?' cried Lady Margaret, dropping my palsied arm, and gazing on me as if she had expected me to talk like a hero.

"'Oh,' said I, 'Eh—e—m, eh—e—m, I will exp—lain to-morrow, ehem, e—h—e—m.' I made to the door ; all the eyes in the room seemed turned into burning glasses, and blistered the very skin on my face. I heard a gentle shriek as I left the apartment ; Lady Margaret fainting, I suppose ! There ended my courtship and my adventures in 'the best society.' I felt melancholy at the ill success of my scheme. You must allow, it was a magnificent project. What moral courage ! I admire myself when I think of

[1] Fact.

it. Without an introduction, without knowing a soul, to become, all by my own resolution, free of the finest houses in London, dancing with earls' daughters, and all but carrying off an earl's daughter myself as my wife. If I had, the friends *must* have done something for me; and Lady Margaret Tomlinson might perhaps have introduced the youthful genius of her Augustus to parliament or the ministry. Oh what a fall was there! yet faith, ha! ha! ha! I could not help laughing, despite of my chagrin, when I remembered that for three months I had imposed on these 'delicate exclusives,' and been literally invited by many of them, who would not have asked the younger sons of their own cousins; merely because I lived in a good street, avowed myself an only child, and talked of my property in Yorkshire! Ha, ha! how bitter the mercenary dupes must have felt, when the discovery was made! what a pill for the good matrons who had coupled my image with that of some filial Mary or Jane,—ha! ha! ha! the triumph was almost worth the mortification. However, as I said before, I fell melancholy on it, especially as my duns became menacing. So, I went to consult with my cousin the bookseller, he recommended me to compose for the journals, and obtained me an offer. I went to work very patiently for a short time, and contracted some agreeable friendships with gentlemen whom I met at an ordinary in St. James's. Still, my duns, though I paid them by driblets, were the plague of my life: I confessed as much to one of my new friends. 'Come to Bath with me,' quoth he, 'for a week, and you shall return as rich as a Jew.' I accepted the offer, and went to Bath in my friend's chariot. He took the name of Lord Dunshunner, an Irish peer who had never been out of Tipperary, and was not therefore likely to be known at Bath. He took also a house for a year, filled it with wines, books, and a sideboard of plate: as he talked vaguely of setting up his younger brother to stand for the town at the next Parliament, he bought these goods of the townspeople, in order to encourage their trade: I managed secretly to transport them to London and sell them; and as we disposed of them fifty per cent. under cost price, our customers, the pawnbrokers, were not very inquisitive. We lived a jolly life at Bath for a couple of months, and departed one night, leaving our housekeeper to answer all interrogatories. We had taken the precaution to wear disguises, stuffed ourselves out, and changed the hues of our hair: my noble friend was an adept in these transformations, and though the police did not sleep on the business, they never stumbled on us. I am especially glad we were not discovered, for I liked Bath excessively, and I intend to return there some of these days and retire from the world—on an heiress!

" Well, Paul, shortly after this adventure, I made your acquaintance. I continued ostensibly my literary profession, but only as a
mask for the labours I did not profess. A circumstance obliged me
to leave London rather precipitately. Lord Dunshunner joined me
in Edinburgh. D—— it, instead of doing anything *there*, we were
done ! The veriest urchin that ever crept through the High Street
is more than a match for the most scientific of Englishmen. With
us it is art ; with the Scotch it is nature. They pick your pockets,
without using their fingers for it ; and they prevent reprisal, by
having nothing for you to pick.

" We left Edinburgh with very long faces, and at Carlisle we
found it necessary to separate. For my part, I went as a valet to a
nobleman who had just lost his last servant at Carlisle by a fever :
my friend gave me the best of characters ! My new master was a
very clever man. He astonished people at dinner by the impromptus
he prepared at breakfast ;—in a word, he was a wit. He soon saw,
for he was learned himself, that I had received a classical education,
and he employed me in the confidential capacity of finding quotations
for him. I classed these alphabetically and under three heads :
' Parliamentary, Literary, Dining-out.' These were again sub-
divided, into ' Fine,'—' Learned,' and ' Jocular ' so that my master
knew at once where to refer for genius, wisdom, and wit. He was
delighted with my management of his intellects. In compliment to
him, I paid more attention to politics than I had done before, for he
was a 'great Whig,' and uncommonly liberal in everything,—but
money ! Hence, Paul, the origin of my political principles ; and, I
thank Heaven, there is not now a rogue in England who is a better,
that is to say, more of a moderate, Whig than your humble servant !
I continued with him nearly a year. He discharged me for a fault
worthy of my genius,—other servants may lose the watch or the
coat of their master ; I went at nobler game and lost him—*his
private character !*"

" How do you mean ?"

" Why I was enamoured of a lady who would not have looked
at me as Mr. Tomlinson ; so I took my master's clothes, and
occasionally his carriage, and made love to my nymph, as Lord
——. Her vanity made her indiscreet. The Tory papers got
hold of it ; and my master, in a change of ministers, was declared
by George the Third to be ' too gay for a Chancellor of the Ex-
chequer.' An old gentleman who had had fifteen children by a
wife like a Gorgon, was chosen instead of my master : and although the new minister was a fool in his public capacity, the
moral public were perfectly content with him, because of his *private
virtues !*

"My master was furious, made the strictest inquiry, *found* me out, and *turned* me out too!

"A Whig not in place has an excuse for disliking the constitution. My distress almost made me a republican; but, true to my creed, I must confess that I would only have levelled upwards. I especially disaffected the inequality of riches: I looked moodily on every carriage that passed: I even frowned like a second Catilline at the steam of a gentleman's kitchen! My last situation had not been lucrative; I had neglected my perquisites, in my ardour for politics. My master, too, refused to give me a character:—who would take me without one?

"I was asking myself this melancholy question one morning, when I suddenly encountered one of the fine friends I had picked up at my old haunt, the ordinary, in St. James's. His name was Pepper."

"Pepper!" cried Paul.

Without heeding the exclamation, Tomlinson continued.

"We went to a tavern and drank a bottle together. Wine made me communicative; it also opened my comrade's heart. He asked me to take a ride with him that night towards Hounslow: I did so, and found a purse."

"How fortunate! Where?"

"In a gentleman's pocket.—I was so pleased with my luck, that I went the same road twice a-week, in order to see if I could pick up any *more* purses. Fate favoured me, and I lived for a long time the life of the blest. Oh, Paul, you know not—you know not what a glorious life is that of a highwayman: but you shall taste it one of these days; you shall, on my honour."

"I now lived with a club of honest fellows: we called ourselves 'The Exclusives,' for we were mighty reserved in our associates, and only those who did business on a grand scale were admitted into our set. For my part, with all my love for my profession, I liked ingenuity still better than force, and preferred what the vulgar call swindling, even to the highroad. On an expedition of this sort, I rode once into a country town, and saw a crowd assembled in one corner,—I joined it, and,—guess my feelings! beheld my poor friend, Viscount Dunshunner, just about to be hanged! I rode off as fast as I could,—I thought I saw Jack Ketch at my heels. My horse threw me at a hedge, and I broke my collar-bone. In the confinement that ensued, gloomy ideas floated before me. I did not like to be hanged! so I reasoned against my errors, and repented. I recovered slowly, returned to town, and repaired to my cousin the bookseller. To say truth, I had played him a little trick: collected some debts of his by a mistake—very natural in the confusion incident on my distresses. However, he was extremely unkind about it; and the mistake, natural as it was, had cost me his acquaintance.

"I went now to him with the penitential aspect of the prodigal son, and, 'faith, he would not have made a bad representation of the fatted calf about to be killed on my return : so corpulent looked he, and so dejected ! 'Graceless reprobate !' he began, 'your poor father is dead !' I was exceedingly shocked ! but—never fear, Paul, I am not about to be pathetic. My father had divided his fortune among all his children; my share was 500*l.* The possession of this sum made my penitence seem much more sincere in the eyes of my good cousin ! and after a very pathetic scene, he took me once more into favour. I now consulted with him as to the best method of laying out my capital and recovering my character. We could not devise any scheme at the first conference; but the second time I saw him, my cousin said, with a cheerful countenance, 'Cheer up, Augustus, I have got thee a situation. Mr. Asgrave, the banker, will take thee as a clerk. He is a most worthy man; and having a vast deal of learning, he will respect thee for thy acquirements.' The same day I was introduced to Mr. Asgrave, who was a little man with a fine bald benevolent head; and after a long conversation which he was pleased to hold with me, I became one of his quill-drivers. I don't know how it was, but by little and little I rose in my master's good graces: I propitiated him, I fancy, by disposing of my 500*l.* according to his advice : he laid it out for me, on what he said was famous security, on a landed estate. Mr. Asgrave was of social habits,—he had a capital house and excellent wines. As he was not very particular in his company, nor ambitious of visiting the great, he often suffered me to make one of his table, and was pleased to hold long arguments with me about the ancients. I soon found out that my master was a great moral philosopher; and being myself in weak health, sated with the ordinary pursuits of the world in which my experience had forestalled my years, and naturally of a contemplative temperament, I turned my attention to the moral studies which so fascinated my employer. I read through nine shelves full of metaphysicians, and knew exactly the points in which those illustrious thinkers quarrelled with each other, to the great advance of the science. My master and I used to hold many a long discussion about the nature of good and evil; and as by help of his benevolent forehead, and a clear dogged voice, he always seemed to our audience to be the wiser and better man of the two, he was very well pleased with our disputes. This gentleman had an only daughter, an awful shrew with a face like a hatchet : but philosophers overcome personal defects; and thinking only of the good her wealth might enable me to do to my fellow-creatures, I secretly made love to her. You will say, that was playing my master but a scurvy trick for his kindness . not at all, my master himself had convinced me, that there was no such virtue as gratitude. It was an error of vulgar moralists. I yielded to his arguments, and at length privately espoused his daughter. The day after this took place, he summoned me to his study. 'So, Augustus,' said he, very mildly, 'you have married my daughter : nay, never look confused ; I saw a long time ago that you were resolved to do so, and I was very glad of it.'

"I attempted to falter out something like thanks. 'Never interrupt me !' said he. 'I had two reasons for being glad :—1st, Because my daughter was the plague of my life, and I wanted some one to take her off my hands ;—2dly, Because I required your assistance on a particular point, and I could not venture to ask it of any one but my son-in-law. In fine, I wish to take you into partnership ! ! !'

"'Partnership !' cried I, falling on my knees. 'Noble—generous man !'

"'Stay a bit,' continued my father-in law. 'What funds do you think requisite for carrying on a bank ? You look puzzled ! Not a shilling ! You will put in just as much as I do. You will put in rather more ; for you once put in five hundred pounds, which has been spent long ago. *I* don't put in a shilling of my own. I live on my clients, and I very willingly offer you half of them !'

"Imagine, dear Paul, my astonishment, my dismay ! I saw myself married to a hideous shrew—son-in-law to a penniless scoundrel, and cheated out of my whole fortune ! Compare this view of the question with that which had blazed on me when I contemplated being son-in-law to the rich Mr Asgrave. I stormed at first. Mr. Asgrave took up Bacon *On the Advancement of Learning*, and made no reply till I was cooled by explosion. You will perceive that, when passion subsided, I necessarily saw that nothing was left for me but adopting my father-in-law's proposal. Thus, by the fatality which attended me, at the very time I meant to reform, I was forced into scoundrelism, and I was driven into defrauding a vast number of persons by the accident of being son-in-law to a great moralist. As Mr. Asgrave was an indolent man, who passed his mornings in speculations on virtue, I was made the active partner. I spent the day at the counting-house ; and when I came home for recreation, my wife scratched my eyes out "

"But were you never recognised as 'the stranger,' or 'the adventurer,' in your new capacity ?"

"No ; for, of course, I assumed, in all my changes, both aliases and disguises. And, to tell you the truth, my marriage so altered me that, what with a snuff-coloured coat and a brown scratch wig, with a pen in my right ear, I looked the very picture of staid respectability. My face grew an inch longer every day. Nothing is so respectable as a long face! and a subdued expression of countenance is the surest sign of commercial prosperity. Well, we went on splendidly enough for about a year. Meanwhile I was wonderfully improved in philosophy. You have no idea how a scolding wife sublimes and rarifies one's intellect. Thunder clears the air, you know! At length, unhappily for my fame (for I contemplated a magnificent moral history of man, which, had she lived a year longer, I should have completed), my wife died in child-bed. My father-in-law and I were talking over the event, and finding fault with civilisation, by the enervating habits by which women die of their children, instead of bringing them forth without being even conscious of the circumstance;—when a bit of paper, sealed awry, was given to my partner: he looked over it—finished the discussion, and then told me our bank had stopped payment. 'Now, Augustus,' said he, lighting his pipe with the bit of paper, 'you see the good of having nothing to lose?'

"We did not pay quite sixpence in the pound; but my partner was thought so unfortunate that the British public raised a subscription for him, and he retired on an annuity, greatly respected and very much compassionated. As I had not been so well known as a moralist, and had not the prepossessing advantage of a bald benevolent head, nothing was done for *me*, and I was turned once more on the wide world, to moralise on the vicissitudes of fortune. My cousin the bookseller was no more, and his son cut me. I took a garret in Warwick Court, and, with a few books, my only consolation, I endeavoured to nerve my mind to the future. It was at this time, Paul, that my studies really availed me. I meditated much, and I became a true philosopher, viz, a practical one. My actions were henceforth regulated by principle; and, at some time or other, I will convince you, that the road of true morals never avoids the pockets of your neighbour. So soon as my mind had made the grand discovery which Mr. Asgrave had made before me, that one should live according to a system,—for if you do wrong, it is then your system that errs, not you —I took to the road, without any of those stings of conscience which had hitherto annoyed me in such adventures. I formed one of a capital knot of 'Free Agents,' whom I will introduce to you some day or other, and I soon rose to distinction among them. But, about six weeks ago, not less than formerly preferring by-ways to highways, I attempted to possess myself of a carriage, and sell it at discount. I was acquitted on the felony; but sent hither by Justice Burnflat on the misdemeanour.

Thus far, my young friend, hath as yet proceeded the life of Augustus Tomlinson."

The history of this gentleman made a deep impression on Paul. The impression was strengthened by the conversations subsequently holden with Augustus. That worthy was a dangerous and subtle persuader. He had really read a good deal of history, and something of morals; and he had an ingenious way of defending his rascally practices by syllogisms from the latter, and examples from the former. These theories he clenched, as it were, by a reference to the existing politics of the day. Cheaters of the public, on false pretences, he was pleased to term *" moderate Whigs ;"* bullying demanders of your purse were *" high Tories ;"* and thieving in gangs was *" the effect of the spirit of party."* There was this difference between Augustus Tomlinson and Long Ned : Ned was the acting knave ; Augustus, the reasoning one ; and we may see, therefore, by a little reflection, that Tomlinson was a far more perilous companion than Pepper, for showy theories are always more seductive to the young and clever than suasive examples, and the vanity of the youthful makes them better pleased by being convinced of a thing, than by being enticed to it.

A day or two after the narrative of Mr. Tomlinson, Paul was again visited by Mrs. Lobkins ; for the regulations against frequent visitors were not then so strictly enforced as we understand them to be now ; and the good dame came to deplore the ill success of her interview with Justice Burnflat.

We spare the tender-hearted reader a detail of the affecting interview that ensued. Indeed, it was but a repetition of the one we have before narrated. We shall only say, as a proof of Paul's tenderness of heart, that when he took leave of the good matron, and bade " God bless her," his voice faltered, and the tears stood in his eyes,—just as they were wont to do in the eyes of George the Third, when that excellent monarch was pleased graciously to encore " God save the King !"

" I'll be hanged," soliloquised our hero, as he slowly bent his course towards the subtle Augustus,—" I'll be hanged (humph ! the denunciation is prophetic), if I don't feel as grateful to the old lady for her care of me as if she had never ill-used me. As for my parents, I believe I have little to be grateful for, or proud of, in that quarter. My poor mother, by all accounts, seems scarcely to have had even the brute virtue of maternal tenderness ; and in all human likelihood I shall never know whether I had one father or fifty. But what matters it ? I rather like the better to be independent ; and, after all, what do nine-tenths of us ever get from our parents but an ugly name, and advice which, if we follow, we are wretched,—and if we neglect, we are disinherited ?"

Comforting himself with these thoughts, which perhaps took their philosophical complexion from the conversations he had lately held with Augustus, and which broke off into the muttered air of

"Why should we quarrel for riches?"

Paul repaired to his customary avocations.

In the third week of our hero's captivity, Tomlinson communicated to him a plan of escape that had occurred to his sagacious brain. In the yard appropriated to the amusements of the gentlemen "misdemeaning," there was a water-pipe that, skirting the wall, passed over a door, through which, every morning, the pious captives passed, in their way to the chapel. By this, Tomlinson proposed to escape; for to the pipe which reached from the door to the wall, in a slanting and easy direction, there was a sort of skirting-board; and a dexterous and nimble man might readily, by the help of this board, convey himself along the pipe, until the progress of that useful conductor (which was happily very brief) was stopped by the summit of the wall, where it found a sequel in another pipe, that descended to the ground on the opposite side of the wall. Now, on this opposite side was the garden of the prison; in this garden was a watchman; and this watchman was the hobgoblin of Tomlinson's scheme: "For, suppose us safe in the garden," said he, "what shall we do with this confounded fellow?"

"But that is not all," added Paul; "for even were there no watchman, there is a terrible wall, which I noted especially last week, when we were set to work in the garden, and which has no pipe, save a perpendicular one, that a man must have the legs of a fly to be able to climb."

"Nonsense!" returned Tomlinson: "I will show you how to climb the stubbornest wall in Christendom, if one has but the coast clear: it is the watchman—the watchman, we must——"

"What?" asked Paul, observing his comrade did not conclude the sentence.

It was some time before the sage Augustus replied; he then said, in a musing tone—

"I have been thinking, Paul, whether it would be consistent with virtue, and that strict code of morals by which all my actions are regulated, to—slay the watchman!"

"Good heavens!" cried Paul, horror-stricken.

"And I have decided," continued Augustus, solemnly, without regard to the exclamation, "that the action would be perfectly justifiable!"

"Villain!" exclaimed Paul, recoiling to the other end of the stone box—(for it was night)—in which they were cooped.

"But," pursued Augustus, who seemed soliloquising, and whose voice, sounding calm and thoughtful, like Young's in the famous monologue in *Hamlet*, denoted that he heeded not the uncourteous interruption—"but opinion does not always influence conduct; and although it may be virtuous to murder the watchman, I have not the heart to do it. I trust in my future history I shall not, by discerning moralists, be too severely censured for a weakness for which my physical temperament is alone to blame!"

Despite the turn of the soliloquy, it was a long time before Paul could be reconciled to further conversation with Augustus; and it was only from the belief that the moralist had leaned to the jesting vein that he at length resumed the consultation.

The conspirators did not, however, bring their scheme that night to any ultimate decision. The next day, Augustus, Paul, and some others of the company, were set to work in the garden; and Paul then observed that his friend, wheeling a barrow close by the spot where the watchman stood, overturned its contents. The watchman was good-natured enough to assist him in refilling the barrow; and Tomlinson profited so well by the occasion, that, that night, he informed Paul, that they would have nothing to dread from the watchman's vigilance. "He has promised," said Augustus, "for certain con-si-de-ra-tions, to allow me to knock him down: he has also promised to be so much hurt, as not to be able to move, until we are over the wall. Our main difficulty now, then, is, the first step,—namely, to climb the pipe unperceived!"

"As to that," said Paul, who developed, through the whole of the scheme, organs of sagacity, boldness, and invention, which charmed his friend, and certainly promised well for his future career; —"as to that, I think we may manage the first ascent with less danger than you imagine: the mornings, of late, have been very foggy; they are almost dark at the hour we go to chapel Let you and I close the file · the pipe passes just above the door, our hands, as we have tried, can reach it; and a spring of no great agility will enable us to raise ourselves up to a footing on the pipe and the skirting-board. The climbing, then, is easy; and, what with the dense fog, and our own quickness, I think we shall have little difficulty in gaining the garden. The only precautions we need use are, to wait for a very dark morning, and to be sure that we are the last of the file, so that no one behind may give the alarm——"

"Or attempt to follow our example, and spoil the pie by a superfluous plum!" added Augustus. "You counsel admirably; and one of these days, if you are not hung in the meanwhile, will, I venture to augur, be a great logician"

The next morning was clear and frosty; but the day after was, to use Tomlinson's simile, "as dark as if all the negroes of Africa had been stewed down into air." "You might have cut the fog with a knife," as the proverb says. Paul and Augustus could not even see how significantly each looked at the other

It was a remarkable trait of the daring temperament of the former, that, young as he was, it was fixed that he should lead the attempt. At the hour, then, for chapel—the prisoners passed as usual through the door. When it came to Paul's turn he drew himself by his hands to the pipe, and then creeping along its sinuous course, gained the wall before he had even fetched his breath. Rather more clumsily, Augustus followed his friend's example; once his foot slipped, and he was all but over. He extended his hands involuntarily, and caught Paul by the leg. Happily our hero had then gained the wall to which he was clinging, and for once in a way, one rogue raised himself without throwing over another. Behold Tomlinson and Paul now seated for an instant on the wall to recover breath! the latter then,—the descent to the ground was not very great,—letting his body down by his hands, dropped into the garden.

"Hurt?" asked the prudent Augustus in a hoarse whisper before he descended from his "bad eminence," being even willing

> "To bear those ills he had,
> Than fly to others that he knew not of,"

without taking every previous precaution in his power.

"No!" was the answer in the same voice, and Augustus dropped.

So soon as this latter worthy had recovered the shock of his fall, he lost not a moment in running to the other end of the garden: Paul followed. By the way Tomlinson stopped at a heap of rubbish, and picked up an immense stone; when they came to the part of the wall they had agreed to scale, they found the watchman, about whom they needed not, by the by, to have concerned themselves; for had it not been arranged that he was to have met them, the deep fog would have effectually prevented him from seeing them: this faithful guardian Augustus knocked down, not with the stone, but with ten guineas; he then drew forth from his dress a thickish cord, which he had procured some days before, from the turnkey, and fastening the stone firmly to one end, threw that end over the wall. Now the wall had (as walls of great strength mostly have) an overhanging sort of battlement on either side, and the stone, when flung over and drawn to the tether of the cord to which it was attached, necessarily hitched against this projection; and thus the cord was, as it were, fastened to the wall, and Tomlinson was enabled by it to draw himself up to the top of the barrier. He performed this feat with gymnastic address, like one who had often practised it ; albeit, the discreet adventurer had not mentioned in his narrative to Paul any previous occasion for the practice. As soon as he had gained the top of the wall, he threw down the cord to his companion, and, in consideration of Paul's inexperience in that manner of climbing, gave the fastening of the rope an additional security by holding it himself. With slowness and labour Paul hoisted himself up ; and then, by transferring the stone to the other side of the wall, where it made, of course, a similar hitch, our two adventurers were enabled successively to slide down, and consummate their escape from the house of correction.

" Follow me now ! " said Augustus, as he took to his heels ; and Paul pursued him through a labyrinth of alleys and lanes, through which he shot and dodged with a variable and shifting celerity that, had not Paul kept close upon him, would very soon (combined with the fog) have snatched him from the eyes of his young ally. Happily the immaturity of the morning, the obscurity of the streets passed through, and, above all, the extreme darkness of the atmosphere, prevented that detection and arrest which their prisoners' garb would otherwise have insured them. At length, they found themselves in the fields ; and, skulking along hedges, and diligently avoiding the highroad, they continued to fly onward, until they had advanced several miles into "the bowels of the land." At that time "the bowels" of Augustus Tomlinson began to remind him of their demands ; and he accordingly suggested the *desirability* of their seizing the first peasant they encountered, and causing him to exchange clothes with one of the fugitives, who would thus be enabled to enter a public-house and provide for their mutual necessities. Paul agreed to this proposition, and, accordingly, they watched their opportunity and *caught* a ploughman. Augustus stripped him of his frock, hat, and worsted stockings ; and Paul, hardened by necessity and companionship, helped to tie the poor ploughman to a tree. They then continued their progress for about an hour, and, as the shades of evening fell around them, they discovered a public-house. Augustus entered, and returned in a few minutes laden with bread and cheese, and a bottle of beer. Prison fare cures a man of daintiness, and the two fugitives dined on these homely viands with considerable complacency They then resumed their journey, and at length, wearied with exertion, they arrived at a lonely haystack, where they resolved to repose for an hour or two.

CHAPTER X.

" Unlike the riba'd, whose licentious jest
Pollutes his banquet, and insults his guest ,
From wealth and grandeur easy to descend,
Thou joy'st to lose the master in the friend :
We round thy board the cheerful menials see,
Gay with the smile of bland equality ;
No social care the gracious lord disdains ;
Love prompts to love, and reverence reverence gains."

Translation of LUCAN to PISO, prefixed to the
Twelfth Paper of ' The Rambler '

OYLY shone down the bashful stars upon our adventurers, as, after a short nap behind the haystack, they stretched themselves, and, looking at each other, burst into an involuntary and hilarious laugh at the prosperous termination of their exploit.

Hitherto they had been too occupied, first by their flight, then by hunger, then by fatigue, for self-gratulation ; now they rubbed their hands, and joked like runaway schoolboys, at their escape.

By degrees their thoughts turned from the past to the future ; and " Tell me, my dear fellow," said Augustus, " what you intend to do. I trust I have long ago convinced you, that it is no sin ' to serve our friends ' and to ' be true to our party ;' and therefore, I suppose, you will decide upon taking to the road ! "

" It is very odd," answered Paul, " that I should have any scruples left after your lectures on the subject ; but I own to you frankly, that, somehow or other, I have doubts whether thieving be really the honestest profession I could follow."

" Listen to me, Paul," answered Augustus ; and his reply is not unworthy of notice. " All crime and all excellence depend upon a good choice of words. I see you look puzzled ; I will explain. If you take money from the public, and say you have robbed, you have indubitably committed a great crime ; but if you do the same, and say you have *been relieving the necessities of the poor*, you have done an excellent action : if, in afterwards dividing this money with your companions, you say you have been sharing booty, you have committed an offence against the laws of your country ; but if you observe that *you have been sharing with your friends the gains of your industry*, you have been performing one of the noblest actions of humanity. To knock a man on the head is neither virtuous nor guilty, but it depends upon the language applied to the action to make it murder or glory.[1] Why not say, then, that you have testified '*the courage of a hero*,' rather than '*the atrocity of a ruffian?*' This is perfectly clear, is it not?"

"It seems so," answered Paul.

"It is so self-evident, that it is the way all governments are carried on. Wherefore, my good Paul, we only do what all other legislators do. We are never rogues so long as we call ourselves honest fellows, and we never commit a crime so long as we can term it a virtue! What say you now?"

Paul smiled, and was silent a few moments before he replied:

"There is very little doubt but that you are wrong; yet if you are, so are all the rest of the world. It is of no use to be the only white sheep of the flock. Wherefore, my dear Tomlinson, I will in future be an excellent citizen, *relieve the necessities of the poor*, and *share the gains of my industry with my friends.*"

"Bravo!" cried Tomlinson. "And now that that is settled, the sooner you are inaugurated the better. Since the starlight has shone forth, I see that I am in a place I ought to be very well acquainted with; or, if you like to be suspicious, you may believe that I have brought you purposely in this direction; but first let me ask if you feel any great desire to pass the night by this haystack, or whether you would like a song and the punch-bowl almost as much as the open air, with the chance of being eat up in a pinch of hay by some strolling cow!"

"You may conceive my choice," answered Paul.

"Well, then, there is an excellent fellow near here, who keeps a public-house, and is a firm ally and generous patron of the lads of the cross. At certain periods they hold weekly meetings at his house: this is one of the nights. What say you? shall I introduce you to the club?"

"I shall be very glad, if they will admit me!" returned Paul, whom many and conflicting thoughts rendered laconic.

"Oh! no fear of that, under my auspices. To tell you the truth, though we are a tolerant sect, we welcome every new proselyte with enthusiasm. But are you tired?"

"A little; the house is not far, you say?"

"About a mile off," answered Tomlinson "Lean on me."

---

[1] We observe in a paragraph from an American paper, copied without comment into the *Morning Chronicle*, a singular proof of the truth of Tomlinson's philosophy. "Mr. Rowland Stephenson (so runs the extract', *the celebrated* English banker, has just purchased a considerable tract of land," &c. Most philosophical of paragraphists! "*Celebrated English banker!*" that sentence is a better illustration of verbal fallacies than all Bentham's treatises put together. "*Celebrated!*" O Mercury, what a dexterous epithet!

Our wanderers now leaving the haystack, struck across part of Finchley Common ; for the abode of the worthy publican was felicitously situated, and the scene in which his guests celebrated their festivities was close by that on which they often performed their exploits.

As they proceeded, Paul questioned his friend touching the name and character of "mine host ;" and the all-knowing Augustus Tomlinson answered him, Quaker-like, by a question,—

"Have you never heard of Gentleman George?"

"What ! the noted head of a flash public-house in the country? To be sure I have, often ; my poor nurse, Dame Lobkins, used to say he was the best-spoken man in the trade !"

"Ay, so he is still. In his youth George was a very handsome fellow, but a little too fond of his lass and his bottle to please his father, a very staid old gentleman, who walked about on Sundays in a bob-wig and a gold-headed cane, and was a much better farmer on week-days than he was head of a public house. George used to be a remarkably smart-dressed fellow, and so he is to this day. He has a great deal of wit, is a very good whist-player, has a capital cellar, and is so fond of seeing his friends drunk that he bought some time ago a large pewter measure in which six men can stand upright. The girls, or rather the old women, to which last he used to be much more civil of the two, always liked him ; they say, nothing is so fine as his fine speeches, and they give him the title of ' *Gentleman* George.' He is a nice, kind-hearted man in many things. Pray Heaven we shall have no cause to miss him when he departs. But, to tell you the truth, he takes more than his share of our common purse."

"What, is he avaricious ?"

"Quite the reverse ; but he's so cursedly fond of building, he invests all *his* money (and wants us to invest all *ours*) in houses , and there's one confounded dog of a bricklayer, who runs him up terrible bills,—a fellow called ' Cunning Nat,' who is equally adroit in spoiling ground and improving *ground rent*."

"What do you mean ?"

"Ah ! thereby hangs a tale. But we are near the place now ; you will see a curious set."

As Tomlinson said this, the pair approached a house standing alone, and seemingly without any other abode in the vicinity. It was of curious and grotesque shape, painted white with a Gothic chimney, a Chinese sign-post (on which was depicted a gentleman fishing, with the words "The Jolly Angler" written beneath), and a porch that would have been Grecian, if it had not been Dutch. It stood in a little field, with a hedge behind it, and the common in front ! Augustus stopped at the door, and while he paused, bursts of laughter rang cheerily within.

"Ah, the merry boys ! " he muttered : " I long to be with them ! " and then with his clenched fist he knocked four times at the door. There was a sudden silence which lasted about a minute, and was broken by a voice within, asking who was there. Tomlinson answered by some cabalistic word ; the door was opened, and a little boy presented himself.

"Well, my lad," said Augustus, "and how is your master ?— Stout and hearty, if I may judge by his voice."

"Ay, Master Tommy, ay he's boosing away at a fine rate in the back-parlour, with Mr. Pepper and fighting Attie, and half-a-score more of them. He'll be woundy glad to see you, I'll be bound."

"Show this gentleman into the bar," rejoined Augustus, "while I go and pay my respects to honest Geordie ! "

The boy made a sort of a bow, and leading our hero into the bar, consigned him to the care of Sal, a buxom barmaid, who reflected credit on the taste of the landlord, and who received Paul with marked distinction and a gill of brandy.

Paul had not long to play the amiable, before Tomlinson rejoined him with the imformation that Gentleman George would be most happy to see him in the back-parlour, and that he would there find an old friend in the person of Mr Pepper

"What ! is he here ?" cried Paul. " The sorry knave ! to let me be caged in his stead ! "

"Gently, gently, no misapplication of terms," said Augustus ; " that was not knavery, that was *prudence*, the greatest of all virtues and the rarest. But come along, and Pepper shall *explain* to-morrow."

Threading a gallery or passage, Augustus preceded our hero, opened a door, and introduced him into a long low apartment, where sat, round a table spread with pipes and liquor, some ten or a dozen men, while at the top of the table, in an arm-chair, presided Gentleman George. That dignitary was a portly and comely gentleman, with a knowing look, and a Welsh wig, worn, as the *Morning Chronicle* says of his Majesty's hat, "in a *dégagé* manner, on one side." Being afflicted with the gout, his left foot reclined on a stool ; and the attitude developed, despite of a lamb's-wool stocking, the remains of an exceedingly good leg.

As Gentleman George was a person of majestic dignity among the Knights of the Cross, we trust we shall not be thought irreverent in applying a few of the words by which the aforesaid *Morning Chronicle* depicted his Majesty, on the day he laid the first stone of his father's monument, to the description of Gentleman George.

"He had on a handsome blue coat, and a white waistcoat;" moreover, "he laughed most good-humouredly," as, turning to Augustus Tomlinson, he saluted him with—

"So, this is the youngster you present to us?—Welcome to the Jolly Angler! Give us thy hand, young sir;—I shall be happy to blow a cloud with thee."

"With all due submission," said Mr. Tomlinson, "I think it may first be as well to introduce my pupil and friend to his future companions."

"You speak like a leary cove," cried Gentleman George, still squeezing our hero's hand; and, turning round in his elbow-chair, he pointed to each member, as he severally introduced his guests to Paul:

"Here," said he,—"here's a fine chap at my right hand—(the person thus designated was a thin military-looking figure, in a shabby riding frock, and with a commanding, bold, aquiline countenance, a little the worse for wear)—here's a fine chap for you; Fighting Attie we calls him: he's a devil on the road. 'Halt—deliver—must and shall—can't and shan't—do as I bid you, or go to the devil,'—that's all Fighting Attie's palaver; and, 'sdeath, it has a wonderful way of coming to the point! A famous cull is my friend Attie—an old soldier—has seen the world, and knows what is what; has lots of gumption, and devil a bit of blarney. Howsomever, the highflyers doesn't like him; and when he takes people's money, he need not be quite so cross about it!—Attie, let me introduce a new pal to you." Paul made his bow.

"Stand at ease, man!" quoth the veteran, without taking the pipe from his mouth.

Gentleman George then continued; and, after pointing out four or five of the company (among whom our hero discovered, to his surprise, his old friends, Mr. Eustace Fitzherbert and Mr. William Howard Russell), came, at length, to one with a very red face, and a lusty frame of body. "That gentleman," said he, "is Scarlet Jem; a dangerous fellow for a *press*, though he says he likes robbing alone now, for a general press is not half such a good thing as it used to be formerly. You have no idea what a hand at disguising himself Scarlet Jem is. He has an old wig which he generally does business in; and you would not go for to know him again, when he conceals himself under the *wig*. Oh, he's a precious rogue, is Scarlet Jem!—As for the cove on t'other side," continued the host of the Jolly Angler, pointing to Long Ned, "all I can say of him, good, bad, or indifferent, is, that he has an unkimmon fine head of hair: and now, youngster, as you knows him, spose you goes and sits by him, and he'll introduce you to the rest; for, split my wig!

(Gentleman George was a bit of a swearer) if I ben't tired, and so here's to your health ; and if so be as your name's Paul, may you alway rob *Peter* [1] in order to pay *Paul!*"

This witticism of mine host's being exceedingly well received, Paul went, amidst the general laughter, to take possession of the vacant seat beside Long Ned. That tall gentleman, who had hitherto been cloud-compelling (as Homer calls Jupiter) in profound silence, now turned to Paul with the warmest cordiality, declared himself overjoyed to meet his old friend once more, and congratulated him alike on his escape from Bridewell, and his admission to the councils of Gentleman George. But Paul, mindful of that exertion of "prudence" on the part of Mr. Pepper, by which he had been left to his fate and the mercy of Justice Burnflat, received his advances very sullenly. This coolness so incensed Ned, who was naturally choleric, that he turned his back on our hero, and being of an aristocratic spirit, muttered something about "upstart, and vulgar cly-fakers being admitted to the company of swell tobymen." This murmur called all Paul's blood into his cheek ; for though he had been punished as a clyfaker (or pickpocket), nobody knew better than Long Ned whether or not he was innocent ; and a reproach from him came therefore with double injustice and severity. In his wrath, he seized Mr. Pepper by the ear, and, telling him he was a shabby scoundrel, challenged him to fight.

So pleasing an invitation not being announced *sotto voce*, but in a tone suited to the importance of the proposition, every one around heard it ; and before Long Ned could answer, the full voice of Gentleman George thundered forth—

"Keep the peace there, you youngster? What ! are you just admitted into our merry-makings, and must you be wrangling already? Harkye, gemmen, I have been plagued enough with your quarrels before now, and the first cove as breaks the present quiet of the Jolly Angler, shall be turned out neck and crop—shan't he, Attie?"

"Right about, march," said the hero.

"Ay, that's the word, Attie," said Gentleman George. "And now, Mr. Pepper, if there be any ill blood 'twixt you and the lad there, wash it away in a bumper of bingo, and let's hear no more whatsomever about it."

"I'm willing," cried Long Ned, with the deferential air of a courtier, and holding out his hand to Paul. Our hero, being somewhat abashed by the novelty of his situation and the rebuke of Gentleman George, accepted, though with some reluctance, the proffered courtesy.

[1] Peter : a portmanteau.

Order being thus restored, the conversation of the convivialists began to assume a most fascinating bias. They talked with infinite *goût* of the sums they had levied on the public, and the peculations they had committed for what one called the "*good of the community*," and another, the "*established order*,"—meaning themselves. It was easy to see in what school the discerning Augustus Tomlinson had learned the value of words.

There was something edifying in hearing the rascals! So nice was their language, and so honest their enthusiasm for their own interests, you might have imagined you were listening to a coterie of cabinet ministers conferring on taxes, or debating on perquisites.

"Long may the *Commons* flourish!" cried punning Georgie, filling his glass; "it is by the commons we're fed, and may they never know cultivation!"

"Three times three!" shouted Long Ned: and the toast was drunk as Mr. Pepper proposed.

"A little moderate cultivation of the commons, to speak frankly," said Augustus Tomlinson modestly, "might not be amiss; for it would decoy people into the belief that they might travel safely; and, after all, a hedge or a barley-field is as good for us as a barren heath, where we have no shelter if once pursued!"

"You talks nonsense, you spooney!" cried a robber of note, called Bagshot; who, being aged, and having been a lawyer's footboy, was sometimes denominated "Old Bags." "You talks nonsense; these innovating ploughs are the ruin of us. Every blade of corn in a common is an encroachment on the constitution and rights of the gemmen highwaymen. I'm old, and mayn't live to see these things; but, mark my words, a time will come when a man may go from Lunnun to Johnny Groat's without losing a penny by one of us; when Hounslow will be safe, and Finchley secure. My eyes, what a sad thing for us that'll be!"

The venerable old man became suddenly silent, and the tears started to his eyes. Gentleman George had a great horror of blue devils, and particularly disliked all disagreeable subjects.

"Thunder and oons, Old Bags!" quoth mine host of the Jolly Angler, "this will never do: we're all met here to be merry, and not to listen to your mullancolly taratarantarums. I says, Ned Pepper, spose you tips us a song, and I'll beat time with my knuckles."

Long Ned, taking the pipe from his mouth, attempted, like Walter Scott's Lady Heron, one or two pretty excuses; these being drowned by an universal shout, the handsome purloiner gave the following song, to the tune of "Time has not thinned my flowing hair."

LONG NED'S SONG.

1.

"Oh, if my hands adhere to cash,
My gloves at least are clean,
And rarely have the gentry flash
In sprucer clothes been seen.

2.

Sweet Public, since your coffers must
Afford our wants relief,
Oh ! soothes it not to yield the dust
To such a charming thief?

3.

I never robbed a single coach
But with a lover's air ,
And though you might my *course* reproach,
You never could my *hair*.

4.

John Bull, who loves a harmless joke,
Is apt at me to grin,
But why be cross with laughing folk,
Unless they laugh and win ?

5.

John Bull has money in his box ,
And though his wit's divine,
Yet let me laugh at Johnny's *locks*—
And John may laugh at mine !"

" 'And John may laugh at mine,' excellent !" cried Gentleman George, lighting his pipe and winking at Attie, "I hears as how you be a famous fellow with the lasses."

Ned smiled and answered,—"No man should boast ; but——" Pepper paused significantly, and then glancing at Attie, said— "Talking of lasses, it is my turn to knock down a gentleman for a song, and I knock down Fighting Attie."

"I never sing," said the warrior.

"Treason, treason," cried Pepper. "It is the law, and you must obey the law ;—so begin."

"It is true, Attie," said Gentleman George.

There was no appeal from the honest publican's fiat ; so, in a quick and laconic manner, it being Attie's favourite dogma, that the least said is the soonest mended, the warrior sung as follows :—

FIGHTING ATTIE'S SONG.

Air.—" He was famed for deeds of arms."

" Rise at six—dine at two—
  Rob your man without ado—
  Such my maxims—if you doubt
  Their wisdom, to the rightabout ! "

> (*Signing to a sallow gentleman on
> the same side of the table to send
> up the brandy bowl.*)

" Pass round the bingo,—of a gun,
  You musty, dusky, *husky son !* " [1]

> (*The sallow gentleman in a hoarse voice,*)

" Attie—the bingo's now with me,
  I can't resign it yet, d'ye see ! "

> (*Attie, seizing the bowl,*)

" Resign, resign it—cease your dust ! "

> (*Wresting it away, and fiercely re-
> garding the sallow gentleman ,*

" You have resigned it—and you must."

CHORUS.

" You have resigned it—and you must."

While the chorus, laughing at the discomfited tippler, yelled forth the emphatic words of the heroic Attie, that personage emptied the brandy at a draught, resumed his pipe, and, in as few words as possible, called on Bagshot for a song. The excellent old highwayman, with great diffidence, obeyed the request, cleared his throat, and struck off with a ditty somewhat to the tune of " The Old Woman."

OLD BAGS' SONG.

" Are the days then gone, when on Hounslow Heath,
    We flashed our nags?
  When the stoutest bosoms quail'd beneath
    The voice of Bags?
  Ne'er was my work half undone, lest
    I should be nabb'd
  Slow was old Bags, but he never ceased
    'Till the whole was grabb'd.

CHORUS.

'Till the whole was grabb'd.

---

[1] Much of whatever amusement might be occasioned by the not (we trust) ill-natured travesties of certain eminent characters in this part of our work when first published, like all political allusions, loses point and becomes obscure as the applications cease to be familiar. It is already necessary, perhaps, to say, that Fighting Attie herein typifies or illustrates the Duke of Wellington's abrupt dismissal of Mr. Huskisson

When the slow coach paused, and the gemmen storm'd,
    I bore the brunt—
And the only sound which my grave lips form'd
    Was 'blunt'—still 'blunt!'
Oh! those jovial days are ne'er forgot'—
    But the tape lags—
When I be's dead, you'll drink one pot
    To poor old Bags!

CHORUS.
To poor old Bags!"

"Ay, that we will, my dear Bagshot," cried Gentleman George, affectionately; but, observing a tear in the fine old fellow's eye, he added, "Cheer up. What, ho! cheer up! Times will improve, and Providence may yet send us one good year, when you shall be as well off as ever! You shakes your poll. Well, don't be humdurgeoned, but knock down a gemman."

Dashing away the drop of sensibility, the veteran knocked down Gentleman George himself.

"Oh, dang it!" said George, with an air of dignity, "I ought to skip, since I finds the lush: but howsomever here goes."

GENTLEMAN GEORGE'S SONG

Air.—"Old King Cole."

"I be's the cove—the merry old cove,
    Of whose max all the *rufflers* sing
And a lushing cove, I thinks, by Jove,
    Is as great as a sober king!

CHORUS.
Is as great as a sober king.

Whatever the noise as is made by the boys
    At the bar as they lush away;
The devil a noise my peace alloys,
    As long as the rascals pay!

CHORUS.
As long as the rascals pay!

What if I sticks my stones and my bricks
    With mortar I takes from the snobbish?
All who can feel for the public weal,
    Likes the public-house to be bobbish.

CHORUS.
Likes the public-house to be bobbish."

"There, gemmen!" said the publican, stopping short, "that's the pith of the matter, and split my wig but I'm short of breath now. So, send round the brandy, Augustus; you sly dog, you keeps it all to yourself."

By this time the whole conclave were more than half-seas over, or, as Augustus Tomlinson expressed it, "their more austere qualities were relaxed by a pleasing and innocent indulgence." Paul's eyes reeled, and his tongue ran loose. By degrees the room swam round, the faces of his comrades altered, the countenance of Old Bags assumed an awful and menacing air. He thought Long Ned insulted him, and that Old Bags took the part of the assailant, doubled his fists, and threatened to put the plaintiff's nob into chancery, if he disturbed the peace of the meeting. Various other imaginary evils beset him. He thought he had robbed a mail-coach in company with Pepper; that Tomlinson informed against him, and that Gentleman George ordered him to be hanged; in short, he laboured under a temporary delirium, occasioned by a sudden reverse of fortune—from water to brandy; and the last thing of which he retained any recollection, before he sunk under the table, in company with Long Ned, Scarlet Jem, and Old Bags, was, the bearing his part in the burthen, of what appeared to him a chorus of last dying speeches and confessions, but what in reality was a song made in honour of Gentleman George, and sung by his grateful guests as a finale to the festivities: It ran thus :—

THE ROBBER'S GRAND TOAST.

" A tumbler of blue ruin, fill, fill for me !
　Red tape those as likes it may drain,
But whatever the lush, it a bumper must be,
　If we ne'er drinks a bumper again !
Now—now in the crib, where a *ruffler* may lie,
　Without fear that the *traps* should d stress him,
With a drop in the mouth, and a drop in the eye,
　Here's to Gentleman George—God bless him !
　　God bless him—God bless him !
　Here's to Gentleman George—God bless him !

'Mong the pals of the Prince, I have heard it's the go,
　Before they have tippled enough,
To smarten their punch with the best curaçoa,
　More conish to render the stuff !
I boast not such lush !—but whoever his glass
　Does not like, I'll be hanged if I press him !
Upstanding, my kiddies—round, round let it pass !
　Here's to Gentleman George—God bless him !
　　God bless him—God bless him !
　Here's to Gentleman George—God bless him !

See—see—the fine fellow grows weak on the stumps,
　Assist him, ye rascals, to stand !
Why, ye stir not a peg !— Are you all in the dumps?—
　Fighting Attie, go, lend him a hand ! "

　　(*The robbers crowd around Gentleman George,
　　each, under pretence of supporting him,
　　hustling him first one way and then another.*)

Come, lean upon me—at your service I am !
  Get away from his elbow, you whelp !—him
You'll only upset—them 'ere fellows but sham !
  Here's to Gentleman George,—God help him !
    God help him—God help him !—
  Here's to Gentleman George—God help him !'"

CHAPTER XI.

"I boast no song in magic wonders rife,
* But yet, O Nature ! is there nought to prize,*
Familiar in thy bosom scenes of life ?
And dwells in daylight truth's salubrious skies
No form with which the soul may sympathise ?
Young, innocent, on whose sweet forehead mild
The parted ringlet shone in simplest guise,
An inmate in the home of Albert smiled,
Or blest his noonday walk—she was his only child."

'GERTRUDE OF WYOMING.'

TIME, thou hast played strange tricks with us ! and we bless the stars that made us a novelist, and permit us now to retaliate. Leaving Paul to the instructions of Augustus Tomlinson and the festivities of the Jolly Angler, and suffering him, by slow but sure degrees, to acquire the graces and the reputation of the accomplished and perfect appropriator of other men's possessions, we shall pass over the lapse of years with the same heedless rapidity with which they have glided over us, and summon our reader to a very different scene from those which would be likely to greet his eyes, were he following the adventures of our new Telemachus. Nor wilt thou, dear reader, whom we make the umpire between ourself and those who never read—the critics ;—thou who hast, in the true spirit of gentle breeding, gone with us among places where the novelty of the scene has, we fear, scarcely atoned for the coarseness, not giving thyself the airs of a dainty abigail,—not prating, lacquey-like, on the low company thou hast met ;—nor wilt thou, dear and friendly reader, have cause to dread that we shall weary thy patience by a "damnable iteration" of the same localities. Pausing for a moment to glance over the divisions of our story, which lies before us like a map, we feel that we may promise in future to conduct thee among aspects of society more familiar to thy habits ;—where events flow to their allotted gulf through landscapes of more pleasing variety, and among tribes of a more luxurious civilisation.

Upon the banks of one of fair England's fairest rivers, and about fifty miles distant from London, still stands an old-fashioned abode, which we shall here term Warlock Manor-house. It is a building of brick, varied by stone copings, and covered in great part with ivy and jasmine. Around it lie the ruins of the elder part of the fabric, and these are sufficiently numerous in extent, and important in appearance, to testify that the mansion was once not without pretensions to the magnificent. These remains of power, some of which bear date as far back as the reign of Henry the Third, are sanctioned by the character of the country immediately in the vicinity of the old manor-house. A vast tract of waste land, interspersed with groves of antique pollards, and here and there irregular and sinuous ridges of green mound, betoken to the inexperienced eye the evidence of a dismantled chase or park, which must originally have been of no common dimensions. On one side of the house the lawn slopes towards the river, divided from a terrace, which forms the most important embellishment of the pleasure-grounds, by that fence to which has been given the ingenious and significant name of "ha-ha!" A few scattered trees of giant growth are the sole obstacles that break the view of the river, which has often seemed to us, at that particular passage of its course, to glide with unusual calmness and serenity. On the opposite side of the stream there is a range of steep hills, celebrated for nothing more romantic than their property of imparting to the flocks that browse upon their short, and seemingly stinted herbage, a flavour peculiarly grateful to the lovers of that pastoral animal which changes its name into mutton after its decease. Upon these hills the vestige of human habitation is not visible; and at times, when no boat defaces the lonely smoothness of the river, and the evening has stilled the sounds of labour and of life, we know few scenes so utterly tranquil, so steeped in quiet, as that which is presented by the old, quaint-fashioned house and its antique grounds, —the smooth lawn, the silent, and (to speak truly, though disparagingly) the somewhat sluggish river, together with the large hills (to which we know, from simple, though metaphysical causes, how entire an idea of quiet, and immovability, peculiarly attaches itself), and the white flocks—those most peaceful of God's creatures, —that in fleecy clusters stud the ascent.

In Warlock House, at the time we refer to, lived a gentleman of the name of Brandon. He was a widower, and had attained his fiftieth year, without casting much regret on the past, or feeling much anxiety for the future. In a word, Joseph Brandon was one of those careless, quiescent, indifferent men, by whom a thought upon any subject is never recurred to without a very urgent necessity.

He was good-natured, inoffensive, and weak ; and if he was not an incomparable citizen, he was, at least, an excellent vegetable. He was of a family of high antiquity, and formerly of considerable note. For the last four or five generations, however, the proprietors of Warlock House, gradually losing something alike from their acres and their consequence, had left to their descendants no higher rank than that of a small country squire. One had been a Jacobite, and had drunk out half a dozen farms in honour of Charley over the water ;—Charley over the water was no very dangerous person, but Charley over the wine was rather more ruinous. The next Brandon had been a fox-hunter, and fox-hunters live as largely as patriotic politicians. Pausanias tells us, that the same people who were the most notorious for their love of wine, were also the most notorious for their negligence of affairs. Times are not much altered since Pausanias wrote, and the remark holds as good with the English as it did with the Phigalei. After this Brandon came one who, though he did not scorn the sportsman, rather assumed the fine gentleman. He married an heiress, who, of course, assisted to ruin him : wishing *no* assistance in so pleasing an occupation, he overturned her (*perhaps* not on purpose), in a new sort of carriage which he was learning to drive, and the good lady was killed on the spot. She left the fine gentleman two sons, Joseph Brandon, the present thane, and a brother some years younger. The elder, being of a fitting age, was sent to school, and somewhat escaped the contagion of the paternal mansion. But the younger Brandon, having only reached his fifth year at the time of his mother's decease, was retained at home. Whether he was handsome, or clever, or impertinent, or like his father about the eyes (that greatest of all merits), we know not ; but the widower became so fond of him, that it was at a late period, and with great reluctance, that he finally intrusted him to the providence of a school.

Among harlots, and gamblers, and lords, and sharpers, and gentlemen of the guards, together with their frequent accompaniments—guards of the gentlemen—viz., bailiffs, William Brandon passed the first stage of his boyhood. He was about thirteen when he was sent to school ; and being a boy of remarkable talents, he recovered lost time so well, that when, at the age of nineteen, he adjourned to the university, he had scarcely resided there a single term before he had borne off two of the highest prizes awarded to academical merit. From the university he departed on the "grand tour," at that time thought so necessary to complete the gentleman : he went in company with a young nobleman, whose friendship he had won at the university, stayed abroad more than two years, and on his return he settled down to the profession of the law.

Meanwhile his father died, and his fortune, as a younger brother, being literally next to nothing, and the family estate (for his brother was not *unwilling* to assist him) being terribly involved, it was believed that he struggled for some years with very embarrassed and penurious circumstances. During this interval of his life, however, he was absent from London, and by his brother supposed to have returned to the Continent . at length, it seems, he profited by a renewal of his friendship with the young nobleman who had accompanied him abroad, reappeared in town, and obtained, through his noble friend, one or two legal appointments of reputable emolument : soon afterwards he got a brief on some cause where a major had been raising a corps to his brother officer, with the better consent of the brother-officer's wife than of the brother officer himself. Brandon's abilities here, for the first time in his profession, found an adequate vent ; his reputation seemed made at once, he rose rapidly in his profession, and, at the time we now speak of, he was sailing down the full tide of fame and wealth, the envy and the oracle of all young Templars and barristers, who, having been starved themselves for ten years, began now to calculate on the possibility of starving their clients. At an early period in his career he had, through the good offices of the nobleman we have mentioned, obtained a seat in the House of Commons ; and though his eloquence was of an order much better suited to the bar than the senate, he had nevertheless acquired a very considerable reputation in the latter, and was looked upon by many as likely to win to the same brilliant fortunes as the courtly Mansfield—a great man, whose political principles and urbane address Brandon was supposed especially to affect as his own model. Of unblemished integrity in public life—for, as he supported all things that exist with the most unbending rigidity, he could not be accused of inconsistency—William Brandon was (as we have said in a former place of unhappy memory to our hero) esteemed in private life the most honourable, the most moral, even the most austere of men ; and his grave and stern repute on this score, joined to the dazzle of his eloquence and forensic powers, had baffled in great measure the rancour of party hostility, and obtained for him a character for virtues almost as high and as enviable as that which he had acquired for abilities.

While William was thus treading a noted and an honourable career, his elder brother, who had married into a clergyman's family, and soon lost his consort, had with his only child, a daughter named Lucy, resided in his paternal mansion in undisturbed obscurity. The discreditable character and habits of the preceding lords of Warlock, which had sunk their respectability in the county, as well as curtailed their property, had rendered the surrounding gentry little anxious to

cultivate the intimacy of the present proprietor ; and the heavy mind
and retired manners of Joseph Brandon were not calculated to
counterbalance the faults of his forefathers, nor to reinstate the name
of Brandon in its ancient popularity and esteem. Though dull and
little cultivated, the squire was not without his "proper pride ; "
he attempted not to intrude himself where he was unwelcome,
avoided county meetings and county balls, smoked his pipe with the
parson, and not unoften with the surgeon and the solicitor, and
suffered his daughter Lucy to educate herself, with the help of the
parson's wife, and to ripen (for Nature was more favourable to her
than Art) into the very prettiest girl that the whole county—we long
to say the whole country—at that time could boast of. Never did
glass give back a more lovely image than that of Lucy Brandon at
the age of nineteen. Her auburn hair fell in the richest luxuriance
over a brow never ruffled, and a cheek where the blood never slept ;
with every instant the colour varied, and at every variation that
smooth, pure, virgin cheek seemed still more lovely than before. She
had the most beautiful laugh that one who loved music could imagine,
—silvery, low, and yet so full of joy ! all her movements, as the old
parson said, seemed to keep time to that laugh ; for mirth made a
great part of her innocent and childish temper ; and yet the mirth
was feminine, never loud, nor like that of young ladies who had
received the last finish at Highgate seminaries Everything joyous
affected her, and at once ,—air,—flowers,—sunshine,—butterflies.
Unlike heroines in general, she very seldom cried, and she saw
nothing charming in having the vapours. But she never looked so
beautiful as in sleep ! and as the light breath came from her parted
lips, and the ivory lids closed over those eyes which only in sleep
were silent—and her attitude in her sleep took that ineffable grace
belonging solely to childhood, or the fresh youth into which childhood merges,—she was just what you might imagine a sleeping
Margaret, before that most simple and gentle of all a poet's visions
of womanhood had met with Faust, or her slumbers been ruffled with
a dream of love.

We cannot say much for Lucy's intellectual acquirements ; she
could, thanks to the parson's wife, spell indifferently well, and write
a tolerable hand ; she made preserves, and sometimes riddles—it was
more difficult to question the excellence of the former than to answer
the queries of the latter. She worked to the admiration of all who
knew her, and we beg leave to say that we deem that "an excellent
thing in woman." She made caps for herself and gowns for the poor,
and now and then she accomplished the more literary labour of a
stray novel that had wandered down to the Manor-house, or an
abridgment of ancient history, in which was omitted every thing but

the proper names. To these attainments she added a certain modicum of skill upon the spinet, and the power of singing old songs with the richest and sweetest voice that ever made one's eyes moisten, or one's heart beat.

Her moral qualities were more fully developed than her mental. She was the kindest of human beings ; the very dog that had never seen her before, knew that truth at the first glance, and lost no time in making her acquaintance. The goodness of her heart reposed upon her face like sunshine, and the old wife at the lodge said poetically and truly of the effect it produced, that "one felt warm when one looked on her." If we could abstract from the description a certain chilling transparency, the following exquisite verses of a forgotten poet[1] might express the purity and lustre of her countenance :—

> " Her face was like the milky way i' the sky,
> A meeting of gentle lights without a name."

She was surrounded by pets of all kinds, ugly and handsome, from Ralph the raven to Beauty the pheasant, and from Bob, the sheep-dog without a tail, to Beau, the Blenheim with blue ribands round his neck ; all things loved her, and she loved all things. It seemed doubtful at that time whether she would ever have sufficient steadiness and strength of character. Her beauty and her character appeared so essentially womanlike—soft, yet lively, buoyant, yet caressing,—that you could scarcely place in her that moral dependence that you might in a character less amiable, but less yieldingly feminine. Time, however, and circumstance, which alter and harden, were to decide whether the inward nature did not possess some latent, and yet undiscovered properties. Such was Lucy Brandon, in the year ——, and in that year, on a beautiful autumnal evening, we first introduce her personally to our readers.

She was sitting on a garden-seat by the river side with her father, who was deliberately conning the evening paper of a former week, and gravely seasoning the ancient news with the inspirations of that weed which so bitterly excited the royal indignation of our British Solomon. It happens, unfortunately for us,—for outward peculiarities are scarcely worthy the dignity to which comedy, whether in the drama or the narrative, aspires,—that Squire Brandon possessed so few distinguishing traits of mind, that he leaves his delineator little whereby to designate him, save a confused and parenthetical habit of speech, by which he very often appeared to those who did not profit by long experience, or close observation, to say exactly, and somewhat ludicrously, that which *he* did not mean to convey.

[1] Suckling

r

"I say, Lucy," observed Mr. Brandon, but without lifting his eyes from the paper; "I say, corn has fallen—think of that, girl, think of that! These times, in my opinion, (ay, and in the opinion of wiser heads than mine, though I do not mean to say that I have not some experience in these matters, which is more than can be said of *all our neighbours*,) *are very curious, and even dangerous.*"

"Indeed, papa!" answered Lucy.

"And I say, Lucy, dear," resumed the squire after a short pause, "there has been (and very strange it is, too, when one considers the crowded neighbourhood—Bless me! what times these are!) a shocking murder *committed upon* (*the tobacco-stopper*—there it is)—think, you know, girl—just by Epping!—an old gentleman!"

"Dear, how shocking! by whom?"

"Ay, that's the question! The coroner's inquest has (what a blessing it is to live in a civilised country, where a man does not die without knowing the why and the wherefore!) sat on the body, and declared (it is very strange, but they don't seem to have made much discovery; for why? we knew as much before,) that the body was found (it was found on the floor, Lucy,) murdered; *murderer or murderers* (*in the bureau*, which was broken open, they found the money left quite untouched,)—unknown!"

Here there was again a slight pause, and passing to another side of the paper, Mr. Brandon resumed in a quicker tone—

"Ha! well, now this is odd! But he's a deuced clever fellow, Lucy! that brother of mine has (and in a very honourable manner too, which I am sure is highly creditable to the family, though he has not taken too much notice of me lately;—a circumstance which, considering I am his elder brother, I am a little angry at;)—distinguished himself in a speech, remarkable, the paper says, for its great legal—(I wonder, by the by, whether William could get me that agistment-money! 'tis a heavy thing to lose; but going to law, as my poor father used to say, is like fishing for gudgeons [not a bad little fish, *we can have some for supper*,] *with guineas*)—knowledge, as well as its splendid and overpowering—(I do love Will for keeping up the family honour; I am sure it is more than I have done—heigh-ho!)—eloquence!"

"And on what subject has he been speaking, papa?"

"Oh, a very fine subject; what you call a—(it is astonishing that in this country there should be such a wish for taking away people's characters, which, for my part, I don't see is a bit more entertaining than what you are always doing—playing with those stupid birds)—libel!"

"But is not my uncle William coming down to see us? He

promised to do so, and it made you quite happy, papa, for two days. I hope he will not disappoint you; and I am sure that it is not his fault if he ever seems to neglect you. He spoke of you to me, when I saw him, in the kindest and most affectionate manner. I do think, my dear father, that he loves you very much."

"Ahem!" said the squire, evidently flattered, and yet not convinced. "My brother Will is a very acute fellow, and I make no—my dear little girl—question, but that—(when you have seen as much of the world as I have, you will grow suspicious,)—he thought that any good word said of me to my daughter would—(you see, Lucy, I am as clear-sighted as my neighbours, though I don't give myself all their airs; which I very well might do, considering my great great great grandfather, Hugo Brandon, had a hand in detecting the gunpowder plot,)—be told to me again!"

"Nay, but I am quite sure my uncle never spoke of you to me with that intention."

"Possibly, my dear child; but when (the evenings are much shorter than they were!) did you talk with your uncle about me?"

"Oh, when staying with Mrs. Warner, in London; to be sure, it is six years ago; but I remember it perfectly. I recollect, in particular, that he spoke of you very handsomely to Lord Mauleverer, who dined with him one evening when I was there, and when my uncle was so kind as to take me to the play. I was afterwards quite sorry that he was so good-natured, as he lost—(you remember I told you the story)—a very valuable watch."

"Ay, ay, I remember all about that, and so,—how long friendship lasts with some people!— Lord Mauleverer dined with William! What a fine thing it is for a man—(it is what I never did, indeed, I like being what they call 'Cock of the Walk'—let me see, now I think of it, Pillum comes to-night to play a hit at backgammon)—to make friends with a great man early in (yet Will did not do it very early, poor fellow! he struggled first with a great deal of sorrow———hardship that is———) life! It is many years now since Will has been hand-and-glove with my ('tis a bit of a puppy) Lord Mauleverer,—what did you think of his lordship?"

"Of Lord Mauleverer? Indeed I scarcely observed him; but he seemed a handsome man, and was very polite. Mrs. Warner said he had been a very wicked person when he was young, but he seems good-natured enough now, papa."

"By the by," said the squire, "his lordship has just been made—(this new ministry seems very unlike the old, which rather puzzles me; for I think it my duty, d'ye see, Lucy, always to vote for his Majesty's government, especially seeing that old Hugo Brandon had a hand in detecting the gunpowder plot; and it is a little odd, at least, at first, to think that good now, which one has always before been thinking abominable) Lord Lieutenant of the county."

"Lord Mauleverer our Lord Lieutenant?"

"Yes, child; and since his lordship is such a friend of my brother's, I should think, considering especially what an old family in the county we are,—not that I wish to intrude myself where I am not thought as fine as the rest,—that he would be more attentive to us than Lord —— was; but that, my dear Lucy, puts me in mind of Pillum, and so, perhaps, you would like to walk to the parson's as it is a fine evening. John shall come for you at nine o'clock *with* (*the moon* is not up then) the lantern"

Leaning on his daughter's willing arm, the good old man then rose and walked homeward; and so soon as she had wheeled round his easy chair, placed the backgammon board on the table, and wished the old gentleman an easy victory over his expected antagonist, the apothecary, Lucy tied down her bonnet, and took her way to the rectory.

When she arrived at the clerical mansion, and entered the drawing-room, she was surprised to find the parson's wife, a good, homely, lethargic old lady, run up to her, seemingly in a state of great nervous agitation and crying,

"Oh, my dear Miss Brandon! which way did you come? Did you meet nobody by the road? Oh, I am so frightened! Such an accident to poor dear Dr. Slopperton! Stopped in the king's highway, robbed of some tithe-money he had just received from Farmer Slowforth: if it had not been for that dear angel, good, young man, God only knows whether I might not have been a disconsolate widow by this time!"

While the affectionate matron was thus running on, Lucy's eye glancing round the room discovered in an armchair the round and oily little person of Dr. Slopperton, with a countenance from which all the carnation hues, save in one circular excrescence on the nasal member, that was left, like the last rose of summer, blooming alone, were faded into an aspect of miserable pallor: the little man tried to conjure up a smile while his wife was narrating his misfortune, and to mutter forth some syllable of unconcern; but he looked, for all his bravado, so exceedingly scared, that Lucy would, despite herself, have laughed outright, had not her eye rested upon the figure of a young man who had been seated beside the reverend gentleman, but who had risen at Lucy's entrance, and who now stood gazing upon her intently, but with an air of great respect. Blushing deeply, and involuntarily, she turned her eyes hastily away, and approaching the good doctor, made her inquiries into the present state of his nerves, in a graver tone than she had a minute before imagined it possible that she should have been enabled to command.

"Ah! my good young lady," said the doctor, squeezing her hand, "I—may, I may say the church—for am I not its minister?—was in imminent danger:—but this excellent gentleman prevented the sacrilege, at least in great measure. I only lost some of my dues—my rightful dues—for which I console myself with thinking that the infamous and abandoned villain will suffer hereafter."

"There cannot be the least doubt of *that*," said the young man: "had he only robbed the mail coach, or broken into a gentleman's house, the offence might have been expiable; but to rob a clergyman, and a rector, too!—Oh, the sacrilegious dog!"

"Your warmth does you honour, sir," said the doctor, beginning now to recover; "and I am very proud to have made the acquaintance of a gentleman of such truly religious opinions!"

"Ah!" cried the stranger, "my foible, sir—if I may so speak—is a sort of enthusiastic fervour for the Protestant Establishment. Nay, sir, I never come across the very *nave* of the church, without feeling an indescribable emotion—a kind of sympathy, as it were—with—with—you understand me, sir—I fear I express myself ill."

"Not at all, not at all!" exclaimed the doctor: "such sentiments are uncommon in one so young."

"Sir, I learned them early in life from a friend and preceptor of mine, Mr. Mac Grawler, and I trust they may continue with me to my dying day."

Here the doctor's servant entered with (we borrow a phrase from the novel of * * * *) "the tea-equipage," and Mrs. Slopperton, betaking herself to its superintendence, inquired with more composure than hitherto had belonged to her demeanour, what sort of a looking creature the ruffian was?

"I will tell you, my dear, I will tell you, Miss Lucy, all about it. I was walking home from Mr. Slowforth's, with his money in my pocket, thinking, my love, of buying you that topaz cross you wished to have."

"Dear, good man!" cried Mrs. Slopperton; "what a fiend it must have been to rob so excellent a creature."

"And," resumed the doctor, "it also occurred to me that the Madeira was nearly out—the Madeira, I mean, with the red seal; and I was thinking it might not be amiss to devote part of the money to buy six dozen more; and the remainder, my love, which would be about one pound eighteen, I thought I would divide,—'for he that giveth to the poor lendeth to the Lord!' among the thirty poor families on the common : that is, if they behaved well, and the apples in the back garden were not feloniously abstracted !"

"Excellent, charitable man !" ejaculated Mrs. Slopperton.

"While I was thus meditating, I lifted my eyes, and saw before me two men ; one of prodigious height, and with a great profusion of hair about his shoulders; the other was smaller, and wore his hat slouched over his face, it was a very large hat. My attention was arrested by the singularity of the tall person's hair, and while I was smiling at its luxuriance, I heard him say to his companion,—' Well, Augustus, as you are such a moral dog, he is in your line, not mine ; so I leave him to you.'—Little did I think those words related to me. No sooner were they uttered, than the tall rascal leaped over a gate and disappeared ; the other fellow then, marching up to me, very smoothly asked me the way to the church, and while I was explaining to him to turn first to the right and then to the left, and so on—for the best way is, you know, exceedingly crooked—the hypocritical scoundrel seized me by the collar, and cried out—'Your money or your life !' I do assure you, that I never trembled so much ; not, my dear Miss Lucy, so much for my own sake, as for the sake of the thirty poor families on the common, whose wants it had been my intention to relieve. I gave up the money, finding my prayers and expostulations were in vain ; and the dog then, brandishing over my head an enormous bludgeon, said—what abominable language !—'I think, doctor, I shall put an end to an existence derogatory to yourself and useless to others.' At that moment the young gentleman beside me sprang over the very gate by which the tall ruffian had disappeared, and cried, 'Hold, villain !' On seeing my deliverer, the coward started back, and plunged into a neighbouring wood. The good young gentleman pursued him for a few minutes, but then returning to my aid, conducted me home ; and as we used to say at school :—

"'Te redisse incolumem gaudeo'

Which, being interpreted, means,—(sir, excuse a pun, I am sure so great a friend to the church understands Latin)—that I am very glad to get back safe to my tea. He ! he ! And now, Miss Lucy, you must thank that young gentleman for having saved the life of your pastoral teacher, which act will no doubt be remembered at the Great Day !"

As Lucy, looking towards the stranger, said something in compliment, she observed a vague, and, as it were, covert smile upon his countenance, which immediately, and, as if by sympathy, conjured one to her own. The hero of the adventure, however, in a very grave tone, replied to her compliment, at the same time bowing profoundly :—

"Mention it not, madam! I were unworthy of the name of a Briton, and a man, could I pass the highway without relieving the distress, or lightening the burthen, of a fellow-creature. And," continued the stranger, after a momentary pause, colouring while he spoke, and concluding in the high-flown gallantry of the day, "methinks it were sufficient reward, had I saved the whole church, instead of one of its most valuable members, to receive the thanks of a lady, whom I might reasonably take for one of those celestial beings to whom we have been piously taught that the church is especially the care!"

Though there might have been something really ridiculous in this overstrained compliment, coupled as it was with the preservation of Dr. Slopperton, yet, coming from the mouth of one whom Lucy thought the very handsomest person she had ever seen, it appeared to her anything but absurd; and, for a very long time afterwards, her heart thrilled with pleasure when she remembered that the cheek of the speaker had glowed, and his voice had trembled as he spoke it.

The conversation now, turning from robbers in particular, dwelt upon robberies in general. It was edifying to hear the honest indignation with which the stranger spoke of the lawless depredators with whom the country, in that day of Macheaths, was infested.

"A pack of infamous rascals!" said he, in a glow; "who attempt to justify their misdeeds by the example of honest men; and who say, that they do no more than is done by lawyers and doctors, soldiers, clergymen, and ministers of state. Pitiful delusion, or rather shameless hypocrisy!"

"It all comes of educating the poor," said the doctor. "The moment they pretend to judge the conduct of their betters—there's an end of all order! They see nothing sacred in the laws, though we hang the dogs ever so fast; and the very peers of the land, spiritual and temporal, cease to be venerable in their eyes."

"Talking of peers," said Mrs. Slopperton, "I hear that Lord Mauleverer is to pass by this road to-night, on his way to Mauleverer Park. Do you know his lordship, Miss Lucy? he is very intimate with your uncle."

"I have only seen him once," answered Lucy.

"Are you sure that his lordship will come this road?" asked the stranger, carelessly: "I heard something of it this morning, but did not know it was settled"

"Oh, quite so!" rejoined Mrs. Slopperton. "His lordship's gentleman wrote for post-horses to meet his lordship at Wyburn, about three miles on the other side of the village, at ten o'clock to-night. His lordship is very impatient of delay."

"Pray," said the doctor, who had not much heeded this turn in the conversation, and was now "on hospitable cares intent;"— "Pray, sir, if not impertinent, are you visiting, or lodging in the neighbourhood; or, will you take a bed with us?"

"You are extremely kind, my dear sir, but I fear I must soon wish you good evening. I have to look after a little property I have some miles hence, which, indeed, brought me down into this part of the world."

"Property!—in what direction, sir, if I may ask?" quoth the doctor; "I know the country for miles."

"Do you, indeed?—where's my property, you say? Why, it is rather difficult to describe it, and it is, after all, a mere trifle: it is only some common-land near the high-road, and I came down to try the experiment of *hedging and draining.*"

"'Tis a good plan, if one has capital, and does not require a speedy return."

"Yes; but one likes a good interest *for the loss of principal,* and a *speedy return* is always desirable; although, alas! it is often attended with risk!"

"I hope, sir," said the doctor, "if you must leave us so soon, that your property will often bring you into our neighbourhood."

"You overpower me with so much unexpected goodness," answered the stranger. "To tell you the truth, nothing can give me greater pleasure than to meet those again who have once obliged me."

"Whom you have obliged, rather!" cried Mrs. Slopperton, and then added, in a loud whisper to Lucy, "How modest! but it is always so with true courage!"

"I assure you, madam," returned the benevolent stranger, "that I never think twice of the little favours I render my fellow-men—my only hope is, that they may be as forgetful as myself."

Charmed with so much unaffected goodness of disposition, the Dr. and Mrs. Slopperton now set up a sort of duet in praise of their guest: after enduring their commendations and compliments for some minutes with much grimace of disavowal and diffidence, the stranger's modesty seemed at last to take pain at the excess of their gratitude; and, accordingly, pointing to the clock, which was within a few minutes of nine, he said—

"I fear, my respected host, and my admired hostess, that I must now leave you; I have far to go."

"But are you yourself not afraid of the highwaymen?" cried Mrs. Slopperton, interrupting him.

"The highwaymen!" said the stranger, smiling: "No! I do not fear *them;* besides, I have little about me worth robbing."

"Do you superintend your property yourself?" said the doctor, who farmed his own glebe, and who, unwilling to part with so charming a guest, seized him now by the button.

"Superintend it myself!—why, not exactly. There is a *bailiff*, whose views of things don't agree with mine, and who now and then gives me a good deal of trouble!"

"Then why don't you discharge him altogether?"

"Ah! I wish I could : but 'tis a necessary evil. We landed proprietors, my dear sir, must always be plagued with something of the sort. For my part, I have found those cursed bailiffs would take away, if they could, all the little property one has been trying to accumulate. But," abruptly changing his manner into one of great softness, "could I not proffer my services and my companionship to this young lady. Would she allow me to conduct her home, and, indeed, stamp this day upon my memory as one of the few delightful ones I have ever known?"

"Thank you, dear sir," said Mrs. Slopperton, answering at once for Lucy; "it is very considerate of you; and I am sure, my love, I could not think of letting you go home alone with old John, after such an adventure to the poor dear doctor."

Lucy began an excuse which the good lady would not hear. But as the servant whom Mr. Brandon was to send with a lantern to attend his daughter home had not arrived, and as Mrs. Slopperton, despite her prepossessions in favour of her husband's deliverer, did not for a moment contemplate his accompanying, without any other attendance, her young friend across the fields at that unseasonable hour, the stranger was forced, for the present, to re-assume his seat ; an open harpsichord at one end of the room gave him an opportunity to make some remark upon music, and this introducing an eulogium on Lucy's voice from Mrs. Slopperton, necessarily ended in a request to Miss Brandon to indulge the stranger with a song. Never had Lucy, who was not a shy girl—she was too innocent to be bashful—felt nervous hitherto in singing before a stranger ; but now she hesitated and faltered, and went through a whole series of little natural affectations before she complied with the request. She chose a song composed somewhat after the old English school, which at that time was reviving into fashion. The song, though conveying a sort of conceit, was not, perhaps, altogether without tenderness ;—it was a favourite with Lucy, she scarcely knew why, and ran thus :—

LUCY'S SONG.

"Why sleep, ye gentle flowers, ah, why,
When tender eve is falling,
And starlight drinks the happy sigh
Of winds to fairies calling?

J 2

Calling with low and plaining note,
   Most like a ringdove chiding,
Or flute faint-heard from distant boat
   O'er smoothest waters gliding.

Lo, round you steals the wooing breeze—
   Lo, on you falls the dew !
O Sweets, awake, for scarcely these
   Can charm while wanting you !

Wake ye not yet—while fast, below
   The silver time is fleeing ?
O Heart of mine, those flowers but show
   Thine own contented being.

The twilight but preserves the bloom,
   The sun can but decay ,
The warmth that brings the rich perfume,
   But steals the life away

O Heart, enjoy thy present calm,
   Rest peaceful in the shade,
And dread the sun that gives the balm
   To bid the blossom fade ''

When Lucy ended, the stranger's praise was less loud than either the doctor's or his lady's ; but how far more sweet it was : and for the first time in her life Lucy made the discovery, that eyes can praise as well as lips. For our part, we have often thought that that discovery is an epoch in life.

It was now that Mrs. Slopperton declared her thorough conviction that the stranger himself could sing —'' He had that about him,'' she said, ''which made her sure of it.''

''Indeed, dear madam,'' said he, with his usual undefinable half-frank, half-latent smile, ''my voice is but so-so, and my memory so indifferent, that even in the easiest passages I soon come to a stand. My best notes are in the falsetto, and as for my *execution*—but we won't talk of *that*.''

'' Nay, nay ; you are so modest,'' said Mrs. Slopperton : ''I am sure you could oblige us if you would.''

'' Your command,'' said the stranger, moving to the harpsichord, ''is all-sufficient ; and since you, madam '' (turning to Lucy), ''have chosen a song after the old school, may I find pardon if I do the same? My selection is, to be sure, from a lawless song-book, and is supposed to be a ballad by Robin Hood, or, at least, one of his merry men ; a very different sort of outlaws from the knaves who attacked you, sir !''

With this preface, the stranger sung to a wild yet jovial air, with a tolerable voice, the following effusion :—

THE LOVE OF OUR PROFESSION ; OR, THE ROBBER'S LIFE.

"On the stream of the World, the Robber's life
  Is borne on the blithest wave ,
Now it bounds into light in a gladsome strife,
  Now it laughs in its hiding cave.

At his maiden's lattice he stays the rein,
  How still is his courser proud !
(But still as a wind when it hangs o'er the main
  In the breast of the boding cloud;—

With the champed bit and the arched crest,
  And the eye of a listening deer,
Like valour, fretful most in rest,
  Least chaf'd when in career.

Fit slave to a Lord whom all else refuse
  To save at his desperate need ,
By my troth ! I think one whom the world pursues
  Hath a right to a gallant steed.

'Away, my beloved, I hear their feet !
  I blow thee a kiss, my fair,
And I promise to bring thee, when next we meet,
  A braid for thy bonny hair.

'Hurra ! for the booty '—my steed, hurra !
  Thorough bush, thorough brake, go we ;
And the coy Moon smiles on our merry way,
  Like my own love—timidly.'

The Parson he rides with a jingling pouch,
  How it blabs of the rifled poor !
The Courtier he lolls in his gilded coach,
  How it smacks of a sinecure !

The Lawyer revolves in his whirling chaise
  Sweet thoughts of a mischief done ;
And the Lady that knoweth the card she plays
  Is counting her guineas won !

'Ho, Lady '—What, holla, ye sinless men !
  My claim ye can scarce refuse ,
For when honest folk live on their neighbours, then
  They encroach on the Robber's dues !'

The Lady changed cheek like a bashful maid,
  The Lawyer talk'd wondrous fair,
The Parson blasphemed, and the Courtier pray'd,
  And the Robber bore off his share.

'Hurra ! for the revel ! my steed, hurra :
  Thorough bush, thorough brake, go we !
It is ever a virtue, when others pay,
  To ruffle it merrily !'

Oh ! there never was life like the Robber's—so
  Jolly, and bold, and free ,
And its end—why, a cheer from the crowd below,
  And a leap from a leafless tree !'"

This very moral lay being ended, Mrs. Slopperton declared it was excellent; though she confessed she thought the sentiments rather loose. Perhaps the gentleman might be induced to favour them with a song of a more refined and modern turn—something senti-mental, in short. Glancing towards Lucy, the stranger answered, that he only knew one song of the kind Mrs. Slopperton specified, and it was so short, that he could scarcely weary her patience by granting her request.

At this moment, the river, which was easily descried from the windows of the room, glimmered in the starlight, and directing his looks towards the water, as if the scene had suggested to him the verses he sung, he gave the following stanzas in a very low, sweet tone, and with a far purer taste than, perhaps, would have suited the preceding and ruder song :—

THE WISH.

"As sleeps the dreaming Eve below,
   Its holiest star keeps ward above,
And yonder wave begins to glow,
   Like Friendship bright'ning into Love!

Ah! would thy bosom were that stream,
   Ne'er woo'd save by the virgin air!—
Ah! would that I were that star, whose beam
   Looks down and finds its image *there!*"

Scarcely was the song ended, before the arrival of Miss Brandon's servant was announced, and her destined escort starting up, gallantly assisted her with her cloak and her hood—happy, no doubt, to escape, in some measure, the overwhelming compliments of his entertainers.

"But," said the doctor, as he shook hands with his deliverer, "by what name shall I remember and "—(lifting his reverend eyes) —"pray for the gentleman to whom I am so much indebted?"

"You are very kind," said the stranger; "my name is Clifford. Madam" (turning to Lucy), "may I offer my hand down the stairs?"

Lucy accepted the courtesy, and the stranger was half way down the staircase, when the doctor, stretching out his little neck, exclaimed,—

"Good evening, sir! I do hope we shall meet again."

"Fear not," said Mr. Clifford, laughing gaily, "I am too great a traveller to make that hope a matter of impossibility. Take care, madam—one step more."

The night was calm and tolerably clear, though the moon had not yet risen, as Lucy and her companion passed through the fields, with the servant preceding them at a little distance with the lantern.

After a pause of some length, Clifford said, with a little hesitation. "Is Miss Brandon related to the celebrated barrister of her name?"

"He is my uncle," said Lucy; "do you know him?"

"Only your uncle?" said Clifford, with vivacity, and evading Lucy's question. "I feared—hem! hem!—that is, I thought he might have been a nearer relation." There was another, but a shorter pause, when Clifford resumed, in a low voice, "Will Miss Brandon think me very presumptuous if I say, that a countenance like hers, once seen, can never be forgotten; and I believe, some years since, I had the honour to see her in London, at the theatre? It was but a momentary and distant glance that I was then enabled to gain; and yet," he added, significantly, "it sufficed!"

"I was only once at the theatre while in London, some years ago," said Lucy, a little embarrassed; "and, indeed, an unpleasant occurrence which happened to my uncle, with whom I was, is sufficient to make me remember it."

"Ha!—and what was it?"

"Why, in going out of the play-house, his watch was stolen by some dexterous pickpocket."

"Was the rogue caught?" asked the stranger.

"Yes; and was sent the next day to Bridewell. My uncle said he was extremely young, and yet quite hardened. I remember that I was foolish enough, when I heard of his sentence, to beg very hard that my uncle would intercede for him; but in vain."

"Did you, indeed, intercede for him?" said the stranger, in so earnest a tone that Lucy coloured for the twentieth time that night, without seeing any necessity for the blush. Clifford continued in a gayer tone, "Well, it is surprising how rogues hang together! I should not be greatly surprised if the person who despoiled your uncle were one of the same gang as the rascal who so terrified your worthy friend the doctor. But is this handsome old place your home?"

"This is my home," answered Lucy; "but it is an old-fashioned, strange place: and few people, to whom it was not endeared by associations, would think it handsome."

"Pardon me!" said Lucy's companion, stopping, and surveying, with a look of great interest, the quaint pile, which now stood close before them; its dark bricks, gable-ends, and ivied walls, tinged by the starry light of the skies, and contrasted by the river, which rolled in silence below. The shutters to the large oriel window of the room, in which the squire usually sat, were still unclosed, and the steady and warm light of the apartment shone forth, casting a glow, even to the smooth waters of the river : at the same moment, too, the friendly bark of the house-dog was heard, as in welcome ; and was followed by the note of the great bell, announcing the hour for the last meal of the old-fashioned and hospitable family.

"There is a pleasure in this !" said the stranger, unconsciously, and with a half-sigh : "I wish I had a home !"

"And have you not a home?" said Lucy, with *naïveté*.

"As much as a bachelor can have, perhaps," answered Clifford, recovering without an effort his gaiety and self-possession. "But you know we wanderers are not allowed the same boast as the more fortunate Benedicts ; we send our hearts in search of a home, and we lose the one without gaining the other. But I keep you in the cold, and we are now at your door."

"You will come in, of course !" said Miss Brandon, "and partake of our evening cheer."

The stranger hesitated for an instant, and then said in a quick tone,—

"No ! many — many thanks ; it is already late. Will Miss Brandon accept my gratitude for her condescension, in permitting the attendance of one unknown to her ?" As he thus spoke, Clifford bowed profoundly over the hand of his beautiful charge ; and Lucy, wishing him good-night, hastened, with a light step, to her father's side.

Meanwhile, Clifford, after lingering a minute, when the door was closed on him, turned abruptly away ; and muttering to himself, repaired with rapid steps to whatever object he had then in view.

CHAPTER XII.

" Up rouse ye then
My merry, merry men !"—JOANNA BAILLIE.

WHEN the moon rose that night, there was one spot upon which she palely broke, about ten miles distant from Warlock, which the forewarned traveller would not have been eager to pass, but which might not have afforded a bad study to such artists as have caught from the savage painter of the Apennines a love for the wild and the adventurous. Dark trees, scattered far and wide over a broken, but verdant sward, made the background ; the moon shimmered through the boughs as she came slowly forth from her pavilion of cloud, and poured a broader beam on two figures just advanced beyond the trees. More plainly brought into light by her rays than his companion, here a horseman, clad in a short cloak that barely covered the crupper of his steed, was looking to the priming of a large pistol which he had just taken from his holster   A slouched hat, and a mask of black crape, conspired with the action to throw a natural suspicion on the intentions of the rider. His horse, a beautiful dark grey, stood quite motionless, with arched neck, and its short ears quickly moving to and fro, demonstrative of that sagacious and anticipative attention which characterises the noblest of all tamed animals : you would not have perceived the impatience of the steed, but for the white foam that gathered round the bit, and for an occasional and unfrequent toss of the head   Behind this horseman, and partially thrown into the dark shadow of the trees, another man, similarly clad, was busied in tightening the girths of a horse, of great strength and size. As he did so, he hummed, with no unmusical murmur, the air of a popular drinking song.

"'Sdeath, Ned !" said his comrade, who had for some time been plunged in a silent reverie,—"'Sdeath ! why can you not stifle your love for the fine arts, at a moment like this? That hum of thine grows louder every moment, at last I expect it will burst out into a full roar ; recollect we are not at Gentleman George's now !"

"The more's the pity, Augustus," answered Ned. "Soho, Little John ; woaho, sir ; a nice long night like this is made on purpose for drinking. Will you, sir ? keep still then !"

"'Man never is, but always to be blest,'" said the moralising Tomlinson ; "you see you sigh for other scenes even when you have a fine night and the chance of a God-send before you."

"Ay, the night is fine enough," said Ned, who was rather a grumbler, as, having finished his gloom-like operation, he now slowly mounted. "D—— it, Oliver[1] looks out as broadly as if he were going to blab. For my part, I love a *dark* night, with a star here and there winking at us, as much as to say, 'I see you, my boys, but I won't say a word about it,' and a small, pattering, drizzling, mizzling rain, that prevents Little John's hoofs being heard, and covers one's retreat, as it were. Besides, when one is a little wet, it is always necessary to drink the more, to keep the cold from one's stomach when one gets home."

"Or in other words," said Augustus, who loved a maxim from his very heart, "light wet cherishes heavy wet !"

"Good !" said Ned, yawning. "Hang it, I wish the captain would come. Do you know what o'clock it is?—Not far short of eleven, I suppose ?"

[1] The moon.

"About that!—hist, is that a carriage?—no—it is only a sudden rise in the wind."

"Very self-sufficient in Mr. Wind to allow himself to be raised without our help!" said Ned : "by the way, we are of course to go back to the Red Cave."

"So Captain Lovett says—— Tell me, Ned, what do you think of the new tenant Lovett has put into the cave."

"Oh, I have strange doubts there," answered Ned, shaking the hairy honours of his head. "I don't half like it ; consider, the cave is our stronghold, and ought only to be known——"

"To men of tried virtue," interrupted Tomlinson. "I agree with you ; I must try and get Lovett to discard his singular *protégé*, as the French say."

"'Gad, Augustus, how came you by so much learning? You know all the poets by heart, to say nothing of Latin and French."

"Oh, hang it, I was brought up, like the captain, to a literary way of life."

"That's what makes you so thick with him, I suppose. *He* writes (and sings too) a tolerable song, and is certainly a deuced clever fellow. What a rise in the world he has made ! Do you recollect what a poor sort of way he was in when you introduced him at Gentleman George's ? and now he's the Captain Crank of the gang."

"The gang ! the company you mean. Gang, indeed ! One would think you were speaking of a knot of pickpockets. Yes, Lovett is a clever fellow ; and, thanks to me, a very decent philosopher !" It is impossible to convey to our reader the grave air of importance with which Tomlinson made his concluding laudation. "Yes," said he, after a pause, "he has a bold, plain way of viewing things, and, like Voltaire, he becomes a philosopher by being a Man of Sense ! Hist ! see my horse's ears ! some one is coming, though I don't hear him ! Keep watch !"

The robbers grew silent, the sound of distant hoofs was indistinctly heard, and, as it came nearer, there was a crash of boughs, as if a hedge had been ridden through ; presently the moon gleamed picturesquely on the figure of a horseman, approaching through the copse in the rear of the robbers. Now he was half seen among the sinuosities of his forest path ; now in full sight, now altogether hid ; then his horse neighed impatiently ; now he again came in sight, and in a moment more he had joined the pair ! The new comer was of a tall and sinewy frame, and in the first bloom of manhood. A frock of dark green, edged with a narrow silver lace, and buttoned from the throat to the middle, gave due effect to an upright mien, a broad chest, and a slender, but rounded waist, that stood in no need of the compression of the tailor. A short riding-cloak clasped across the throat with a silver buckle, hung pic-turesquely over one shoulder, while his lower limbs were cased in military boots, which, though they rose above the knee, were evidently neither heavy nor embarrassing to the vigorous sinews of the horseman. The caparisons of the steed—the bit, the bridle, the saddle, the holster—were according to the most approved fashion of the day ; and the steed itself was in the highest condition, and of remarkable beauty. The horseman's air was erect and bold ; a small but coal-black mustachio heightened the resolute expression of his short, curved lip ; and from beneath the large hat which over-hung his brow, his long locks escaped, and waved darkly in the keen night air. Altogether, horseman and horse exhibited a gallant and even a chivalrous appearance, which the hour and the scene heightened to a dramatic and romantic effect.

"Ha ! Lovett."

"How are you, my merry men !" were the salutations exchanged.

"What news ?" said Ned.

"Brave news ! look to it. My lord and his carriage will be by in ten minutes at most."

"Have you got anything more out of the parson I frightened so gloriously?" asked Augustus.

"No ; more of that hereafter. Now for our new prey."

"Are you sure our noble friend will be so soon at hand?" said Tomlinson, patting his steed, that now pawed in excited hilarity.

"Sure ! I saw him change horses ; I was in the stable-yard at the time ; he got out for half an hour, to eat, I fancy ;—be sure that I played him a trick in the meanwhile."

"What force ?" asked Ned.

"Self and servant."

"The post-boys ?"

"Ay, I forgot them. Never mind, you must frighten them."

"Forwards !" cried Ned, and his horse sprang from his armed heel.

"One moment," said Lovett ; "I must put on my mask—soho—Robin, soho ! Now for it—forwards !"

As the trees rapidly disappeared behind them, the riders entered, at a hand gallop, on a broad track of waste land interspersed with dykes and occasionally fences of hurdles, over which their horses bounded like quadrupeds well accustomed to such exploits.

Certainly at that moment, what with the fresh air, the fitful moon-light now breaking broadly out, now lost in a rolling cloud, the exciting exercise, and that racy and dancing stir of the blood, which all action, whether evil or noble in its nature, raises in our veins ;

what with all this, we cannot but allow the fascination of that lawless life ;—a fascination so great, that one of the most noted *gentlemen highwaymen* of the day, one too who had received an excellent education, and mixed in no inferior society, is reported to have said when the rope was about his neck, and the good Ordinary was exhorting him to repent of his ill-spent life, "*Ill*-spent, you dog '—Gad ! (smacking his lips) it was *delicious !*"

"Fie ! fie ! Mr. ——, raise your thoughts to Heaven !"

"But a canter across the common—oh !" muttered the criminal ; and his soul cantered off to eternity.

So briskly leaped the heart of the leader of the three, that, as they now came in view of the main road, and the distant wheel of a carriage *whirred* on the ear, he threw up his right hand with a joyous gesture, and burst into a boyish exclamation of hilarity and delight.

"Whist, captain !" said Ned, checking his own spirits with a mock air of gravity, "let us conduct ourselves like gentlemen ; it is only your low fellows who get into such confoundedly high spirits ; men of the world like us should do everything as if their hearts were broken."

"Melancholy[1] ever cronies with Sublimity, and Courage is sublime," said Augustus, with the pomp of a maxim-maker.

[1] A maxim which would have pleased Madame de Stael, who thought that philosophy consisted in fine sentiments. In the *Life of Lord Byron*, just published by Mr Moore, the distinguished biographer makes a similar assertion to that of the sage Augustus : "When did ever a sublime thought spring up in the soul that Melancholy was not to be found, however latent, in its neighbourhood ?" Now, with due deference to Mr. Moore, this is a very sickly piece of nonsense, that has not even an atom of truth to stand on "God said, Let there be light, and there was light !"—We should like to know where lies the Melancholy of that sublime sentence ? "Truth," says Plato, "is the body of God, and Light is his shadow." In the name of common sense, in what possible corner, in the vicinity of that lofty image, lurks the jaundiced face of this eternal *bête noir* of Mr Moore's ? Again, in that sublimest passage in the sublimest of the Latin poets (Lucretius), which bursts forth in honour of Epicurus,[1] is there any thing that speaks to us of sadness ? On the contrary, in the three passages we have referred to, especially in the two first quoted, there is something splendidly luminous and cheering. Joy is often a great source of the sublime, the suddenness of its ventings would alone suffice to make it so. What can be more sublime than the triumphant Psalms of David, intoxicated as they are with an almost delirium of transport? Even in the *gloomiest* passages of the poets, where we recognise sublimity, we do not often find *melancholy* We are stricken by terror, appalled by awe, but seldom softened into sadness. In fact, Melancholy rather belongs to another class of feelings than those excited by a sublime passage or those which engender its composition On one hand, in the

[1] "Primus Graius homo mortaleis tollere, contra," &c
To these instances we might especially add the odes of Pindar, Horace, and Campbell.

"Now for the hedge !" cried Lovett, unheeding his comrades, and his horse sprang into the road.

The three men now were drawn up quite still and motionless by the side of the hedge. The broad road lay before them, curving out of sight on either side ; the ground was hardening under an early tendency to frost, and the clear ring of approaching hoofs sounded on the ear of the robbers, ominous, haply, of the chinks of "more attractive metal" about, if Hope told no flattering tale, to be their own.

Presently the long-expected vehicle made its appearance at the turn of the road, and it rolled rapidly on behind four fleet post-horses.

"You, Ned, with your large steed, stop the horses ; you, Augustus, bully the post-boys ; leave me to do the rest," said the captain.

"As agreed," returned Ned, laconically. "Now, look at me !" and the horse of the vain highwayman sprang from its shelter. So instantaneous were the operations of these experienced tacticians, that Lovett's orders were almost executed in a briefer time than it had cost him to give them

The carriage being stopped, and the post-boys white and

loftiest flights of Homer, Milton, and Shakspeare, we will challenge a critic to discover this "green sickness' which Mr. Moore would convert into the magnificence of the plague. On the other hand, where is the evidence that Melancholy made the habitual temperaments of those divine men? Of Homer we know nothing ; of Shakspeare and Milton, we have reason to believe the ordinary temperament was constitutionally cheerful. The latter boasts of it. A thousand instances, in contradiction to an assertion it were not worth while to contradict, were it not so generally popular, so highly sanctioned, and so eminently pernicious to everything that is manly and noble in literature, rush to our memory But we think we have already quoted enough to disprove the sentence, which the illustrious biographer has himself disproved in more than twenty passages, which, *if* he is pleased to forget, we thank Heaven, posterity never will Now we are on the subject of this Life, so excellent in many respects, we cannot but observe that we think the whole scope of its *philosophy* utterly unworthy of the accomplished mind of the writer ; the philosophy consists of an unpardonable distorting of general truths, to suit the peculiarities of an individual, noble indeed, but proverbially morbid and eccentric. A striking instance of this occurs in the laboured assertion that poets make but sorry domestic characters. What ! because Lord Byron is said to have been a bad husband, was (to go no further back for examples)—was Walter Scott a bad husband ? or was Campbell ? or is Mr. Moore himself ? Why, in the name of justice, should it be insinuated that Milton was a bad husband, when, as far as any one can judge of the matter, it was Mrs. Milton who was the bad wife ? And why, oh ! why should we be told by Mr Moore, a man who, to judge by *Captain Rock* and the *Epicurean*, wants neither learning nor diligence—why are we to be told, with peculiar emphasis, that Lord Bacon never married, when Lord Bacon not only married, but his marriage was so advantageous as to be an absolute epoch in his career ? Really, really, one begins to believe that there is not such a thing as a fact in the world !

trembling, with two pistols (levelled by Augustus and Pepper) cocked at their heads, Lovett dismounting, threw open the door of the carriage, and in a very civil tone, and with a very bland address, accosted the inmate.

"Do not be alarmed, my lord, you are perfectly safe ; we only require your watch and purse."

" Really," answered a voice still softer than that of the robber, while a marked and somewhat *French* countenance, crowned with a fur cap, peered forth at the arrester,—"really, sir, your request is so modest that I were worse than cruel to refuse you. My purse is not very full, and you may as well have it as one of my rascally duns ; but my watch I have a love for, and——"

"I understand you, my lord," interrupted the highwayman. " What do you value your watch at ? "

" Humph—to you it may be worth some twenty guineas."

" Allow me to see it ! "

" Your curiosity is extremely gratifying," returned the nobleman, as with great reluctance he drew forth a gold repeater, set, as was sometimes the fashion of that day, in precious stones. The high-wayman looked slightly at the bauble.

" Your lordship," said he, with great gravity, " was too modest in your calculation—your taste reflects greater credit on you : allow me to assure you that your watch is worth fifty guineas to us at the least. To show you that I think so most sincerely, I will either keep it, and we will say no more on the matter ; or I will return it to you upon your word of honour that you will give me a cheque for fifty guineas payable, by your *real* bankers, to ' bearer for self.' Take your choice ; it is quite immaterial to me ! "

" Upon my honour, sir," said the traveller, with some surprise struggling to his features, " your coolness and self-possession are quite admirable. I see you know the world."

" Your lordship flatters me ! " returned Lovett, bowing. " How do you decide ? "

" Why, is it possible to write drafts without ink, pen, or paper ? "

Lovett drew back, and while he was searching in his pockets for writing implements, which he always carried about him, the traveller seized the opportunity, and, suddenly snatching a pistol from the pocket of the carriage, levelled it full at the head of the robber. The traveller was an excellent and practised shot—he was almost within arm's length of his intended victim—his pistols were the envy of all his Irish friends. He pulled the trigger—the powder flashed in the pan, and the highwayman, not even changing countenance, drew forth a small ink-bottle, and placing a steel pen in it, handed it to the nobleman, saying, with incomparable *sang froid*, "Would you like, my lord, to try the other pistol? If so, oblige me by a quick aim, as you must see the necessity of despatch. If not, here is the back of a letter, on which you can write the draft."

The traveller was not a man apt to become embarrassed in any-thing—save his circumstances; but he certainly felt a little discom-posed and confused as he took the paper, and, uttering some broken words, wrote the cheque. The highwayman glanced over it, saw it was written according to form, and then with a bow of cool respect, returned the watch, and shut the door of the carriage.

Meanwhile the servant had been shivering in front—boxed up in that solitary convenience termed, not euphoniously, a dickey. Him the robber now briefly accosted.

"What have you got about you belonging to your master?"

"Only his pills, your honour! which I forgot to put in the——"

"Pills!—throw them down to me!" The valet tremblingly extracted from his side-pocket a little box, which he threw down, and Lovett caught in his hand.

He opened the box, counted the pills—

"One,—two,—four,—twelve,—Aha!" He reopened the carriage door.

"Are these your pills, my lord?"

The wondering peer, who had begun to resettle himself in the corner of his carriage, answered, "that they were!"

"My lord, I see you are in a high state of fever; you were a little delirious just now when you snapped a pistol in your friend's face. Permit me to recommend you a prescription—swallow off all these pills!"

"My God!" cried the traveller, startled into earnestness: "What do you mean?—twelve of those pills would kill a man!"

"Hear him!" said the robber, appealing to his comrades, who roared with laughter. "What, my lord, would you rebel against your doctor?—Fie, fie! be persuaded."

And with a soothing gesture he stretched the pill-box towards the recoiling nose of the traveller. But though a man who could as well as any one make the best of a bad condition, the traveller was especially careful of his health; and so obstinate was he where that was concerned, that he would rather have submitted to the effectual operation of a bullet, than incurred the chance operation of an extra pill. He, therefore, with great indignation, as the box was still extended towards him, snatched it from the hand of the robber, and, flinging it across the road, said, with dignity:—

"Do your worst, rascals! But, if you leave me alive, you shall repent the outrage you have offered to one of his Majesty's household!" Then, as if becoming sensible of the ridicule of affecting too much in his present situation, he added in an altered tone: "And now, for Heaven's sake, shut the door; and if you must kill somebody, there's my servant on the box—he's paid for it."

This speech made the robbers laugh more than ever; and Lovett, who liked a joke even better than a purse, immediately closed the carriage doors, saying,—

"Adieu! my Lord; and let me give you a piece of advice: whenever you get out at a country inn, and stay half-an-hour while your horses are changing, take your pistols with you, or you may chance to have the charge drawn."

With this admonition the robber withdrew; and seeing that the valet held out to him a long green purse, he said, gently shaking his head,—

"Rogues should not prey on each other, my good fellow. You rob your master—so do we—let each keep what he has got."

Long Ned and Tomlinson, then backing their horses, the carriage was freed; and away started the post-boys at a pace which seemed to show less regard for life than the robbers themselves had evinced.

Meanwhile the captain remounted his steed, and the three confederates, bounding in gallant style over the hedge through which they had previously gained the road, galloped off in the same direction they had come; the moon ever and anon bringing into light their flying figures, and the sound of many a joyous peal of laughter ringing through the distance along the frosty air.

CHAPTER XIII.

" *What is here ?—*
Gold ? . . . .
Th is much of this will make black white—foul fair.'
                        ' TIMON OF ATHENS.

" *Came there a certain lord, neat, trimly drest,*
Fresh as a bridegroom."   ' HENRY THE FOURTH.'

' *I do not know the man I should avoid*
So soon as that spare Cassius !   He reads much.
He is a great observer · and he looks
Quite through the deeds of men
Often he smiles, but smiles in such a sort,
As if he mocked himself or scorned his spirit,
That could be moved to smile at anything."—' JULIUS CÆSAR.'

THE next day, late at noon, as Lucy was sitting with her father, not as usual engaged either in work or in reading, but seemingly quite idle, with her pretty foot upon the squire's gouty stool, and her eyes fixed on the carpet, while her hands (never were hands so soft and so small as Lucy's, though they may have been eclipsed in whiteness) were lightly clasped together and reposed listlessly on her knees,—the surgeon of the village abruptly entered with a face full of news and honor. Old Squire Brandon was one of those persons who always hear news, whatever it may be, later than any of their neighbours, and it was not till all the gossips of the neighbourhood had picked the bone of the matter quite bare, that he was now informed, through the medium of Mr. Pillum, that Lord Mauleverer had on the preceding night been stopped by three highwaymen in his road to his country seat, and robbed to a considerable amount.

The fame of the worthy Dr. Slopperton's mal-adventure having, long ere this, been spread far and wide, the whole neighbourhood was naturally thrown into great consternation.   Magistrates were sent to, large dogs borrowed, blunderbusses cleaned, and a subscription made throughout the parish for the raising of a patrol.   There seemed little doubt but that the offenders, in either case, were members of the same horde ; and Mr. Pillum, in his own mind, was perfectly convinced that they meant to encroach upon his trade, and destroy all the surrounding householders who were worth the trouble.

The next week passed in the most diligent endeavours, on the part

of the neighbouring magistrates and yeomanry, to detect and seize
the robbers, but their labours were utterly fruitless ; and one justice
of peace, who had been particularly active, was himself entirely
" cleaned out " by an old gentleman, who, under the name of Mr.
Bagshot—rather an ominous cognomen—offered to conduct the un-
suspicious magistrate to the very spot where the miscreants might
be seized.   No sooner, however, had he drawn the poor justice away
from his comrades into a lonely part of the road, than he stripped
him to his shirt.   He did not even leave his worship his flannel
drawers, though the weather was as bitter as the dog-days of
eighteen hundred and twenty-nine.

"'Tis not my way," said the hoary ruffian, when the justice
petitioned at least for the latter article of attire ; " 'tis not my way
—I be's slow about my work, but I does it thoroughly—so off with
your rags, old 'un."

This was, however, the only additional instance of aggression in
the vicinity of Warlock Manor-house ; and, by degrees, as the
autumn declined, and no farther enormities were perpetrated, people
began to look out for a new topic of conversation.   This was
afforded them by a piece of unexpected good fortune to Lucy
Brandon.

Mrs. Warner, an old lady to whom she was slightly related, and
with whom she had been residing during her brief and only visit to
London, died suddenly, and in her will declared Lucy to be her sole
heiress.   The property, which was in the funds, and which amounted
to sixty thousand pounds, was to be enjoyed by Miss Brandon immediately on her attaining her twenty-first year ; meanwhile the executors to the will were to pay to the young heiress the annual sum of
six hundred pounds.   The joy which this news created in Warlock
Manor-house may easily be conceived.   The squire projected improvements here, and repairs there ; and Lucy, poor girl, who had
no idea of money for herself, beyond the purchase of a new pony, or
a gown from London, seconded with affectionate pleasure all her
father's suggestions, and delighted herself with the reflection that
those fine plans, which were to make the Brandons greater than the
Brandons ever were before, were to be realised by her own, own
money !   It was at this identical time that the surrounding gentry
made a simultaneous and grand discovery—viz. of the astonishing
merits and great good sense of Mr. Joseph Brandon.   It was a pity,
they observed, that he was of so reserved and shy a turn—it was not
becoming in a gentleman of so ancient a family.   But why should
they not endeavour to draw him from his retirement into those more
public scenes which he was doubtless well calculated to adorn ?

Accordingly, as soon as the first month of mourning had expired, several coaches, chariots, chaises, and horses, which had never been seen at Warlock Manor-house before, arrived there one after the other in the most friendly manner imaginable. Their owners admired everything—the house was such a fine relic of old times!—for their parts they liked an oak staircase!—and those nice old windows!—and what a beautiful peacock!—and, Heaven save the mark! that magnificent chestnut tree was worth a forest!—Mr. Brandon was requested to make one of the county hunt, not that he any longer hunted himself, but that his name would give such consequence to the thing!—Miss Lucy must come to pass a week with her dear friends the Honourable Misses Sansterre!—Augustus, their brother, had *such* a sweet lady's horse!—In short, the customary change which takes place in people's characters after the acquisition of a fortune, took place in the characters of Mr. and Miss Brandon; and when people become suddenly amiable, it is no wonder that they should suddenly gain a vast accession of friends.

But Lucy, though she had seen so little of the world, was not quite blind; and the squire, though rather obtuse, was not quite a fool. If they were not rude to their new visitors, they were by no means overpowered with gratitude at their condescension. Mr. Brandon declined subscribing to the hunt, and Miss Lucy laughed in the face of the Honourable Augustus Sansterre. Among their new guests, however, was one who to great knowledge of the world joined an extreme and even brilliant polish of manners, which at least prevented deceit from being disagreeable, if not wholly from being unseen :—this was the new lieutenant of the county, Lord Mauleverer.

Though possessed of an immense property in that district, Lord Mauleverer had hitherto resided but little on his estates. He was one of those gay lords who are now somewhat uncommon in this country after mature manhood is attained, who live an easy and rakish life, rather among their parasites than their equals, and who yet, by aid of an agreeable manner, natural talents, and a certain graceful and light cultivation of mind (not the less pleasant for its being universally coloured with worldliness, and an amusing rather than offensive regard for self) never lose their legitimate station in society; who are oracles in dress, equipages, cookery, and beauty, and, having no character of their own, are able to fix by a single word a character upon any one else. Thus, while Mauleverer rather lived the dissolute life of a young nobleman, who prefers the company of agreeable demireps to that of wearisome duchesses, than maintained the decorous state befitting a mature age, and an immense interest in the country,—he was quite as popular at court, where he held a situation in the household, as he was in the green-

100m, where he enchanted every actress on the right side of forty
A word from him in the legitimate quarters of power went farther
than an harangue from another; and even the prudes,—at least, all
those who had daughters,—confessed "that his lordship was a very
interesting character." Like Brandon, his familiar friend, he had
risen in the world (from the Irish baron to the English earl) without having ever changed his politics, which were ultra-Tory; and
we need not observe that he was deemed, like Brandon, a model of
public integrity. He was possessed of two places under government, six votes in the House of Commons, and eight livings in the
church; and we must add, in justice to his loyal and religious
principles, that there was not in the three kingdoms a firmer friend
to the existing establishments.

Whenever a nobleman does not marry, people try to take away
his character. Lord Mauleverer had never married; the Whigs
had been very bitter on the subject; they even alluded to it in the
House of Commons, that chaste assembly, where the never-failing
subject of reproach against Mr. Pitt was the not being of an amorous
temperament; but they had not hitherto prevailed against the stout
earl's celibacy. It is true, that if he was devoid of a wife, he had
secured to himself plenty of substitutes; his profession was that of
a man of gallantry; and though he avoided the daughters, it was
only to make love to the mothers. But his lordship had now
attained a certain age, and it was at last circulated among his friends
that he intended to look out for a Lady Mauleverer.

" Spare your caresses," said his toady-in-chief to a certain duchess,
who had three portionless daughters: " Mauleverer has sworn that
he will not choose among your order: you know his high politics,
and you will not wonder at his declaring himself averse in matrimony
as in morals to a *community of goods.*"

The announcement of the earl's matrimonial design, and the
circulation of this anecdote, set all the clergymen's daughters in
England on a blaze of expectation; and when Mauleverer came to
* * * * shire, upon obtaining the honour of the lieutenancy, to
visit his estates and court the friendship of his neighbours, there was
not an old-young lady of forty, who worked in broad-stitch and had
never been to London above a week at a time, who did not deem
herself exactly the sort of person sure to fascinate his lordship. It
was late in the afternoon when the travelling chariot of this distinguished person, preceded by two outriders in the earl's undress
livery of dark green, stopped at the hall door of Warlock House.
The squire was at home, actually and metaphorically; for he never
dreamed of denying himself to any one, gentle or simple. The door
of the carriage being opened, there descended a small slight man,

richly dressed (for lace and silk vestments were not then quite discarded, though gradually growing less the mode), and of an air prepossessing, and *distinguished*, rather than *dignified*. His years,—for his countenance, though handsome, was deeply marked, and evinced the tokens of dissipation,—seemed more numerous than they really were; and, though not actually past middle age, Lord Mauleverer might fairly have received the unpleasing epithet of elderly. However, his step was firm, his gait upright, and his figure was considerably more youthful than his physiognomy. The first compliments of the day having passed, and Lord Mauleverer having expressed his concern that his long and frequent absence from the county had hitherto prevented his making the acquaintance of Mr. Brandon, the brother of one of his oldest and most esteemed friends, conversation became on both sides rather an effort. Mr. Brandon first introduced the subject of the weather, and the turnips—inquired whether his lordship was not very fond—(for his part he used to be, but lately the rheumatism had disabled him, he hoped his lordship was not subject to *that complaint*) *of shooting!*

Catching only the last words,—for, besides the awful complexity of the squire's sentences, Mauleverer was slightly affected by the aristocratic complaint of deafness,—the earl answered with a smile,—

" The complaint of shooting !—Very good indeed, Mr. Brandon ; it is seldom that I have heard so witty a phrase. No, I am not in the least troubled with that epidemic. It is a disorder very prevalent in this county."

" My lord ! " said the squire, rather puzzled—and then observing that Mauleverer did not continue, he thought it expedient to start another subject.

" I was exceedingly grieved to hear that your lordship, in travelling to Mauleverer Park—(that is a very ugly road across the waste land ; the roads in this county are in general pretty good—for my own part, when I was a magistrate I was very strict in that respect) —was robbed. You have not yet, I believe, detected—(for my part, though I do not profess to be much of a politician, I do think that in affairs of robbery there is a great deal of remissness in *the ministers*)—*the villains !* "

" Our friend is disaffected ! " thought the lord-lieutenant, imagining that the last opprobrious term was applied to the respectable personages specified in the parenthesis. Bowing with a polished smile to the squire, Mauleverer replied aloud, that he was extremely sorry that their conduct (meaning the ministers) did not meet with Mr. Brandon's approbation.

" Well," thought the squire, " that is playing the courtier with a vengeance ! " " Meet with my approbation ! " said he, warmly :

"how could your lordship think me—(for though I am none of your saints, I am, I hope, a good Christian ; an excellent one, judging from your words, *your lordship must be !*) *so partial to crime !*"

"*I* partial to crime !" returned Mauleverer, thinking he had stumbled unawares on some outrageous democrat, yet smiling as softly as usual ; "you judge me harshly, Mr. Brandon ! you must do me more justice, and you can only do that by knowing me better."

Whatever unlucky answer the squire might otherwise have made, was cut off by the entrance of Lucy ; and the earl, secretly delighted at the interruption, rose to render her his homage, and to remind her of the introduction he had formerly been so happy as to obtain to her through the friendship of Mr. William Brandon,—"a friendship," said the gallant nobleman, "to which I have often before been indebted, but which was never more agreeably exerted on my behalf."

Upon this Lucy, who, though she had been so painfully bashful during her meeting with Mr. Clifford, felt no overpowering diffidence in the presence of so much greater a person, replied laughingly, and the earl rejoined by a second compliment. Conversation was now no longer an effort ; and Mauleverer, the most consummate of epicures, whom even royalty trembled to ask without preparation, on being invited by the unconscious squire to partake of the family dinner, eagerly accepted the invitation. It was long since the knightly walls of Warlock had been honoured by the presence of a guest so courtly. The good squire heaped his plate with a profusion of boiled beef ; and while the poor earl was contemplating in dismay the alps upon alps which he was expected to devour, the grey-headed butler, anxious to serve him with alacrity, whipped away the overloaded plate, and presently returned it, yet more astoundingly surcharged with an additional world of a composition of stony colour and sudorific aspect, which, after examining in mute attention for some moments, and carefully removing as well as he was able, to the extreme edge of his plate, the earl discovered to be suet pudding.

"You eat nothing, my lord," cried the squire ; "let me give you (this is more underdone ;)" holding between blade and fork in middle air a horrent fragment of scarlet, shaking its gory locks,— "another slice."

Swift at the word dropped upon Mauleverer's plate the happy finger and ruthless thumb of the grey-headed butler.

"Not a morsel more," cried the earl, struggling with the murtherous domestic. "My dear sir, excuse me ; I assure you I have never ate such a dinner before—never !"

"Nay, now!" quoth the squire, expostulating, "you really—(and this air is so keen that your ordship should indulge your appetite, *if you follow the physician's advice,*) *eat nothing!*"

Again Mauleverer was at fault.

"The physicians are right, Mr. Brandon," said he; "very right, and I am forced to live abstemiously: indeed I do not know whether, if I were to exceed at your hospitable table, and attack all that you would bestow upon me, I should ever recover it. You would have to seek a new lieutenant for your charming county, and on the tomb of the last Mauleverer the hypocritical and unrelated heir would inscribe, 'Died of the visitation of Beef, John, Earl, &c.'"

Plain as the meaning of this speech might have seemed to others, the squire only laughed at the effeminate appetite of the speaker, and inclined to think him an excellent fellow for jesting so good-humouredly on his own physical infirmity. But Lucy had the tact of her sex, and, taking pity on the earl's calamitous situation, though she certainly never guessed at its extent, entered with so much grace and ease into the conversation which he sought to establish between them, that Mauleverer's gentleman, who had hitherto been pushed aside by the zeal of the grey-headed butler, found an opportunity, when the squire was laughing and the butler staring, to steal away the overburthened plate unsuspected and unseen

In spite, however, of these evils of board and lodgment, Mauleverer was exceedingly well pleased with his visit; nor did he terminate it till the shades of night had begun to close, and the distance from his own residence conspired with experience to remind him that it was possible for a highwayman's audacity to attack the equipage even of Lord Mauleverer. He then reluctantly re-entered his carriage, and bidding the postilions drive as fast as possible, wrapped himself in his *roquelaire*, and divided his thoughts between Lucy Brandon and the *homard au gratin* with which he purposed to console himself immediately on his return home. However, Fate, which mocks our most cherished hopes, ordained that on arriving at Mauleverer Park the owner should be suddenly afflicted with a loss of appetite, a coldness in the limbs, a pain in the chest, and various other ungracious symptoms of portending malady. Lord Mauleverer went straight to bed; he remained there for some days, and when he recovered his physicians ordered him to Bath. The Whig Methodists, who hated him, ascribed his illness to Providence; and his lordship was firmly of opinion that it should be ascribed to the beef and pudding. However this be, there was an end, for the present, to the hopes of young ladies of forty, and to the intended festivities at Mauleverer Park. "Good Heavens!" said the earl, as his carriage wheels turned from his gates, "what a loss to

country tradesmen may be occasioned by a piece of underdone beef,
especially if it be boiled!"

About a fortnight had elapsed since Mauleverer's meteoric visit
to Warlock House, when the squire received from his brother the
following epistle!—

"MY DEAR JOSEPH,

"You know my numerous avocations, and, amid the press of
business which surrounds me, will, I am sure, forgive me for
being a very negligent and remiss correspondent.   Nevertheless,
I assure you, no one can more sincerely sympathise in that good
fortune which has befallen my charming niece, and of which your
last letter informed me, than I do.   Pray give my best love to
her, and tell her how complacently I look forward to the brilliant
sensation she will create, when her beauty is enthroned upon that
rank which, I am quite sure, it will one day or other command.

"You are not aware, perhaps, my dear Joseph, that I have for
some time been in a very weak and declining state of health.   The
old nervous complaint in my face has of late attacked me grievously,
and the anguish is sometimes so great that I am scarcely able to
bear it.   I believe the great demand which my profession makes
upon a frame of body never strong, and now beginning prematurely
to feel the infirmities of time, is the real cause of my maladies.   At
last, however, I must absolutely punish my pocket, and indulge my
inclinations by a short respite from toil.   The doctors—sworn friends,
you know, to the lawyers—since they make common cause against
mankind, have peremptorily ordered me to lie by, and to try a short
course of air, exercise, social amusements, and the waters of Bath.
Fortunately, this is vacation time, and I can afford to lose a few weeks
of emolument, in order, perhaps, to secure many years of life.   I purpose, then, early next week, repairing to that melancholy reservoir of
the gay, where persons dance out of life and are fiddled across the
Styx.   In a word, I shall make one of the adventurers after health,
who seek the goddess at King Bladud's pump-room.   Will you and
dear Lucy join me there?   I ask it of your friendship, and I am quite
sure that neither of you will shrink aghast at the proposal of solacing
your invalid relation.   At the same time that I am recovering health,
my pretty niece will be avenging Pluto, by consigning to his dominions
many a better and younger hero in my stead.   And it will be a double
pleasure to me to see all the hearts, &c.—I break off, for what can
I say on that subject which the little coquette does not anticipate?
It is high time that Lucy should see the world; and though there
are many at Bath, above all places, to whom the heiress will be an
object of interested attentions, yet there are also many in that

crowded city by no means undeserving her notice. What say you, dear Joseph?—But I know already; you will not refuse to keep company with me in my little holiday, and Lucy's eyes are already sparkling at the idea of new bonnets, Milsom Street, a thousand adorers, and the Pump-room.

"Ever, dear Joseph,

"Yours affectionately,

"WILLIAM BRANDON.

"P.S.—I find that my friend Lord Mauleverer is at Bath; I own that is an additional reason to take me thither; by a letter from him, received the other day, I see that he has paid you a visit, and he now raves about his host and the heiress. Ah, Miss Lucy, Miss Lucy! are you going to conquer him whom all London has, for years more than I care to tell (yet not many, for Mauleverer is still young), assailed in vain? Answer me!"

This letter created a considerable excitement in Warlock House The old squire was extremely fond of his brother, and grieved to the heart to find that he spoke so discouragingly of his health. Nor did the squire for a moment hesitate at accepting the proposal to join his distinguished relative at Bath. Lucy also,—who had for her uncle, possibly from his profuse yet not indelicate flattery, a very great regard and interest, though she had seen but little of him,— urged the squire to lose no time in arranging matters for their departure, so as to precede the barrister, and prepare everything for his arrival. The father and daughter being thus agreed, there was little occasion for delay; an answer to the invalid's letter was sent by return of post, and on the fourth day from their receipt of the said epistle, the good old squire, his daughter, a country girl, by way of abigail—the grey-headed butler, and two or three live pets, of the size and habits most convenient for travelling, were on their way to a city which at that time was gayer, at least, if somewhat less splendid, than the metropolis.

On the second day of their arrival at Bath, Brandon (as in future, to avoid confusion, we shall call the younger brother, giving to the elder his patriarchal title of squire) joined them.

He was a man seemingly rather fond of parade, though at heart he disrelished and despised it. He came to their lodging, which had not been selected in the very best part of the town, in a carriage and six, but attended only by one favourite servant.

They found him in better looks and better spirits than they had anticipated. Few persons, when he liked it, could be more agreeable than William Brandon; but at times there mixed with his conversation a bitter sarcasm, probably a habit acquired in his profession, or an occasional tinge of morose and haughty sadness, possibly the consequence of his ill-health. Yet his disorder, which was somewhat approaching to that painful affliction the *tic doulou-reux*, though of fits more rare in occurrence than those of that complaint ordinarily are, never seemed even for an instant to operate upon his mood, whatever that might be That disease worked unseen; not a muscle of his face appeared to quiver; the smile never vanished from his mouth, the blandness of his voice never grew faint as with pain, and, in the midst of intense torture, his resolute and stern mind conquered every external indication; nor could the most observant stranger have noted the moment when the fit attacked or released him. There was something inscrutable about the man. You felt that you took his character upon trust, and not on your own knowledge. The acquaintance of years would have left you equally dark as to his vices or his virtues. He varied often, yet in each variation he was equally undiscoverable. Was he performing a series of parts, or was it the ordinary changes of a man's true temperament that you beheld in him? Commonly smooth, quiet, attentive, flattering in social intercourse; he was known in the senate and courts of law for a cold asperity, and a caustic venom,—scarcely rivalled even in those arenas of contention. It seemed as if the bitterer feelings he checked in private life, he delighted to indulge in public. Yet, even there, he gave not way to momentary petulance or gushing passion; all seemed with him systematic sarcasm, or habitual sternness. He outraged no form of ceremonial, or of society. He stung, without appearing conscious of the sting; and his antagonist writhed not more beneath the torture of his satire, than the crushing contempt of his self-command. Cool, ready, aimed and defended on all points, sound in knowledge, unfailing in observation, equally consummate in sophistry when needed by himself, and instantaneous in detecting sophistry in another; scorning no art, however painful,—begrudging no labour, however weighty,—minute in detail, yet not the less comprehending the whole subject in a grasp; such was the legal and public character William Brandon had established, and such was the fame he joined to the unsullied purity of his moral reputation. But to his friends he seemed only the agreeable, clever, lively, and, if we may use the phrase *innocently*, the *worldly* man,—never affecting a superior sanctity, or an over-anxiety to forms, except upon great occasions; and rendering his austerity of manners the more admired, because he made it seem so unaccompanied by hypocrisy.

"Well," said Brandon, as he sat after dinner alone with his

relations, and had seen the eyes of his brother close in diurnal slumber,—"tell me, Miss Lucy, what you think of Lord Mauleverer ; do you find him agreeable?"

"Very; too much so, indeed!"

"Too much so! that is an uncommon fault, Lucy ; unless you mean to insinuate that you find him too agreeable for your peace of mind."

"Oh, no! there is little fear of that. All that I meant to express was, that he seems to make it the sole business of his life to be agreeable ; and that one imagines he had gained that end by the loss of certain qualities which one would have liked better."

"Umph! and what are they?"

"Truth, sincerity, independence, and honesty of mind."

"My dear Lucy, it has been the professional study of my life to discover a man's character, especially so far as truth is concerned, in as short a time as possible ; but you excel me by intuition, if you can tell whether there be sincerity in a courtier's character at the first interview you have with him."

"Nevertheless, I am sure of my opinion," said Lucy, laughing ; "and I will tell you one instance I observed among a hundred. Lord Mauleverer is rather deaf, and he imagined, in conversation, that my father said one thing—it was upon a very trifling subject—the speech of some member of parliament (the lawyer smiled), when in reality he meant to say another. Lord Mauleverer, in the warmest manner in the world, chimed in with him, appeared thoroughly of his opinion, applauded his sentiments, and wished the whole country of his mind. Suddenly my father spoke, Lord Mauleverer bent down his ear, and found that the sentiments he had so lauded were exactly those my father the least favoured. No sooner did he make this discovery, than he wheeled round again, dexterously and gracefully, I allow ; condemned all that he had before extolled, and extolled all that he had before abused!"

"And is that all, Lucy?" said Brandon, with a keener sneer on his lip than the occasion warranted. "Why, that is what every one does ; only some more gravely than others. Mauleverer in society ; I, at the bar ; the minister in parliament ; friend to friend ; lover to mistress ; mistress to lover ; half of us are employed in saying white is black, and the other half in swearing that black is white. There is only one difference, my pretty niece, between the clever man and the fool ; the fool says what is false while the colours stare in his face and give him the lie ; but the clever man takes, as it were, a brush, and literally turns the black into white, and the white into black, before he makes the assertion, which is *then true*. The fool changes, and is a liar ; the clever man makes the colours change, and is a genius. But this is not for your young years yet, Lucy."

F

"But, I can't see the necessity of seeming to agree with people," said Lucy, simply; "surely they would be just as well pleased if you differed from them civilly and with respect?"

"No, Lucy," said Brandon, still sneering; "to be liked, it is not necessary to be anything but compliant; lie, cheat, make every word a snare, and every act a forgery—but never contradict. Agree with people, and they make a couch for you in their hearts. You know the story of Dante and the buffoon. Both were entertained at the court of the vain pedant, who called himself Prince Scaliger; the former poorly, the latter sumptuously. 'How comes it,' said the buffoon to the poet, 'that I am so rich and you so poor?' 'I shall be as rich as you,' was the stinging and true reply, 'whenever I can find a patron as like myself as Prince Scaliger is like you!'"

"Yet my birds," said Lucy, caressing the goldfinch, which nestled to her bosom, "are not like me, and I love them. Nay, I often think I could love those better who differ from me the most. I feel it so in books;—when, for instance, I read a novel or a play; and you, uncle, I like almost in proportion to my perceiving in myself nothing in common with you."

"Yes," said Brandon, "you have in common with me a love for old stories of Sir Hugo, and Sir Rupert, and all the other 'Sirs' of our mouldered and by-gone race. So you shall sing me the ballad about Sir John de Brandon, and the dragon he slew in the Holy Land. We will adjourn to the drawing-room, not to disturb your father."

Lucy agreed, took her uncle's arm, repaired to the drawing-room, and, seating herself at the harpsichord, sang to an inspiriting, yet somewhat rude air, the family ballad her uncle had demanded.

It would have been amusing to note in the rigid face of the hardened and habitual man of peace and parchments, a certain enthusiasm which ever and anon crossed his cheek, as the verses of the ballad rested on some allusion to the knightly House of Brandon, and its old renown. It was an early prejudice, breaking out despite of himself—a flash of character, stricken from the hard fossil in which it was imbedded One would have supposed that the silliest of all prides (for the pride of money, though meaner, is less senseless), family pride, was the last weakness which at that time the callous and astute lawyer would have confessed, even to himself.

"Lucy," said Brandon, as the song ceased, and he gazed on his beautiful niece with a certain pride in his aspect,—"I long to witness your first appearance in the world. This lodging, my dear, is not fit——but pardon me! what I was about to say is this: your father and yourself are here at my invitation, and in my house you must dwell: you are my guests, not mine host and hostess. I have, therefore, already directed my servant to secure me a house, and provide the necessary establishment; and I make no doubt, as he is a quick fellow, that within three days all will be ready. You must then be the magnet of my abode, Lucy; and, meanwhile, you must explain this to my brother, and, for you know his jealous hospitality, obtain his acquiescence."

"But ——" began Lucy.

"But me no buts," said Brandon, quickly, but with an affectionate tone of wilfulness; "and now, as I feel very much fatigued with my journey, you must allow me to seek my own room."

"I will conduct you to it myself," said Lucy, for she was anxious to show her father's brother the care and forethought which she had lavished on her arrangements for his comfort. Brandon followed her into an apartment, which his eye knew at a glance had been subjected to that female superintendence which makes such uses from what men reject as insignificant; and he thanked her with more than his usual amenity, for the grace which had presided over, and the kindness which had dictated, her preparations. As soon as he was left alone, he wheeled his arm-chair near the clear, bright fire, and resting his face upon his hand, in the attitude of a man who prepares himself, as it were, for the indulgence of meditation, he muttered :—

"Yes! these women are, first, what Nature makes them, and that is good : next, what *we* make them, and that is evil! Now, could I persuade myself that we ought to be nice as to the use we put these poor puppets to, I should shrink from enforcing the destiny which I have marked for this girl. But that is a pitiful consideration, and he is but a silly player who loses his money for the sake of preserving his counters. So the young lady must go as another score to the fortunes of William Brandon. After all, who suffers? —Not she. She will have wealth, rank, honour : *I* shall suffer, to yield so pretty and pure a gem to the coronet of—faugh! How I despise that dog! but how I could hate, crush, mangle him, could I believe that he despised me! Could he do so? Umph! No, I have resolved myself, that is impossible. Well, let me hope *that* matrimonial point will be settled; and now, let me consider what next step I shall take for myself—myself!—ay—only myself!—with me perishes the last male of Brandon. But the light shall not go out under a bushel."

As he said this, the soliloquist sunk into a more absorbed, and a silent reverie, from which he was disturbed by the entrance of his servant. Brandon, who was never a dreamer, save when alone, broke at once from his reflections.

"You have obeyed my orders, Barlow?" said he.

"Yes, sir," answered the domestic. "I have taken the best house yet unoccupied, and when Mrs. Roberts (Brandon's house-keeper) arrives from London, every thing will, I trust, be exactly to your wishes."

"Good! And you gave my note to Lord Mauleverer?"

"With my own hands, sir; his lordship will await you at home all to-morrow."

"Very well! and now, Barlow, see that your room is within call (bells, though known, were not common at that day), and give out that I am gone to bed, and must not be disturbed. What's the hour?"

"Just on the stroke of ten, sir."

"Place on that table my letter-case and the inkstand. Look in, to help me to undress, at half-past one; I shall go to bed at that hour. And—stay—be sure, Barlow, that my brother believes me retired for the night. He does not know my habits, and will vex himself if he thinks I sit up so late in my present state of health."

Drawing the table with its writing appurtenances near to his master, the servant left Brandon once more to his thoughts or his occupations.

CHAPTER XIV.

"SERVANT. *Get away, I say, wid dat nasty bell.*
PUNCH   *Do you call this a bell?* (patting it). *It is an organ.*
SERVANT *I say it is a bell—a nasty bell!*
PUNCH.   *I say it is an organ* (striking him with it).—*What do you say it is now?*
SERVANT. *An organ, Mr Punch!*"

'THE TRAGICAL COMEDY OF PUNCH AND JUDY.'

THE next morning, before Lucy and her father had left their apartments, Brandon, who was a remarkably early riser, had disturbed the luxurious Mauleverer in his first slumber. Although the courtier possessed a villa some miles from Bath, he preferred a lodging in the town, both as being warmer than a rarely inhabited country-house, and as being to an indolent man more immediately convenient for the gaieties and the waters of the medicinal city. As soon as the earl had rubbed his eyes, stretched himself, and prepared himself for the untimeous colloquy, Brandon poured forth his excuses for the hour he had chosen for a visit.

"Mention it not, my dear Brandon," said the good-natured nobleman, with a sigh; "I am glad at any hour to see you, and I am very sure that what you have to communicate is always worth listening to."

"It was only upon public business, though of rather a more important description than usual, that I ventured to disturb you," answered Brandon, seating himself on a chair by the bedside. "This morning—an hour ago—I received by private express a letter from London, stating that a new arrangement will positively be made in the cabinet—nay, naming the very promotions and changes. I confess, that as my name occurred, as also your own, in these nominations, I was anxious to have the benefit of your necessarily accurate knowledge on the subject, as well as of your advice."

"Really, Brandon," said Mauleverer, with a half-peevish smile, "any other hour in the day would have done for 'the business of the nation,' as the newspapers call that troublesome farce we go through; and I had imagined you would not have broken my nightly slumbers, except for something of real importance—the discovery of a new beauty, or the invention of a new dish."

"Neither the one nor the other could you have expected from *me*, my dear lord," rejoined Brandon. "You know the dry trifles in which a lawyer's life wastes itself away; and beauties and dishes have no attraction for us, except the former be damsels deserted, and the latter patents invaded. But my news, after all, is worth hearing, unless you have heard it before."

"Not I! but I suppose I shall hear it in the course of the day: pray Heaven I be not sent for to attend some plague of a council. Begin!"

"In the first place, Lord Duberly resolves to resign, unless this negotiation for peace be made a cabinet question."

"Pshaw! let him resign. I have opposed the peace so long, that it is out of the question. Of course, Lord Wanstead will not think of it, and he may count on my boroughs. A peace! shameful, disgraceful, dastardly proposition!"

"But, my dear lord, my letter says, that this unexpected firmness on the part of Lord Duberly has produced so great a sensation, that, seeing the impossibility of forming a durable cabinet without him, the king has consented to the negotiation, and Duberly stays in!"

"The devil!—what next?"

"Raffden and Sternhold go out in favour of Baldwin and Charlton, and in the hope that you will lend your aid to——"

"I!" said Lord Mauleverer, very angrily, "I lend my aid to Baldwin, the Jacobin, and Charlton, the son of a brewer!"

"Very true!" continued Brandon. "But in the hope that you might be persuaded to regard the new arrangements with an indulgent eye, you are talked of instead of the Duke of —— for the vacant garter and the office of chamberlain."

"You don't mean it!" cried Mauleverer, starting from his bed.

"A few other (but, I hear, chiefly legal) promotions are to be made. Among the rest, my learned brother, the democrat Sarsden, is to have a silk gown; Cromwell is to be attorney-general; and, between ourselves, they have offered me a judgeship."

"But the garter!" said Mauleverer, scarcely hearing the rest of the lawyer's news,—"the whole object, aim, and ambition of my life. How truly kind in the king! After all," continued the earl, laughing, and throwing himself back, "opinions are variable—truth is not uniform—the times change, not we—and we must have peace instead of war!"

"Your maxims are indisputable, and the conclusion you come to is excellent," said Brandon.

"Why, you and I, my dear fellow," said the earl, "who know men, and who have lived all our lives in the world, *must* laugh behind the scenes at the cant we wrap in tinsel, and send out to stalk across the stage. We know that our Coriolanus of Tory integrity is a corporal kept by a prostitute; and the Brutus of Whig liberty is a lacquey turned out of place for stealing the spoons; but we must not tell this to the world. So, Brandon, you must write me a speech for the next session, and be sure it has plenty of general maxims, and concludes with 'my bleeding country!'"

The lawyer smiled. "You consent then to the expulsion of Sternhold and Raffden? for, after all, that is the question. Our British vessel, as the d——d metaphor-mongers call the state, carries the public good safe in the hold like brandy; and it is only when fear, storm, or the devil makes the rogues quarrel among themselves, and break up the casks, that one gets above a thimblefull at a time. We should go on fighting with the rest of the world for ever, if the ministers had not taken to fight among themselves."

"As for Sternhold," said the earl, "'tis a vulgar dog, and voted for economical reform. Besides, I don't know him; he may go to the devil for aught I care: but Raffden must be dealt handsomely with, or, despite the garter, I will fall back among the Whigs, who, after all, give tolerable dinners."

"But why, my lord, must Raffden be treated better than his brother recusant?"

"Because he sent me, in the handsomest manner possible, a pipe of that wonderful Madeira, which you know I consider the chief grace of my cellars, and he gave up a canal navigation bill, which would have enriched his whole county, when he knew that it would injure my property. No, Brandon, curse public cant ; we know what that is. But we are gentlemen, and our private friends must not be thrown overboard,—unless, at least, we do it in the civilest manner we can."

"Fear not," said the lawyer; "you have only to say the word, and the cabinet can cook up an embassy to Owhyhee, and send Raffden there with a stipend of five thousand a-year."

"Ah ! that's well thought of; or we might give him a grant of a hundred thousand acres in one of the colonies, or let him buy crown land at a discount of eighty per cent. So that's settled."

"And now, my dear friend," said Brandon, "I will tell you frankly why I come so early ; I am required to give a hasty answer to the proposal *I* have received, namely, of the judgeship. Your opinion ?"

"A judgeship ! *you* a judge? What ! forsake your brilliant career for so petty a dignity?—you jest !"

"Not at all,—listen. You know how bitterly I have opposed this peace, and what hot enemies I have made among the new friends of the administration : on the one hand, these enemies insist on sacrificing me ; and on the other, if I *were* to stay in the Lower House and speak for what I have before opposed, I should forfeit the support of a great portion of my own party : hated by one body, and mistrusted by the other, a seat in the House of Commons ceases to be an object. It is proposed that I should retire on the dignity of a judge, with the positive and pledged, though secret, promise of the first vacancy among the chiefs. The place of chief justice or chief baron is indeed the only fair remuneration for my surrender of the gains of my profession, and the abandonment of my parliamentary and legal career ; the title, which will of course be attached to it, might go (at least, by an exertion of interest), to the eldest son of my niece, in case she married a commoner :—or," added he, after a pause, "her second son in case she married a peer."

"Ha—true !" said Mauleverer quickly, and as if struck by some sudden thought ; "and your charming niece, Brandon, would be worthy of any honour either to her children or herself. You do not know how struck I was with her ; there is something so graceful in her simplicity ; and in her manner of smoothing down the little rugosities of Warlock House, there was so genuine and so easy a dignity, that I declare I almost thought myself young again, and capable of the self-cheat of believing myself in love. But, oh ! Brandon, imagine me at your brother's board !—me, for whom ortolans are too substantial, and who feel, when I tread, the slightest inequality in the carpets of Tournay !—imagine me, dear Brandon,

in a black wainscot room, hung round with your ancestors in brown
wigs with posies in their button-holes,—an immense fire on one side,
and a thorough draught on the other,—a huge circle of beef before
me, smoking like Vesuvius, and twice as large,—a plateful (the
plate was pewter—is there not a metal so called?) of this mingled
flame and lava sent under my very nostril, and upon pain of ill-
breeding to be despatched down my proper mouth,—an old gentleman in fustian breeches and worsted stockings, by way of a butler,
filling me a can of ale,—and your worthy brother asking me if I
would not prefer port,—a lean footman in livery (such a livery, ye
gods!) scarlet, blue, yellow, and green, a rainbow ill made! on the
opposite side of the table looking at the 'Lord' with eyes and
mouth equally open, and large enough to swallow me,—and your
excellent brother himself at the head of the table glowing through
the mists of the beef, like the rising sun in a sign-post ;—and then,
Brandon, turning from this image, behold beside me the fair, delicate, aristocratic, yet simple loveliness of your niece, and—but you
look angry—I have offended you."

It was high time for Mauleverer to ask that question ; for, during
the whole of the earl's recital, the dark face of his companion had
literally burnt with rage : and here we may observe how generally
selfishness, which *makes* the man of the world, *prevents* its possessor,
by a sort of paradox, from being *consummately* so.   For Mauleverer,
occupied by the pleasure he felt at his own wit, and never having
that magic sympathy with others, which creates the incessantly keen
observer, had not, for a moment, thought that he was offending to
the quick the hidden pride of the lawyer.   Nay, so little did he
suspect Brandon's real weaknesses, that he thought him a philosopher, who would have laughed alike at principles and people,
however near to him might be the latter, and however important
the former.   Mastering by a single effort, which restored his cheek
to its usual steady hue, the outward signs of his displeasure, Brandon
rejoined.

"Offend me! by no means, my dear lord   I do not wonder at
your painful situation in an old country gentleman's house, which
has not for centuries offered scenes fit for the presence of so distinguished a guest.   Never, I may say, since the time when Sir
Charles de Brandon entertained Elizabeth at Warlock ; and your
ancestor (you know my old musty studies on those points of obscure
antiquity), John Mauleverer, who was a noted goldsmith of London,
supplied the plate for the occasion."

"Fairly retorted," said Mauleverer, smiling ; for though the
earl had a great contempt for low birth, set on high places, in
other men, he was utterly void of pride in his own family.   "Fairly

retorted! but I never meant anything else but a laugh at your brother's housekeeping; a joke, surely, permitted to a man whose own fastidiousness on these matters is so standing a jest. But, by heavens, Brandon! to turn from these subjects, your niece is the prettiest girl I have seen for twenty years; and if she would forget my being the descendant of John Mauleverer, the noted goldsmith of London, she may be Lady Mauleverer as soon as she pleases."

"Nay, now, let us be serious, and talk of the judgeship," said Brandon, affecting to treat the proposal as a joke.

"By the soul of Sir Charles de Brandon, I am serious!" cried the earl; "and as a proof of it, I hope you will let me pay my respects to your niece to-day—not with my offer in my hand, yet —for it must be a love match on *both* sides." And the earl, glancing towards an opposite glass, which reflected his attenuated but comely features, beneath his velvet night-cap, trimmed with *Mechlin*, laughed half-triumphantly as he spoke.

A sneer just passed the lips of Brandon, and as instantly vanished; while Mauleverer continued :—

"And as for the judgeship, dear Brandon, I advise you to accept it, though you know best; and I do think no man will stand a fairer chance of the chief-justiceship: or, though it be somewhat unusual for 'common' lawyers, why not the woolsack itself? As you say, the second son of your niece might inherit the dignity of the peerage!"

"Well, I will consider of it favourably," said Brandon, and soon afterwards he left the nobleman to renew his broken repose.

"I can't laugh at that man," said Mauleverer to himself, as he turned round in his bed, "though he has much that I should laugh at in another; and faith, there is one little matter I might well scorn him for, if I were not a philosopher. 'Tis a pretty girl, his niece, and with proper instructions might do one credit; besides she has 60,000*l.* ready money; and, faith, I have not a shilling for my own pleasure, though I have, or alas! had, fifty thousand a-year for that of my establishment! In all probability, she will be the lawyer's heiress, and he must have made, at least, as much again as her portion; nor is *he*, poor devil, a very good life. Moreover, if he rise to the peerage? and the second son—Well! well! it will not be such a bad match for the goldsmith's descendant either!"

With that thought, Lord Mauleverer fell asleep. He rose about noon, dressed himself with unusual pains, and was just going forth on a visit to Miss Brandon, when he suddenly remembered that her uncle had not mentioned her address or his own. He referred to the lawyer's note of the preceding evening; no direction was insciibed on it; and Mauleverer was forced, with much chagrin, to forego for that day the pleasure he had promised himself.

In truth, the wary lawyer, who, as we have said, despised show and outward appearances as much as any man, was yet sensible of their effect even in the eyes of a lover; and moreover, Lord Mauleveier was one whose habits of life were calculated to arouse a certain degiee of vigilance on points of household pomp, even in the most unobservant. Biandon therefore resolved that Lucy should not be visited by her admirer, till the removal to their new abode was effected; nor was it till the third day from that on which Mauleverer had held with Brandon the interview we have iecorded, that the eail received a note from Brandon, seemingly turning only on political matters, but inscribed with the address and direction in full foim.

Mauleverer answered it in person. He found Lucy at home, and more beautiful than ever; and from that day his mind was made up, as the mammas say, and his visits became constant.

CHAPTER XV.

"*There is a festival where knights and dames,*
And aught that wealth or lofty lineage claims,
Appear.   *   *   *
  *   *   *   *   *
'*Tis he—how came he thence?—what doth he here?*"—'LARA.'

THERE are two charming situations in life for a woman: one, the fiist freshness of heiress-ship and beauty; the other, youthful widowhood, with a large jointure. It was at least Lucy's fortune to enjoy the first. No sooner was she fairly launched into the gay world, than she became the object of universal idolatry. Crowds followed her wherever she moved: nothing was talked of, or dreamed of, toasted, or betted on, but Lucy Biandon; even her simplicity, and utter ignorance of the aits of fine life, enhanced the *éclat* of her reputation. Somehow oi other, *young* people of the gentler sex are iarely ill-bred, even in their eccentricities; and there is often a great deal of grace in inexperience. Her uncle, who accompanied her eveiywhere, himself no slight magnet of attraction, viewed her success with a complacent triumph which he suffeied no one but her father or herself to detect. To the smooth coolness of his manner, nothing would have seemed more foreign than pride at the notice gained by a beauty, or exultation at any favour won from the caprices of fashion. As for the good old squire, one would have imagined him far more the invalid than his brother. He was scarcely ever seen ; for though he went everywhere, he was one of those persons who sink into a corner the moment they enter a room. Whoever discovered him in his retreat, held out their hands, and exclaimed, "God bless me !— *you* here ! we have not seen you for this age !" Now and then, if in a very dark niche of the room a card-table had been placed, the worthy gentleman toiled through an obscure rubber, but more frequently he sat with his hands clasped, and his mouth open, counting the number of candles in the room, or calculating "when that stupid music would be over."

Lord Mauleverer, though a polished and courteous man, whose great object was necessarily to ingratiate himself with the father of his intended bride, had a horror of being bored, which surpassed all other feelings in his mind. He could not, therefore, persuade himself to submit to the melancholy duty of listening to the squire's "linked *speeches* long drawn out." He always glided by the honest man's station, seemingly in an exceeding hurry, with a "Ah, my *dear* sir, how do you do? How delighted I am to see you !—And your incomparable daughter ?—Oh, there she is !—pardon me, dear sir—you see my attraction !"

Lucy, indeed, who never forgot any one (except herself occasionally), sought her father's retreat as often as she was able ; but her engagements were so incessant, that she no sooner lost one partner, than she was claimed and carried off by another. However, the squire bore his solitude with tolerable cheerfulness, and always declared that "he was very well amused ; although balls and concerts were necessarily a little dull to one who came from a fine old place like Warlock Manor-house, and it was not the same thing that pleased young ladies (for, to them, that fiddling and giggling till two o'clock in the morning might be *a very pretty way of killing time*), *and their papas !*"

What considerably added to Lucy's celebrity, was the marked notice and admiration of a man so high in rank and *ton* as Lord Mauleverer. That personage, who still retained much of a youthful mind and temper, and who was in his nature more careless than haughty, preserved little or no state in his intercourse with the social revellers at Bath. He cared not whither he went, so that he was in the train of the young beauty ; and the most fastidious nobleman of the English court was seen in every second and third rate set of a great watering-place, the attendant, the flirt, and often the ridicule of the daughter of an obscure and almost insignificant country squire. Despite the honour of so distinguished a lover, and despite all the novelties of her situation, the pretty head of Lucy Brandon was as yet, however, perfectly unturned ; and as for her heart, the only impression that it had ever received, was made by that wandering guest of the village rector, whom she had never again seen, but who yet clung to her imagination, invested not only with all the graces which in right of a singularly handsome person he possessed, —but with those to which he never could advance a claim,—more dangerous to her peace, from the very circumstance of their origin in her fancy, not his merits.

They had now been some little time at Bath, and Brandon's brief respite was pretty nearly expired, when a public ball of uncommon and manifold attraction was announced. It was to be graced not only by the presence of all the surrounding families, but also by that of royalty itself ; it being an acknowledged fact, that people dance much better, and eat much more supper, when any relation to a king is present.

"I must stay for this ball, Lucy,' said Brandon, who, after spending the day with Lord Mauleverer, returned home in a mood more than usually cheerful : "I must stay for this one ball, Lucy, and witness your complete triumph, even though it will be necessary to leave you the very next morning."

"*So* soon !" cried Lucy.

"So soon !" echoed the uncle with a smile. "How good you are to speak thus to an old valetudinarian, whose company must have fatigued you to death ! nay, no pretty denials ! But the great object of my visit to this place is accomplished : I have seen you, I have witnessed your *début* in the great world, with, I may say, more than a father's exultation, and I go back to my dry pursuits with the satisfaction of thinking our old and withered genealogical tree has put forth one blossom worthy of its freshest day."

"Uncle !" said Lucy, reprovingly, and holding up her taper finger with an arch smile, mingling with a blush, in which the woman's vanity spoke, unknown to herself.

"And why that look, Lucy ?" said Brandon.

"Because—because—well, no matter ! you have been bred to that trade in which, as you say yourself, men tell untruths for others, till they lose all truth for themselves. But, let us talk of you, not me ; are you really well enough to leave us ?"

Simple and even cool as the words of Lucy's question, when written, appear ; in her mouth they took so tender, so anxious a tone, that Brandon, who had no friend, nor wife, nor child, nor any one in his household, in whom interest in his health or welfare was a thing of course, and who was consequently wholly unaccustomed to the accent of kindness, felt himself of a sudden touched and stricken.

" Why, indeed, Lucy," said he, in a less artificial voice than that in which he usually spoke, " I should like still to profit by your cares, 'and forget my infirmities and pains in your society; but I cannot : the tide of events, like that of nature, waits not our pleasure ! "

" But we may take our own time for setting sail ! " said Lucy.

" Ay, this comes of talking in metaphor," rejoined Brandon, smiling ; "they who begin it, always get the worst of it. In plain words, dear Lucy, I can give no more time to my own ailments. A lawyer cannot play truant in term time without——"

" Losing a few guineas ! " said Lucy, interrupting him.

" Worse than that—his practice and his name ' "

" Better those than health and peace of mind."

"Out on you—no ! " said Brandon, quickly, and almost fiercely ; —" we waste all the greenness and pith of our life in striving to gain a distinguished slavery ; and when it is gained, we must not think that an humble independence would have been better ! If we ever admit that thought, what fools—what lavish fools we have been ! —No ! " continued Brandon, after a momentary pause, and in a tone milder and gayer, though not less characteristic of the man's stubbornness of will—" after losing all youth's enjoyments and manhood's leisure, in order that in age, the mind, the all-conquering mind, should break its way at last into the applauding opinions of men, I should be an effeminate idler indeed, did I suffer,—so long as its jarring parts hold together, or so long as I have the power to command its members,—this weak body to frustrate the labour of its better and nobler portion, and command that which it is ordained to serve."

Lucy knew not while she listened, half in fear, half in admiration, to her singular relation, that at the very moment he thus spoke, his disease was preying upon him in one of its most relentless moods, without the power of wringing from him a single outward token of his torture. But she wanted nothing to increase her pity and affec- tion for a man who, in consequence, perhaps, of his ordinary surface of worldly and cold properties of temperament, never failed to leave an indelible impression on all who had ever seen that temperament broken through by deeper, though often by more evil feelings.

" Shall you go to Lady ——'s rout ? " asked Brandon, easily sliding back into common topics. " Lord Mauleverer requested me to ask you."

" That depends on you and my father ! "

" If on me, I answer yes ! " said Brandon. "I like hearing

Mauleverer, especially among persons who do not understand him : there is a refined and subtle sarcasm running through the commonplaces of his conversation, which cuts the good fools, like the invisible sword in the fable, that lopped off heads, without occasioning the owners any other sensation than a pleasing and self-complacent titillation. How immeasurably superior he is in manner and address to all we meet here ; does it not strike you ?"

"Yes—no—I can't say that it does exactly," rejoined Lucy.

"Is that confusion tender ?" thought Brandon.

"In a word," continued Lucy, "Lord Mauleverer is one whom I think pleasing, without fascination ; and amusing, without brilliancy. He is evidently accomplished in mind, and graceful in manner ; and withal, the most uninteresting person I ever met."

"Women have not often thought so !" said Brandon.

"I cannot believe that they can think otherwise."

A certain expression, partaking of scorn, played over Brandon's hard features. It was a noticeable trait in him, that while he was most anxious to impress Lucy with a favourable opinion of Lord Mauleverer, he was never quite able to mask a certain satisfaction at any jest at the Earl's expense, or any opinion derogatory to his general character for pleasing the opposite sex ; and this satisfaction was no sooner conceived, than it was immediately combated by the vexation he felt, that Lucy did not seem to share his own desire that she should become the wife of the courtier. There appeared as if, in that respect, there was a contest in his mind between interest on one hand, and private dislike, or contempt, on the other.

"You judge women wrongly !" said Brandon. "Ladies never know each other ; of all persons, Mauleverer is best calculated to win them, and experience has proved my assertion. The proudest lot I know of for a woman would be the thorough conquest of Lord Mauleverer ; but it is impossible. He may be gallant, but he will never be subdued. He defies the whole female world, and with justice and impunity. Enough of him. Sing to me, dear Lucy."

The time for the ball approached, and Lucy, who was a charming girl, and had nothing of the angel about her, was sufficiently fond of gaiety, dancing, music, and admiration, to feel her heart beat high at the expectation of the event.

At last, the day itself came. Brandon dined alone with Mauleverer, having made the arrangement that he, with the earl, was to join his brother and niece at the ball. Mauleverer, who hated state, except on great occasions, when no man displayed it with a better grace, never suffered his servants to wait at dinner when he was alone, or with one of his peculiar friends. The attendants remained without, and were summoned at will by a bell laid beside the host.

The conversation was unrestrained.

"I am perfectly certain, Brandon," said Mauleverer, "that if you were to live tolerably well, you would soon get the better of your nervous complaints. It is all poverty of blood, believe me.—Some more of the fins, eh?—No!—oh, hang your abstemiousness, it is d—d unfriendly to eat so little! Talking of fins and friends— heaven defend me from ever again forming an intimacy with a pedantic epicure, especially if he puns!"

"Why—what has a pedant to do with fins?"

"I will tell you—(Ah, this Madeira!)—I suggested to Lord Dareville, who affects the gourmand, what a capital thing a dish all fins—(turbot's fins)—might be made. 'Capital!' said he, in a rapture, 'dine on it with me to-morrow.' '*Volontiers!*' said I. The next day, after indulging in a pleasing reverie all the morning as to the manner in which Dareville's cook, who is not without genius, would accomplish the grand idea, I betook myself punctually to my engagement. Would you believe it? When the cover was removed, the sacrilegious dog of an Amphitryon had put into the dish Cicero *de Finibus*. 'There is a work all fins!' said he."

"Atrocious jest!" exclaimed Brandon, solemnly.

"Was it not? Whenever the gastronomists set up a religious inquisition, I trust they will roast every impious rascal who treats the divine mystery with levity. Pun upon cooking, indeed! *A propos* of Dareville, he is to come into the administration."

"You astonish me!" said Brandon; "I never heard that; I don't know him. He has very little power; has he any talent?"

"Yes, a very great one,—*acquired* though!"

"What is it?"

"A pretty wife!"

"My lord!" exclaimed Brandon, abruptly, and half rising from his seat.

Mauleverer looked up hastily, and, on seeing the expression of his companion's face, coloured deeply; there was a silence for some moments.

"Tell me," said Brandon, indifferently, helping himself to vege- tables, for he seldom touched meat; and a more amusing contrast can scarcely be conceived, than that between the earnest epicurism of Mauleverer, and the careless contempt of the sublime art mani- fested by his guest:—"tell me, you who necessarily know every- thing, whether the government really is settled,—whether you are to have the garter, and I—(mark the difference!)—the judgeship."

"Why so, I imagine, it will be arranged; viz. if you will consent to hang up the rogues, instead of living by the fools!"

"One may unite both!" returned Brandon. "But I believe, in

general, it is *vice versâ*, for we live by the rogues, and it is only the fools we are able to hang up. You ask me if I will take the judgeship. I would not—no, I would rather cut my hand off—(and the lawyer spoke with great bitterness)—forsake my present career, despite all the obstacles that now encumber it, did I think that this miserable body would suffer me for two years longer to pursue it."

"You shock me!" said Mauleverer, a little affected, but nevertheless applying the cayenne to his cucumber with his unusual unerring nicety of tact; "you shock me, but you are considerably better than you were."

"It is not," continued Brandon, who was rather speaking to himself than to *his friend*—"it is not that I am unable to conquer the pain, and to master the recreant nerves; but I feel myself growing weaker and weaker beneath the continual exertion of my remaining powers, and I shall die before I have gained half my objects, if I do not leave the labours which are literally tearing me to pieces."

"But," said Lord Mauleverer, who was the idlest of men, "the judgeship is not an easy sinecure."

"No! but there is less demand on the mind in that station, than in my present one;" and Brandon paused before he continued. "Candidly, Mauleverer, you do not think they will deceive me? you do not think they mean to leave me to this political death without writing 'Resurgam' over the hatchment?"

"They dare not!" said Mauleverer, quaffing his fourth glass of Madeira.

"Well! I have decided on my change of life," said the lawyer, with a slight sigh.

"So have I on my change of opinion," chimed in the earl. "I will tell you what opinions seem to me like."

"What?" said Brandon, abstractedly.

"*Trees!*" answered Mauleverer, quaintly. "If they can be made serviceable by standing, don't part with a stick; but when they are of that growth that sells well, or whenever they shut out a *fine prospect*, cut them down, and pack them off by all manner of means!—And now for the second course."

"I wonder," said the earl, when our political worthies were again alone, "whether there ever existed a minister who cared three straws for the people—*many* care for *their party*, but as for the country——"

"It is all fiddlestick!" added the lawyer, with more significance than grace.

"Right; it is all fiddlestick, as you tersely express it. King, Constitution, and Church, for ever! which, being interpreted, means—first, King, or Crown influence, judgeships, and gaiters,—

secondly, Constitution, or fees to the lawyer, places to the states-man, laws for the rich, and Game Laws for the poor;—thirdly, Church, or livings for our younger sons, and starvings for their curates!"

"Ha, ha!" said Brandon, laughing sardonically; "*we* know human nature!"

"And how it may be gulled!" quoth the courtier. "Here's a health to your niece! and may it not be long before you hail her as your friend's bride!"

"Bride, *et cætera*," said Brandon, with a sneer, meant only for his own satisfaction. "But, mark me, my dear lord, do not be too sure of her—she is a singular girl, and of more independence than the generality of women. She will not think of your rank and station in estimating you; she will think only of their owner; and pardon me if I suggest to you, who know the sex so well, one plan that it may not be unadvisable for you to pursue. Don't let her fancy you entirely hers; rouse her jealousy, pique her pride—let her think you unconquerable, and, unless she is unlike all women, she will want to conquer you."

The earl smiled. "I must take my chance!" said he, with a confident tone.

"The hoary coxcomb!" muttered Brandon between his teeth: "now will his folly spoil all."

"And that reminds me," continued Mauleverer, "that time wanes, and dinner is not over; let us not hurry, but let us be silent, to enjoy the more. These truffles in champagne—*do* taste them, they would raise the dead."

The lawyer smiled, and accepted the kindness, though he left the delicacy untouched; and Mauleverer, whose soul was in his plate, saw not the heartless rejection

Meanwhile, the youthful beauty had already entered the theatre of pleasure, and was now seated with the squire, at the upper end of the half-filled ball-room.

A gay lady of the fashion at that time, and of that half and half rank to which belonged the aristocracy of Bath,—one of those curious persons we meet with in the admirable novels of Miss Burney, as appertaining to the order of fine ladies,—made the trio with our heiress and her father, and pointed out to them by name the various characters that entered the apartments. She was still in the full tide of scandal, when an unusual sensation was visible in the environs of the door; three strangers of marked mien, gay dress, and an air which, though differing in each, was in all alike remark-able for a sort of "dashing" assurance, made their *entrée*. One was of uncommon height, and possessed of an exceedingly fine head of hair; another was of a more quiet and unpretending aspect, but, nevertheless, he wore upon his face a supercilious, yet not ill-humoured expression; the third was many years younger than his companions, strikingly handsome in face and figure, altogether of a better taste in dress, and possessing a manner that, though it had equal ease, was not equally noticeable for impudence and swagger.

"Who can those be?" said Lucy's female friend in a wondering tone. "I never saw them before—they must be great people—they have all *the airs of persons of quality!*—Dear, how odd that I should not know them!"

While the good lady, who, like all good ladies of that stamp, thought people of quality had airs, was thus lamenting her ignorance of the new comers, a general whisper of a similar import was already circulating round the room;—"Who are they?" and the universal answer was, "Can't tell—never saw them before!"

Our strangers seemed by no means displeased with the evident and immediate impression they had made. They stood in the most conspicuous part of the room, enjoying, among themselves, a low conversation, frequently broken by fits of laughter; tokens, we need not add, of their super-eminently good breeding. The handsome figure of the youngest stranger, and the simple and seemingly un-conscious grace of his attitudes, were not, however, unworthy of the admiration he excited; and even his laughter, rude as it really was, displayed so dazzling a set of teeth, and was accompanied by such brilliant eyes, that before he had been ten minutes in the room, there was scarcely a young lady under thirty-nine not disposed to fall in love with him.

Apparently heedless of the various remarks which reached their ears, our strangers, after they had from their station sufficiently surveyed the beauties of the ball, strolled arm-in-arm through the rooms. Having sauntered through the ball and card-rooms, they passed the door that led to the entrance passage, and gazed, with other loiterers, upon the new comers ascending the stairs. Here the two younger strangers renewed their whispered conversation, while the eldest, who was also the tallest one, carelessly leaning against the wall, employed himself for a few moments in thrusting his fingers through his hair. In finishing this occupation, the peculiar state of his ruffles forced itself upon the observation of our gentleman, who, after gazing for some moments on an envious rent in the right ruffle, muttered some indistinct words, like, "the cock of that confounded pistol," and then tucked up the mutilated ornament with a peculiarly nimble motion of the fingers of his left hand: the next moment, diverted by a new care, the stranger applied his digital members to the arranging and caressing of a remarkably splendid brooch, set in the bosom of a shirt, the rude texture of which formed a singular contrast with the magnificence of the embellishment, and the fineness of the one ruffle suffered by our modern Hyperion to make its appearance beneath his cinnamon-coloured coat-sleeve. These little personal arrangements completed, and a dazzling snuff-box released from the confinement of a side-pocket, tapped thrice, and lightened of two pinches of its titillating luxury, the stranger now, with the guardian eye of friendship, directed a searching glance to the dress of his friends. *There*, all appeared meet for his strictest scrutiny, save, indeed, that the supercilious-looking stranger having just drawn forth his gloves, the lining of his coat-pocket—which was rather soiled into the bargain—had not returned to its internal station; the tall stranger, seeing this little inelegance, kindly thrust three fingers with a sudden and light dive into his friend's pocket, and effectually repulsed the forwardness of the intrusive lining. The supercilious stranger no sooner felt the touch, than he started back, and whispered his officious companion,—

"What! among friends, Ned! Fie now; curb the nature of thee for one night, at least."

Before he of the flowing locks had time to answer, the master of the ceremonies, who had for the last three minutes been eyeing the strangers through his glass, stepped forward with a sliding bow, and the handsome gentleman taking upon himself the superiority and precedence over his comrades, was the first to return the courtesy. He did this with so good a grace, and so pleasing an expression of countenance, that the censor of bows was charmed at once, and, with a second and more profound salutation, announced himself and his office.

"You would like to dance, probably, gentlemen?" he asked, glancing at each, but directing his words to the one who had prepossessed him.

"You are very good," said the comely stranger; "and, for my part, I shall be extremely indebted to you for the exercise of your powers in my behalf. Allow me to return with you to the ball-room, and I can there point out to you the objects of my especial admiration."

The master of the ceremonies bowed as before, and he and his new acquaintance strolled into the ball-room, followed by the two comrades of the latter.

"Have you been long in Bath, sir?" inquired the monarch of the rooms.

"No, indeed! we only arrived this evening."

"From London?"

"No, we made a little tour across the country."

"Ah! very pleasant, this fine weather."

"Yes; especially in the evenings."

"Oho!—romantic!" thought the man of balls, as he rejoined aloud, "Why the nights *are* agreeable, and the moon is particularly favourable to us."

"Not always!" quoth the stranger.

"True—true, the night before last was dark; but, in general, surely the moon has been very bright."

The stranger was about to answer, but checked himself, and simply bowed his head as in assent

"I wonder who they are!" thought the master of the ceremonies "Pray, sir," said he, in a low tone, "is that gentleman—that *tall* gentleman, any way related to Lord ——? I cannot but think I see a family likeness."

"Not in the least related to his lordship," answered the stranger: "but he is of a family that have made a noise in the world; though he (as well as my other friend) is merely a commoner!" laying a stress on the last word.

"Nothing, sir, can be more respectable than a commoner of family," returned the polite Mr. ——, with a bow.

"I agree with you, sir," answered the stranger, with another. "But, heavens!"—and the stranger started; for at that moment his eye caught for the first time, at the far end of the room, the youthful and brilliant countenance of Lucy Brandon,—"do I see rightly? or is that Miss Brandon?"

"It is indeed that lovely young lady," said Mr ——. "I congratulate you on knowing one so admired. I suppose that you, being blessed with her acquaintance, do not need the formality of my introduction."

"Umph!" said the stranger, rather shortly and uncourteously— "No! Perhaps you had better present me!"

"By what name shall I have that honour, sir?" discreetly inquired the nomenclator.

"Clifford!" answered the stranger; "Captain Clifford!"

Upon this, the prim master of the ceremonies, threading his path through the now fast-filling room, approached towards Lucy to obey Mr. Clifford's request. Meanwhile, that gentleman, before he followed the steps of the tutelary spirit of the place, paused, and said to his friends, in a tone careless, yet not without command, "Hark ye, gentlemen, oblige me by being as civil and silent as ye are able, and don't thrust yourselves upon me, as you are accustomed to do, whenever you see *no* opportunity of indulging me with that honour with the least show of propriety!" So saying, and waiting no reply, Mr. Clifford hastened after the master of the ceremonies.

"Our friend grows mighty imperious!" said Long Ned, whom our readers have already recognised in the tall stranger.

"'Tis the way with your rising geniuses," answered the moralising Augustus Tomlinson, "Suppose we go to the card-room, and get up a rubber!"

"Well thought of," said Ned, yawning,—a thing he was very apt to do in society; "and I wish nothing worse to those who try our *rubbers*, than that they may be well cleaned by them." Upon this witticism the Colossus of Roads, glancing towards the glass, strutted off, arm-in-arm with his companion, to the card-room.

During this short conversation the re-introduction of Mr. Clifford (the stranger of the Rectory and deliverer of Dr. Slopperton) to Lucy Brandon had been effected, and the hand of the heiress was already engaged (according to the custom of that time) for the *two* ensuing dances.

It was about twenty minutes after the above presentation had taken place, that Lord Mauleverer and William Brandon entered the rooms; and the buzz created by the appearance of the noted peer and the distinguished lawyer had scarcely subsided, before the royal personage expected to grace the "festive scene" (as the newspapers say of a great room with plenty of miserable-looking people in it) arrived. The most attractive persons in Europe may be found among the royal family of England, and the great personage then at Bath, in consequence of certain political intrigues, wished, at that time especially, to make himself as popular as possible. Having gone the round of the old ladies, and assured them, as the *Court Journal* assures the old ladies at this day, that they were "morning stars," and "swan-like wonders," the Prince espied Brandon, and immediately beckoned to him with a familiar gesture. The smooth but saturnine lawyer approached the royal presence with the manner that peculiarly distinguished him, and which blended, in no ungraceful mixture, a species of stiffness, that passed with the crowd for native independence, with a supple insinuation, that was usually deemed the token of latent benevolence of heart. There was something, indeed, in Brandon's address that always pleased the great; and they liked him the better, because, though he stood on no idle political points, mere differences in the view taken of a hair-breadth, —such as a corn-law, or a Catholic bill; alteration in the church, or a reform in parliament; yet he invariably talked so like a man of honour (except when with Mauleverer), that his urbanity seemed attachment to individuals; and his concessions to power, sacrifices of private opinion for the sake of obliging his friends.

"I am very glad, indeed," said the royal personage, "to see Mr. Brandon looking so much better Never was the crown in greater want of his services ; and, if rumour speak true, they will soon be required in another department of his profession."

Brandon bowed, and answered :—

" So, please your royal highness, they will always be at the command of a king from whom I have experienced such kindness, in any capacity for which his Majesty may deem them fitting."

" It *is* true, then !" said his royal highness, significantly. " I congratulate you ! The quiet dignity of the bench must seem to you a great change after a career so busy and restless ?"

" I fear I shall feel it so at first, your royal highness," answered Brandon, " for I like even the toil of my profession ; and at this moment, when I am in full practice, it more than ever—but (checking himself at once) his Majesty's wishes, and my satisfaction in complying with them, are more than sufficient to remove any momentary regret I might otherwise have felt in quitting those toils which have now become to me a second nature."

" It is possible," rejoined the Prince, " that his Majesty took into consideration the delicate state of health which, in common with the whole public, I grieve to see the papers have attributed to one of the most distinguished ornaments of the bar."

" So, please your royal highness," answered Brandon, coolly, and with a smile which the most piercing eye could not have believed the mask to the agony then gnawing at his nerves, " it is the interest of my rivals to exaggerate the little ailments of a weak constitution. I thank Providence that I am now entirely recovered ; and at no time of my life have I been less unable to discharge—so far as my *native* and *mental* incapacities will allow—the duties of any occupation, however arduous. Nay, as the brute grows accustomed to the mill, so have I grown wedded to business ; and even the brief relaxation I have now allowed myself seems to me rather irksome than pleasurable."

" I rejoice to hear you speak thus," answered his royal highness warmly ; " and I trust for many years, and," added he, in a lower tone, " in the highest chamber of the senate, that we may profit by your talents. The times are those in which many occasions occur, that oblige all true friends of the constitution to quit minor employment for that great constitutional one that concerns us all, the highest and the meanest ; and (the royal voice sank still lower) I feel justified in assuring you, that the office of chief justice alone is not considered by his Majesty as a sufficient reward for your generous sacrifice of present ambition to the difficulties of government."

Brandon's proud heart swelled, and that moment the veriest pains of hell would scarcely have been felt.

While the aspiring schemer was thus agreeably engaged, Mauleverer, sliding through the crowd with that grace which charmed every one, old and young, and addressing to all he knew some lively or affectionate remark, made his way to the dancers, among whom he had just caught a glimpse of Lucy. "I wonder," he thought, "whom she is dancing with. I hope it is that ridiculous fellow, Mossop, who tells a good story against himself; or that handsome ass, Belmont, who looks at his own legs, instead of seeming to have eyes for no one but his partner. Ah! if Tarquin had but known women as well as I do, he would have had no reason to be rough with Lucretia. 'Tis a thousand pities that experience comes, in women, as in the world, just when it begins to be no longer of use to us!"

As he made these moral reflections, Mauleverer gained the dancers, and beheld Lucy listening, with downcast eyes and cheeks that *evidently* blushed, to a young man, whom Mauleverer acknowledged at once to be one of the best-looking fellows he had ever seen. The stranger's countenance, despite an extreme darkness of complexion, was, to be sure, from the great regularity of the features, rather effeminate; but, on the other hand, his figure, though slender and graceful, betrayed to an experienced eye an extraordinary proportion of sinew and muscle: and even the dash of effeminacy in the countenance was accompanied by so manly and frank an air, and was so perfectly free from all coxcombry or self-conceit, that it did not in the least decrease the prepossessing effect of his appearance. An angry and bitter pang shot across that portion of Mauleverer's frame which the earl thought fit, for want of another name, to call his heart. "How cursedly pleased she looks!" muttered he. "By heaven! that stolen glance under the left eye-lid, dropped as suddenly as it is raised! and *he*—ha!—how firmly he holds that little hand. I think I see him paddle with it; and then the dog's earnest, intent look—and she all blushes! though she dare not look up to meet his gaze, feeling it by intuition. Oh! the demure, modest, shamefaced hypocrite! How silent she is!—she can prate enough to *me!* I would give my promised garter if she would but talk to him. Talk—talk—laugh—prattle—only simper, in God's name, and I shall be happy. But that bashful, blushing silence—it is insupportable. Thank Heaven, the dance is over! Thank Heaven, again! I have not felt such pains since the last nightmare I had, after dining with her father!"

With a face all smiles, but with a mien in which more dignity than he ordinarily assumed was worn, Mauleverer now moved towards Lucy, who was leaning on her partner's arm. The earl, who had ample tact where his consummate selfishness did not warp it, knew well how to act the lover, without running ridiculously into the folly of seeming to play the hoary dangler. He sought rather to be lively than sentimental ; and beneath the wit to conceal the suitor.

Having paid, then, with a careless gallantry, his first compliments, he entered into so animated a conversation, interspersed with so many *naïve* yet palpably just observations on the characters present, that perhaps he had never appeared to more brilliant advantage. At length, as the music was about to recommence, Mauleverer, with a careless glance at Lucy's partner, said, "Will Miss Brandon now allow me the agreeable duty of conducting her to her father?"

"I believe," answered Lucy, and her voice suddenly became timid, "that, according to the laws of the rooms, I am engaged to this gentleman for another dance."

Clifford, in an assured and easy tone, replied in assent.

As he spoke, Mauleverer honoured him with a more accurate survey than he had hitherto bestowed on him ; and whether or not there was any expression of contempt or superciliousness in the survey, it was sufficient to call up the indignant blood to Clifford's cheek. Returning the look with interest, he said to Lucy, "I believe, Miss Brandon, that the dance is about to begin ;" and Lucy, obeying the hint, left the aristocratic Mauleverer to his own meditations.

At that moment the master of the ceremonies came bowing by, half afraid to address so great a person as Mauleverer, but willing to show his respect by the profoundness of his salutation.

"Aha ! my dear Mr. —— !" said the earl, holding out both his hands to the Lycurgus of the rooms ; "how are you? Pray can you inform me who that young—*man* is, now dancing with Miss Brandon ?"

"It is—let me see—Oh ! it is a Captain Clifford, my lord ! a very fine young man, my lord ! Has your lordship never met him ?"

"Never ! who is he? One under your more especial patronage ?" said the earl, smiling.

"Nay, indeed !" answered the master of the ceremonies, with a simper of gratification ; "I scarcely know who he is yet ; the captain only made his appearance here to-night for the first time. He came with two other gentlemen—ah ! there they are !" and he pointed the earl's scrutinising attention to the elegant forms of Mr. Augustus Tomlinson and Mr. Ned Pepper, just emerging from the card-rooms. The swagger of the latter gentleman was so peculiarly important, that Mauleverer, angry as he was, could scarcely help laughing. The master of the ceremonies noted the earl's countenance, and remarked, that "that fine-looking man seemed disposed to give himself *airs!*"

"Judging from the gentleman's appearance," said the earl, dryly (Ned's face, to say truth, did betoken his affection for the bottle), "I should imagine that he was much more accustomed to give himself *thorough draughts!*"

"Ah!" renewed the *arbiter elegantiarum*, who had not heard Mauleverer's observation, which was uttered in a very low voice,— "Ah! they seem real dashers!"

"Dashers!" repeated Mauleverer: "true, *haberdashers!*"

Long Ned now, having in the way of his profession acquitted himself tolerably well at the card-table, thought he had purchased the right to parade himself through the rooms, and show the ladies what stuff a Pepper could be made of.

Leaning with his left hand on Tomlinson's arm, and employing the right in fanning himself furiously with his huge *chapeau bras*, the lengthy adventurer stalked slowly along,—now setting out one leg jauntily—now the other, and ogling "the ladies" with a kind of Irish look, viz., a look between a wink and a stare.

Released from the presence of Clifford, who kept a certain check on his companions, the apparition of Ned became glaringly conspicuous; and wherever he passed, a universal whisper succeeded.

"Who can he be?" said the widow Matemore; "'tis a droll creature: but what a head of hair!"

"For my part," answered the Spinster Sneerall, "I think he is a linendraper in disguise; for I heard him talk to his companion of 'tape.'"

"Well, well," thought Mauleverer, "it would be but kind to seek out Brandon, and hint to him in what company his niece seems to have fallen!" And, so thinking, he glided to the corner where, with a grey-headed old politician, the astute lawyer was conning the affairs of Europe.

In the interim, the second dance had ended, and Clifford was conducting Lucy to her seat, each charmed with the other, when he found himself abruptly tapped on the back, and, turning round in alarm,—for such taps were not unfamiliar to him,—he saw the cool countenance of Long Ned, with one finger sagaciously laid beside the nose.

"How now?" said Clifford, between his ground teeth, "did I not tell thee to put that huge bulk of thine as far from me as possible?"

"Humph!" grunted Ned, "if these are my thanks, I may as well keep my kindness to myself; but know you, my kid, that lawyer Brandon is here, peering through the crowd, at this very moment, in order to catch a glimpse of that woman's face of thine."

"Ha!" answered Clifford, in a very quick tone, "begone, then ! I will meet you without the rooms immediately."

Clifford now turned to his partner, and bowing very low, in reality to hide his face from those sharp eyes which had once seen it in the court of Justice Burnflat, said, "I trust, madam, I shall have the honour to meet you again ;—is it, if I may be allowed to ask, with your celebrated uncle that you are staying, or ——"

"With my father," answered Lucy, concluding the sentence Clifford had left unfinished ; "but my uncle has been with us, though I fear he leaves us to-morrow."

Clifford's eyes sparkled ; he made no answer, but, bowing again, receded into the crowd and disappeared. Several times that night did the brightest eyes in Somersetshire rove anxiously round the rooms in search of our hero ; but he was seen no more.

It was on the stairs that Clifford encountered his comrades ; taking an arm of each, he gained the door without any adventure worth noting—save that, being kept back by the crowd for a few moments, the moralising Augustus Tomlinson, who honoured the moderate Whigs by enrolling himself among their number, took up, *pour passer le temps*, a tall gold-headed cane, and, weighing it across his finger with a musing air, said, "Alas ! among our supporters we often meet heads as heavy—but of what a different metal !" The crowd now permitting, Augustus was walking away with his companions, and, in that absence of mind characteristic of philosophers, unconsciously bearing with him the gold-headed object of his reflection, when a stately footman stepping up to him, said, "Sir, my cane !"

"Cane, fellow !" said Tomlinson. "Ah, I am so absent !— Here is thy cane.—Only think of my carrying off the man's cane, Ned ! ha ! ha !"

"Absent, indeed !" grunted a knowing chairman, watching the receding figures of the three gentlemen : "Body o' me ! but it was *the cane* that was about to be absent !"

CHAPTER XVI.

WHACKUM —"*My dear rogues, dear boys, Bluster and Dingboy! you are the bravest fellows that ever scoured yet!*" SHADWELL'S ' Scourers.'

"*Cato, the Thessalian, was wont to say, that some things may be done unjustly, that many things may be done justly*"
LORD BACON (being a justification of every rascality)

ALTHOUGH our three worthies had taken unto themselves a splendid lodging in Milsom Street, which to please Ned was over a hair-dresser's shop; yet, instead of returning thither, or repairing to such taverns as might seem best befitting their fashion and garb, they struck at once from the gay parts of the town, and tarried not till they reached a mean-looking alehouse in a remote suburb.

The door was opened to them by an elderly lady; and Clifford, stalking before his companions into an apartment at the back of the house, asked if the other gentlemen were come yet.

"No," returned the dame. "Old Mr. Bags came in about ten minutes ago; but, hearing more work might be done, he went out again."

"Bring the lush and the pipes, old blone!" cried Ned, throwing himself on a bench; "we are never at a loss for company!"

"You, indeed, never can be, who are always inseparably connected with the object of your admiration," said Tomlinson, dryly, and taking up an old newspaper. Ned, who, though choleric, was a capital fellow, and could bear a joke on himself, smiled, and, drawing forth a little pair of scissors, began trimming his nails.

"Curse me," said he, after a momentary silence, "if this is not a devilish deal pleasanter than playing the fine gentleman in that great room with a rose in one's button-hole! What say you, Master Lovett?"

Clifford (as henceforth, despite his other aliases, *we* shall denominate our hero), who had thrown himself at full length on a bench at the far end of the room, and who seemed plunged into a sullen reverie, now looked up for a moment, and then, turning round and presenting the dorsal part of his body to Long Ned, muttered, "Pish!"

"Harkye, Master Lovett!" said Long Ned, colouring. "I don't know what has come over you of late; but I would have you to learn that gentlemen are entitled to courtesy and polite behaviour : and so, d'ye see, if you ride your high horse upon me, splice my extremities if I won't have satisfaction !"

"Hist, man, be quiet," said Tomlinson, philosophically snuffing the candles—

> "' For companions to quarrel,
> Is extremely immoral.'

Don't you see that the captain is in a reverie ? what good man ever loves to be interrupted in his meditations ?—Even Alfred the Great could not bear it ! Perhaps, at this moment, with the true anxiety of a worthy chief, the captain is designing something for our welfare !"

"Captain, indeed !" muttered Long Ned, darting a wrathful look at Clifford, who had not deigned to pay any attention to Mr. Pepper's threat ; "for my part I cannot conceive what was the matter with us when we chose this green slip of the gallows-tree for our captain of the district. To be sure, he did very well at first, and that robbery of the old lord was not ill-planned—but lately——"

"Nay, nay," quoth Augustus, interrupting the gigantic grumbler, "the nature of man is prone to discontent. Allow that our present design of setting up the gay Lothario, and trying our chances at Bath for an heiress, is owing as much to Lovett's promptitude as to our invention."

"And what good will come of it ?" returned Ned, as he lighted his pipe : "answer me that. Was I not dressed as fine as a lord—and did not I walk three times up and down that great room without being a jot the better for it ?"

"Ah ! but you know not how many secret conquests you may have made : you cannot win a prize by looking upon it."

"Humph !" grunted Ned, applying himself discontentedly to the young existence of his pipe

"As for the captain's partner," renewed Tomlinson, who maliciously delighted in exciting the jealousy of the handsome "tax-collector," for that was the designation by which Augustus thought proper to style himself and companions—"I will turn Tory if she be not already half in love with him ; and did you hear the old gentleman who cut into our rubber say what a fine fortune she had ? Faith, Ned, it is lucky for us two that we all agreed to go shares in our marriage speculations ; I fancy the worthy captain will think it a bad bargain for himself"

"I am not so sure of that, Mr. Tomlinson," said Long Ned, sourly eyeing his comrade.

" Some women may be caught by a smooth skin and a showy
manner, but *real* masculine beauty,—eyes, colour, and hair,—Mr.
Tomlinson, must ultimately make its way : so hand me the brandy
and cease your jaw."

" Well, well," said Tomlinson, " I'll give you a toast—' The
prettiest girl in England ;'—and that's Miss Brandon ! ' "

" You shall give no such toast, sir ! " said Clifford, starting from
the bench.—" What the devil is Miss Brandon to you ?—And now,
Ned,"—(seeing that the tall hero looked on him with an unfavourable aspect),—" here's my hand, forgive me if I was uncivil.
Tomlinson will tell you, in a maxim, men are changeable. Here's
to your health ; and it shall not be my fault, gentlemen, if we have
not a merry evening ! "

This speech, short as it was, met with great applause from the
two friends ; and Clifford, as president, stationed himself in a huge
chair at the head of the table. Scarcely had he assumed this dignity,
before the door opened, and half-a-dozen of the gentlemen confederates trooped somewhat noisily into the apartment.

" Softly, softly, messieurs," said the president, recovering all his
constitutional gaiety, yet blending it with a certain negligent command—" respect for the chair, if you please ! 'Tis the way with
all assemblies where the public purse is a matter of deferential
interest ! "

" Hear him ! " cried Tomlinson.

" What, my old friend Bags ! " said the president : " you have
not come empty-handed, I will swear ; your honest face is like the
table of contents to the good things in your pockets ! "

" Ah, Captain Clifford," said the veteran, groaning, and shaking
his reverend head, " I have seen the day when there was not a lad
in England forked so largely, so comprehensively-like, as I did.
But, as King Lear says at Common Garden, ' I be's old now ! ' "

" But your zeal is as youthful as ever, my fine fellow," said the
captain, soothingly ; " and if you do not clean out the public as
thoroughly as heretofore, it is not the fault of your inclinations."

" No, that it is not ! " cried the " tax-collectors" unanimously.
" And if ever a pocket is to be picked neatly, quietly, and effect-
ively," added the complimentary Clifford, " I do not know to this
day, throughout the three kingdoms, a neater, quieter, and more
effective set of fingers than Old Bags's ! "

The veteran bowed disclaimingly, and took his seat among the
heartfelt good wishes of the whole assemblage.

" And now, gentlemen," said Clifford, as soon as the revellers
had provided themselves with their wonted luxuries, potatory and
fumous, " let us hear your adventures, and rejoice our eyes with

their produce. The gallant Attic shall begin—but first, a toast,—
'May those who leap from a hedge never leap from a tree!'"

This toast being drunk with enthusiastic applause, Fighting Attie
began the recital of his little history.

"You sees, captain," said he, putting himself in a martial position,
and looking Clifford full in the face, "that I'm not addicted to much
blarney. Little cry and much wool is my motto. At ten o'clock
A.M. saw the enemy—in the shape of a Doctor of Divinity. 'Blow
me,' says I to Old Bags, 'but I'll do his reverence!'—'Blow me,'
says Old Bags, 'but you sha'n't—you'll have us scragged if you
touches the church.'—'My grandmother!' says I. Bags tells the
pals—all in a fuss about it—what care I?—I puts on a decent dress,
and goes to the doctor as a decayed soldier, wot supplies the shops
in the turning line. His reverence—a fat jolly dog as ever you see
—was at dinner over a fine roast pig. So I tells him I have some
bargains at home for him. Splice me, if the doctor did not think
he had got a prize! so he puts on his boots, and he comes with me
to my house. But when I gets him into a lane, out come my pops.
'Give up, doctor,' says I; 'others must share the goods of the
church now.' You has no idea what a row he made: but I did the
thing, and there's an end on't."

"Bravo, Attie!" cried Clifford, and the word echoed round the
board. Attie put a purse on the table, and the next gentleman was
called to confession.

"It skills not, boots not," gentlest of readers, to record each of
the narratives that now followed one another. Old Bags, in especial,
preserved his well-earned reputation, by emptying six pockets,
which had been filled with every possible description of petty
valuables. Peasant and prince appeared alike to have come under
his hands; and, perhaps, the good old man had done in one town
more towards effecting an equality of goods among different ranks,
than all the Reformers, from Cornwall to Carlisle. Yet so keen
was his appetite for the sport, that the veteran appropriator absolutely burst into tears at not having "forked more."

"I love a warm-hearted enthusiasm," cried Clifford, handling the
movables, while he gazed lovingly on the ancient purloiner:—"May
new cases never teach us to forget Old Bags!"

As soon as this "sentiment" had been duly drunk, and Mr.
Bagshot had dried his tears and applied himself to his favourite
drink—which, by the way, was "blue ruin," the work of division
took place. The discretion and impartiality of the captain in this
arduous part of his duty attracted universal admiration; and each
gentleman having carefully pouched his share, the youthful president
hemmed thrice, and the society became aware of a purposed speech.

"Gentlemen!" began Clifford,—and his main supporter, the sapient Augustus, shouted out "Hear!"—"Gentlemen, you all know that when, some months ago, you were pleased,—partly at the instigation of Gentleman George,—God bless him!—partly from the exaggerated good opinion expressed of me by my friends, —to elect me to the high honour of the command of this district, I myself was by no means ambitious to assume that rank, which I knew well was far beyond my merits, and that responsibility which I knew, with equal certainty, was too weighty for my powers. Your voices, however, overruled my own; and as Mr. Muddlepud, the great metaphysician, in that excellent paper, 'The Asinæum,' was wont to observe, 'the susceptibilities, innate, extensible, incomprehensible, and eternal,' existing in my bosom, were infinitely more powerful than the shallow suggestions of reason—that ridiculous thing which all wise men and judicious Asinæans sedulously stifle."

"Plague take the man, what is he talking about?" said Long Ned, who we have seen was of an envious temper, in a whisper to Old Bags. Old Bags shook his head.

"In a word, gentlemen," renewed Clifford, "your kindness overpowered me; and, despite my cooler inclinations, I accepted your flattering proposal. Since then I have endeavoured, so far as I have been able, to advance your interests; I have kept a vigilant eye upon all my neighbours; I have, from county to county, established numerous correspondents; and our exertions have been carried on with a promptitude that has ensured success.

"Gentlemen, I do not wish to boast, but on these nights of periodical meetings, when every quarter brings us to go halves— when we meet in private to discuss the affairs of the public—show our earnings, as it were, in privy council, and divide them amicably, as it were, in the cabinet—('Hear! hear!' from Mr. Tomlinson), —it is customary for your captain for the time being to remind you of his services, engage your pardon for his deficiencies, and your good wishes for his future exertions.—Gentlemen! has it ever been said of Paul Lovett that he heard of a prize and forgot to tell you of his news?—('Never! never!' loud cheering.)—Has it ever been said of him that he sent others to seize the booty, and stayed at home to think how it should be spent? ('No! no!' repeated cheers.)—Has it ever been said of him that he took less share than his due of your danger, and more of your guineas?—(Cries in the negative, accompanied with vehement applause.)—Gentlemen, I thank you for these flattering and audible testimonials in my favour; but the points on which I have dwelt, however necessary to my honour, would prove but little for my merits; they might be worthy notice in your comrade, you demand more subtle duties in your chief.

Gentlemen! has it ever been said of Paul Lovett that he sent out
brave men on forlorn hopes? that he hazarded your own heads by
rash attempts in acquiring pictures of King George's? that zeal, in
short, was greater in him than caution? or that his love of a *quid*[1]
ever made him neglectful of your just aversion to a *quod?*[2]—
(Unanimous cheering.)

"Gentlemen! since I have had the honour to preside over your
welfare, Fortune, which favours the bold, has not been unmerciful
to you! But three of our companions have been missed from our
peaceful festivities. One, gentlemen, I myself expelled from our
corps for ungentlemanlike practices: he picked pockets of *fogles*[3]—
it was a vulgar employment. Some of you, gentlemen, have done
the same for amusement—Jack Littlefork did it for occupation. I
expostulated with him in public and in private; Mr. Pepper cut his
society; Mr. Tomlinson read him an essay on Real Greatness of Soul:
all was in vain. He was pumped by the mob for the theft of a
bird's eye wipe. The fault I had borne with—the detection was
unpardonable; I expelled him.—Who's here so base as would be a
fogle-hunter? If any, speak; for him have I offended! Who's
here so rude as would not be a gentleman? If any, speak; for him
have I offended! I pause for a reply! What, none! then none
have I offended. (Loud cheers.) Gentlemen, I may truly add, that
I have done no more to Jack Littlefork than you should do to Paul
Lovett! The next vacancy in our ranks was occasioned by the
loss of Patrick Blunderbull. You know, gentlemen, the vehement
exertions that I made to save that misguided creature, whom I had
made exertions no less earnest to instruct. But he chose to swindle
under the name of the 'Honourable Captain Smico;' the Peerage
gave him the lie at once; his case was one of aggravation, and he
was so remarkably ugly, that he 'created no interest.' He left us for
a foreign exile; and if, as a man, I lament him, I confess to you,
gentlemen, as a 'tax-collector,' I am easily consoled.

"Our third loss must be fresh in your memory. Peter Popwell,
as bold a fellow as ever breathed, is no more! (A movement in the
assembly.)—Peace be with him! He died on the field of battle;
shot dead by a Scotch Colonel, whom poor Popwell thought to rob
of nothing with an empty pistol. His memory, gentlemen — in
solemn silence!

"These make the catalogue of our losses,"—(resumed the youthful chief, so soon as the "red cup had crowned the memory" of
Peter Popwell),—"I am proud, even in sorrow, to think that the
blame of those losses rests not with me. And now, friends and
followers! Gentlemen of the Road, the Street, the Theatre, and

---

[1] Quid—a guinea.   [2] Quod—a prison.   [3] Handkerchiefs.

the Shop ! Prigs, Toby-men, and Squires of the Cross ! According to the laws of our Society, I resign into your hands that power which for two quarterly terms you have confided to mine, ready to sink into your ranks as a comrade, nor unwilling to renounce the painful honour I have borne ;—borne with much infirmity, it is true ; but at least with a sincere desire to serve that cause with which you have entrusted me."

So saying, the Captain descended from his chair amidst the most uproarious applause : and as soon as the first burst had partially subsided, Augustus Tomlinson rising, with one hand in his breeches' pocket, and the other stretched out, said :

"Gentlemen, I move that Paul Lovett be again chosen as our Captain for the ensuing term of three months.—(Deafening cheers.) —Much might I say about his surpassing merits ; but why dwell upon that which is obvious? Life is short ! Why should speeches be long ? Our lives, perhaps, are shorter than the lives of other men : why should not our harangues be of a suitable brevity? Gentlemen, I shall say but one word in favour of my excellent friend ; of mine, say I? ay, of mine, of yours. He is a friend to all of us ! A prime minister is not more useful to his followers, and more burthensome to the public than I am proud to say is—Paul Lovett !—(Loud plaudits.)—What I shall urge in his favour is simply this . the man whom opposite parties unite in praising must have supereminent merit. Of all your companions, gentlemen, Paul Lovett is the only man who to that merit can advance a claim. —(Applause.)—You all know, gentlemen, that our body has long been divided into two factions ; each jealous of the other—each desirous of ascendancy—and each emulous which shall put the greatest number of fingers into the public pie. In the language of the vulgar, the one faction would be called 'swindlers,' and the other 'highwaymen.' I, gentlemen, who am fond of finding new names for things, and for persons, and am a bit of a politician, call the one *Whigs*, and the other *Tories*.—(Clamorous cheering.)—Of the former body, I am esteemed no uninfluential member ; of the latter faction, Mr. Bags is justly considered the most shining orna- ment. Mr. Attie and Mr. Edward Pepper can scarcely be said to belong entirely to either : they unite the good qualities of both : 'British compound' some term them : I term them *Liberal Aris- tocrats !*—(Cheers.)—I now call upon you all, Whig or Swindler, Tory or Highwayman ; 'British Compounds' or Liberal Aristocrats ; I call upon you all, to name me one man whom you will all agree to elect ?"

All—"Lovett for ever !"

"Gentlemen !" continued the sagacious Augustus, "that shout is

sufficient ; without another word, I propose, as your Captain, Mr.
Paul Lovett."

"And I seconds the motion !" said old Mr. Bags.

Our hero, being now, by the unanimous applause of his confederates, restored to the chair of office, returned thanks in a neat
speech ; and Scarlet Jem declared, with great solemnity, that it did
equal honour to his head and heart.

The thunders of eloquence being hushed, *flashes of lightning*, or,
as the vulgar say, "glasses of gin," gleamed about.   Good old Mr.
Bags stuck, however, to his blue ruin, and Attie to the bottle of
bingo : some, among whom were Clifford and the wise Augustus,
called for wine ; and Clifford, who exerted himself to the utmost in
supporting the gay duties of his station, took care that the song
should vary the pleasures of the bowl.   Of the songs we have only
been enabled to preserve two.   The first is by Long Ned ; and,
though we confess we can see but little in it, yet (perhaps from
some familiar allusion or another, with which we are necessarily
unacquainted,) it produced a prodigious sensation,—it ran thus :—

THE ROGUE'S RECIPE.

Your honest fool a rogue to make,
　As great as can be seen, sir,—
Two hackney'd rogues you first must take,
　Then place your fool between, sir.

Virtue 's a dunghill cock, ashamed
　Of self when pair'd with game ones ;
And wildest elephants are tamed
　If stuck betwixt two tame ones."

The other effusion with which we have the honour to favour our
readers is a very amusing duet which took place between Fighting
Attie and a tall thin robber, who was a dangerous fellow in a mob,
and was therefore called Mobbing Francis ; it was commenced by
the latter :—

MOBBING FRANCIS.

"The best of all robbers as ever I know'd,
　Is the bold Fighting Attie, the pride of the road '—
Fighting Attie, my hero, I saw you to-day
　A purse full of yellow boys seize ;
And as, just at present, *I'm low in the lay*,
　I'll borrow a *quid*, if you please.
Oh! bold Fighting Attie—the knowing—the natty—
　By us all it must sure be confest,
Though your shoppers and snobbers are pretty good robbers,
　A soldier is always the best "

FIGHTING ATTIE.

" Stubble your *whids*,[1]
You wants to trick I
Lend you my *quids?*
Not one, by Dickey.'

MOBBING FRANCIS.

"Oh, what a beast is a niggardly ruffler,
  Nabbing—grabbing all for himself,
Hang it, old fellow, I'll hit you a muffler,
  Since you won't give me a pinch of the pelf.
You has not a heart for the *general distress*,—
  You cares not a mag if our party should fall,
And if Scarlet Jem were not good at a press,
  By Goles, it would soon be all up with us all!—
Oh, Scarlet Jem, he is trusty and trim,
  Like his wig to his poll, sticks his conscience to him ,
But I vows I despises the fellow who prizes
  More his own ends than the popular stock, sir ,
And the soldier as bones for himself and his crones,
  Should be boned like a traitor himself at the block, sir."

This severe response of Mobbing Francis's did not in the least ruffle the constitutional calmness of Fighting Attie ; but the wary Clifford, seeing that Francis had lost his temper, and watchful over the least sign of disturbance among the company, instantly called for another song, and Mobbing Francis sullenly knocked down Old Bags.

The night was far gone, and so were the wits of the honest tax-gatherers; when the president commanded silence, and the con-vivialists knew that their chief was about to issue forth the orders for the ensuing term. Nothing could be better timed than such directions,—during merriment, and before oblivion.

"Gentlemen!" said the captain, "I will now, with your leave, impart to you all the plans I have formed for each. You, Attie, shall repair to London : be the Windsor road and the purlieus of Pimlico your especial care. Look you, my hero, to these letters ; they will apprise you of much work : I need not caution you to silence. Like the oyster, you never open your mouth but for something.—Honest Old Bags, a rich grazier will be in Smithfield on Thursday ; his name is Hodges, and he will have somewhat like a thousand pounds in his pouch. He is green, fresh, and avaricious ; offer to assist him in defrauding his neighbours in a bargain, and cease not till thou hast *done* that with him which he wished to do to others. Be—excellent old man,—like the frog-fish, which fishes

[1] Hold your tongue

for other fishes with two horns that resemble baits; the prey dart
at the horns, and are down the throat in an instant!—For thee,
dearest Jem, these letters announce a prize:—fat is Parson Pliant!
full is his purse; and he rides from Henley to Oxford on Friday—
I need say no more! As for the rest of you, gentlemen, on this
paper you will see your destinations fixed. I warrant you, ye will
find enough work till we meet again this day three months. Myself, Augustus Tomlinson, and Ned Pepper, remain at Bath; we
have business in hand, gentlemen, of paramount importance; should
you by accident meet us, never acknowledge us—we are *incog.*;
striking at high game, and putting on falcon's plumes to do it in
character—you understand; but this accident can scarcely occur,
for none of you will remain at Bath; by to-morrow night, may the
road receive you. And now, gentlemen, speed the glass, and I'll
give you a sentiment by way of a spur to it—

> "' Much sweeter than honey
> Is other men's money!'"

Our hero's maxim was received with all the enthusiasm which
agreeable truisms usually create. And old Mr Bags rose to address
the chair; unhappily for the edification of the audience, the veteran's
foot slipped before he had proceeded farther than "Mr. President,"
he fell to the earth with a sort of reel—

> "Like shooting stars he fell to rise no more!"

His body became a capital footstool for the luxurious Pepper.
Now Augustus Tomlinson and Clifford, exchanging looks, took
every possible pains to promote the hilarity of the evening; and,
before the third hour of morning had sounded, they had the satisfaction of witnessing the effects of their benevolent labours in the
prostrate forms of all their companions. Long Ned, naturally more
capacious than the rest, succumbed the last.

"As leaves of trees," said the chairman, waving his hand—

> "' As leaves of trees the race of man is found,
> Now *fresh with dew*, new withering on the ground.'"

"Well said, my Hector of Highways!" cried Tomlinson; and
then helping himself to the wine, while he employed his legs in
removing the supine forms of Scarlet Jem and Long Ned, he
continued the Homeric quotation, with a pompous and self-
gratulatory tone,—

> "' So flourish *these* when *those* have passed away!'"

"We managed to get rid of our friends," began Clifford—
"Like Whigs in place," interrupted the politician.

"Right, Tomlinson, thanks to the milder properties of our drink, and, perchance, to the stronger qualities of our heads; and now tell me, my friend, what think you of our chance of success? Shall we catch an heiress or not?"

"Why really," said Tomlinson, "women are like those calculations in arithmetic, which one can never bring to an exact account; for my part, I shall stuff my calves, and look out for a widow. You, my good fellow, seem to stand a fair chance with Miss ——"

"Oh, name her not!" cried Clifford, colouring, even through the flush which wine had spread over his countenance. "Ours are not the lips by which her name should be breathed; and faith, when I think of her, I do it anonymously."

"What, *have* you ever thought of her before this evening?"

"Yes, for months," answered Clifford. "You remember, some time ago, when we formed the plan for robbing Lord Mauleverer, how, rather for frolic than profit, you robbed Dr. Slopperton, of Warlock, while I compassionately walked home with the old gentleman. Well, at the parson's house, I met Miss Brandon;—mind, if I speak of her by name, *you* must not; and, by Heaven!—but I won't swear.—I accompanied her home. You know, before morning we robbed Lord Mauleverer; the affair made a noise, and I feared to endanger you all if I appeared in the vicinity of the robbery. Since then, business diverted my thoughts; we formed the plan of trying a matrimonial speculation at Bath. I came hither —guess my surprise at seeing *her*——"

"And your delight," added Tomlinson, "at hearing she is as rich as she is pretty."

"No!" answered Clifford, quickly; "that thought gives me no pleasure—you stare. I will try and explain. You know, dear Tomlinson, I'm not much of a canter, and yet my heart shrinks when I look on that innocent face, and hear that soft, happy voice, and think that my love to her can be only ruin and disgrace; nay, that my very address is contamination, and, my very glance towards her an insult."

"Hey-day!" quoth Tomlinson; "have you been under my instructions, and learned the true value of words? and can you have any scruples left on so easy a point of conscience? True, you may call your representing yourself to her as an unprofessional gentleman, and so winning her affections, deceit; but why call it deceit when a '*genius for intrigue*' is so much neater a phrase: in like manner, by marrying the young lady, if you say *you have ruined her*, you justly deserve to be annihilated; but why not say you have '*saved yourself*,' and then, my dear fellow, you will have done the most justifiable thing in the world."

"Pish, man!" said Clifford, peevishly; "none of thy sophisms and sneers!"

"By the soul of Sir Edward Coke, I am serious!—But look you, my friend, this is not a matter where it is *convenient* to have a tender-footed conscience. You see these fellows on the ground!—all d—d clever, and so-forth; but you and I are of a different order. I have had a classical education, seen the world, and mixed in decent society; you, too, had, not been long a member of our club, before you distinguished yourself above us all. Fortune smiled on your youthful audacity. You grew particular in horses and dress, frequented public haunts, and being a deuced good-looking fellow, with an inborn air of gentility, and some sort of education, you became sufficiently well received to acquire, in a short time, the manner and tone of a——what shall I say,—a gentleman, and the taste to like suitable associates. This is my case too! Despite our labours for the public weal, the ungrateful dogs see that we are above them; a single envious breast is sufficient to give us to the hangman; we have agreed that we are in danger, we have agreed to make an honourable retreat! we cannot do so without money; you know the vulgar distich among our set. Nothing can be truer—

> "'Hanging is 'nation
> More nice than starvation!'

You will not carry off some of the common stock, though I think you justly might, considering how much you have put into it. What, then, shall we do? Work we cannot! Beg we will not! And, between you and me, we are cursedly extravagant! What remains but marriage?"

"It is true!" said Clifford, with a half sigh.

"You may well sigh, my good fellow, marriage is a lacka-daisical proceeding at best; but there is no resource: and now, when you have got a liking to a young lady who is as rich as a she-Crœsus, and so gilded the pill as bright as a lord mayor's coach, what the devil have you to do with scruples?"

Clifford made no answer, and there was a long pause; perhaps he would not have spoken so frankly as he had done, if the wine had not opened his heart.

"How proud," renewed Tomlinson, "the good old matron at Thames Court would be if you marry a lady! You have not seen her lately?"

"Not for years," answered our hero. "Poor old soul! I believe that she is well in health, and I take care that she should not be poor in pocket."

"But why not visit her? Perhaps, like all great men, especially of a liberal turn of mind, you are ashamed of old friends, eh?"

"My good fellow, is that like me? Why, you know the beaux of our set look askant on me for not keeping up my dignity, robbing only in company with well-dressed gentlemen, and swindling under the name of a lord's nephew; no, my reasons are these:—first, you must know, that the old dame had set her heart on my turning out an honest man."

"And so you have!" interrupted Augustus; "honest to your party: what more would you have from either prig or politician?"

"I believe," continued Clifford, not heeding the interruption, "that my poor mother, before she died, desired that I might be reared honestly; and, strange as it may seem to you, Dame Lobkins is a conscientious woman in her own way—it is not her fault if I have turned out as I have done. Now I know well that it would grieve her to the quick to see me what I am. Secondly, my friend, under my new names, various as they are,—Jackson and Howard, Russell and Pigwiggin, Villiers and Gotobed, Cavendish and Solomons,—you may well suppose that the good persons in the neighbourhood of Thames Court have no suspicion that the adventurous and accomplished ruffler, at present captain of this district, under the new appellation of Lovett, is in reality no other than the obscure and surnameless Paul of the Mug. Now you and I, Augustus, have read human nature, though in the *black letter;* and I know well that were I to make my appearance in Thames Court, and were the old lady—(as she certainly would, not from unkindness, but insobriety, not that she loves me less, but heavy wet more)—to divulge the secret of that appearance——"

"You know well," interrupted the vivacious Tomlinson, "that the identity of your former meanness with your present greatness would be easily traced; the envy and jealousy of your early friends aroused; a hint of your whereabout and aliases given to the police, and yourself grabbed, with a slight possibility of a hempen consummation."

"You conceive me exactly!" answered Clifford: "the fact is, that I have observed in nine cases out of ten our bravest fellows have been taken off by the treachery of some early sweetheart or the envy of some boyish friend. My destiny is not yet fixed; I am worthy of better things than a ride in the cart with a nosegay in my hand; and though I care not much about death in itself, I am resolved, if possible, not to die a highwayman: hence my caution, and that prudential care for secresy and safe asylums, which men, less wise than you, have so often thought an unnatural contrast to my conduct on the road."

"Fools!" said the philosophical Tomlinson; "what has the bravery of a warrior to do with his insuring his house from fire?"

"However," said Clifford, "I send my good nurse a fine gift every now and then to assure her of my safety; and thus, notwithstanding my absence, I show my affection by my *presents*;—excuse a pun."

"And have you never been detected by any of your quondam associates?"

"Never!—remember in what a much more elevated sphere of life I have been thrown; and who could recognise the scamp Paul with a fustian jacket in gentleman Paul with a laced waistcoat? Besides, I have diligently avoided every place where I was likely to encounter those who saw me in childhood. You know how little I frequent flash houses, and how scrupulous I am in admitting new confederates into our band; you and Pepper are the only two of my associates— (save my *protégé*, as you express it, who never deserts the cave)—that possess a knowledge of my identity with the lost Paul; and as ye have both taken that dread oath in silence, which to disobey, until, indeed, I be in gaol or on the gibbet, is almost to be assassinated, I consider my secret is little likely to be broken, save with my own consent."

"True," said Augustus, nodding; "one more glass, and to bed, Mr. Chairman."

"I pledge you, my friend; our last glass shall be philanthropically quaffed;—'All fools, and may their money soon be parted!'"

"All fools!" cried Tomlinson, filling a bumper; "but I quarrel with the wisdom of your toast;—may fools be rich, and rogues will never be poor! I would make a better livelihood of a rich fool than a landed estate."

So saying, the contemplative and ever-sagacious Tomlinson tossed off his bumper; and the pair, having kindly rolled by pedal applications the body of Long Ned into a safe and quiet corner of the room, mounted the stairs, arm-in-arm, in search of somnambular accommodations.

CHAPTER XVII.

" That contrast of the hardened and mature,
The calm brow brooding o'er the project dark,
With the clear loving heart, and spirit pure
Of youth—I love—yet, hating, love to mark!"

H. FLETCHER.

N the forenoon of the day after the ball, the carriage of William Brandon, packed and prepared, was at the door of his abode at Bath; meanwhile, the lawyer was closeted with his brother. "My dear Joseph," said the barrister, "I do not leave you without being fully sensible of your kindness evinced to me, both in coming hither, contrary to your habits, and accompanying me everywhere, despite of your tastes."

"Mention it not, my dear William," said the kind-hearted squire, "for your delightful society is to me the most agreeable—(and that's what I can say of very few people like you; for, for my own part, I generally find the cleverest men *the most unpleasant*)—*in the world!* And I think lawyers in particular—(very different, indeed, from your tribe *you are!*)—*perfectly intolerable!*"

"I have, now," said Brandon, who with his usual nervous quickness of action was walking with rapid strides to and fro the apartment, and scarcely noted his brother's compliment—"I have now another favour to request of you.—Consider this house and these servants yours, for the next month or two at least. Don't interrupt me—it is no compliment—I speak for our family benefit." And then seating himself next to his brother's arm-chair, for a fit of the gout made the squire a close prisoner, Brandon unfolded to his brother his cherished scheme of marrying Lucy to Lord Mauleverer. Notwithstanding the constancy of the earl's attentions to the heiress, the honest squire had never dreamt of their palpable object; and he was overpowered with surprise when he heard the lawyer's expectations.

"But, my dear brother," he began, "so great a match for my Lucy, the Lord-Lieutenant of the Coun——"

"And what of that?" cried Brandon proudly, and interrupting his brother; "is not the race of Brandon, which has matched its scions with royalty, far nobler than that of the upstart stock of Mauleverer?—What is there presumptuous in the hope that the descendant of the Earls of Suffolk should regild a faded name with some of the precious dust of the quondam silversmiths of London?

G 2

—"Besides," he continued, after a pause, "Lucy will be rich—very rich—and before two years my rank may possibly be of the same order as Mauleverer's!"

The squire stared; and Brandon, not giving him time to answer, resumed.—It is needless to detail the conversation; suffice it to say, that the artful barrister did not leave his brother till he had gained his point—till Joseph Brandon had promised to remain at Bath in possession of the house and establishment of his brother; to throw no impediment on the suit of Mauleverer; to cultivate society as before; and, above all, not to alarm Lucy, who evidently did not yet favour Mauleverer exclusively, by hinting to her the hopes and expectations of her uncle and father. Brandon, now taking leave of his brother, mounted to the drawing-room in search of Lucy. He found her leaning over the gilt cage of one of her feathered favourites, and speaking to the little inmate in that pretty and playful language in which all thoughts, innocent, yet fond, should be clothed. So beautiful did Lucy seem, as she was thus engaged in her girlish and caressing employment, and so utterly unlike one meet to be the instrument of ambitious designs, and the sacrifice of worldly calculations, that Brandon paused, suddenly smitten at heart, as he beheld her: he was not, however, slow in recovering himself; he approached. "Happy he," said the man of the world, "for whom caresses and words like these are reserved!"

Lucy turned. "It is ill!" she said, pointing to the bird, which sat with its feathers stiff and erect, mute and heedless even of that voice which was as musical as its own.

"Poor prisoner!" said Brandon; "even gilt cages and sweet tones cannot compensate to thee for the loss of the air and the wild woods!"

"But," said Lucy, anxiously, "it is not confinement which makes it ill! If you think so, I will release it instantly."

"How long have you had it?" asked Brandon.

"For three years!" said Lucy.

"And is it your *chief* favourite?"

"Yes; it does not sing so prettily as the other—but it is far more sensible, and *so* affectionate."

"Can you release it then?" asked Brandon, smiling. "Would it not be better to see it die in your custody, than to let it live and to see it no more?"

"Oh, no, no!" said Lucy, eagerly; "when I love any one— any thing—I wish that to be happy, not me!"

As she said this, she took the bird from the cage; and bearing it to the open window, kissed it, and held it on her hand in the air. The poor bird turned a languid and sickly eye around it, as if the sight of the crowded houses and busy streets presented nothing familiar or inviting ; and it was not till Lucy, with a tender courage, shook it gently from her, that it availed itself of the proffered liberty. It flew first to an opposite balcony ; and then recovering from a short, and, as it were, surprised pause, took a brief circuit above the houses ; and after disappearing for a few minutes, flew back, circled the window, and re-entering, settled once more on the fair form of its mistress and nestled into her bosom.

Lucy covered it with kisses. "You see it will not leave me!" said she.

"Who can?" said the uncle, warmly, charmed for the moment from every thought, but that of kindness for the young and soft creature before him—"Who can," he repeated with a sigh, "but an old and withered ascetic like myself? I must leave you indeed ; see, my carriage is at the door! Will my beautiful niece, among the gaieties that surround her, condescend now and then to re-member the crabbed lawyer, and assure him by a line of her hap-piness and health? Though I rarely write any notes but those upon cases, *you*, at least, may be sure of an answer. And tell me, Lucy, if there be in all this city one so foolish as to think that these idle gems, useful only as a vent for my pride in you, can add a single charm to a beauty above all ornament?"

So saying, Brandon produced a leathern case ; and touching a spring, the imperial flash of diamonds, which would have made glad many a patrician heart, broke dazzlingly on Lucy's eyes.

"No thanks, Lucy," said Brandon, in answer to his niece's dis-claiming and shrinking gratitude ; "I do honour to myself, not you ; and now bless you, my dear girl. Farewell! Should any occasion present itself in which you require an immediate adviser, at once kind and wise, I beseech you, my dearest Lucy, as a parting request, to have no scruples in consulting Lord Mauleverer. Besides his friendship for me, he is much interested in you, and you may con-sult him with the more safety and assurance ; because (and the lawyer smiled) he is perhaps the only man in the world whom my Lucy could not make in love with her. His gallantry may appear adulation, but it is never akin to love. Promise me, that you will not hesitate in this?"

Lucy gave the promise readily, and Brandon continued in a care-less tone—"I hear that you danced last night with a young gentle-man whom no one knew, and whose companions bore a very strange appearance. In a place like Bath, society is too mixed not to render the greatest caution in forming acquaintances absolutely necessary. You must pardon me, my dearest niece, if I remark that a young lady owes it not only to herself, but to her relations, to

observe the most rigid circumspection of conduct. This is a wicked
world, and the peach-like bloom of character is easily rubbed away.
In these points Mauleverer can be of great use to you. His knowledge of character—his penetration into men—and his tact in manners—are unerring. Pray, be guided by him: whomsoever he
warns you against, you may be sure is unworthy of your acquaintance. God bless you! you *will* write to me often and frankly, dear
Lucy; tell me all that happens to you—all that interests, nay, all
that displeases."

Brandon then, who had seemingly disregarded the blushes with
which, during his speech, Lucy's cheeks had been spread, folded his
niece in his arms, and hurried, as if to hide his feeling, into his
carriage. When the horses had turned the street, he directed the
postilions to stop at Lord Mauleverer's. "Now," said he to himself, "if I can get this clever coxcomb to second my schemes, and
play according to my game, and not according to his own vanity, I
shall have a knight of the garter for my nephew-in-law!"

Meanwhile Lucy, all in tears, for she loved her uncle greatly, ran
down to the squire to show him Brandon's magnificent present.

"Ah!" said the squire, with a sigh, "few men were born with
more good, generous, and great qualities—(pity only that his chief
desire was to get on in the world; for my part, I think *no motive
makes greater and more cold-hearted rogues)—than my brother
William!*"

CHAPTER XVIII.

*" Why did she love him?—Curious fool, be still!
Is human love the growth of human will?
To her he might be gentleness!"*—LORD BYRON.

IN three weeks from the time of his arrival, Captain Clifford
was the most admired man in Bath. It is true, the gentlemen, who have a quicker tact as to the respectability of
their own sex than women, might have looked a little shy
upon him, had he not himself especially shunned appearing intrusive,
and indeed rather avoided the society of men than courted it; so
that after he had fought a duel with a baronet (the son of a shoemaker), who called him *one* Clifford; and had exhibited a flea-
bitten horse, allowed to be the finest in Bath, he rose insensibly into
a certain degree of respect with the one sex as well as popularity
with the other. But what always attracted and kept alive suspicion,

was his intimacy with so peculiar and *dashing* a gentleman as Mr. Edward Pepper. People could get over a certain frankness in Clifford's address, but the most lenient were astounded by the swagger of Long Ned. Clifford, however, not insensible to the ridicule attached to his acquaintances, soon managed to pursue his occupations alone ; nay, he took a lodging to himself, and left Long Ned and Augustus Tomlinson (the latter to operate as a check on the former) to the quiet enjoyment of the hair-dresser's apartments. He himself attended all public gaieties ; and his mien, and the appearance of wealth which he maintained, procured him access into several private circles, which pretended to be exclusive : as if people who had daughters ever could be exclusive ! Many were the kind looks, nor few the inviting letters, which he received ; and if his sole object had been to marry an heiress, he would have found no difficulty in attaining it. But he devoted himself entirely to Lucy Brandon ; and to win one glance from her, he would have renounced all the heiresses in the kingdom. Most fortunately for him, Mauleverer, whose health was easily deranged, had fallen ill the very day William Brandon left Bath ; and his lordship was thus rendered unable to watch the movements of Lucy, and undermine, or totally prevent, the success of her lover. Miss Brandon, indeed, had at first, melted by the kindness of her uncle, and struck with the sense of his admonition (for she was no self-willed young lady, who was determined to be in love), received Captain Clifford's advances with a coldness which, from her manner the first evening they had met at Bath, occasioned him no less surprise than mortification. He retreated, and recoiled on the squire, who, patient and bold, as usual, was sequestered in his favourite corner. By accident, Clifford trod on the squire's gouty digital ; and in apologising for the offence, was so struck by the old gentleman's good nature and peculiarity of expressing himself, that without knowing who he was, he entered into conversation with him. There was an off-hand sort of liveliness and candour, not to say wit, about Clifford, which always had a charm for the elderly, who generally like frankness, above all the cardinal virtues ; the squire was exceedingly pleased with him. The acquaintance, once begun, was naturally continued without difficulty when Clifford ascertained who was his new friend ; and next morning, meeting in the pump-room, the squire asked Clifford to dinner. The *entrée* to the house thus gained, the rest was easy. Long before Mauleverer recovered his health, the mischief effected by his rival was almost beyond redress ; and the heart of the pure, the simple, the affectionate Lucy Brandon, was more than half lost to the lawless and vagrant cavalier who officiates as the hero of this tale.

One morning, Clifford and Augustus strolled out together. " Let us," said the latter, who was in a melancholy mood, "leave the busy streets, and indulge in a philosophical conversation on the nature of man, while we are enjoying a little fresh air in the country." Clifford assented to the proposal, and the pair slowly sauntered up one of the hills that surround the city of Bladud.

" There are certain moments," said Tomlinson, looking pensively down at his kerseymere gaiters, " when we are like the fox in the nursery rhyme, 'The fox had a wound, he could not tell where'— we feel extremely unhappy, and we cannot tell *why!*—a dark and sad melancholy grows over us—we shun the face of man—we wrap ourselves in our thoughts like silkworms—we mutter fag-ends of dismal songs—tears come into our eyes—we recall all the misfortunes that have ever happened to us—we stoop in our gait, and bury our hands in our breeches-pockets—we say ' what is life?—a stone to be shied into a horsepond !' We pine for some congenial heart—and have an itching desire to talk prodigiously about ourselves : all *other* subjects seem weary, stale, and unprofitable—we feel as if a fly could knock us down, and are in a humour to fall in love, and make a very sad piece of business of it. Yet with all this weakness we have, at these moments, a finer opinion of ourselves than we ever had before. We call our megrims the melancholy of a sublime soul—the yearnings of an indigestion we denominate yearnings after immortality— nay, sometimes 'a proof of the nature of the soul!' May I find some biographer who understands such sensations well, and may he style those melting emotions the offspring of the poetical character,[1] which, in reality, are the offspring of—a mutton-chop ! "

" You jest pleasantly enough on your low spirits," said Clifford ; " but I have a cause for mine."

" What then ? " cried Tomlinson. " So much the easier is it to cure them. The mind can cure the evils that spring *from* the mind ; it is only a fool, and a quack, and a driveller, when it professes to heal the evils that spring from the body :—*my* blue devils spring from the body—consequently, my mind, which, as you know, is a particularly wise mind, wrestles not against them. Tell me frankly," renewed Augustus, after a pause, "do you ever repent? Do you

---

[1] Vide Moore's *Life of Byron.* In which it is satisfactorily shown that, if a man fast forty eight hours, then eat three lobsters, and drink Heaven knows how many bottles of claret—if, when he wake the next morning, he sees himself abused as a demon by half the periodicals of the country—if, in a word, he be broken in his health, irregular in his habits, unfortunate in his affairs, unhappy in his home—and if then he should be so extremely eccentric as to be low-spirited and misanthropical, the low-spirits and the misanthropy are by no means to be attributed to the above agreeable circumstances, but—God wot—to the " poetical character ! "

ever think, if you had been a shop-boy with a white apron about your middle, that you would have been a happier and a better member of society than you now are?"

"Repent!" said Clifford, fiercely; and his answer opened more of his secret heart, its motives, its reasonings, and its peculiarities, than were often discernible. "Repent—that is the idlest word in our language. No,—the moment I repent, that moment I reform! Never can it seem to me an atonement for crime merely to regret it —my mind would lead me not to regret, but to repair!—Repent!— no, not yet. The older I grow, the more I see of men and of the callings of social life—the more I, an open knave, sicken at the glossed and covert dishonesties around. I acknowledge no allegiance to society. From my birth to this hour, I have received no single favour from its customs or its laws;—openly I war against it, and patiently will I meet its revenge. This may be crime; but it looks light in my eyes when I gaze around, and survey on all sides the masked traitors who acknowledge large debts to society, — who profess to obey its laws—adore its institutions—and, above all—oh, how righteously!—attack all those who attack it, and who yet lie, and cheat, and defraud, and peculate—publicly reaping all the comforts, privately filching all the profits. Repent!—of what? I come into the world friendless and poor—I find a body of laws hostile to the friendless and the poor! To those laws hostile to me, then, I acknowledge hostility in my turn. Between us are the conditions of war. Let them expose a weakness—I insist on my right to seize the advantage: let them defeat me, and I allow their right to destroy." [1]

"Passion," said Augustus coolly, "is the usual enemy of reason —in your case it is the friend!"

The pair had now gained the summit of a hill which commanded a view of the city below. Here Augustus, who was a little short-winded, paused to recover breath. As soon as he had done so, he pointed with his fore-finger to the scene beneath, and said enthusiastically—"What a subject for contemplation!"

Clifford was about to reply, when suddenly the sound of laughter and voices was heard behind—"Let us fly!" cried Augustus; "on this day of spleen man delights me not—nor woman either."

"Stay!" said Clifford, in a trembling accent; for among those voices he recognised one which had already acquired over him an irresistible and bewitching power. Augustus sighed, and reluctantly remained motionless. Presently a winding in the road brought into view a party of pleasure, some on foot, some on horseback, others

[1] The author need not, he hopes, observe, that these sentiments are Mr Paul Clifford's—not his.

in little vehicles which even at that day haunted watering places,
and called themselves "Flies" or "Swallows."

But among the gay procession Clifford had only eyes for one!
Walking with that elastic step which so rarely survives the first
epoch of youth, by the side of the heavy chair in which her father
was drawn, the fair beauty of Lucy Brandon threw, at least in the
eyes of her lover, a magic and a lustre over the whole group.   He
stood for a moment, stilling the heart that leaped at her bright looks
and the gladness of her innocent laugh ; and then recovering himself, he walked slowly, and with a certain consciousness of the effect of
his own singularly handsome person, towards the party.   The good
squire received him with his usual kindness, and informed him,
according to that *lucidus ordo* which he so especially favoured, of
the whole particulars of their excursion   There was something
worthy of an artist's sketch in the scene at that moment—the old
squire in his chair, with his benevolent face turned towards Clifford,
and his hands resting on his cane—Clifford himself bowing down
his stately head to hear the details of the father ; — the beautiful
daughter on the other side of the chair, her laugh suddenly stilled,
her gait insensibly more composed, and blush chasing blush over
the smooth and peach-like loveliness of her cheek ;—the party, of
all sizes, ages, and attire, affording ample scope for the caricaturist ;
and the pensive figure of Augustus Tomlinson (who, by-the-by, was
exceedingly like Liston) standing apart from the rest, on the brow
of the hill where Clifford had left him, and moralising on the motley
procession, with one hand hid in his waistcoat, and the other caressing his chin, which slowly and pendulously with the rest of his head
moved up and down.

As the party approached the brow of the hill, the view of the city
below was so striking, that there was a general pause for the purpose
of survey.   One young lady, in particular, drew forth her pencil, and
began sketching, while her mamma looked complacently on, and
abstractedly devoured a sandwich.   It was at this time, in the general
applause, that Clifford and Lucy found themselves—Heaven knows
how ! next to each other, and at a sufficient distance from the squire
and the rest of the party to feel, in some measure, alone.   There was
a silence in both which neither dared to break ; when Lucy, after
looking at and toying with a flower that she had brought from the
place which the party had been to see, accidentally dropped it ; and
Clifford and herself stooping at the same moment to recover it, their
hands met.   Involuntarily, Clifford detained the soft fingers in his
own ; his eyes, that encountered hers, so spell-bound and arrested
them that for once they did not sink beneath his gaze ; his lips
moved, but many and vehement emotions so suffocated his voice

that no sound escaped them. But all the heart was in the eyes of each ; that moment fixed their destinies. Henceforth there was an era from which they dated a new existence ; a nucleus around which their thoughts, their remembrances, and their passions, clung. The great gulf was passed ; they stood on the same shore ; and felt, that though still apart and disunited, on that shore was no living creature but themselves ! Meanwhile, Augustus Tomlinson, on finding himself surrounded by persons eager to gaze and to listen, broke from his moodiness and reserve. Looking full at his next neighbour, and flourishing his right hand in the air, till he suffered it to rest in the direction of the houses and chimneys below, he repeated that moral exclamation which had been wasted on Clifford, with a more solemn and a less passionate gravity than before—

"What a subject, ma'am, for contemplation !"

"Very sensibly said, indeed, sir," said the lady addressed, who was rather of a serious turn.

"I never," resumed Augustus in a louder key, and looking round for auditors,—"I never see a great town from the top of a hill, without thinking of an apothecary's shop !"

"Lord, sir !" said the lady. Tomlinson's end was gained :— struck with the quaintness of the notion, a little crowd gathered instantly around him, to hear it farther developed.

"Of an apothecary's shop, ma'am !" repeated Tomlinson. "There lie your simples, and your purges, and your cordials, and your poisons ; all things to heal, and to strengthen, and to destroy. There are drugs enough in that collection to save you, to cure you all ; but none of you know how to use them, nor what medicines to ask for, nor what portions to take ; so that the greater part of you swallow the wrong dose, and die of the remedy !"

"But if the town be the apothecary's shop, what, in the plan of your idea, stands for the apothecary?" asked an old gentleman, who perceived at what Tomlinson was driving.

"The apothecary, sir," answered Augustus, stealing his notion from Clifford, and sinking his voice, lest the true proprietor should overhear him—Clifford was otherwise employed—"The apothecary, sir, is the LAW ! It is the law that stands behind the counter, and dispenses to each man the dose he should take. To the poor, it gives bad drugs gratuitously ; to the rich, pills to stimulate the appetite ; to the latter, premiums for luxury ; to the former, only speedy refuges from life ! Alas ! either your apothecary is but an ignorant quack, or his science itself is but in its cradle. He blunders as much as you would do if left to your own selection. Those who have recourse to him seldom speak gratefully of his skill. He relieves you, it is true —but of your money, not your malady ; and the only branch of his profession in which he is an adept, is that which enables him to *bleed* you!—O Mankind!" continued Augustus, "what noble creatures you ought to be! You have keys to all sciences, all arts, all mysteries, but one! You have not a notion how you ought to be governed!— you cannot frame a tolerable law for the life and soul of you! You make yourselves as uncomfortable as you can by all sorts of galling and vexatious institutions, and you throw the blame upon 'Fate' You lay down rules it is impossible to comprehend, much less to obey ; and you call each other monsters, because you cannot conquer the impossibility ! You invent all sorts of vices, under pretence of making laws for preserving virtue ; and the anomalous artificialities of conduct yourselves produce, you say you are born with ;—you make a machine by the perversest art you can think of, and you call it, with a sigh, 'Human Nature.' With a host of good dispositions struggling at your breasts, you insist upon libelling the Almighty, and declaring that He meant you to be wicked. Nay, you even call the man mischievous and seditious who begs and implores you to be one jot better than you are.—O Mankind ! you are like a nosegay bought at Covent Garden. The flowers are lovely, the scent delicious ; —mark that glorious hue ; contemplate that bursting petal !—how beautiful, how redolent of health, of nature, of the dew and breath and blessing of Heaven, are you all ! But as for the dirty piece of string that ties you together, one would think you had picked it out of the kennel."

So saying, Tomlinson turned on his heel, broke away from the crowd, and solemnly descended the hill. The party of pleasure slowly followed ; and Clifford, receiving an invitation from the squire to partake of his family dinner, walked by the side of Lucy, and felt as if his spirit were drunk with the airs of Eden.

A brother squire, who, among the gaieties of Bath, was almost as forlorn as Joseph Brandon himself, partook of the Lord of Warlock's hospitality. When the three gentlemen adjourned to the drawing-room, the two elder sat down to a game at backgammon, and Clifford was left to the undisturbed enjoyment of Lucy's conversation. She was sitting by the window when Clifford joined her. On the table by her side were scattered books, the charm of which (they were chiefly poetry) she had only of late learned to discover ; *there* also were strewn various little masterpieces of female ingenuity, in which the fairy fingers of Lucy Brandon were especially formed to excel. The shades of evening were rapidly darkening over the empty streets ; and in the sky, which was cloudless and transparently clear, the stars came gradually out one by one, until,

> " As water does a sponge, so *their soft light*
> Fill'd the void, hollow, universal air "

Beautiful Evening ! (if we, as well as Augustus Tomlinson, may indulge in an apostrophe)—Beautiful Evening ! For thee all poets have had a song, and surrounded thee with rills, and waterfalls, and dews, and flowers, and sheep, and bats, and melancholy, and owls ; yet we must confess that to us, who in this very sentimental age are a bustling, worldly, hardminded person, jostling our neighbours, and thinking of the main chance ;—to us, thou art never so charming, as when we meet thee walking in thy grey hood, through the emptying streets, and among the dying sounds of a city. We love to feel the stillness, where all, two hours back, was clamour. We love to see the dingy abodes, of Trade and Luxury, those restless patients of earth's constant fever, contrasted and canopied by a heaven full of purity, and quietness, and peace. We love to fill our thought with speculations on man,—even though the man be the muffin-man,—rather than with inanimate objects—hills and streams—things to dream about, not to meditate on. Man is the subject of far nobler contemplation, of far more glowing hope, of a far purer and loftier vein of sentiment, than all the " floods and fells " in the universe ;—and that, sweet Evening ! is one reason why we like that the earnest and tender thoughts thou excitest within us, should be rather surrounded by the labours and tokens, of our species, than by sheep, and bats, and melancholy, and owls. But whether, most blessed Evening ! thou delightest us in the country or in the town, thou equally disposest us to make and to feel love !—thou art the cause of more marriages, and more divorces, than any other time in the twenty-four hours. Eyes, that were common eyes to us before, touched by thy enchanting and magic shadows, become inspired, and preach to us of heaven. A softness settles on features that were harsh to us while the sun shone ; a mellow "light of love" reposes on the complexion, which by day we would have steeped "full fathom five" in a sea of Mrs. Gowland's lotion.—What, then, thou modest hypocrite ! to those who *already* and deeply love—what, then, of danger and of paradise dost thou bring ?

Silent, and stilling the breath which heaved in both quick and fitfully, Lucy and Clifford sat together. The streets were utterly deserted, and the loneliness, as they looked below, made them feel the more intensely not only the emotions which swelled within them, but the undefined and electric sympathy which, in uniting them, divided them from the world. The quiet around was broken by a distant strain of rude music ; and as it came nearer, two forms of no poetical order grew visible : the one was a poor blind man, who was drawing from his flute tones in which the melancholy beauty of the air compensated for any deficiency (the deficiency was but slight) in the execution. A woman much younger than the musician, and with

something of beauty in her countenance, accompanied him, holding
a tattered hat, and looking wistfully up at the windows of the silent
street.   We said two forms—we did the injustice of forgetfulness to
another—a rugged and simple friend, it is true, but one that both
minstrel and wife had many and moving reasons to love.   This was
a little wiry terrier, with dark piercing eyes, that glanced quickly
and sagaciously in all quarters from beneath the shaggy covert that
surrounded them ;   slowly the animal moved onward, pulling gently
against the string by which he was held, and by which he guided
his master.   Once his fidelity was tempted : another dog invited
him to play ;   the poor terrier looked anxiously and doubtingly round,
and then uttering a low growl of denial, pursued

> " The noiseless tenour of his way."

The little procession stopped beneath the window where Lucy and
Clifford sat ;   for the quick eye of the woman had perceived them,
and she laid her hand on the blind man's arm, and whispered him.
He took the hint, and changed his air into one of love.   Clifford
glanced at Lucy—her cheek was dyed in blushes.   The air was
over,—another succeeded—it was of the same kind ; a third—the
burden was still unaltered ; and then Clifford threw into the street
a piece of money, and the dog wagged his abridged and dwarfed
tail, and darting forward, picked it up in his mouth ; and the woman
(she had a kind face !) patted the officious friend, even before she
thanked the donor, and then she dropped the money with a cheering
word or two into the blind man's pocket, and the three wanderers
moved slowly on.   Presently they came to a place where the street
had been mended, and the stones lay scattered about.   Here the
woman no longer trusted to the dog's guidance, but anxiously
hastened to the musician, and led him with evident tenderness and
minute watchfulness over the rugged way.   When they had passed
the danger, the man stopped ; and before he released the hand
which had guided him, he pressed it gratefully, and then both the
husband and the wife stooped down and caressed the dog.   This
little scene—one of those rough copies of the loveliness of human
affections, of which so many are scattered about the highways of the
world—both the lovers had involuntarily watched ; and now as they
withdrew their eyes—those eyes settled on each other—Lucy's swam
in tears.

"To be loved and tended by the one I love," said Clifford, in a
low voice, " I would walk blind and barefoot over the whole earth ! "

Lucy sighed very gently ; and placing her pretty hands (the one
clasped over the other) upon her knee, looked down wistfully on

them, but made no answer. Clifford drew his chair nearer, and gazed on her as she sat ; the long dark eyelash drooping over her eyes, and contrasting the ivory lids ; her delicate profile half turned from him, and borrowing a more touching beauty from the soft light that dwelt upon it ; and her full yet still scarcely developed bosom heaving at thoughts which she did not analyse, but was content to feel at once vague and delicious : he gazed and his lips trembled— he longed to speak—he longed to say but those words which convey what volumes have endeavoured to express, and have only weakened by detail—"*I love.*" How he resisted the yearnings of his heart, we know not—but he did resist ; and Lucy, after a confused and embarrassed pause, took up one of the poems on the table, and asked him some questions about a particular passage in an old ballad which he had once pointed to her notice   The passage related to a border chief, one of the Armstrongs of old, who, having been seized by the English and condemned to death, vented his last feelings in a passionate address to his own home—his rude tower— and his newly-wedded bride. "Do you believe," said Lucy, as their conversation began to flow, "that one so lawless and eager for bloodshed and strife, as this robber is described to be, could be so capable of soft affections?"

"I do," said Clifford ; "because he was not sensible that he was as criminal as you esteem him.   If a man cherish the idea that his actions are not evil, he will retain at his heart all its better and gentler sensations as much as if he had never sinned.   The savage murders his enemy, and when he returns home is not the less devoted to his friend, or the less anxious for his children.   To harden and embrute the kindly dispositions, we must not only indulge in guilt, but feel that we are guilty.   Oh! many that the world load with their opprobrium are capable of acts—nay, have committed acts, which in others the world would reverence and adore.   Would you know whether a man's heart be shut to the power of love ; ask what he is—not to his foes, but to his friends!   Crime, too," continued Clifford, speaking fast and vehemently, while his eyes flashed and the dark blood rushed to his cheek—"Crime—what is crime? Men embody their worst prejudices, their most evil passions, in a heterogeneous and contradictory code, and whatever breaks this code they term a crime.   When they make no distinction in the penalty—that is to say, in the estimation—awarded both to murder and to a petty theft imposed on the weak will by famine, we ask nothing else to convince us that they are ignorant of the very nature of guilt, and that they make up in ferocity for the want of wisdom."

Lucy looked in alarm at the animated and fiery countenance of the speaker.   Clifford recovered himself after a moment's pause, and rose from his seat, with the gay and frank laugh which made one of his peculiar characteristics. "There is a singularity in politics, Miss Brandon," said he, "which I dare say you have often observed, viz. that those who are least important, are always most noisy; and that the chief people who lose their temper, are those who have nothing to gain in return."

As Clifford spoke, the doors were thrown open, and some visitors to Miss Brandon were announced. The good squire was still immersed in the vicissitudes of his game, and the sole task of receiving and entertaining "the company," as the chambermaids have it, fell, as usual, upon Lucy. Fortunately for her, Clifford was one of those rare persons who possess eminently the talents of society. There was much in his gay and gallant temperament, accompanied as it was with sentiment and ardour, that resembled our *beau idéal* of those chevaliers, ordinarily peculiar to the Continent—heroes equally in the drawing-room and the field. Observant, courteous, witty, and versed in the various accomplishments that combine (that most unfrequent of all unions!) vivacity with grace, he was especially formed for that brilliant world from which his circumstances tended to exclude him. Under different auspices, he might have been—Pooh! We are running into a most pointless commonplace;—what might any man be under auspices different from those by which his life has been guided? Music soon succeeded to conversation, and Clifford's voice was of necessity put into requisition. Miss Brandon had just risen from the harpsichord, as he sat down to perform his part; and she stood by him with the rest of the group while he sung. Only twice his eye stole to that spot which her breath and form made sacred to him; once when he began, and once when he concluded his song. Perhaps the recollection of their conversation inspired him; certainly it dwelt upon his mind at the moment—threw a richer flush over his brow, and infused a more meaning and heartfelt softness into his tone.

STANZAS.

"When I leave thee, oh! ask not the world what that heart
  Which adores thee to others may be!
I know that I sin when from thee I depart,
  But my guilt shall not light upon thee!

My life is a river which glasses a ray
  That hath deign'd to descend from above;
Whatever the banks that o'ershadow its way,
  It mirrors the light of thy love.

Though the waves may run high when the night wind awakes,
  And hurries the stream to its fall:
Though broken and wild be the billows it makes,
  Thine image still trembles on all!"

While this ominous love between Clifford and Lucy was thus finding fresh food in every interview and every opportunity, the unfortunate Mauleverer, firmly persuaded that his complaint was a relapse of what he termed the "Warlock dyspepsia," was waging dire war with the remains of the beef and pudding, which he tearfully assured his physicians "were lurking in his constitution." As Mauleverer, though complaisant—like most men of unmistakable rank—to all his acquaintances, whatever might be their grade,— possessed but very few friends intimate enough to enter his sick chamber, and none of that few were at Bath, it will readily be perceived that he was in blissful ignorance of the growing fortunes of his rival ; and to say the exact truth, illness, which makes a man's thoughts turn very much upon himself, banished many of the most tender ideas usually floating in his mind around the image of Lucy Brandon. His pill superseded his passion ; and he felt that there are draughts in the world more powerful in their effects than those in the phials of Alcidonis.[1] He very often thought, it is true, how pleasant it would be for Lucy to smooth his pillow, and Lucy to prepare that mixture ; but then Mauleverer had an excellent valet, who hoped to play the part enacted by Gil Blas towards the honest Licentiate ; and to nurse a legacy while he was nursing his master. And the earl, who was tolerably good-tempered, was forced to confess that it would be scarcely possible for any one "to know his ways better than Smoothson." Thus, during his illness, the fair form of his intended bride little troubled the peace of the noble adorer. And it was not till he found himself able to eat three good dinners consecutively, with a tolerable appetite, that Mauleverer recollected that he was violently in love. As soon as this idea was fully reinstated in his memory, and he had been permitted by his doctor to allow himself "a little cheerful society," Mauleverer resolved to go to the rooms for an hour or two.

It may be observed that most great personages have some favourite place, some cherished Baiæ, at which they love to throw off their state, and to play the amiable instead of the splendid ; and Bath at that time, from its gaiety, its ease, the variety of character to be found in its haunts, and the obliging manner in which such characters exposed themselves to ridicule, was exactly the place calculated to please a man like Mauleverer, who loved at once to be admired and to satirise. He was therefore an idolised person at the city of Bladud ; and as he entered the rooms he was surrounded by a whole band of imitators and sycophants, delighted to find his lordship looking so much better and declaring himself so convalescent. As soon as the earl had bowed and smiled, and shaken hands

[1] See Marmontel's pretty tale of *Les Quatres Flacons.*

sufficiently to sustain his reputation, he sauntered towards the dancers in search of Lucy. He found her not only exactly in the same spot in which he had last beheld her, but dancing with exactly the same partner who had before provoked all the gallant nobleman's jealousy and wrath. Mauleverer, though not by any means addicted to preparing his compliments beforehand, had just been conning a delicate speech for Lucy; but no sooner did the person of her partner flash on him than the whole flattery vanished at once from his recollection. He felt himself grow pale; and when Lucy turned, and seeing him near, addressed him in the anxious and soft tone which she thought due to her uncle's friend on his recovery, Mauleverer bowed, confused and silent; and that green-eyed passion, which would have convulsed the *mind* of a true lover, altering a little the course of its fury, effectually disturbed the *manner* of the courtier.

Retreating to an obscure part of the room, where he could see all without being conspicuous, Mauleverer now employed himself in watching the motions and looks of the young pair. He was naturally a penetrating and quick observer, and in this instance jealousy sharpened his talents; he saw enough to convince him that Lucy was already attached to Clifford; and being, by that conviction, fully persuaded that Lucy was necessary to his own happiness, he resolved to lose not a moment in banishing Captain Clifford from her presence, or at least, in instituting such inquiries into that gentleman's relatives, rank, and respectability, as would, he hoped, render such banishment a necessary consequence of the research.

Fraught with this determination, Mauleverer repaired at once to the retreat of the squire, and engaging him in conversation, bluntly asked him, "Who the deuce Miss Brandon was dancing with?"

The squire, a little piqued at this *brusquerie*, replied by a long eulogium on Paul; and Mauleverer, after hearing it throughout with the blandest smile imaginable, told the squire, very politely, that he was sure Mr. Brandon's good nature had misled him. "Clifford!" said he, repeating the name,—"Clifford! It is one of those names which are particularly selected by persons nobody knows; first, because the name is good, and secondly, because it is common. My long and dear friendship with your brother makes me feel peculiarly anxious on any point relative to his niece; and, indeed, my dear William, overrating, perhaps, my knowledge of the world, and my influence in society,—but not my affection for him,—besought me to assume the liberty of esteeming myself a friend, nay, even a relation of yours and Miss Brandon's; so that I trust you do not consider my caution impertinent."

The flattered squire assured him that he was particularly honoured, so far from deeming his lordship—(which never could be the case with people so distinguished as *his lordship was, especially !*)—*impertinent.*

Lord Mauleverer, encouraged by this speech, artfully renewed, and succeeded, if not in convincing the squire that the handsome captain was a suspicious character, at least in persuading him that common prudence required that he should find out exactly who the handsome captain was, especially as he was in the habit of dining with the squire thrice a-week, and dancing with Lucy every night.

"See," said Mauleverer, "he approaches you now : I will retreat to the chair by the fireplace, and you shall cross-examine him—I have no doubt you will do it with the utmost delicacy."

So saying, Mauleverer took possession of a seat where he was not absolutely beyond hearing (slightly deaf as he was) of the ensuing colloquy, though the position of his seat screened him from sight. Mauleverer was esteemed a man of the most punctilious honour in private life, and he would not have been seen in the act of listening to other people's conversation for the world.

Hemming with an air and resettling himself as Clifford approached, the squire thus skilfully commenced the attack : "Ah, ha ! my good Captain Clifford, and how do you do? I saw you—(and I am *very glad, my friend, as every one else is, to see you*)—*at a distance.* And where have you left my daughter?"

"Miss Brandon is dancing with Mr. Muskwell, sir," answered Clifford.

"Oh ! she is !—Mr. Muskwell—humph !—Good family the Muskwells—came from Primrose Hall. Pray, Captain,—not that I want to know for my own sake, for I am a strange, odd person, I believe, and I am thoroughly convinced—(some people are sensorious, and others, thank God, are not !)—of your respectability, —what family do you come from ? You won't think my—my caution impertinent ?" added the shrewd old gentleman, borrowing that phrase which he thought so friendly in the mouth of Lord Mauleverer.

Clifford coloured for a moment, but replied with a quiet archness of look, "Family ! oh, my dear sir, I come from an old family,—a very old family indeed."

"So I always thought ; and in what part of the world?"

"Scotland, sir—all our family come from Scotland ; viz. all who live long do—the rest die young."

"Ay, particular air does agree with particular constitutions. I, for instance, could not live in all countries ; not—you take me—in the North !"

"Few honest men *can* live there," said Clifford, dryly.

"And," resumed the squire, a little embarrassed by the nature of his task, and the cool assurance of his young friend—

"And pray, Captain Clifford, what regiment do you belong to?"

"Regiment?—oh, the Rifles!" answered Clifford. ("Deuce is in me," muttered he—"if I can resist a jest, though I break my neck over it.")

"A very gallant body of men?" said the squire.

"No doubt of that, sir!" rejoined Clifford.

"And do you think, Captain Clifford," renewed the squire, "that it is a good corps for getting on?"

"It is rather a bad one for getting off," muttered the Captain; and then aloud, "Why, we have not much interest at court, sir."

"Oh! but then there is a wider scope, as my brother the lawyer says—and no man knows better—for merit. I dare say you have seen many a man elevated from the ranks?"

"Nothing more common, sir, than such elevation; and so great is the virtue of our corps, that I have also known not a few willing to transfer the honour to their comrades."

"You don't say so!" exclaimed the squire, opening his eyes at such disinterested magnanimity.

"But," said Clifford, who began to believe he might carry the equivoque too far, and who thought, despite of his jesting, that it was possible to strike out a more agreeable vein of conversation— "but, sir, if you remember, you have not yet finished that youthful hunting adventure of yours, when the hounds were lost at Burnham Copse."

"Oh, very true," cried the squire, quite forgetting his late suspicions; and forthwith he began a story that promised to be as long as the chase it recorded. So charmed was he when he had finished it, with the character of the gentleman who had listened to it so delightedly, that on rejoining Mauleverer, he told the earl, with an important air, that he had strictly examined the young captain, and that he had fully convinced himself of the excellence of his family, as well as the rectitude of his morals. Mauleverer listened with a countenance of polite incredulity; he had heard but little of the conversation that had taken place between the pair; but on questioning the squire upon sundry particulars of Clifford's birth, parentage, and property, he found him exactly as ignorant as before. The courtier, however, seeing further expostulation was in vain, contented himself with patting the squire's shoulder, and saying, with a mysterious urbanity, "Ah, sir, you are too good!"

With these words he turned on his heel, and, not yet despairing, sought the daughter. He found Miss Brandon just released from dancing, and with a kind of paternal gallantry, he offered his arm to parade the apartments.   After some preliminary flourish, and reference, for the thousandth time, to his friendship for William Brandon, the earl spoke to her about that "fine-looking young man, who called himself Captain Clifford."

Unfortunately for Mauleverer, he grew a little too unguarded, as his resentment against the interference of Clifford warmed with his language, and he dropped in his anger one or two words of caution, which especially offended the delicacy of Miss Brandon.

"Take care how I encourage, my lord!" said Lucy, with glowing cheeks, repeating the words which had so affronted her, "I really must beg you——"

"You mean, dear Miss Brandon," interrupted Mauleverer, squeezing her hand with respectful tenderness, "that you must beg me to apologise for my inadvertent expression.   I do most sincerely.   If I had felt less interest in your happiness, believe me, I should have been more guarded in my language."

Miss Brandon bowed stiffly, and the courtier saw, with secret rage, that the country beauty was not easily appeased, even by an apology from Lord Mauleverer.   "I have seen the time," thought he, "when young unmarried ladies would have deemed *an affront* from *me* an honour   They would have gone into hysterics at an *apology!*" Before he had time to make his peace, the squire joined them; and Lucy taking her father's arm, expressed her wish to return home. The squire was delighted at the proposition.   It would have been but civil in Mauleverer to offer his assistance in those little attentions preparatory to female departure from balls.   He hesitated for a moment—"It keeps one so long in those cursed thorough draughts," thought he, shivering.   "Besides, it is just possible that I may not marry her, and it is no good risking a cold (above all, at the beginning of winter) for nothing!"   Fraught with this prudential policy, Mauleverer then resigned Lucy to her father, and murmuring in her ear that "her displeasure made him the most wretched of men," concluded his adieu by a bow penitentially graceful.

About five minutes afterwards, he himself withdrew.   As he was wrapping his corporeal treasure in his *roquelaire* of sables, previous to immersing himself in his chair, he had the mortification of seeing Lucy, who with her father, from some cause or other, had been delayed in the hall, handed to the carriage by Captain Clifford. Had the earl watched more narrowly than in the anxious cares due to himself he was enabled to do, he would, to his consolation, have noted that Lucy gave her hand with an averted and cool air, and that Clifford's expressive features bore rather the aspect of mortification than triumph

He did not, however, see more than the action ; and as he was borne homeward with his flambeaux and footmen preceding him, and the watchful Smoothson by the side of the little vehicle, he muttered his determination of writing by the very next post to Brandon, all his anger for Lucy, and all his jealousy of her evident lover.

While this doughty resolve was animating the great soul of Mauleverer, Lucy reached her own room, bolted the door, and throwing herself on her bed, burst into a long and bitter paroxysm of tears. So unusual were such visitors to her happy and buoyant temper, that there was something almost alarming in the earnestness and obstinacy with which she now wept.

" What ! " said she, bitterly, " have I placed my affections upon a man of uncertain character ' and is my infatuation so clear, that an acquaintance dare hint at its imprudence ? And yet his manner— his tone ! No, no, there can be no reason for shame in loving him ! " And as she said this, her heart smote her for the coldness of her manner towards Clifford, on his taking leave of her for the evening. " Am I," she thought, weeping yet more vehemently than before— " am I so worldly, so base, as to feel altered towards him the moment I hear a syllable breathed against his name ? Should I not, on the contrary. have clung to his image with a greater love, if he were attacked by others ? But my father, my dear father, and my kind, prudent uncle, something is due to them ; and they would break their hearts if I loved one whom they deemed unworthy. Why should I not summon courage, and tell him of the suspicions respecting him ? One candid word would dispel them Surely it would be but kind in me towards him, to give him an opportunity of disproving all false and dishonouring conjectures. And why this reserve, when so often, by look and hint, if not by open avowal, he has declared that he loves me, and knows—he *must* know—that he is not indifferent to me ? Why does he never speak of his parents, his relations, his home ? "

And Lucy, as she asked this question, drew from a bosom whose hue and shape might have rivalled hers who won Cymon to be wise,[1] a drawing which she herself had secretly made of her lover, and which, though inartificially and even rudely done, yet had caught the inspiration of memory, and breathed the very features and air that were stamped already ineffaceably upon a heart too holy for so sullied an idol. She gazed upon the portrait as if it could answer her question of the original ; and as she looked, and looked, her tears slowly ceased, and her innocent countenance relapsed gradually into its usual and eloquent serenity. Never, perhaps,

[1] See Dryden's poem of *Cymon and Iphigenia.*

could Lucy's own portrait have been taken at a more favourable moment. The unconscious grace of her attitude ; her dress loosened ; the modest and youthful voluptuousness of her beauty ; the tender cheek to which the virgin bloom, banished for awhile, was now all glowingly returning ; the little white soft hand on which that cheek leaned, while the other contained the picture upon which her eyes fed ; the half smile just conjured to her full, red, dewy lips, and gone the moment after, yet again restored ; all made a picture of such enchanting loveliness, that we question whether Shakespeare himself could have fancied an earthly shape more meet to embody the vision of a Miranda or a Viola. The quiet and maiden neatness of the apartment gave effect to the charm ; and there was a poetry even in the snowy furniture of the bed, the shutters partly unclosed and admitting a glimpse of the silver moon, and the solitary lamp just contending with the purer ray of the skies, and so throwing a mixed and softened light around the chamber.

She was yet gazing on the drawing, when a faint stream of music stole through the air beneath her window, and it gradually rose till the sound of a guitar became distinct and clear, suiting with, not disturbing, the moonlit stillness of the night. The gallantry and romance of a former day, though at the time of our story subsiding, were not quite dispelled ; and nightly serenades under the casements of a distinguished beauty were by no means of unfrequent occurrence. But Lucy, as the music floated upon her ear, blushed deeper and deeper, as if it had a dearer source to her heart than ordinary gallantry ; and raising herself on one arm from her incumbent position, she leaned forward to catch the sound with a greater and more unerring certainty.

After a prelude of some moments, a clear and sweet voice accompanied the instrument, and the words of the song were as follows : —

CLIFFORD'S SERENADE.

" There is a world where every night
My spirit meets and walks with thine ;
And hopes—I dare not tell thee—light
Like stars of Love—that world of mine !

Sleep !—to the waking world my heart
Hath now, methinks, a stranger grown
Ah, sleep ! that I may feel thou art
Within *one* world that is my own."

As the music died away, Lucy sank back once more, and the drawing which she held was pressed (with cheeks glowing, though unseen, at the act) to her lips. And though the character of her

lover was uncleared, though she herself had come to no distinct
resolution even to inform him of the rumours against his name, yet
so easily restored was her trust in him, and so soothing the very
thought of his vigilance and his love, that before an hour had passed,
her eyes were closed in sleep ; the drawing was laid, as a spell
against grief, under her pillow ; and in her dreams she murmured
his name, and unconscious of reality and the future, smiled tenderly
as she did so !

CHAPTER XIX.

" Come, the plot thickens ! and another fold
Of the warm cloak of mystery wraps us around.
　　*　　*　　*　　*
　*　　　　*　　　　*　　　　*

And for their loves ?
　Behold the seal is on them !"—' TANNER OF TYBURN.'

WE must not suppose that Clifford's manner and tone were
towards Lucy Brandon such as they seemed to others.
Love refines every roughness ; and that truth which
nurtures tenderness is never barren of grace.   Whatever
the habits and comrades of Clifford's life, he had at heart many good
and generous qualities.   They were not often perceptible it is true—
first, because he was of a gay and reckless turn ; secondly, because
he was not easily affected by any external circumstances ; and
thirdly, because he had the policy to affect among his comrades only
such qualities as were likely to give him influence with them.   Still,
however, his better genius broke out whenever an opportunity presented itself.   Though no " Corsair," romantic and unreal, an
Ossianic shadow becoming more vast in proportion as it recedes
from substance ; though no grandly-imagined lie to the fair proportions of human nature, but an erring man in a very prosaic and
homely world ; Clifford still mingled a certain generosity and
chivalric spirit of enterprise even with the practices of his profession.
Although the name of Lovett, by which he was chiefly known, was
one peculiarly distinguished in the annals of the adventurous, it
had never been coupled with rumours of cruelty or outrage ; and it
was often associated with anecdotes of courage, courtesy, good
humour, or forbearance.   He was one whom a real love was peculiarly calculated to soften and to redeem. The boldness, the candour,
the unselfishness of his temper, were components of nature upon

which affection invariably takes a strong and deep hold. Besides, Clifford was of an eager and aspiring turn; and the same temper and abilities which had in a very few years raised him in influence and popularity far above all the chivalric band with whom he was connected, when once inflamed and elevated by a higher passion, were likely to arouse his ambition from the level of his present pursuits, and reform him, ere too late, into a useful, nay, even an honourable, member of society. We trust that the reader has already perceived that, despite his early circumstances, his manner and address were not such as to unfit him for a lady's love. The comparative refinement of his exterior is easy of explanation, for he possessed a natural and inborn gentility, a quick turn for observation, a ready sense both of the ridiculous and the graceful; and these are materials which are soon and lightly wrought from coarseness into polish. He had been thrown, too, among the leaders and heroes of his band; many not absolutely low in birth, nor debased in habit. He had associated with the Barringtons of the day: gentlemen who were admired at Ranelagh, and made speeches worthy of Cicero when they were summoned to trial. He had played his part in public places; and, as Tomlinson was wont to say after his classic fashion, "the triumphs accomplished in the field had been planned in the ball-room." In short, he was one of those accomplished and elegant highwaymen of whom we yet read wonders, and by whom it would have been delightful to have been robbed: and the aptness of intellect which grew into wit with his friends, softened into sentiment with his mistress. There is something, too, in beauty (and Clifford's person, as we have before said, was possessed of even uncommon attractions) which lifts a beggar into nobility; and there was a distinction in his gait and look which supplied the air of rank, and the tone of courts. Men, indeed, skilled like Mauleverer in the subtleties of manner, might perhaps have easily detected in him the want of that indescribable essence possessed only by persons reared in good society; but that want being shared by so many persons of indisputable birth and fortune, conveyed no particular reproach. To Lucy, indeed, brought up in seclusion, and seeing at Warlock none calculated to refine her taste in the fashion of an air or phrase to a very fastidious standard of perfection, this want was perfectly imperceptible: she remarked in her lover only a figure everywhere unequalled—an eye always eloquent with admiration—a step from which grace could never be divorced—a voice that spoke in a silver key, and uttered flatteries delicate in thought and poetical in word: —even a certain originality of mind, remark, and character, occasionally approaching to the *bizarre*, yet sometimes also to the elevated, possessed a charm for the imagination of a young and not

unenthusiastic female, and contrasted favourably, rather than the
reverse, with the dull insipidity of those she ordinarily saw.   Nor
are we sure that the mystery thrown about him, irksome as it was to
her, and discreditable as it appeared to others, was altogether ineffectual in increasing her love for the adventurer; and thus Fate,
which transmutes in her magic crucible all opposing metals into
that one which she is desirous to produce, swelled the wealth of an
ill-placed and ominous passion by the very circumstances which
should have counteracted and destroyed it.

We are willing, by what we have said, not to defend Clifford, but
to redeem Lucy in the opinion of our readers for loving so unwisely;
and when they remember her youth, her education, her privation of
a mother, of all female friendship, even of the vigilant and unrelaxing care of some protector of the opposite sex, we do not think
that what was so natural will be considered by any inexcusable.

Mauleverer woke the morning after the ball in better health than
usual, and, consequently, more in love than ever.   According to his
resolution the night before, he sat down to write a long letter to
William Brandon : it was amusing and witty as usual; but the wily
nobleman succeeded, under the cover of wit, in conveying to Brandon's mind a serious apprehension lest his cherished matrimonial
project should altogether fail.   The account of Lucy and of Captain
Clifford, contained in the epistle, instilled, indeed, a double portion
of sourness into the professionally acrid mind of the lawyer; and as
it so happened that he read the letter just before attending the court
upon a case in which he was counsel to the crown, the witnesses on
the opposite side of the question felt the full effects of the barrister's
ill-humour.

The case was one in which the defendant had been engaged in
swindling transactions to a very large amount; and, among his
agents and assistants, was a person of the very lowest orders—
but who, seemingly enjoying large connexions, and possessing
natural acuteness and address, appeared to have been of great use
in receiving and disposing of such goods as were fraudulently obtained.   As a witness against the latter person appeared a pawnbroker, who produced certain articles that had been pledged to him
at different times by this humble agent.   Now, Brandon, in examining the guilty go-between, became the more terribly severe,
in proportion as the man evinced that semblance of unconscious
stolidity which the lower orders can so ingeniously assume, and
which is so peculiarly adapted to enrage and to baffle the gentlemen of the bar.   At length, Brandon entirely subduing and
quelling the stubborn hypocrisy of the culprit, the man turned
towards him a look between wrath and beseechingness, muttering :—

"Aha!—*if* so be, Counsellor Brandon, you knew vat I knows, you vould not go for to bully *I* so!"

"And pray, my good fellow, what is it that you know that should make me treat you as if I thought you an honest man?"

The witness had now relapsed into sullenness, and only answered by a sort of grunt. Brandon, who knew well how to sting a witness into communicativeness, continued his questioning, till the witness, rearoused into anger, and, it may be, into indiscretion, said, in a low voice,—

"Hax Mr. Swoppem (the pawnbroker) what I sold 'im on the 15th hof February, exactly twenty-three yearn ago?"

Brandon started back, his lips grew white, he clenched his hands with a convulsive spasm; and while all his features seemed distorted with an earnest, yet fearful intensity of expectation, he poured forth a volley of questions, so incoherent and so irrelevant, that he was immediately called to order by his learned brother on the opposite side. Nothing farther could be extracted from the witness. The pawnbroker was resummoned: he appeared somewhat disconcerted by an appeal to his memory so far back as twenty-three years; but after taking some time to consider, during which the agitation of the usually cold and possessed Brandon was remarkable to all the court, he declared that he recollected no transaction whatsoever with the witness at that time. In vain were all Brandon's efforts to procure a more elucidatory answer. The pawnbroker was impenetrable, and the lawyer was compelled reluctantly to dismiss him. The moment the witness left the box, Brandon sunk into a gloomy abstraction— he seemed quite to forget the business and the duties of the court; and so negligently did he continue to conclude the case, so purposeless was the rest of his examination and cross-examination, that the cause was entirely marred, and a verdict "Not guilty" returned by the jury.

The moment he left the court, Brandon repaired to the pawnbroker's; and after a conversation with Mr. Swoppem, in which he satisfied that honest tradesman that his object was rather to reward than intimidate, Swoppem confessed that, twenty-three years ago, the witness had met him at a public-house in Devereux Court, in company with two other men, and sold him several articles in plate, ornaments, &c. The great bulk of these articles had, of course, long left the pawnbroker's abode; but he still thought a stray trinket or two—not of sufficient worth to be re-set or remodelled, nor of sufficient fashion to find a ready sale—lingered in his drawers. Eagerly, and with trembling hands, did Brandon toss over the motley contents of the mahogany reservoirs which the pawnbroker now submitted to his scrutiny. Nothing on earth is so melancholy a prospect as a pawnbroker's drawer! Those little, quaint, valueless ornaments,—those

H

true-lovers' knots, those oval lockets, those battered rings, girdled by initials, or some brief inscription of regard or of grief,—what tales of past affections, hopes, and sorrows, do they not tell ! But no sentiment of so general a sort ever saddened the hard mind of William Brandon, and now less than at any time could such reflections have occurred to him. Impatiently he threw on the table, one after another, the baubles once hoarded, perchance, with the tenderest respect, till, at length, his eyes sparkled, and with a nervous gripe he seized upon an old ring, which was inscribed with letters, and circled a heart containing hair. The inscription was simply, " W. B. to Julia." Strange and dark was the expression that settled on Brandon's face as he regarded this seemingly worthless trinket. After a moment's gaze, he uttered an inarticulate exclamation, and thrusting it into his pocket, renewed his search. He found one or two other trifles of a similar nature ; one was an ill-done miniature set in silver, and bearing at the back sundry half-effaced letters, which Brandon construed at once (though no other eye could) into "Sir John Brandon, 1635, Ætat. 28 ;" the other was a seal stamped with the noble crest of the house of Brandon, ' A bull's head, ducally crowned and armed, Or.' As soon as Brandon had possessed himself of these treasures, and arrived at the conviction that the place held no more, he assured the conscientious Swoppem of his regard for that person's safety, and rewarded him munificently, and went his way to Bow Street for a warrant against the witness who had commended him to the pawnbroker. On his road thither, a new resolution occurred to him : " Why make all public," he muttered to himself, "if it *can* be avoided ? and it *may* be avoided !" He paused a moment,—then retraced his way to the pawnbroker's, and, after a brief mandate to Mr Swoppem, returned home. In the course of the same evening, the witness we refer to was brought to the lawyer's house by Mr. Swoppem, and there held a long and private conversation with Brandon ; the result of this seemed a compact to their mutual satisfaction, for the man went away safe, with a heavy purse and a light heart, although sundry shades and misgivings did certainly ever and anon cross the latter ; while Brandon flung himself back in his seat, with the triumphant air of one who has accomplished some great measure, and his dark face betrayed in every feature a joyousness and hope, which were unfrequent guests, it must be owned, either to his countenance or his heart.

So good a man of business, however, was William Brandon, that he allowed not the event of that day to defer beyond the night his attentions to his designs for the aggrandisement of his niece and house. By daybreak the next morning he had written to Lord Mauleverer, to his brother, and to Lucy. To the last, his letter, couched in all the anxiety of fondness, and the caution of affectionate experience, was well calculated to occasion that mingled shame and soreness which the wary lawyer rightly judged would be the most effectual enemy to an incipient passion. "I have accidentally heard," he wrote, "from a friend of mine, just arrived from Bath, of the glaring attentions paid to you by a Captain Clifford; I will not, my dearest niece, wound you by repeating what also I heard of your manner in receiving them. I know the ill-nature and the envy of the world; and I do not for a moment imagine that my Lucy, of whom I am so justly proud, would countenance, from a petty coquetry, the advances of one whom she could never marry, or evince to any suitor partiality unknown to her relations, and certainly placed in a quarter which could never receive their approbation. I do not credit the reports of the idle, my dear niece; but if I discredit you must not slight them. I call upon your prudence, your delicacy, your discretion, your sense of right, at once, and effectually, to put a stop to all impertinent rumours. dance with this young man no more; do not let him be of your party in any place of amusement, public or private; avoid even seeing him if you are able, and throw in your manner towards him that decided cold-ness which the world cannot mistake." Much more did the skilful uncle write, but all to the same purpose, and for the furtherance of the same design. His letter to his brother was no less artful. He told him at once that Lucy's preference of the suit of a handsome fortune-hunter was the public talk, and besought him to lose not a moment in quelling the rumour. "You may do so easily," he wrote, "by avoiding the young man; and should he be very importunate, return at once to Warlock; your daughter's welfare must be dearer to you than anything."

To Mauleverer, Brandon replied by a letter which turned first on public matters, and then slid carelessly into the subject of the earl's information.

Among the admonitions which he ventured to give Mauleverer, he dwelt, not without reason, on the want of tact displayed by the earl, in not manifesting that pomp and show which his station in life enabled him to do. "Remember," he urged, "you are not among your equals, by whom unnecessary parade begins to be considered an ostentatious vulgarity. The surest method of dazzling our inferiors is by splendour —not taste. All young persons—all women in particular, are caught by show, and enamoured of magnificence. Assume a greater state, and you will be more talked of; and notoriety wins a woman's heart more than beauty or youth. You have, forgive me, played the boy too long; a certain dignity becomes your manhood: women will not respect you if you suffer yourself to become 'stale and cheap to vulgar company.' You are like a man who has fifty advantages, and uses only one of them to gain his point, when you rely on your conversation and your manner, and throw away the resources of your wealth and your station. Any private gentleman may be amiable and witty; but any private gentleman cannot call to his aid the Aladdin's lamp possessed in England by a wealthy peer. Look to this, my dear lord; Lucy at heart is vain, or she is not a woman. Dazzle her, then,—dazzle! Love may be blind, but it must be made so by excess of light. You have a country-house within a few miles of Bath. Why not take up your abode there instead of in a paltry lodging in the town? Give sumptuous entertainments,—make it necessary for all the world to attend them,—exclude, of course, this Captain Clifford; you will then meet Lucy without a rival. At present, excepting only your title, you fight on a level ground with this adventurer, instead of an eminence from which you could in an instant sweep him away Nay, he is stronger than you; he has the opportunities afforded by a partnership in balls where you cannot appear to advantage; he is, you say, in the first bloom of youth,— he is handsome. Reflect!—your destiny, so far as Lucy is concerned, is in your hands. I turn to other subjects," &c.

As Brandon re-read, ere he signed, this last letter, a bitter smile sat on his harsh, yet handsome features. "If," said he, mentally, "I can effect this object; if Mauleverer does marry this girl, why so much the better that she has another, a fairer, and a more welcome lover. By the great principle of scorn within me, which has enabled me to sneer at what weaker minds adore, and make a footstool of that worldly honour which fools set up as a throne, it would be to me more sweet than fame,—ay, or even than power— to see this fine-spun lord a gibe in the mouths of men,—a cuckold— a cuckold!" and as he said the last word Brandon laughed outright. "And he thinks, too," added he, "that he is sure of my fortune; otherwise, perhaps, he, the goldsmith's descendant, would not dignify our house with his proposals; but he may err there—he may err there;"—and finishing his soliloquy, Brandon finished also his letter by—"Adieu, my dear lord, your most affectionate friend!"

It is not difficult to conjecture the effect produced upon Lucy by Brandon's letter: it made her wretched; she refused for days to go out; she shut herself up in her apartment, and consumed the time in tears and struggles with her own heart. Sometimes, what she conceived to be her duty conquered, and she resolved to forswear her lover; but the night undid the labour of the day: for at night, every night, the sound of her lover's voice, accompanied by music, melted away her resolution, and made her once more all tenderness and trust. The words, too, sung under her window, were especially suited to affect her; they breathed a melancholy which touched her the more from its harmony with her own

thoughts.   One while they complained of absence, at another they
hinted at neglect; but there was always in them a tone of humiliation, not reproach : they bespoke a sense of unworthiness in the
lover, and confessed that even the love was a crime : and in proportion as they owned the want of desert, did Lucy more firmly
cling to the belief that her lover was deserving,

The old squire was greatly disconcerted by his brother's letter.
Though impressed with the idea of self-consequence, and the love
of tolerably pure blood common to most country squires, he was
by no means ambitious for his daughter.   On the contrary, the same
feeling which at Warlock had made him choose his companions
among the inferior gentry, made him averse to the thought of a
son-in-law from the peerage.   In spite of Mauleverer's good nature,
the very ease of the earl annoyed him, and he never felt at home in
his society.   To Clifford he had a great liking ; and having convinced himself that there was nothing to suspect in the young
gentleman, he saw no earthly reason why so agreeable a companion
should not be an agreeable son-in-law.   "If he be poor," thought
the squire, "though he does not seem so, Lucy is rich!"   And
this truism appeared to him to answer every objection.   Nevertheless, William Brandon possessed a remarkable influence over the
weaker mind of his brother ; and the squire, though with great
reluctance, resolved to adopt his advice.   He shut his doors against
Clifford, and when he met him in the streets, instead of greeting
him with his wonted cordiality, he passed him with a hasty "Good
day, captain!" which, after the first day or two, merged into a
distant bow.   Whenever very good-hearted people are rude, and
unjustly so, the rudeness is in the extreme.   The squire felt it so
irksome to be less familiar than heretofore with Clifford, that his
only remaining desire was now to drop him altogether ; and to this
consummation of acquaintance the gradually cooling salute appeared
rapidly approaching.   Meanwhile, Clifford, unable to see Lucy,
shunned by her father, and obtaining in answer to all inquiry rude
looks from the footman, whom nothing but the most resolute command over his muscles prevented him from knocking down, began
to feel, perhaps, for the first time in his life, that an equivocal
character is at least no equivocal misfortune.   To add to his distress,
"the earnings of his previous industry"—we use the expression
cherished by the wise Tomlinson—waxed gradually less and less,
beneath the expenses of Bath ; and the murmuring voices of his
two comrades began already to reproach their chief for his inglorious
idleness, and to hint at the necessity of a speedy exertion

CHAPTER XX.

"WHACKUM   *Look you there, now !   Well, all Europe cannot show a knot
of finer wits and braver gentlemen.*
DINGBOY. *Faith, they are pretty smart men* "

SHADWELL'S ' Scourers.'

THE world of Bath was of a sudden delighted by the intelligence that Lord Mauleverer had gone to Beauvale (the beautiful seat possessed by that nobleman in the neighbourhood of Bath), with the intention of there holding a series of sumptuous entertainments.

The first persons to whom the gay earl announced his "hospitable purpose" were Mr. and Miss Brandon ; he called at their house, and declared his resolution of not leaving it till Lucy (who was in her own room) consented to gratify him with an interview, and a promise to be the queen of his purposed festival.   Lucy, teased by her father, descended to the drawing-room spiritless and pale ; and the earl, struck by the alteration of her appearance, took her hand, and made his inquiries with so interesting and feeling a semblance of kindness, as prepossessed the father, for the first time, in his favour, and touched even the daughter.   So earnest, too, was his request that she would honour his festivities with her presence, and with so skilful a flattery was it conveyed, that the squire undertook to promise the favour in her name ; and when the earl, declaring he was not contented with that promise from another, appealed to Lucy herself, her denial was soon melted into a positive, though a reluctant assent.

Delighted with his success, and more struck with Lucy's loveliness, refined as it was by her paleness, than he had ever been before, Mauleverer left the house, and calculated, with greater accuracy than he had hitherto done, the probable fortune Lucy would derive from her uncle.

No sooner were the cards issued for Lord Mauleverer's *fête*, than nothing else was talked of among the circles which, at Bath, people were pleased to term " the World."

But, in the interim, caps are making, and talk flowing, at Bath ; and when it was found that Lord Mauleverer—the good-natured Lord Mauleverer !—the obliging Lord Mauleverer !—was really going to be exclusive, and out of a thousand acquaintances to select only eight hundred, it is amazing how his popularity deepened into

, respect. Now, then, came anxiety and triumph; she who was asked turned her back upon her who was not,—old friendships dissolved,—Independence wrote letters for a ticket,—and, as England is the freest country in the world, all the Mistresses Hodges and Snodges begged to take the liberty of bringing their youngest daughters.

Leaving the enviable Mauleverer—the god-like occasion of so much happiness and woe, triumph and dejection, ascend with us, O reader, into those elegant apartments over the hairdresser's shop, tenanted by Mr. Edward Pepper, and Mr. Augustus Tomlinson :—the time was that of evening; Captain Clifford had been dining with his two friends; the cloth was removed, and conversation was flowing over a table graced by two bottles of port, a bowl of punch for Mr. Pepper's especial discussion, two dishes of filberts, another of devilled biscuits, and a fourth of three Pomarian crudities, which nobody touched.

The hearth was swept clean, the fire burned high and clear, the curtains were let down, and the light excluded. Our three adventurers and their room seemed the picture of comfort. So thought Mr Pepper; for, glancing round the chamber, and putting his feet upon the fender, he said,—

"Were my portrait to be taken, gentlemen, it is just as I am now that I would be drawn!"

"And," said Tomlinson, cracking his filberts—Tomlinson was fond of filberts—"were I to choose a home, it is in such a home as this that I would be always quartered."

"Ah! gentlemen," said Clifford, who had been for some time silent, "it is more than probable that both your wishes may be heard, and that ye may be drawn, quartered, and something else, too, in the very place of your *desert!*"

"Well!" said Tomlinson, smiling gently, "I am happy to hear you jest again, captain, though it be at our expense."

"Expense!" echoed Ned; "Ay! there's the rub! Who the deuce is to pay the expense of our dinner?"

"And our dinners for the last week?" added Tomlinson ;—"this empty nut looks ominous; it certainly has one grand feature, strikingly resembling my pockets."

"Heigho!" sighed Long Ned—turning his waistcoat commodities inside-out with a significant gesture, while the accomplished Tomlinson, who was fond of plaintive poetry, pointed to the disconsolate vacua, and exclaimed,—

> " E'en while Fashion's brightest arts decoy,
> The heart desponding asks if *this* be joy!"

"In truth, gentlemen," added he, solemnly depositing his nut-crackers on the table, and laying, as was his wont, when about to be luminous, his right finger on his sinister palm—"in truth, gentlemen, affairs are growing serious with us, and it becomes necessary forth-with to devise some safe means of procuring a decent competence."

"I am dunned confoundedly," cried Ned.

"And," continued Tomlinson, "no person of delicacy likes to be subjected to the importunity of vulgar creditors; we must, therefore, raise money for the liquidation of our debts. Captain Lovett, or Clifford, whichever you be styled, we call upon you to assist us in so praiseworthy a purpose."

Clifford turned his eyes first to one, and then on the other, but made no answer.

"*Imprimis*," said Tomlinson, "let us each produce our stock in hand: for my part, I am free to confess—for what shame is there in that poverty which our exertions are about to relieve?—that I have only two guineas, four shillings, and threepence halfpenny!"

"And I," said Long Ned, taking a China ornament from the chimney-piece, and emptying its contents in his hand, "am in a still more pitiful condition. See, I have only three shillings and a bad guinea. I gave the guinea to the waiter at the White Hart, yesterday; the dog brought it back to me to-day, and I was forced to change it with my last shiner. Plague take the thing; I bought it of a Jew for four shillings, and have lost one pound five by the bargain!"

"Fortune frustrates our wisest schemes!" rejoined the moralising Augustus. "Captain, will *you* produce the scanty wrecks of your wealth?"

Clifford, still silent, threw a purse on the table; Augustus care-fully emptied it, and counted out five guineas; an expression of grave surprise settled on Tomlinson's contemplative brow, and extending the coins towards Clifford, he said in a melancholy tone,—

> —"'All your pretty ones?
> Did you say all?'"

A look from Clifford answered the interesting interrogatory.

"These, then," said Tomlinson, collecting in his hand the common wealth—"these, then, are all our remaining treasures!"—As he spoke, he jingled the coins mournfully in his palm, and gazing upon them with a parental air, exclaimed,—

> "Alas! regardless of their doom, the little victims play!"

"Oh, d—— it!' said Ned, "no sentiment! Let us come to

business at once. To tell you the truth, I, for one, am tired of this heiress-hunting, and a man may spend a fortune in the chase before he can win one."

"You despair then, positively, of the widow you have courted so long?" asked Tomlinson.

"Utterly!" rejoined Ned, whose addresses had been limited solely to the dames of the middling class, and who had imagined himself at one time, as he punningly expressed it, sure of a *dear rib* from *Cheapside*. "Utterly; she was very civil to me at first, but when I proposed, asked me, with a blush, for my 'references.'— 'References?' said I; 'why, I want the place of your husband, my charmer, not your footman!'—The dame was inexorable, said she could not take me without a character, but hinted that I might be the lover instead of the bridegroom; and when I scorned the suggestion, and pressed for the parson, she told me point blank, with her unlucky city pronunciation, 'that she would never accompany me to the *h*alter!'"

"Ha, ha, ha!" cried Tomlinson, laughing. "One can scarcely blame the good lady for that. Love rarely brooks such permanent *ties*. But have you no other lady in your eye?"

"Not for matrimony:—all roads but those to the church!"

While this dissolute pair were thus conversing, Clifford, leaning against the wainscot, listened to them with a sick and bitter feeling of degradation, which, till of late days, had been a stranger to his breast. He was at length aroused from his silence by Ned, who, bending forward, and placing his hand upon Clifford's knee, said abruptly,—

"In short, captain, you must lead us once more to glory. We have still our horses, and I keep my mask in my pocket-book, together with my comb. Let us take the road to-morrow night, dash across the country towards Salisbury, and after a short visit in that neighbourhood to a band of old friends of mine—bold fellows, who would have stopped the devil himself when he was at work upon Stonehenge,—make a tour by Reading and Henley, and end by a plunge into London."

"You have spoken well, Ned!" said Tomlinson, approvingly. "Now, noble captain, your opinion?"

"Messieurs," answered Clifford, "I highly approve of your intended excursion, and I only regret that I cannot be your companion."

"Not! and why?" cried Mr. Pepper, amazed.

"Because I have business here that renders it impossible; perhaps, before long, I may join you in London."

"Nay," said Tomlinson, "there is no necessity for our going to

H 2

London, if you wish to remain here ; nor need we at present recur
to so desperate an expedient as the road—a little quiet business at
Bath will answer our purpose , and for my part, as you well know,
I love exerting my wits in some scheme more worthy of them than
the highway ;—a profession meeter for a bully than a man of genius.
Let us then, captain, plan a project of enrichment on the property
of some credulous tradesman ! why have recourse to rough measures,
so long as we can find easy fools ? "

Clifford shook his head. "I will own to you fairly," said he,
"that I cannot at present take a share in your exploits : nay, as
your chief, I must lay my positive commands on you to refrain from
all exercise of your talents at Bath.   Rob, if you please : the world
is before you : but this city is sacred."

"Body o' me ! " cried Ned, colouring, "but this is too good.   I
will not be dictated to in this manner."

" But, sir," answered Clifford, who had learned in his oligarchical
profession the way to command, "but, sir, you shall ; or if you
mutiny, you leave our body, and then will the hangman have no
petty chance of your own.   Come ! come ! ingrate as you are, what
would you be without me ?   How many times have I already saved
that long carcass of thine from the rope, and now would you have
the baseness to rebel ?   Out on you ! "

Though Mr. Pepper was still wroth, he bit his lip in moody
silence, and suffered not his passion to have its way ; while Clifford
rising, after a short pause, continued .   "Look you, Mr. Pepper,
you know my commands ; consider them peremptory.   I wish you
success, and plenty !   Farewell, gentlemen ! "

"Do you leave us already ? " cried Tomlinson.   "You are
offended."

"Surely not ! " answered Clifford, retreating to the door.   "But
an engagement elsewhere, you know ! "

"Ay, I take you ! " said Tomlinson, following Clifford out of the
room, and shutting the door after him.

"Ay, I take you ! " added he, in a whisper, as he arrested Clifford
at the head of the stairs.   "But tell me, how do you get on with the
heiress ? "

Smothering that sensation at his heart which made Clifford, reckless as he was, enraged and ashamed, whenever, through the lips of
his comrades, there issued any allusion to Lucy Brandon, the chief
replied, " I fear, Tomlinson, that I am already suspected by the old
squire !   All of a sudden, he avoids me, shuts his door against me ;
Miss Brandon goes nowhere : and even if she did, what could I
expect from her after this sudden change in the father ? "

Tomlinson looked blank and disconcerted.   "But," said he, after a moment's silence, "why not put a good face on the matter? walk up to the squire, and ask him the reason of his unkindness?"

"Why, look you, my friend; I am bold enough with all others, but this girl has made me as bashful as a maid in all that relates to herself. Nay, there are moments when I think I can conquer all selfish feeling, and rejoice for her sake that she has escaped me. Could I but see her once more—I could—yes! I feel—I feel I could—resign her for ever!"

"Humph!" said Tomlinson; "and what is to become of *us?* Really, my captain, your sense of duty should lead you to exert yourself; your friends starve before your eyes, while you are shilly-shallying about your mistress. Have you no bowels for friendship?"

"A truce with this nonsense!" said Clifford, angrily.

"It is sense,—sober sense,—and sadness too," rejoined Tomlinson. "Ned is discontented, our debts are imperious. Suppose, now,—just suppose,—that we take a moonlight flitting from Bath, will that tell well for you whom we leave behind? Yet this we must do, if you do not devise some method of refilling our purses. Either, then, consent to join us in a scheme meet for our wants, or pay our debts in this city, or fly with us to London, and dismiss all thoughts of that love which is so seldom friendly to the projects of ambition."

Notwithstanding the manner in which Tomlinson made this three-fold proposition, Clifford could not but acknowledge the sense and justice contained in it; and a glance at the matter sufficed to show how ruinous to his character, and, therefore, to his hopes, would be the flight of his comrades and the clamour of their creditors.

"You speak well, Tomlinson," said he, hesitating; "and yet for the life of me I cannot aid you in any scheme which may disgrace us by detection. Nothing can reconcile me to the apprehension of Miss Brandon's discovering who and what was her suitor."

"I feel for you," said Tomlinson, "but give me and Pepper at least permission to shift for ourselves; trust to my known prudence for finding some method to raise the wind without creating a dust: in other words—(this cursed Pepper makes one so vulgar!)—of preying on the public without being discovered."

"I see no alternative," answered Clifford, reluctantly, "but, if possible, be quiet for the present; bear with me for a few days longer, give me only sufficient time once more to see Miss Brandon, and I will engage to extricate you from your difficulties!"

"Spoken like yourself, frankly and nobly!" replied Tomlinson: "no one has a greater confidence in your genius, once excited, than I have!"

So saying, the pair shook hands and parted. Tomlinson rejoined Mr. Pepper.

"Well, have you settled anything?" quoth the latter.

"Not exactly; and though Lovett has promised to exert himself in a few days, yet, as the poor man is in love, and his genius under a cloud, I have little faith in his promises."

"And I have none!" said Pepper; "besides, time presses! A few days!—a few devils! We are certainly scented here, and I walk about like a barrel of beer at Christmas, under hourly apprehension of being *tapped!*"

"It is very strange," said the philosophic Augustus; "but I think there is an instinct in tradesmen by which they can tell a rogue at first sight; and I can get (dress I ever so well) no more credit with my laundress than my friends the Whigs can with the people."

"In short, then," said Ned, "we must recur at once to the road; and on the day after to-morrow there will be an excellent opportunity: the old earl with the hard name gives a breakfast, or feast, or some such mummery. I understand people will stay till after nightfall; let us watch our opportunity, we are famously mounted, and some carriage later than the general string may furnish us with all our hearts can desire!"

"Bravo!" cried Tomlinson, shaking Mr. Pepper heartily by the hand; "I give you joy of your ingenuity, and you may trust to me to make our peace afterwards with Lovett. Any enterprise that seems to him gallant he is always willing enough to forgive; and as he never practises any other branch of the profession than that of the road,—(for which I confess that I think him foolish,)—he will be more ready to look over our exploits in that line than in any other more subtle but less heroic."

"Well, I leave it to you to propitiate the cove or not, as you please; and now that we have settled the main point, let us finish the lush!"

"And," added Augustus, taking a pack of cards from the chimney-piece, "we can in the meanwhile have a quiet game at cribbage for shillings."

"Done!" cried Ned, clearing away the dessert.

If the redoubted hearts of Mr. Edward Pepper, and that Ulysses of robbers, Augustus Tomlinson, beat high as the hours brought on Lord Mauleverer's *fête*, their leader was not without anxiety and expectation for the same event. He was uninvited, it is true, to the gay scene; but he had heard in public that Miss Brandon, recovered from her late illness, was certainly to be there; and Clifford, torn with suspense, and eager once more, even if for the last time, to see the only person who had ever pierced his soul with a keen sense of his errors, or crimes, resolved to risk all obstacles, and meet her at Mauleverer's.

"My life," said he, as he sat alone in his apartment, eyeing the falling embers of his still and lethargic fire, "may soon approach its termination; it is, indeed, out of the chances of things that I can long escape the doom of my condition; and when, as a last hope to raise myself from my desperate state into respectability and reform, I came hither, and meditated purchasing independence by marriage, I was blind to the cursed rascality of the action! Happy, after all, that my intentions were directed against one whom I so soon and so adoringly learned to love! Had I wooed one whom I loved less, I might not have scrupled to deceive her into marriage. As it is!—well!—it is idle in me to think thus of my resolution, when I have not even the option to choose; when her father, perhaps, has already lifted the veil from my assumed dignities, and the daughter already shrinks in horror from my name. Yet I will see her! I will look once more upon that angel face—I will hear from her own lips the confession of her scorn—I will see that bright eye flash hatred upon me, and I can then turn once more to my fatal career, and forget that I have ever repented that it was begun. Yet, what else could have been my alternative? Friendless, homeless, nameless—an orphan, worse than an orphan—the son of a harlot, my father even unknown! yet cursed with early aspirings and restlessness, and a half glimmering of knowledge, and an entire lust of whatever seemed enterprise—what wonder that I chose anything rather than daily labour and perpetual contumely? After all, the fault is in fortune, and the world, not me! Oh, Lucy! had I but been born in your sphere, had I but possessed the claim to merit you, what would I not have done, and dared, and conquered, for your sake!"

Such, or similar to these, were the thoughts of Clifford during the interval between his resolution of seeing Lucy and the time of effecting it. The thoughts were of no pleasing, though of an exciting nature; nor were they greatly soothed by the ingenious occupation of cheating himself into the belief that, if he was a highwayman, it was altogether the fault of the highways.

CHAPTER XXI.

"DREAM. *Let me but see her, dear Leontius.*"
'HUMOROUS LIEUTENANT.'

"HEMPSKIRKE. *It was the fellow, sure.*
WOLFORT. *What are you, sirrah?*"—'BEGGAR'S BUSH.'

 THOU divine spirit, that burnest in every breast, inciting
each with the sublime desire to be *fine!* that stirrest up
the great to become little in order to seem greater, and
that makest a duchess woo insult for a voucher! Thou
that delightest in so many shapes, multifarious, yet the same ; spirit
that makest the high despicable, and the lord meaner than his valet!
equally great whether thou cheatest a friend, or cuttest a father!
lackering all thou touchest with a bright vulgarity, that thy votaries
imagine to be gold!—thou that sendest the few to fashionable balls
and the many to fashionable novels ;—that smitest even Genius as
well as Folly, making the favourites of the Gods boast an acquaintance they have not with the graces of a mushroom peerage, rather
than the knowledge they have of the Muses of an eternal Helicon!
—thou that leavest in the great ocean of our manners no dry spot
for the foot of independence ;—that pallest on the jaded eye with a
moving and girdling panorama of daubed vilenesses, and fritterest
away the souls of free-born Britons into a powder smaller than the
angels which dance in myriads on a pin's point. Whether, O
spirit! thou callest thyself Fashion, or Ton, or Ambition, or Vanity,
or Cringing, or Cant, or any title equally lofty and sublime—would
that from thy wings we could gain but a single plume! Fain
would we, in fitting strain, describe the festivities of that memorable
day, when the benevolent Lord Mauleverer received and blessed the
admiring universe of Bath.

But to be less poetical, as certain writers say, when they have been
writing nonsense—but to be less poetical, and more exact, the morning, though in the depth of winter, was bright and clear, and Lord
Mauleverer found himself in particularly good health Nothing
could be better planned than the whole of his arrangements : unlike
those which are ordinarily chosen for the express reason of being
as foreign as possible to the nature of our climate, all at Lord
Mauleverer's were made suitable to a Greenland atmosphere. The
temples and summer-houses, interspersed through the grounds, were

fitted up, some as Esquimaux huts, others as Russian pavilions; fires were carefully kept up; the musicians, Mauleverer took care should have as much wine as they pleased; they were set skilfully in places where they were unseen, but where they could be heard. One or two temporary buildings were erected for those who loved dancing; and as Mauleverer, miscalculating on the principles of human nature, thought *gentlemen* might be averse from ostentatious exhibition, he had hired persons to skate minuets and figures of eight upon his lakes, for the amusement of those who were fond of skating. All people who would be kind enough to dress in strange costumes, and make odd noises, which they called singing, the earl had carefully engaged, and planted in the best places for making them look still stranger than they were.

There was also plenty to eat, and more than plenty to drink. Mauleverer knew well that our countrymen and countrywomen, whatever be their rank, like to have their spirits exalted. In short, the whole *déjeûner* was so admirably contrived, that it was probable the guests would not look much more melancholy during the amusements, than they would have done had they been otherwise engaged at a funeral.

Lucy and the squire were among the first arrivals.

Mauleverer, approaching the father and daughter with his most courtly manner, insisted on taking the latter under his own escort, and being her cicerone through the round of preparations.

As the crowd thickened, and it was observed how gallant were the attentions testified towards Lucy by the host, many and envious were the whispers of the guests! Those good people, naturally angry at the thought that two individuals should be married, divided themselves into two parties; one abused Lucy, and the other Lord Mauleverer; the former vituperated *her* art, the latter *his* folly. "I thought she would play her cards well—deceitful creature!" said the one. "January and May," muttered the other; "the man's sixty!" It was noticeable that the party against Lucy was chiefly composed of ladies, that against Mauleverer of men; that conduct must indeed be heinous which draws down the indignation of one's own sex!

Unconscious of her crimes, Lucy moved along, leaning on the arm of the gallant earl, and languidly smiling, with her heart far away, at his endeavours to amuse her. There was something interesting in the mere contrast of the pair; so touching seemed the beauty of the young girl, with her delicate cheek, maiden form, drooping eyelid, and quiet simplicity of air, in comparison to the worldly countenance and artificial grace of her companion.

After some time, when they were in a sequestered part of the

grounds, Mauleverer, observing that none were near, entered a rude
hut ; and so fascinated was he at that moment by the beauty of his
guest, and so meet to him seemed the opportunity of his confession,
that he with difficulty suppressed the avowal rising to his lips, and
took the more prudent plan of first sounding and preparing, as it
were, the way.

"I cannot tell you, my dear Miss Brandon," said he, slightly
pressing the beautiful hand leaning on his arm, "how happy I am
to see you the guest—the queen, rather—of my house ! Ah ! could
the bloom of youth return with its feelings ! Time is never so cruel
as when, while stealing from us the power to please, he leaves us in
full vigour the unhappy privilege to be charmed ! "

Mauleverer expected at least a blushing contradiction to the
implied application of a sentiment so affectingly expressed : he was
disappointed. Lucy, less alive than usual to the sentimental, or
its reverse, scarcely perceived his meaning, and answered simply,
"That it was very true." "This comes of being, like my friend
Burke, too refined for one's audience," thought Mauleverer, wincing
a little from the unexpected reply. "And yet!" he resumed, "I
would not forego my power to admire, futile—nay, painful as it is.
Even now, while I gaze on you, my heart tells me that the pleasure
I enjoy, it is at your command, at once, and for ever, to blight into
misery ; but while it tells me, I gaze on ! "

Lucy raised her eyes, and something of her natural archness
played in their expression.

"I believe, my lord," said she, moving from the hut, "that it
would be better to join your guests : walls have ears ; and what
would be the gay Lord Mauleverer's self-reproach, if he heard again
of his fine compliments to——?"

"The most charming person in Europe ! " cried Mauleverer
vehemently, and the hand which he before touched he now clasped :
at that instant Lucy saw opposite to her, half hid by a copse of ever-
greens, the figure of Clifford His face, which seemed pale and wan,
was not directed towards the place where she stood ; and he evidently did not perceive Mauleverer or herself, yet so great was the
effect that this glimpse of him produced on Lucy, that she trembled
violently, and, unconsciously uttering a faint cry, snatched her hand
from Mauleverer.

The earl started, and, catching the expression of her eyes, turned
instantly towards the spot to which her gaze seemed riveted. He
had not heard the rustling of the boughs, but he saw, with his
habitual quickness of remark, that they still trembled, as if lately
displaced ; and he caught through their interstices the glimpse of a
receding figure He sprang forward with an agility very uncommon

to his usual movements; but before he gained the copse, every
vestige of the intruder had vanished.

What slaves we are to the moment! As Mauleverer turned back
to rejoin Lucy, who, agitated almost to fainting, leaned against the
rude wall of the hut, he would as soon have thought of flying as of
making that generous offer of self, &c. which the instant before he
had been burning to render Lucy. The vain are always sensitively
jealous, and Mauleverer, remembering Clifford, and Lucy's blushes
in dancing with him, instantly accounted for her agitation and its
cause. With a very grave air he approached the object of his late
adoration, and requested to know if it were not some abrupt intruder
that had occasioned her alarm. Lucy, scarcely knowing what she
said, answered in a low voice, "That it was, indeed!" and begged
instantly to rejoin her father. Mauleverer offered his arm with
great dignity, and the pair passed into the frequented part of the
grounds, where Mauleverer once more brightened into smiles and
courtesy to all around him.

"He is certainly accepted!" said Mr. Shrewd to Lady Simper.

"What an immense match for the girl!" was Lady Simper's
reply.

Amidst the music, the dancing, the throng, the noise, Lucy found
it easy to recover herself; and, disengaging her arm from Lord
Mauleverer, as she perceived her father, she rejoined the squire, and
remained a patient listener to his remarks till, late in the noon, it
became an understood matter that people were expected to go into
a long room in order to eat and drink. Mauleverer, now alive to
the duties of his situation, and feeling exceedingly angry with Lucy,
was more reconciled than he otherwise might have been to the
etiquette which obliged him to select for the object of his hospitable
cares an old dowager duchess, instead of the beauty of the *fête;* but
he took care to point out to the squire the places appointed for himself and daughter, which were, though at some distance from the
earl, under the providence of his vigilant survey.

While Mauleverer was deifying the Dowager Duchess, and
refreshing his spirits with a chicken, and a medicinal glass of
Madeira, the conversation near Lucy turned, to her infinite dismay,
upon Clifford. Some one had seen him in the grounds, booted, and
in a riding undress,—(in *that* day, people seldom rode and danced
in the same conformation of coat,)—and as Mauleverer was a precise
person about those little matters of *etiquette*, this negligence of
Clifford's made quite a subject of discussion. By degrees the conversation changed into the old inquiry as to who this Captain
Clifford was; and just as it had reached that point, it reached also
the gently deafened ears of Lord Mauleverer.

"Pray, my lord," said the old duchess, "since he is one of your guests, you, who know who and what every one is, can possibly inform us of the real family of this beautiful Mr. Clifford?"

"One of my guests, did you say?" answered Mauleverer, irritated greatly beyond his usual quietness of manner: "really, your grace does me wrong. He may be a guest of my valet, but he assuredly is not mine; and should I encounter him, I shall leave it to my valet to give him his *congé* as well as his invitation!"

Mauleverer, heightening his voice as he observed athwart the table an alternate paleness and flush upon Lucy's face, which stung all the angrier passions, generally torpid in him, into venom, looked round, on concluding, with a haughty and sarcastic air: so loud had been his tone, so pointed the insult, and so dead the silence at the table while he spoke, that every one felt that the affront must be carried at once to Clifford's hearing, should he be in the room. And after Mauleverer had ceased, there was an universal nervous and indistinct expectation of an answer and a scene; all was still, and it soon became certain that Clifford was not in the apartment. When Mr. Shrewd had fully convinced himself of this fact—(for there was a daring spirit about Clifford which few wished to draw upon themselves),—that personage broke the pause by observing that no man, who pretended to be a gentleman, would intrude himself, unasked and unwelcome, into any society; and Mauleverer, catching up the observation, said—(drinking wine at the same time with Mr. Shrewd),—that undoubtedly such conduct fully justified the rumours respecting Mr. Clifford, and utterly excluded him from that rank to which it was before more than suspected he had no claim.

So luminous and satisfactory an opinion from such an authority, once broached, was immediately and universally echoed; and, long before the repast was over, it seemed to be tacitly agreed that Captain Clifford should be sent to Coventry, and if he murmured at the exile, he would have no right to insist upon being sent thence to the devil.

The good old squire, mindful of his former friendship for Clifford, and not apt to veer, was about to begin a speech on the occasion, when Lucy, touching his arm, implored him to be silent; and so ghastly was the paleness of her cheek while she spoke, that the squire's eyes, obtuse as he generally was, opened at once to the real secret of her heart. As soon as the truth flashed upon him, he wondered, recalling Clifford's great personal beauty and marked attentions, that it had not flashed upon him sooner; and leaning back on his chair, he sunk into one of the most unpleasant reveries he had ever conceived.

At a given signal the music for the dancers recommenced, and, at a hint to that effect from the host, persons rose without ceremony to repair to other amusements, and suffer such guests as had hitherto been excluded from eating to occupy the place of the relinquishers. Lucy, glad to escape, was one of the first to resign her situation, and with the squire she returned to the grounds. During the banquet, evening had closed in, and the scene now really became fairy-like and picturesque ;—lamps hung from many a tree, reflecting the light through the richest and softest hues,—the music itself sounded more musically than during the day,—gipsy-tents were pitched at wild corners and copses, and the bright wood-fires burning in them blazed merrily upon the cold yet cheerful air of the increasing night. The view was really novel and inviting ; and as it had been an understood matter that ladies were to bring furs, cloaks, and boots, all those who thought they looked well in such array made little groups, and scattered themselves about the grounds and in the tents. They, on the contrary, in whom "the purple light of love" was apt by the frost to be propelled from the cheeks to the central ornament of the face, or who thought a fire in a room quite as agreeable as a fire in a tent, remained within, and contemplated the scene through the open windows.

Lucy longed to return home, nor was the squire reluctant ; but, unhappily, it wanted an hour to the time at which the carriage had been ordered, and she mechanically joined a group of guests, who had persuaded the good-natured squire to forget his gout, and venture forth to look at the illuminations. Her party was soon joined by others, and the group gradually thickened into a crowd ; the throng was stationary for a few minutes before a little temple, in which fireworks had just commenced an additional attraction to the scene. Opposite to this temple, as well as in its rear, the walks and trees had been purposely left in comparative darkness, in order to heighten the effect of the fireworks.

" I declare," said Lady Simper, glancing down one of the alleys which seemed to stretch away into blackness— " I declare it seems quite a lovers' walk ! how kind in Lord Mauleverer !—such a delicate attention——"

" To your ladyship ! " added Mr. Shrewd with a bow.

While, one of this crowd, Lucy was vacantly eyeing the long trains of light which ever and anon shot against the sky, she felt her hand suddenly seized, and at the same time a voice whispered, " For God's sake, read this now and grant my request ! "

The voice, which seemed to rise from the very heart of the speaker, Lucy knew at once ; she trembled violently, and remained for some minutes with eyes which did not dare to look from the

ground. A note she felt had been left in her hand, and the agonized
and earnest tone of that voice, which was dearer to her ear than the
fulness of all music, made her impatient yet afraid to read it. As
she recovered courage she looked around, and seeing that the attention of all was bent on the fireworks, and that her father, ·in
particular, leaning on his cane, seemed to enjoy the spectacle
with a child's engrossed delight, she glided softly away, and entering
unperceived one of the alleys, she read, by a solitary lamp that
burned at its entrance, the following lines written in pencil and in
a hurried hand, apparently upon a leaf torn from a pocket-book :—

"I implore—I entreat you, Miss Brandon, to see me, if but for a
moment. I purpose to tear myself away from the place in which
you reside—to go abroad—to leave even the spot hallowed by your
footstep. After this night, my presence, my presumption, will
degrade you no more. But this night, for mercy's sake, see me, or
I shall go mad! I will but speak to you one instant : this is all I
ask. If you grant me this prayer, the walk to the left where you
stand, at the entrance to which there is one purple lamp, will afford
an opportunity to your mercy. A few yards down that walk I will
meet you—none can see or hear us. Will you grant this? I know
not—I dare not think : but under any case, your name shall be the
last upon my lips.   P.C."

As Lucy read this hurried scrawl, she glanced towards the lamp
above her, and saw that she had accidentally entered the very walk
indicated in the note. She paused—she hesitated ;—the impropriety
—the singularity of the request, darted upon her at once ; on the
other hand, the anxious voice still ringing in her ear, the incoherent
vehemence of the note, the risk, the opprobrium Clifford had incurred,
solely—her heart whispered—to see her, all aided her simple temper,
her kind feelings, and her love for the petitioner, in inducing her to
consent. She cast one glance behind,—all seemed occupied with far
other thoughts than that of notice towards her ; she looked anxiously
before,—all looked gloomy and indistinct ; but suddenly, at some
little distance, she descried a dark figure in motion. She felt her
knees shake under her, her heart beat violently ; she moved onward
a few paces, again paused, and looked back ; the figure before her
moved as in approach, she resumed courage, and advanced—the
figure was by her side.

"How generous, how condescending, is this goodness in Miss
Brandon!" said the voice, which so struggled with secret and strong
emotion, that Lucy scarcely recognised it as Clifford's. "I did not
dare to expect it ; and now—now that I meet you ——" Clifford

paused, as if seeking words ; and Lucy, even through the dark, perceived that her strange companion was powerfully excited ; she waited for him to continue, but observing that he walked on in silence, she said, though with a trembling voice, " Indeed, Mr. Clifford, I fear that it is very, very improper in me to meet you thus ; nothing but the strong expressions in your letter—and—and —in short, my fear that you meditated some desperate design, at which I could not guess, caused me to yield to your wish for an interview." She paused, and Clifford, still preserving silence, she added, with some little coldness in her tone, " If you have really aught to say to me, you must allow me to request that you speak it quickly. This interview, you must be sensible, ought to end almost as soon as it begins."

" Hear me, then ! " said Clifford, mastering his embarrassment, and speaking in a firm and clear voice—" is that true, which I have but just heard,—is it true that I have been spoken of in your presence in terms of insult and affront ? "

It was now for Lucy to feel embarrassed ; fearful to give pain, and yet anxious that Clifford should know, in order that he might disprove, the slight and the suspicion which the mystery around him drew upon his name, she faltered between the two feelings, and, without satisfying the latter, succeeded in realising the fear of the former.

" Enough ! " said Clifford, in a tone of deep mortification, as his quick ear caught and interpreted, yet more humiliatingly than the truth, the meaning of her stammered and confused reply. " Enough ! I see that it is true, and that the only human being in the world to whose good opinion I am not indifferent has been a witness of the insulting manner in which others have dared to speak of me ! "

" But," said Lucy, eagerly, " why give the envious or the idle any excuse ? Why not suffer your parentage and family to be publicly known ? Why are you here "—(and her voice sunk into a lower key)—" this very day, unasked, and therefore subject to the cavils of all who think the poor distinction of an invitation an honour ? Forgive me, Mr. Clifford, perhaps I offend,—I hurt you by speaking thus frankly ; but your good name rests with yourself, and your friends cannot but feel angry that you should trifle with it."

" Madam ! " said Clifford, and Lucy's eyes, now growing accustomed to the darkness, perceived a bitter smile upon his lips, " my name, good or ill, is an object of little care to me. I have read of philosophers who pride themselves in placing no value in the opinions of the world. Rank me among that sect—but I am, I own I am, anxious that you alone, of all the world, should not despise me ;— and now that I feel you do—that you must—everything worth living or hoping for is past ! "

"Despise you!" said Lucy, and her eyes filled with tears—
"indeed you wrong me and yourself. But listen to me, Mr. Clifford :
I have seen, it is true, but little of the world, yet I have seen enough
to make me wish I could have lived in retirement for ever ; the
rarest quality among either sex, though it is the simplest, seems to
me, good-nature ; and the only occupation of what are termed
fashionable people appears to be speaking ill of one another :
nothing gives such a scope to scandal as mystery ; nothing disarms
it like openness. I know—your friends know, Mr. Clifford, that
your character can bear inspection ; and I believe, for my own part,
the same of your family. Why not, then, declare who and what
you are?"

"That candour would indeed be my best defender," said Clifford,
in a tone which ran displeasingly through Lucy's ear ; "but in
truth, madam, I repeat, I care not one drop of this worthless blood
what men say of me ; that time has passed and for ever : perhaps it
never keenly existed for me—no matter. I came hither, Miss
Brandon, not wasting a thought on these sickening fooleries, or on
the hoary idler by whom they are given ! I came hither only once
more to see you—to hear you speak—to watch you move—to tell
you—(and the speaker's voice trembled, so as to be scarcely audible)
—to tell you, if any reason for the disclosure offered itself, that I
have had the boldness—the crime to love—to love—O God ! to
adore you ! and then to leave you for ever !"

Pale, trembling, scarcely preserved from falling by the tree against
which she leaned, Lucy listened to this abrupt avowal.

"Dare I touch this hand," continued Clifford, as he knelt and
took it, timidly and reverently : "you know not, you cannot dream,
how unworthy is he who thus presumes—yet, not all unworthy, while
he is sensible of so deep, so holy a feeling as that which he bears to
you. God bless you, Miss Brandon !—Lucy, God bless you!—And
if, hereafter, you hear me subjected to still blacker suspicions, or
severer scrutiny, than that which I now sustain—if even your charity
and goodness can find no defence for me,—if the suspicion become
certainty, and the scrutiny end in condemnation, believe, at least,
that circumstances have carried me beyond my nature ; and that
under fairer auspices I might have been other than I am !" Lucy's
tear dropped upon Clifford's hand, as he spoke ; and while his heart
melted within him as he felt it, and knew his own desperate and
unredeemed condition, he added,—

"Every one courts you—the proud, the rich, the young, the high-
born, all are at your feet ! You will select one of that number for
your husband : may he watch over you as I would have done !—love
you as I do he *cannot!* Yes, I repeat it!" continued Clifford,

vehemently, "he *cannot!* None amidst the gay, happy, silken crowd of your equals and followers *can* feel for you that single and overruling passion, which makes you to me what all combined—country, power, wealth, reputation, an honest name, peace, common safety, the quiet of the common air, alike the least blessing and the greatest—are to all others! Once more, may God in heaven watch over you and preserve you! I tear myself, on leaving you, from all that cheers, or blesses, or raises, or might have saved me!—Farewell!"

The hand which Lucy had relinquished to her strange suitor was pressed ardently to his lips, dropped in the same instant, and she knew that she was once more alone.

But Clifford, hurrying rapidly through the trees, made his way towards the nearest gate which led from Lord Mauleverer's domain; when he reached it, a crowd of the more elderly guests occupied the entrance, and one of these was a lady of such distinction, that Mauleverer, in spite of his aversion to any superfluous exposure to the night air, had obliged himself to conduct her to her carriage. He was in a very ill humour with this constrained politeness, especially as the carriage was very slow in relieving him of his charge, when he saw, by the lamplight, Clifford passing near him, and winning his way to the gate. Quite forgetting his worldly prudence which should have made him averse to scenes with any one, especially with a flying enemy, and a man with whom, if he believed aright, little glory was to be gained in conquest, much less in contest; and only remembering Clifford's rivalship, and his own hatred towards him for the presumption, Mauleverer, uttering a hurried apology to the lady on his arm, stepped forward, and opposing Clifford's progress, said, with a bow of tranquil insult, "Pardon me, sir, but is it at *my* invitation, or that of one of my servants, that you have honoured me with your company this day?"

Clifford's thoughts at the time of this interruption were of that nature before which all petty misfortunes shrink into nothing; if, therefore, he started for a moment at the earl's address, he betrayed no embarrassment in reply, but bowing with an air of respect, and taking no notice of the affront implied in Mauleverer's speech, he answered,—

"Your lordship has only to deign a glance at my dress, to see that I have not intruded myself on your grounds, with the intention of claiming your hospitality. The fact is, and I trust to your lordship's courtesy to admit the excuse, that I leave this neighbourhood to-morrow, and for some length of time. A person whom I was very anxious to see before I left was one of your lordship's

guests ; I heard this, and knew that I should have no other opportunity of meeting the person in question before my departure ; and
I must now throw myself on the well-known politeness of Lord
Mauleverer, to pardon a freedom originating in a business very
much approaching to a necessity."

Lord Mauleverer's address to Clifford had congregated an immediate crowd of eager and expectant listeners, but so quietly respectful and really gentlemanlike were Clifford's air and tone in excusing
himself, that the whole throng were smitten with a sudden disappointment.

Lord Mauleverer himself, surprised by the temper and deport-
ment of the unbidden guest, was at a loss for one moment ; and
Clifford was about to take advantage of that moment and glide
away, when Mauleverer, with a second bow, more civil than the
former one, said :

"I cannot but be happy, sir, that my poor place has afforded
you any convenience ; but, if I am not very impertinent, will you
allow me to inquire the name of my guest with whom you required
a meeting ? "

"My lord," said Clifford, drawing himself up, and speaking
gravely and sternly, though still with a certain deference—"I need
not surely point out to your lordship's good sense and good feeling, that your very question implies a doubt, and, consequently, an
affront, and that the tone of it is not such as to justify that con-
cession on my part which the farther explanation you require would
imply ! "

Few spoken sarcasms could be so bitter as that silent one which
Mauleverer could command by a smile, and, with this complimentary expression on his thin lips and raised brow, the earl
answered : "Sir, I honour the skill testified by your reply ; it must
be the result of a profound experience in these affairs I wish you,
sir, a very good night ; and the next time you favour me with a
visit, I am quite sure that your motives for so indulging me will be
no less creditable to you than at present."

With these words, Mauleverer turned to rejoin his fair charge.
But Clifford was a man who had seen in a short time a great deal
of the world, and knew tolerably well the theories of society, if not
the practice of its minutiæ ; moreover, he was of an acute and
resolute temper, and these properties of mind, natural and acquired,
told him that he was now in a situation in which it had become
more necessary to defy than to conciliate. Instead therefore of
retiring he walked deliberately up to Mauleverer, and said :

"My lord, I shall leave it to the judgment of your guests to
decide whether you have acted the part of a nobleman and a

gentleman in thus, in your domains, insulting one who has given you such explanation of his trespass as would fully excuse him in the eyes of all considerate or courteous persons. I shall also leave it to them to decide whether the tone of your inquiry allowed me to give you any farther apology. But I shall take it upon *myself*, my lord, to demand from *you* an immediate explanation of your last speech."

"Insolent!" cried Mauleverer, colouring with indignation, and almost for the first time in his life losing absolute command over his temper; "do you bandy words with me?—Begone, or I shall order my servants to thrust you forth!"

"Begone, sir!—begone!" cried several voices in echo to Mauleverer, from those persons who deemed it now high time to take part with the powerful.

Clifford stood his ground, gazing around with a look of angry and defying contempt, which, joined to his athletic frame, his dark and fierce eye, and a heavy riding-whip, which, as if mechanically, he half raised, effectually kept the murmurers from proceeding to violence.

"Poor pretender to breeding and to sense!" said he, disdainfully turning to Mauleverer; "with one touch of this whip I could shame you for ever, or compel you to descend from the level of your rank to that of mine, and the action would be but a mild return to your language. But I love rather to teach you than to correct. According to my creed, my lord, he conquers most in good breeding who forbears the most—*scorn* enables *me* to forbear!—Adieu!"

With this, Clifford turned on his heel and strode away. A murmur, approaching to a groan, from the younger or sillier part of the parasites (the mature and the sensible have no extra emotion to throw away), followed him as he disappeared.

CHAPTER XXII.

"Outlaw. *Stand, sir, and throw us that you have about you!*
Val. *Ruffians, forego that rude, uncivil touch!*"

'The Two Gentlemen of Verona.'

N leaving the scene in which he had been so unwelcome a guest, Clifford hastened to the little inn where he had left his horse. He mounted and returned to Bath. His thoughts were absent, and he unconsciously suffered the horse to direct its course whither it pleased. This was naturally towards the nearest halting-place which the animal remembered;

and this halting-place was at that illustrious tavern, in the suburbs of the town, in which we have before commemorated Clifford's re-election to the dignity of chief. It was a house of long-established reputation; and here news of any of the absent confederates was always to be obtained. This circumstance, added to the excellence of its drink, its ease, and the electric chain of early habits, rendered it a favourite haunt, even despite their present gay and modish pursuits, with Tomlinson and Pepper; and here, when Clifford sought the pair at unseasonable hours, was he for the most part sure to find them. As his meditations were interrupted by the sudden stopping of his horse beneath the well-known sign, Clifford, muttering an angry malediction on the animal, spurred it onward in the direction of his own home. He had already reached the end of the street, when his resolution seemed to change, and muttering to himself, "Ay, I might as well arrange this very night for our departure!" he turned his horse's head backward, and was once more at the tavern door. He threw the bridle over an iron railing, and knocking with a peculiar sound at the door, was soon admitted.

"Are —— and —— here?" asked he of the old woman, as he entered, mentioning the cant words by which, among friends, Tomlinson and Pepper were usually known. "They are both gone on the sharps to-night," replied the old lady, lifting her unsnuffed candle to the face of the speaker with an intelligent look; "Oliver[1] is sleepy, and the lads will take advantage of his nap."

"Do you mean," answered Clifford, replying in the same key, which we take the liberty to paraphrase, "that they are out on any actual expedition?"

"To be sure," rejoined the dame. "They who lag late on the road may want money for supper!"

"Ha! which road?"

"You are a pretty fellow for captain!" rejoined the dame, with a good-natured sarcasm in her tone. "Why, Captain Gloak, poor fellow! knew every turn of his men to a hair, and never needed to ask what they were about. Ah, he *was* a fellow! none of your girl-faced mudgers, who make love to ladies, forsooth—a pretty woman need not look far for a kiss when he was in the room, I warrant, however coarse her duds might be; and lauk! but the captain was a sensible man, and liked a cow as well as a calf."

"So, so! on the road are they?" cried Clifford, musingly, and without heeding the insinuated attack on his decorum. "But answer me, what is the plan?—Be quick."

[1] The moon

"Why," replied the dame, "there's some swell cove of a lord gives a blow-out to-day, and the lads, dear souls! think to play the queer on some straggler."

Without uttering a word, Clifford darted from the house, and was remounted before the old lady had time to recover her surprise.

"If you want to see them," cried she, as he put spurs to his horse, "they ordered me to have supper ready at ——" The horse's hoofs drowned the last words of the dame, and carefully re-bolting the door, and muttering an invidious comparison between Captain Clifford and Captain Gloak, the good landlady returned to those culinary operations destined to rejoice the hearts of Tomlinson and Pepper.

Return we ourselves to Lucy. It so happened that the squire's carriage was the last to arrive; for the coachman, long uninitiated among the shades of Warlock into the dissipation of fashionable life, entered on his *début* at Bath, with all the vigorous heat of matured passions for the first time released, into the festivities of the ale-house, and having a milder master than most of his comrades, the fear of displeasure was less strong in his aurigal bosom than the love of companionship; so that during the time this gentleman was amusing himself, Lucy had ample leisure for enjoying all the thousand-and-one reports of the scene between Mauleverer and Clifford, which regaled her ears. Nevertheless, whatever might have been her feelings at these pleasing recitals, a certain vague joy predominated over all. A man feels but slight comparative happiness in being loved, if he know that it is in vain. But to a woman that simple knowledge is sufficient to destroy the memory of a thousand distresses, and it is not till she has told her heart again and again that she is loved, that she will even begin to ask if it be in vain.

It was a partially starlit, yet a dim and obscure night, for the moon had for the last hour or two been surrounded by mist and cloud, when at length the carriage arrived; and Mauleverer, for the second time that evening playing the escort, conducted Lucy to the vehicle. Anxious to learn if she had seen or been addressed by Clifford, the subtle earl, as he led her to the gate, dwelt particularly on the intrusion of that person, and by the trembling of the hand which rested on his arm, he drew no delicious omen for his own hopes. "However," thought he, "the man goes to-morrow, and then the field will be clear; the girl's a child yet, and I forgive her folly." And with an air of chivalric veneration, Mauleverer bowed the object of his pardon into her carriage.

As soon as Lucy felt herself alone with her father, the emotions so long pent within her forced themselves into vent, and leaning

back against the carriage, she wept, though in silence, tears, burning
tears, of sorrow, comfort, agitation, anxiety.

The good old squire was slow in perceiving his daughter's emotion ; it would have escaped him altogether, if, actuated by a kindly
warming of the heart towards her, originating in his new suspicion
of her love for Clifford, he had not put his arm round her neck ;
and this unexpected caress so entirely unstrung her nerves, that Lucy
at once threw herself upon her father's breast, and her weeping,
hitherto so quiet, became distinct and audible.

"Be comforted, my dear, dear child !" said the squire, almost
affected to tears himself ; and his emotion, arousing him from his
usual mental confusion, rendered his words less involved and equivocal than they were wont to be. "And now I do hope that you
won't vex yourself ; the young man is indeed—and, I do assure you,
I always thought so—a very charming gentleman, there's no denying it. But what can we do ? You see what they all say of him,
and it really was—we must allow that—very improper in him to
come without being asked. Moreover, my dearest child, it is very
wrong, very wrong, indeed, to love any one, and not know who he
is ; and—and—but don't cry, my dear love, don't cry so ; all will
be very well, I am sure—quite sure !"

As he said this, the kind old man drew his daughter nearer him,
and feeling his hand hurt by something she wore unseen which
pressed against it, he inquired, with some suspicion that the love
might have proceeded to love-gifts, what it was.

"It is my mother's picture," said Lucy, simply, and putting it
aside.

The old squire had loved his wife tenderly, and when Lucy made
this reply, all the fond and warm recollections of his youth rushed
upon him : he thought, too, how earnestly on her death-bed that
wife had recommended to his vigilant care their only child now
weeping on his bosom ; he remembered how, dwelling on that which
to all women seems the grand epoch of life, she had said, "Never
let her affections be trifled with,—never be persuaded by your ambitious brother to make her marry where she loves not, or to oppose
her, without strong reason, where she does : though she be but a
child now, I know enough of her to feel convinced that if ever she
love, she will love too well for her own happiness, even with all
things in her favour." These words, these recollections, joined to
the remembrance of the cold-hearted scheme of William Brandon,
which he had allowed himself to favour, and of his own supineness
towards Lucy's growing love for Clifford, till resistance became at
once necessary and too late, all smote him with a remorseful sorrow,
and fairly sobbing himself, he said, "Thy mother, child ! ah, would

that she were living, she would never have neglected thee as I have done !"

The squire's self-reproach made Lucy's tears cease on the instant, and, as she covered her father's hand with kisses, she replied only by vehement accusations against herself, and praises of his too great fatherly fondness and affection. This little burst, on both sides, of honest and simple-hearted love, ended in a silence full of tender and mingled thoughts : and as Lucy still clung to the breast of the old man, uncouth as he was in temper, below even mediocrity in intellect, and altogether the last person in age, or mind, or habit, that seemed fit for a confidant in the love of a young and enthusiastic girl, she felt the old homely truth, that under all disadvantages there are, in this hollow world, few in whom trust can be so safely reposed, few who so delicately and subtilely respect the confidence, as those from whom we spring.

The father and daughter had been silent for some minutes, and the former was about to speak, when the carriage suddenly stopped. The squire heard a rough voice at the horses' heads ; he looked forth from the window to see, through the mist of the night, what could possibly be the matter, and he encountered in this action, just one inch from his forehead, the protruded and shining barrel of a horse-pistol. We may believe, without a reflection on his courage, that Mr. Brandon threw himself back into his carriage with all possible despatch ; and at the same moment the door was opened, and a voice said, not in a threatening, but a smooth accent, "Ladies and gentlemen, I am sorry to disturb you, but want is imperious : oblige me with your money, your watches, your rings, and any other little commodities of a similar nature !"

So delicate a request the squire had not the heart to resist, the more especially as he knew himself without any weapons of defence ; accordingly he drew out a purse, not very full it must be owned, together with an immense silver hunting-watch, with a piece of black riband attached to it : "There, sir," said he, with a groan, "don't frighten the young lady."

The gentle applicant, who indeed was no other than the specious Augustus Tomlinson, slid the purse into his waistcoat pocket, after feeling its contents with a rapid and scientific finger. "Your watch, sir," quoth he, and as he spoke he thrust it carelessly into his coat-pocket, as a school-boy would thrust a peg-top, "is heavy ; but trusting to experience, since an accurate survey is denied me, I fear it is more valuable from its weight than its workmanship : however, I will not wound your vanity by affecting to be fastidious. But surely the young lady, as you call her,—(for I pay you the compliment of believing your word as to her age, inasmuch as the night

is too dark to allow me the happiness of a personal inspection,)—
the young lady has surely some little trinket she can dispense with;
'Beauty when unadorned,' you know, &c."

Lucy, who, though greatly frightened, lost neither her senses nor
her presence of mind, only answered by drawing forth a little silk
purse, that contained still less than the leathern convenience of the
squire; to this she added a gold chain; and Tomlinson, taking
them with an affectionate squeeze of the hand, and a polite apology,
was about to withdraw, when his sagacious eyes were suddenly
stricken by the gleam of jewels. The fact was, that in altering the
position of her mother's picture, which had been set in the few
hereditary diamonds possessed by the Lord of Warlock, Lucy had
allowed it to hang on the outside of her dress, and bending forward
to give the robber her other possessions, the diamonds at once came
in full sight, and gleamed the more invitingly from the darkness of
the night.

"Ah, madam!" said Tomlinson, stretching forth his hand, "you
would play me false, would you? Treachery should never go
unpunished. Favour me instantly with the little ornament round
your neck!"

"I cannot—I cannot!" said Lucy, grasping her treasure with both
her hands,—"it is my mother's picture and my mother is dead!"

"The wants of others, madam," returned Tomlinson, who could
not for the life of him *rob immorally,* "are ever more worthy your
attention than family prejudices. Seriously, give it, and that
instantly; we are in a hurry, and your horses are plunging like
devils: they will break your carriage in an instant—dispatch!"

The squire was a brave man on the whole, though no hero, and
the nerves of an old fox-hunter soon recover from a little alarm.
The picture of his buried wife was yet more inestimable to him
than it was to Lucy, and at this new demand his spirit was roused
within him.

He clenched his fists, and advancing himself, as it were, on his
seat, he cried in a loud voice:—

"Begone, fellow!—I have given you—for my own part I think
so—too much already; and by G—d you shall not have the
picture!"

"Don't force me to use violence!" said Augustus, and putting
one foot on the carriage-step, he brought his pistol within a few
inches of Lucy's breast, rightly judging, perhaps, that the show
of danger to her would be the best method to intimidate the
squire. At that instant the valorous moralist found himself suddenly seized with a powerful gripe on the shoulder, and a low
voice, trembling with passion, hissed in his ear. Whatever might

be the words that startled his organs, they operated as an instantaneous charm; and to their astonishment, the squire and Lucy beheld their assailant abruptly withdraw. The door of the carriage was clapped to, and scarcely two minutes had elapsed before, the robber having remounted, his comrade—(hitherto stationed at the horses' heads)—set spurs to his own steed, and the welcome sound of receding hoofs smote upon the bewildered ears of the father and daughter.

The door of the carriage was again opened, and a voice, which made Lucy paler than the preceding terror, said,—

"I fear, Mr. Brandon, the robbers have frightened your daughter. There is now, however, nothing to fear—the ruffians are gone."

"God bless me!" said the squire: "why, is that Captain Clifford?"

"It is! and he conceives himself too fortunate to have been of the smallest service to Mr. and Miss Brandon."

On having convinced himself that it was indeed to Mr. Clifford that he owed his safety, as well as that of his daughter, whom he believed to have been in a far more imminent peril than she really was,—(for to tell thee the truth, reader, the pistol of Tomlinson was rather calculated for show than use, having a peculiarly long bright barrel with nothing in it,)—the squire was utterly at a loss how to express his gratitude; and when he turned to Lucy to beg she would herself thank their gallant deliverer, he found that, overpowered with various emotions, she had, for the first time in her life, fainted away.

"Good Heavens!" cried the alarmed father, "she is dead,—my Lucy—my Lucy—they have killed her!"

To open the door nearest to Lucy, to bear her from the carriage in his arms, was to Clifford the work of an instant; utterly unconscious of the presence of any one else—unconscious even of what he said, he poured forth a thousand wild, passionate, yet half-audible expressions; and as he bore her to a bank by the roadside, and seating himself, supported her against his bosom, it would be difficult, perhaps, to say, whether something of delight—of burning and thrilling delight—was not mingled with his anxiety and terror. He chafed her small hands in his own—his breath, all trembling and warm, glowed upon her cheek, and once, and but once, his lips drew nearer, and breathing aside the dishevelled richness of her tresses, clung in a long and silent kiss to her own.

Meanwhile, by the help of his footman, who had now somewhat recovered his astonished senses, the squire descended from his carriage, and approached with faltering steps the place where his daughter reclined. At the instant that he took her hand, Lucy began to revive, and the first action, in the bewildered unconsciousness of awaking, was to throw her arm around the neck of her supporter.

Could all the hours and realities of hope, joy, pleasure, in Clifford's previous life have been melted down and concentrated into a single emotion, that emotion would have been but tame to the rapture of Lucy's momentary and innocent caress! And at a later, yet no distant, period, when in the felon's cell the grim visage of Death scowled upon him, it may be questioned whether his thoughts dwelt not far more often on the remembrance of that delightful moment, than on the bitterness and ignominy of an approaching doom!

"She breathes—she moves—she wakes!" cried the father; and Lucy, attempting to rise, and recognising the squire's voice, said faintly, "Thank God, my dear father, you are not hurt! And are they really gone?—and where—where are *we*?"

The squire, relieving Clifford of his charge, folded his child in his arms, while in his own elucidatory manner he informed her where she was, and with whom. The lovers stood face to face to each other, but what delicious blushes did the night, which concealed all but the outline of their forms, hide from the eyes of Clifford!

The honest and kind heart of Mr. Brandon was glad of a release to the indulgent sentiments it had always cherished towards the suspected and maligned Clifford, and turning now from Lucy, it fairly poured itself forth upon her deliverer. He grasped him warmly by the hand, and insisted upon his accompanying them to Bath in the carriage, and allowing the footman to ride his horse. This offer was still pending, when the footman, who had been to see after the health and comfort of his fellow-servant, came to inform the party in a dolorous accent, of something which, in the confusion and darkness of the night, they had not yet learned,—namely, that the horses and coachman were—gone!

"Gone!" said the squire—"gone!—why the villains can't—(for my part, I never believe, though I have heard such wonders of, those sleights of hand)—have bagged them!"

Here a low groan was audible, and the footman, sympathetically guided to the spot whence it emanated, found the huge body of the coachman safely deposited, with its face downward, in the middle of the kennel. After this worthy had been lifted to his legs, and had shaken himself into intelligence, it was found that when the robber had detained the horses, the coachman, who required very little to conquer his more bellicose faculties, had—(he himself said, by a violent blow from the ruffian, though, perhaps, the cause lay nearer home)—quitted the coach-box for the kennel, the horses grew frightened, and after plunging and rearing till he cared no longer to occupy himself with their arrest, the highwayman had very quietly cut the traces, and by the time present, it was not impossible that the horses were almost at the door of their stables at Bath.

The footman who had apprised the squire of this misfortune was, unlike most news-tellers, the first to offer consolation.

"There be an excellent public," quoth he, "about a half a mile on, where your honour could get horses ; or, mayhap, if Miss Lucy, poor heart, be faint, you may like to stop for the night."

Though a walk of half a mile in a dark night, and under other circumstances, would not have seemed a grateful proposition, yet, at present, when the squire's imagination had only pictured to him the alternatives of passing the night in the carriage, or of crawling on foot to Bath, it seemed but a very insignificant hardship. And tucking his daughter's arm under his own, while in a kind voice he told Clifford " to support her on the other side," the squire ordered the footman to lead the way with Clifford's horse, and the coachman to follow or be d—d, which ever he pleased.

In silence Clifford offered his arm to Lucy, and silently she accepted the courtesy. The squire was the only talker, and the theme he chose was not ungrateful to Lucy, for it was the praise of her lover. But Clifford scarcely listened, for a thousand thoughts and feelings contested within him ; and the light touch of Lucy's hand upon his arm would alone have been sufficient to distract and confuse his attention. The darkness of the night, the late excitement, the stolen kiss that still glowed upon his lips, the remembrance of Lucy's flattering agitation in the scene with her at Lord Maul-everer's, the yet warmer one of that unconscious embrace, which still tingled through every nerve of his frame, all conspired with the delicious emotion which he now experienced at her presence and her contact to intoxicate and inflame him. Oh, those burning moments in love, when romance has just mellowed into passion, and without losing any thing of its luxurious vagueness, mingles the enthusiasm of its dreams with the ardent desires of reality and earth ! *That* is the exact time, when love has reached its highest point,—when all feelings, all thoughts, the whole soul, and the whole mind, are seized and engrossed,—when every difficulty weighed in the opposite scale seems lighter than dust,—when to renounce the object beloved is the most deadly and lasting sacrifice,—and when in so many breasts, where honour, conscience, virtue, are far stronger than we can believe them ever to have been in a criminal like Clifford, honour, conscience, virtue, have perished at once and suddenly into ashes before that mighty and irresistible fire.

The servant, who had had previous opportunities of ascertaining the topography of the " public " of which he spake, and who was

I

perhaps tolerably reconciled to his late terror in the anticipation of renewing his intimacy with the "spirits of the past," now directed the attention of our travellers to a small inn just before them. Mine host had not yet retired to repose, and it was not necessary to knock twice before the door was opened.

A bright fire, an officious landlady, a commiserate landlord, a warm potation, and the promise of excellent beds, all appeared to our squire to make ample amends for the intelligence that the inn was not licensed to let post-horses; and mine host having promised forthwith to send two stout fellows a rope, and a cart-horse, to bring the carriage under shelter (for the squire valued the vehicle *because* it was twenty years old), and, moreover, to have the harness repaired, and the horses ready by an early hour the next day, the good humour of Mr. Brandon rose into positive hilarity. Lucy retired under the auspices of the landlady to bed, and the squire having drunk a bowl of bishop, and discovered a thousand new virtues in Clifford, especially that of never interrupting a good story, clapped the captain on the shoulder, and making him promise not to leave the inn till he had seen him again, withdrew also to the repose of his pillow. Clifford remained below, gazing abstractedly on the fire for some time afterwards; nor was it till the drowsy chambermaid had thrice informed him of the prepared comforts of his bed, that he adjourned to his chamber. Even then it seems that sleep did not visit his eyelids, for a wealthy glazier, who lay in the room below, complained bitterly the next morning of some person walking overhead "in all manner of strides, just for all the world like a happarition in boots."

CHAPTER XXIII.

"VIOLA.—*And dost thou love me?*
LYSANDER. . . . *Love thee, Viola?*
Do I not fly thee when my being drinks
Light from thine eyes?—that flight is all my answer!'
'THE BRIDE,' Act II., Scene 1.

THE curtain meditations of the squire had not been without the produce of a resolve. His warm heart at once reopened to the liking he had formerly conceived for Clifford; he longed for an opportunity to atone for his past unkindness, and to testify his present gratitude; moreover, he felt at once indignant at, and ashamed of, his late conduct in joining the popular, and, as he now fully believed, the causeless prepossession against his young friend, and before a more present and a stronger sentiment his habitual deference for his brother's counsels faded easily away. Coupled with these favourable feelings towards Clifford were his sagacious suspicions, or rather certainty, of Lucy's attachment to her handsome deliverer; and he had at least sufficient penetration to perceive that she was not likely to love him the less for the night's adventure. To all this was added the tender recollection of his wife's parting words; and the tears and tell-tale agitation of Lucy in the carriage were sufficient to his simple mind, which knew not how lightly maiden's tears are shed and dried, to confirm the prediction of the dear deceased. Nor were the squire's more generous and kindly feelings utterly unmixed with selfish considerations. *Proud*, but not the least *ambitious*, he was always more ready to confer an honour than receive one, and at heart he was secretly glad at the notion of exchanging, as a son-in-law, the polished and *unfamiliar* Mauleverer for the agreeable and social Clifford. Such, in "admired disorder," were the thoughts which rolled through the teeming brain of Joseph Brandon, and before he had turned on his left side, which he always did preparatory to surrendering himself to slumber, the squire had fully come to a determination most fatal to the schemes of the lawyer and the hopes of the earl.

The next morning, as Lucy was knitting

"The loose train of her amber-dropping hair"

before the little mirror of her chamber, which even through its dimmed and darkened glass gave back a face which might have shamed a Grecian vision of Aurora, a gentle tap at her door announced her father. There was in his rosy and comely countenance that expression generally characteristic of a man pleased with himself, and persuaded that he is about to give pleasure.

"My dear child," said the squire, fondly stroking down the luxuriance of his Lucy's hair, and kissing her damask cheek, "I am come to have some little conversation with you: sit down now, and (for my part, I love to talk at my ease; and, by the by, shut the window, my love, it is an easterly wind) I wish that we may come to a clear and distinct understanding. Hem!—give me your hand, my child,—I think on these matters one can scarcely speak too precisely and to the purpose; although I am well aware—(for, for my own part, I always wish to act to every one, to you especially, my dearest child, with the greatest consideration)—that we must go to work with as much delicacy as conciseness. You know this Captain Clifford,—'tis a brave youth, is it not?—well—nay, never blush so deeply, there is nothing (for in these matters one can't have all one's

wishes,—one can't have *everything*) *to be ashamed of!* Tell me
now, child, dost think he is in love with thee?"

If Lucy did not immediately answer by words, her pretty lips
moved as if she could readily reply; and, finally, they settled into
so sweet and so assured a smile, that the squire, fond as he was of
"precise" information, was in want of no fuller answer to his
question.

"Ay, ay, young lady," said he, looking at her with all a father's
affection, "I see how it is. And, come now,—what do you turn
away for? Dost think if, as I believe, though there are envious
persons in the world, as there always are when a man's handsome,
or clever, or brave; though, by the way, which is a very droll thing
in my eyes, they don't envy, at least not ill-naturedly, a man for
being a lord, or rich; but, quite on the contrary, rank and money
seem to make them think one has all the cardinal virtues. Humph!
—If I say, this Mr. Clifford should turn out to be a gentleman of
family,—for you know that is essential, since the Brandons have,
as my brother has probably told you, been a great race many
centuries ago;—dost think, my child, that thou couldst give up (the
cat is out of the bag) this old lord, and many a simple gentleman?"

The hand which the squire had held was now with an arch tenderness applied to his mouth, and when he again seized it Lucy hid
her glowing face in his bosom; and it was only by a whisper, as if
the very air was garrulous, that he could draw forth (for now he
insisted on a verbal reply) her happy answer.

We are not afraid that our reader will blame us for not detailing
the rest of the interview between the father and daughter: it did not
last above an hour longer; for the squire declared that, for his own
part, he hated more words than were necessary. Mr. Brandon was
the first to descend to the breakfast, muttering as he descended the
stairs, "Well now, hang me if I am not glad that's off (for I do not
like to think much of so silly a matter) my mind. And as for my
brother, I shan't tell him till it's all over and settled. And if he
is angry, he and the old lord may, though I don't mean to be
unbrotherly, go to the devil together!"

When the three were assembled at the breakfast-table, there could
not, perhaps, have been found any where a stronger contrast than
that which the radiant face of Lucy bore to the haggard and worn
expression that disfigured the handsome features of her lover. So
marked was the change that one night seemed to have wrought
upon Clifford, that even the squire was startled and alarmed at it.
But Lucy, whose innocent vanity pleased itself with accounting for
the alteration, consoled herself with the hope of soon witnessing a
very different expression on the countenance of her lover; and though

she was silent, and her happiness lay quiet and deep within her, yet in her eyes and lip there was that which seemed to Clifford an insult to his own misery, and stung him to the heart. However, he exerted himself to meet the conversation of the squire, and to mask as well as he was able the evidence of the conflict which still raged within him.

The morning was wet and gloomy ; it was that drizzling and misty rain which is so especially nutritious to the growth of blue devils, and the jolly squire failed not to rally his young friend upon his feminine susceptibility to the influences of the weather. Clifford replied jestingly, and the jest, if bad, was good enough to content the railer. In this facetious manner passed the time, till Lucy, at the request of her father, left the room to prepare for their return home.

Drawing his chair near to Clifford's, the squire then commenced in real and affectionate earnest his operations—these he had already planned—in the following order : they were, first, to inquire into, and to learn, Clifford's rank, family, and prospects ; secondly, having ascertained the proprieties of the outer man, they were to examine the state of the inner one ; and thirdly, should our skilful inquirer find his guesses at Clifford's affection for Lucy confirmed, they were to expel the modest fear of a repulse, which the squire allowed was natural enough, and to lead the object of the inquiry to a knowledge of the happiness that, Lucy consenting, might be in store for him. While, with his wonted ingenuity, the squire was pursuing his benevolent designs, Lucy remained in her own room, in such meditation and such dreams as were natural to a heart so sanguine and enthusiastic.

She had been more than half-an-hour alone, when the chamber-maid of the hostelry knocked at her door, and delivered a message from the squire, begging her to come down to him in the parlour. With a heart that beat so violently it almost seemed to wear away its very life, Lucy slowly, and with tremulous steps, descended to the parlour. On opening the door she saw Clifford standing in the recess of the window : his face was partly turned from her, and his eyes downcast. The good old squire sat in an elbow chair, and a sort of puzzled and half-satisfied complacency gave expression to his features.

"Come hither, child," said he, clearing his throat ; "Captain Clifford—a-hem !—has done you the honour—to—and I dare say you will be very much surprised—not that, for my own part, I think there is much to wonder at in it, but such may be my partial opinion (and *it is certainly very natural in me*)—*to make you a declaration of love.* He declares, moreover, that he is the most miserable of men, and that he would die sooner than have the presumption to hope. Therefore you see, my love, I have sent for you, to give him permission to destroy himself in any way he pleases; and I leave him to show cause why (it is a fate that sooner or later happens to all his fellow-men) sentence of death should not be passed against him." Having delivered this speech with more propriety of word than usually fell to his share, the squire rose hastily and hobbled out of the room.

Lucy sank into the chair her father had quitted, and Clifford, approaching towards her, said, in a hoarse and low voice,—

"Your father, Miss Brandon, says rightly, that I would die rather than lift my eyes in hope to you. I thought yesterday that I had seen you for the last time; chance, not my own folly or presumption, has brought me again before you; and even the few hours I have passed under the same roof with you have made me feel as if my love—my madness—had never reached its height till now. Oh, Lucy!" continued Clifford, in a more impassioned tone, and, as if by a sudden and irresistible impulse. throwing himself at her feet; "if I *could* hope to merit you—if I could hope to raise myself—if I could—but no—no—no! I am cut off from all hope, and for ever!"

There was so deep, so bitter, so heartfelt an anguish and remorse in the voice with which these last words were spoken, that Lucy, hurried off her guard, and forgetting every thing in wondering sympathy and compassion, answered, extending her hand towards Clifford, who, still kneeling, seized and covered it with kisses of fire,—

"Do not speak thus, Mr. Clifford; do not accuse yourself of what I am sure, quite sure, you cannot deserve. Perhaps,—forgive me,—your birth, your fortune, are beneath your merits; and you have penetrated into my father's weakness on the former point; or, perhaps, you yourself have not avoided all the errors into which men are hurried; perhaps you have been imprudent or thoughtless; perhaps you have (fashion is contagious) played beyond your means, or incurred debts: these are faults, it is true, and to be regretted, yet not surely irreparable."

For that instant can it be wondered that all Clifford's resolution and self-denial deserted him, and lifting his eyes, radiant with joy and gratitude, to the face which bent in benevolent innocence towards him, he exclaimed, "No, Miss Brandon!—no, Lucy! —dear, angel Lucy! my faults are less venial than these, but perhaps they are no less the consequence of circumstances and contagion; perhaps it may not be too late to repair them. Would you—you indeed deign to be my guardian, I might not despair of being saved!"

"If," said Lucy, blushing deeply, and looking down, while she spoke quick and eagerly, as if to avoid humbling him by her offer, —"if, Mr. Clifford, the want of wealth has in any way occasioned you uneasiness, or—or error, do believe me—I mean *us*—so much your friends as not for an instant to scruple in relieving us of some little portion of our last night's debt to you."

"Dear, noble girl!" said Clifford, while there writhed upon his lips one of those smiles of powerful sarcasm that sometimes distorted his features, and thrillingly impressed upon Lucy a resemblance to one very different in reputation and character to her lover,—"Do not attribute my misfortunes to so petty a source ; it is not money that I shall want while I live, though I shall to my last breath remember this delicacy in you, and compare it with certain base remembrances in my own mind. Yes! all past thoughts and recollections will make me hereafter worship you even more than I do now ; while in your heart they will—unless Heaven grant me one prayer—make you scorn and detest me!"

"For mercy's sake do not speak thus!" said Lucy, gazing in indistinct alarm upon the dark and working features of her lover. "Scorn, detest you! impossible! How could I, after the remembrance of last night?"

"Ay! of last night," said Clifford, speaking through his ground teeth : "there is much in that remembrance to live long in both of us : but you—*you*—fair angel" (and all harshness and irony vanishing at once from his voice and countenance, yielded to a tender and deep sadness, mingled with a respect that bordered on reverence), —"*you* never could have dreamed of more than pity for one like me,—you never could have stooped from your high and dazzling purity to know for me one such thought as that which burns at my heart for you,—you—yes, withdraw your hand, I am not worthy to touch it!" And clasping his own hands before his face, he became abruptly silent ; but his emotions were but ill concealed, and Lucy saw the muscular frame before her heaved and convulsed by passions which were more intense and rending because it was only for a few moments that they conquered his self-will and struggled into vent.

If afterwards,—but *long* afterwards, Lucy recalling the mystery of his words, confessed to herself that they betrayed guilt, she was then too much affected to think of anything but her love and his emotion. She bent down, and with a girlish and fond self-abandonment, which none could have resisted, placed both her hands on his : Clifford started, looked up, and in the next moment he had clasped her to his heart ; and while the only tears he had shed since his career of crime fell fast and hot upon her countenance, he kissed her forehead, her cheek, her lips, in a passionate and wild transport. His voice died within him, he could not trust himself to speak ; only one thought, even in that seeming forgetfulness of her and of himself, stirred and spoke at his breast—*flight*. The more he felt he loved,—the more tender and the more confiding the object of his love, the more urgent became the necessity to leave her. All other duties had been neglected, but he loved with a real love ; and love, which *taught* him *one* duty, *bore* him triumphantly through its bitter ordeal.

"You will hear from me to-night," he muttered ; "believe that I am mad, accursed, criminal, but not utterly a monster! I ask no more merciful opinion !" He drew himself from his perilous position, and abruptly departed.

When Clifford reached his home, he found his worthy coadjutors waiting for him with alarm and terror on their countenances. An old feat, in which they had signalised themselves, had long attracted the rigid attention of the police, and certain officers had now been seen at Bath, and certain inquiries had been set on foot, which portended no good to the safety of the sagacious Tomlinson and the valorous Pepper. They came, humbly and penitentially demanding pardon for their unconscious aggression of the squire's carriage, and entreating their captain's instant advice. If Clifford had before wavered in his disinterested determination,—if visions of Lucy, of happiness, and reform, had floated in his solitary ride too frequently and too glowingly before his eyes, the sight of these men, their conversation, their danger, all sufficed to restore his resolution. "Merciful God !" thought he, "and is it to the comrade of such lawless villains, to a man, like them, exposed hourly to the most ignominious of deaths, that I have for one section of a moment dreamed of consigning the innocent and generous girl, whose trust or love is the only crime that could deprive her of the most brilliant destiny?"

Short were Clifford's instructions to his followers, and so much do we do mechanically, that they were delivered with his usual forethought and precision. "You will leave the town instantly ; go not, for your lives, to London, or to rejoin any of your comrades. Ride for the Red Cave ; provisions are stored there, and, since our late alteration of the interior, it will afford ample room to conceal your horses. On the night of the second day from this I will join you. But be sure that you enter the cave at night, and quit it upon no account till I come !"

"Yes !" said he, when he was alone, "I will join you again, but only to quit you. One more offence against the law, or at least one sum wrested from the swollen hands of the rich sufficient to equip me for a foreign army, and I quit the country of my birth and my crimes. If I cannot deserve Lucy Brandon, I will be somewhat less unworthy. Perhaps (why not?) I am young, my nerves are not weak, my brain is not dull; perhaps I may in some field of honourable adventure win a name, that before my death-bed I may not blush to acknowledge to her!"

While this resolve beat high within Clifford's breast, Lucy sadly and in silence was continuing with the squire her short journey to Bath. The latter was very inquisitive to know why Clifford had gone, and what he had avowed; and Lucy, scarcely able to answer, threw every thing on the promised letter of the night.

"I am glad," muttered the squire to her, "that he is going to write; for, somehow or other, though I questioned him very tightly, he slipped through my cross-examination, and bursting out at once as to his love for you, left me as wise about himself as I was before; no doubt (for my own part I don't see what should prevent his being a great man *incog.*) this letter will explain all!"

Late that night the letter came; Lucy, fortunately for her, was alone in her own room; she opened it, and read as follows :—

CLIFFORD'S LETTER.

"I have promised to write to you, and I sit down to perform that promise. At this moment the recollection of your goodness, your generous consideration, is warm within me; and while I must choose calm and common words to express what I ought to say, my heart is alternately melted and torn by thoughts which would ask words, oh how different! Your father has questioned me often of my parentage and birth,—I have hitherto eluded his interrogatories. Learn now who I am. In a wretched abode, surrounded by the inhabitants of poverty and vice, I recall my earliest recollections. My father is unknown to me as to every one; my mother, to *you* I dare not mention who or what she was,—she died in my infancy. Without a name, but not without an inheritance (my inheritance was large—it was infamy!) I was thrown upon the world: I had received by accident some education, and imbibed some ideas, not natural to my situation; since then I have played many parts in life: books and men I have not so neglected, but that I have gleaned at intervals some little knowledge from both. Hence, if I have seemed to you better than I am, you will perceive the cause: circumstances made me soon my own master; they made me also one whom honest men do not love to look upon; my deeds have been, and my character is, of a par with my birth and my fortunes. I came, in the noble hope to raise and redeem myself by gilding my

I 2

fate with a wealthy marriage, to this city: I saw you, whom I had once before met. I heard you were rich. Hate me, Miss Brandon, hate me !—I resolved to make your ruin the cause of my redemption. Happily for you, I scarcely knew you before I loved you ; that love deepened,—it caught something pure and elevated from yourself. My resolution forsook me ; even now I could throw myself on my knees and thank God that you—you, dearest and noblest of human beings—are not my wife. Now, is my conduct clear to you?—If not, imagine me all that is villanous, save in one point, where *you* are concerned, and not a shadow of mystery will remain. Your kind father, over-rating the paltry service I rendered you, would have consented to submit my fate to your decision. I blush indig-nantly for him—for you—that any living man should have dreamed of such profanation for Miss Brandon. Yet I myself was carried away and intoxicated by so sudden and so soft a hope—even I dared to lift my eyes to you, to press you to this guilty heart, to forget myself, and to dream that you might be mine ! Can you forgive me for this madness ? And hereafter, when in your lofty and glittering sphere of wedded happiness, can you remember my presumption and check your scorn ? Perhaps you think that by so *late* a confession I have already deceived you. Alas ! you know not what it costs me *now* to confess ! I had only one hope in life,—it was that you might still, long after you had ceased to see me, fancy me not utterly beneath the herd with whom you live. This burning yet selfish vanity I tear from me, and now I go where no hope can pursue me. No hope for myself, save one which can scarcely deserve the name, for it is rather a rude and visionary wish than an expectation :—it is, that under another name, and under different auspices, you may hear of me at some distant time ; and when I apprise you that under that name you may recognise one who loves you better than all created things, you may feel *then*, at least, no cause for shame at your lover. What will *you* be then ? A happy wife—a mother—the centre of a thousand joys —beloved, admired—blest when the eye sees you and the ear hears ! And this is what I ought to hope ; this is the consolation that ought to cheer me ;—perhaps a little time hence it will Not that I shall love you less ; but that I shall love you less burningly, and therefore less selfishly. I have now written to you all that it becomes you to receive from me. My horse waits below to bear me from this city, and for ever from your vicinity. For ever !—ay, you are the only blessing *for ever* forbidden me. Wealth I may gain—a fair name— even glory I may perhaps aspire to !—to Heaven itself I may find a path ; but of *you* my very dreams cannot give me the shadow of a hope. I do not say, if you could pierce my soul while I write, that you would pity me. You may think it strange, but I would not have your *pity* for worlds; I think I would even rather have your hate, pity seems so much like contempt. But if you knew what an effort has enabled me to tame down my language, to curb my thoughts, to prevent me from embodying that which now makes my brain whirl, and my hand feel as if the living fire consumed it; if you knew what has enabled me to triumph over the madness at my heart, and spare you what, if writ or spoken, would seem like the ravings of insanity, you would not, and you could not, despise me, though you might abhor.

"And now, Heaven guard and bless you! Nothing on *earth* could injure you. And even the wicked who have looked upon you learn to pray—*I* have prayed for you!"

Thus (abrupt and signatureless) ended the expected letter. Lucy came down the next morning at her usual hour, and, except that she was very pale, nothing in her appearance seemed to announce past grief or emotion. The squire asked her if she had received the promised letter? She answered in a clear, though faint voice, that she had—that Mr. Clifford had confessed himself of too low an origin to hope for marriage with Mr. Brandon's family; that she trusted the squire would keep his secret; and that the subject might never again be alluded to by either. If, in this speech, there was something alien to Lucy's ingenuous character, and painful to her mind, she felt it, as it were a duty to her former lover not to betray the whole of that confession so bitterly wrung from him. Perhaps, too, there was in that letter a charm which seemed to her too sacred to be revealed to any one. And mysteries were not excluded even from a love so ill-placed, and seemingly so transitory as hers.

Lucy's answer touched the squire in his weak point. "A man of decidedly low origin," he confessed, "was utterly out of the question; nevertheless, the young man showed a great deal of candour in his disclosure." He readily promised never to broach a subject necessarily so unpleasant; and though he sighed as he finished his speech, yet the extreme quiet of Lucy's manner reassured him; and when he perceived that she resumed, though languidly, her wonted avocations, he felt but little doubt of her soon overcoming the remembrance of what, he hoped, was but a girlish and fleeting fancy. He yielded, with avidity, to her proposal to return to Warlock; and in the same week as that in which Lucy had received her lover's mysterious letter, the father and daughter commenced their journey home.

CHAPTER XXIV.

"BUTLER.   *What are these, sir?*
YEOMAN.   *And of what nature—to what use?*
LATROC.   *Imagine."*   'THE TRAGEDY OF ROLLO.'

"QUICKLY   *He's in Arthur's bosom, if ever man went to Arthur's bosom."*
                                        'HENRY V.'

THE stream of our narrative now conducts us back to
William Brandon. The law-promotions previously intended were completed ; and, to the surprise of the
public, the envied barrister, undergoing the degradation
of knighthood, had, at the time we return to him, just changed his
toilsome occupations for the serene dignity of the bench.   Whatever
regret this wily and aspiring schemer might otherwise have felt at
an elevation considerably less distinguished than he might reasonably
have expected, was entirely removed by the hopes afforded to him
of a speedy translation to a more brilliant office : it was whispered
among those not unlikely to foresee such events, that the interest of
the government required his talents in the house of peers. Just at
this moment, too, the fell disease, whose ravages Brandon endeavoured, as jealously as possible, to hide from the public, had
appeared suddenly to yield to the skill of a new physician ; and by
the administration of medicines, which a man less stern or resolute
might have trembled to adopt (so powerful and, for the most part,
deadly was their nature), he passed from a state of almost insufferable
torture to an elysium of tranquillity and ease : perhaps, however, the
medicines which altered also decayed his constitution : and it was
observable, that in two cases, where the physician had attained a
like success by the same means, the patients had died suddenly,
exactly at the time when their cure seemed to be finally completed.
However, Sir William Brandon appeared very little anticipative of
danger. His manner became more cheerful and even than it had
ever been before ; there was a certain lightness in his gait, a certain
exhilaration in his voice and eye, which seemed the tokens of one
from whom a heavy burden had been suddenly raised, and who was
no longer prevented from the eagerness of hope by the engrossing
claims of a bodily pain. He had always been bland in society, but
now his courtesy breathed less of artifice,—it took a more hearty
tone. Another alteration was discernible in him, and that was pre-

cisely the reverse of what might have been expected. He became more *thrifty*—more attentive to the expenses of life than he had been. Though a despiser of show and ostentation, and far too *hard* to be luxurious, he was too scientific an architect of the weaknesses of others not to have maintained during his public career an opulent appearance and a hospitable table. The profession he had adopted requires, perhaps, less of externals to aid it than any other; still Brandon had affected to preserve parliamentary as well as legal importance; and, though his house was situated in a quarter entirely professional, he had been accustomed to assemble around his hospitable board all who were eminent, in his political party, for rank or for talent. Now, however, when hospitality, and a certain largeness of expenses, better became his station, he grew closer and more exact in his economy. Brandon never could have degenerated into a *miser*; money, to one so habitually wise as he was, could never have passed from means into an object; but he had, evidently, for some cause or another, formed the resolution to save. Some said it was the result of returning health, and the hope of a prolonged life, to which many objects for which wealth is desirable might occur. But when it was accidentally ascertained that Brandon had been making several inquiries respecting a large estate in the neighbourhood of Warlock, formerly in the possession of his family, the gossips (for Brandon was a man to be gossiped about) were no longer in want of a motive, false or real, for the judge's thrift.

It was shortly after his elevation to the bench, and ere these signs of change had become noticeable, that the same strange ragamuffin whom we have mentioned before, as introduced by Mr. Swoppem to a private conference with Brandon, was admitted to the judge's presence.

"Well," said Brandon, impatiently, the moment the door was closed, "your news?"

"Vy, your onor," said the man, bashfully, twirling a thing that stood proxy for a hat, "I thinks as ow I shall be hable to satisfy your vorship's onor." Then approaching the judge, and assuming an important air, he whispered,—

"'Tis as ow I thought!"

"My God!" cried Brandon, with vehemence. "And he is alive?—and where?"

"I believes," answered the seemly confidant of Sir William Brandon, "that he be's alive! and if he be's alive, may I flash my ivories in a glass case, if I does not ferret him out; but as to saying vhere he be at this nick o' the moment, smash me if I can!"

"Is he in this country?" said Brandon; "or do you believe that he has gone abroad?"

"Vy, much of one and not a little of the other!" said the euphonious confidant.

"How! speak plain, man—what do you mean?"

"Vy, I means, your onor, that I can't say vhere he is."

"And this," said Brandon, with a muttered oath,—"this is your boasted news, is it? Dog! damned, damned dog! if you trifle with me, or play me false, I will hang you,—by the living G—, I will!"

The man shrunk back involuntarily from Brandon's vindictive forehead and kindled eyes; but with the cunning peculiar to low vice answered, though in a humbler tone,—

"And vot good vill that do your onor? If so be as ow you scrags I, vill that put your vorship in the vay of finding *he*?"

Never was there an obstacle in grammar through which a sturdy truth could not break; and Brandon, after a moody pause, said in a milder voice,—"I did not mean to frighten you! Never mind what I said; but you can surely guess whereabouts he is, or what means of life he pursues? perhaps"—and a momentary paleness crossed Brandon's swarthy visage:—"perhaps he may have been driven into dishonesty in order to maintain himself!"

The informant replied with great *naïveté*, that "such a thing was not unpossible!" And Brandon then entered into a series of seemingly careless but artful cross-questionings, which either the ignorance or the craft of the man enabled him to baffle. After some time, Brandon, disappointed and dissatisfied, gave up his professional task; and bestowing on the man many sagacious and minute instructions, as well as a very liberal donation, he was forced to dismiss his mysterious visitor and to content himself with an assured assertion, that if the object of his inquiries should not already be gone to the devil, the strange gentleman employed to discover him would certainly, sooner or later, bring him to the judge.

This assertion, and the interview preceding it, certainly inspired Sir William Brandon with a feeling like complacency, although it was mingled with a considerable alloy.

"I do not," thought he, concluding his meditations when he was left alone,—"I do not see what else I can do! Since it appears that the boy had not even a name when he set out alone from his wretched abode, I fear that an advertisement would have but little chance of even designating, much less of finding him, after so long an absence. Besides, it might make me the prey to impostors; and, in all probability, he has either left the country, or adopted some mode of living which would prevent his daring to disclose himself!" This thought plunged the soliloquist into a gloomy abstraction, which lasted several minutes, and from which he started, muttering aloud,—

"Yes, yes! I dare to believe, to hope it.—Now for the minister, and the peerage!" And from that time the root of Sir William Brandon's ambition spread with a firmer and more extended grasp over his mind.

We grieve very much that the course of our story should now oblige us to record an event which we would willingly have spared ourselves the pain of narrating. The good old Squire of Warlock Manor-house had scarcely reached his home on his return from Bath, before William Brandon received the following letter from his brother's grey-headed butler :—

"HONNURED SUR,

"I send this with all speede, thof with a hevy hart, to axquainte you with the sudden (and it is feered by his loving friends and well-wishers, which latter, to be sur, is all as knows him) dangeros ilness of the Squire.[1] He was seezed, poor deer gentleman (for God never made a better, no offence to your Honnur), the moment he set footing in his Own Hall, and what has hung rond me like a mill-ston ever sin, is that instead of his saying—'How do you do, Sampson?' as was his wont, whenever he returned from forren parts, sich as Bath, Lunnun, and the like ; he said, 'God bless you, Sampson!' which makes me think sumhow that it will be his last wurds ; for he has never spoke sin, for all Miss Lucy be by his bedside continual. She, poor deer, don't take on at all, in regard of crying and such woman's wurk, but looks nevertheless, for all the wurld, just like a copse. I sends Tom the postilion with this hexpress, nowing he is a good hand at a gallop, having, not sixteen years ago, beat some o' the best on un at a raceng. Hoping as yer honnur will lose no time in coming to this 'hous of mourning,'

"I remane, with all respect,
"Your Honnur's humble sarvant to command,
"JOHN SAMPSON."

Sir William Brandon did not give himself time to re-read this letter, in order to make it more intelligible, before he wrote to one of his professional compeers, requesting him to fill his place during his unavoidable absence, on the melancholy occasion of his brother's expected death ; and having so done, he immediately set off for Warlock. Inexplicable even to himself was that feeling, so nearly approaching to real sorrow, which the worldly lawyer felt at the

---

[1] The reader, who has doubtless noticed how invariably servants of long standing acquire a certain tone from that of their master, may observe that honest John Sampson had caught from the squire the habit of parenthetical composition

prospect of losing his guileless and unspeculating brother. Whether it be that turbulent and ambitious minds, in choosing for their wavering affections the very opposites of themselves, feel (on losing the fellowship of those calm, fair characters that have never crossed their rugged path) as if they lost, in losing them, a kind of haven for their own restless thoughts and tempest-worn designs !—be this as it may, certain it is, that when William Brandon arrived at his brother's door, and was informed by the old butler, who, for the first time, was slow to greet him, that the squire had just breathed his last, his austere nature forsook him at once, and he felt the shock with a severity perhaps still keener than that which a more genial and affectionate heart would have experienced.

As soon as he had recovered his self-possession, Sir William made question of his niece ; and finding that after an unrelaxing watch during the whole of the squire's brief illness, nature had failed her at his death, and she had been borne senseless from his chamber to her own, Brandon walked with a step far different from his usual stately gait to the room where his brother lay. It was one of the oldest apartments in the house, and much of the ancient splendour that belonged to the mansion ere its size had been reduced, with the fortunes of its successive owners, still distinguished the chamber. The huge mantel-piece ascended to the carved ceiling in grotesque pilasters, and scroll-work of the blackest oak, with the quartered arms of Brandon and Saville escutcheoned in the centre,—the panelled walls of the same dark wainscot,—the *armorie* of ebony, —the high-backed chairs, with their tapestried seats,—the lofty bed, with its hearselike plumes and draperies of a crimson damask that seemed, so massy was the substance, and so prominent the flowers, as if it were rather a carving than a silk,—all conspired with the size of the room to give it a feudal solemnity, not perhaps suited to the rest of the house, but well calculated to strike a gloomy awe into the breast of the worldly and proud man who now entered the death-chamber of his brother.

Silently William Brandon motioned away the attendants, and silently he seated himself by the bed, and looked long and wistfully upon the calm and placid face of the deceased. It is difficult to guess at what passed within him during the space of time in which he remained alone in that room. The apartment itself he could not, at another period, have tenanted without secret emotion. It was that in which, as a boy, he had himself been accustomed to sleep ; and, even then a schemer and an aspirant, the very sight of the room sufficed to call back all the hopes and visions, the restless projects and the feverish desires, which had now brought him to the envied state of an acknowledged celebrity and a shattered frame.

There must have been something awful in the combination of those active remembrances with the cause which had led him to that apartment; and there was a homily in the serene countenance of the dead, which preached more effectually to the heart of the living than William Brandon would ever have cared to own. He had been more than an hour in the room, and the evening had already begun to cast deep shadows through the small panes of the half-closed window, when Brandon was startled by a slight noise. He looked up, and beheld Lucy opposite to him. She did not see him; but throwing herself upon the bed, she took the cold hand of the deceased, and, after a long silence, burst into a passion of tears.

"My father!" she sobbed,—"my kind, good father! who will love me now?"

"I!" said Brandon, deeply affected; and, passing round the bed, he took his niece in his arms: "I will be your father, Lucy, and you—the last of our race—shall be to me as a daughter!"

CHAPTER XXV.

"*Falsehood in him was not the useless lie*
Of boasting pride or laughing vanity ·
It was the gainful—the persuading art," &c.
*   *   *   *
CRABBE.

"*On with the horses—off to Canterbury*,
Tramp—tramp o'er pebble, and splash—splash thro' puddle;
Hurrah! how swiftly speeds the post so merry!
*   *   *   *   *   *   *
*   *   *   *   *   *   *
'*Here laws are all inviolate; none lay*
Traps for the traveller; every highway's clear;
Here——' *he was interrupted by a knife,*
With '*D—— your eyes!—your money or your life!*'"
'DON JUAN.'

MISFORTUNES are like the creations of Cadmus—they destroy one another! Roused from the torpor of mind occasioned by the loss of her lover at the sudden illness of the squire, Lucy had no thought for herself—no thought for any one—for any thing but her father, till long after the earth had closed over his remains. The very activity of the latter grief was less dangerous than the quiet of the former; and when the first keenness of sorrow passed away, and her mind gradually and mechanically returned to the remembrance of Clifford, it was with an intensity less strong, and less fatal to her health and happiness than before. She thought it unnatural and criminal to allow any thing else to grieve her, while she had so sacred a grief as that of her loss ; and her mind, once aroused into resistance to passion, betrayed a native strength little to have been expected from her apparent character. Sir William Brandon lost no time in returning to town after the burial of his brother. He insisted upon taking his niece with him ; and, though with real reluctance, she yielded to his wishes, and accompanied him. By the squire's will, indeed, Sir William was appointed guardian to Lucy, and she yet wanted more than a year of her majority.

Brandon, with a delicacy very uncommon to him where women (for he was a confirmed woman-hater) were concerned, provided every thing that he thought could in any way conduce to her comfort. He ordered it to be understood in his establishment that she was its mistress. He arranged and furnished, according to what he imagined to be her taste, a suite of apartments for her sole accommodation ; a separate carriage and servants were appropriated to her use ; and he sought, by perpetual presents of books, or flowers, or music, to occupy her thoughts, and atone for the solitude to which his professional duties obliged him so constantly to consign her. These attentions, which showed this strange man in a new light, seemed to bring out many little latent amiabilities, which were usually imbedded in the callosities of his rocky nature ; and, even despite her causes for grief and the deep melancholy which consumed her, Lucy was touched with gratitude at kindness doubly soothing in one who, however urbane and polished, was by no means addicted to the little attentions that are considered so gratifying by women, and yet for which they so often despise, while they like, him who affords them. There was much in Brandon that wound itself insensibly around the heart. To one more experienced than Lucy, this involuntary attraction might not have been incompatible with suspicion, and could scarcely have been associated with esteem ; and yet for all who knew him intimately, even for the penetrating and selfish Mauleverer, the attraction existed : unprincipled, crafty, hypocritical, even base when it suited his purpose ; secretly sneering at the dupes he made, and knowing no code save that of interest and ambition ; viewing men only as machines, and opinions only as ladders,—there was yet a tone of powerful feeling sometimes elicited from a heart that could at the same moment have sacrificed a whole people to the pettiest personal object . and sometimes with Lucy the eloquence or irony of his conversation deepened into a melancholy—a half-suppressed gentleness of sentiment, that accorded with the state of *her own* mind and interested her kind feelings powerfully in *his*. It was these peculiarities in his converse which made Lucy love to hear him ; and she gradually learned to anticipate with a gloomy pleasure the hour in which, after the occupations of the day, he was accustomed to join her.

" You look unwell, uncle, to-night," she said, when one evening he entered the room with looks more fatigued than usual ; and, rising, she leaned tenderly over him, and kissed his forehead.

" Ay ! " said Brandon, utterly unwon by, and even unheeding, the caress ; " our way of life soon passes into the sear and yellow leaf ; and when Macbeth grieved that he might not look to have that which should accompany old age, he had grown doting, and grieved for what was worthless."

" Nay, uncle, 'honour, love, obedience, troops of friends,'— *these* surely were worth the sighing for ? "

" Pooh ! not worth a single sigh ! The foolish wishes we form in youth have something noble, and something *bodily* in them ; but those of age are utter shadows, and the shadows of pigmies ! Why, what is honour, after all ? What is this good name among men ?— Only a sort of heathenish idol, set up to be adored by one set of fools, and scorned by another. Do you not observe, Lucy, that the man you hear most praised by the party you meet to-day, is most abused by that which you meet to-morrow ? Public men are only praised by their party ; and their party, sweet Lucy, are such base minions, that it moves one's spleen to think one is so little as to be useful to them. Thus a good name is only the good name of a sect, and the members of that sect are only marvellous proper knaves."

" But posterity does justice to those who really deserve fame."

" Posterity ! Can you believe that a man who knows what life is, cares for the penny whistles of grown children after his death ? Posterity, Lucy—no ! Posterity is but the same perpetuity of fools and rascals ; and even were justice desirable at their hands, they could *not* deal it. Do men agree whether Charles Stuart was a liar or a martyr ? For how many ages have we believed Nero a monster ! A writer now asks, as if demonstrating a problem, what real historian could doubt that Nero was a paragon ?· The patriarchs of Scripture have been declared by modern philosophy to be a series of astronomical hieroglyphs ; and, with greater show of truth, we are assured that the patriot Tell never existed ! Posterity ! the word has gulled men enough without *my* adding to the number. I, who loathe the living, can scarcely venerate the unborn. Lucy, believe me, that no man can mix largely with men in political life, and not despise every thing that in youth he adored! Age leaves us only one feeling—contempt!"

"Are you belied, then?" said Lucy, pointing to a newspaper, the organ of the party opposed to Brandon: "Are you belied when you are here called 'ambitious?' When they call you 'selfish' and 'grasping' I know they wrong you; but I confess that I *have* thought you ambitious; yet can he who despises men desire their good opinion?"

"Their good opinion!" repeated Brandon, mockingly: "Do we want the bray of the asses we ride?—No!" he resumed, after a pause. "It is *power*, not *honour*; it is the hope of elevating oneself in every respect, in the world without, as well as in the world of one's own mind: it is this hope which makes me labour where I might rest, and will continue the labour to my grave. Lucy," continued Brandon, fixing his keen eyes on his niece, "have you no ambition? have power, and pomp, and place, no charm for your mind?"

"None!" said Lucy, quietly and simply.

"Indeed! yet there are times when I have thought I recognised my blood in your veins. You are sprung from a once noble, but a fallen race. Are you ever susceptible to the weakness of ancestral pride?"

"You say," answered Lucy, "that we should care not for those who live after us; much less, I imagine, should we care for those who have lived ages before!"

"Prettily answered," said Brandon, smiling. "I will tell you at one time or another what effect that weakness you despise already once had, long after your age, upon me. You are early wise on some points—profit by my experience, and be so on *all*."

"That is to say, in despising all men and all things!" said Lucy, also smiling.

"Well, never mind my creed; you may be wise after your own: but trust one, dearest Lucy, who loves you purely and disinterestedly, and who has weighed with scales balanced to a hair all the advantages to be gleaned from an earth, in which I verily think the harvest was gathered before we were put into it;—trust me, Lucy, and never think love—that maiden's dream—so valuable as rank and power: pause well before you yield to the former; accept the latter the moment they are offered you. Love puts you at the feet of another, and that other a tyrant; rank puts others at your feet, and all those thus subjected are your slaves!"

Lucy moved her chair (so that the new position concealed her face) and did not answer; and Brandon, in an altered tone, continued,—

"Would you think, Lucy, that I once was fool enough to imagine that love was a blessing, and to be eagerly sought for? I gave up my hopes, my chances of wealth, of distinction, all that had burned from the years of boyhood into my very heart. I chose poverty, obscurity, humiliation,—but I chose also love. What was my reward? Lucy Brandon, I was deceived—deceived!"

Brandon paused, and Lucy took his hand affectionately, but did not break the silence. Brandon resumed:

"Yes, I was deceived! But I in my turn had a revenge,—and a fitting revenge; for it was not the revenge of hatred, but" (and the speaker laughed sardonically) "of contempt. Enough of this, Lucy! What I wished to say to you is this—grown men and women know more of the truth of things than ye young persons think for. Love is a mere bauble, and no human being ever exchanged for it one solid advantage without repentance. Believe this; and if rank ever puts itself under those pretty feet, be sure not to spurn the footstool."

So saying, with a slight laugh, Brandon lighted his chamber candle, and left the room for the night.

As soon as the lawyer reached his own apartment, he indited to Lord Mauleverer the following epistle:—

"Why, dear Mauleverer, do you not come to town? I want you,—your party wants you; perhaps the K—g wants you; and certainly, if you are serious about my niece, the care of your own love-suit should induce you yourself to want to come hither. I have paved the way for you; and I think, with a little management, you may anticipate a speedy success: but Lucy is a strange girl; and, perhaps, after all, though you ought to be on the spot, you had better leave her as much as possible in my hands. I know human nature, Mauleverer, and that knowledge is the engine by which I will work your triumph. As for the young lover, I am not quite sure whether it be not better for our sake that Lucy should have experienced a disappointment on that score; for when a woman has once loved, and the love is utterly hopeless, she puts all vague ideas of other lovers altogether out of her head; she becomes contented with a husband *whom she can esteem!* Sweet canter! But *you*, Mauleverer, want Lucy *to love you!* And so she will—after you have married her! She will love you partly from the advantages she derives from you, partly from familiarity (to say nothing of your good qualities). For my part, I think domesticity goes so far, that I believe a woman always inclined to be affectionate to a man whom she has once seen in his nightcap. However, you should come to town; my poor brother's recent death allows us to see no one,—the coast will be clear from rivals; grief has softened my niece's heart;—in a word, you could not have a better opportunity.   Come !

"By the way, you say one of the reasons which made you think ill of this Captain Clifford was, your impression that, in the figure of one of his comrades, you recognised something that appeared to you to resemble one of the fellows who robbed you a few months ago.   I understand that, at this moment, the police are in active pursuit of three most accomplished robbers ; nor should I be at all surprised if this very Clifford were to be found the leader of the gang, viz. the notorious Lovett.   I hear that the said leader is a clever and a handsome fellow, of a gentlemanlike address, and that his general associates are two men of the exact stamp of the worthies you have so amusingly described to me.   I heard this yesterday from Nabbem, the police-officer, with whom I once scraped acquaintance on a trial ; and in my grudge against your rival, I hinted at my suspicion that he, Captain Clifford, might not impossibly prove this Rinaldo Rinaldini of the roads.   Nabbem caught at my hint at once ; so that, if it be founded on a true guess, I may flatter my conscience, as well as my friendship, by the hope that I have had some hand in hanging this Adonis of my niece's.   Whether my guess be true or not, Nabbem says he is sure of this Lovett ; for one of his gang has promised to betray him.   Hang these aspiring dogs !   I thought treachery was confined to politics ; and that thought makes me turn to public matters,—in which all people are turning with the most edifying celerity."

     *   *   *   *   *   *   *

     *   *   *   *   *   *   *

     *   *   *   *   *   *   *

Sir William Brandon's epistle found Mauleverer in a fitting mood for Lucy and for London.   Our worthy peer had been not a little chagrined by Lucy's sudden departure from Bath ; and while in doubt whether or not to follow her, the papers had informed him of the squire's death.   Mauleverer, being then fully aware of the impossibility of immediately urging his suit, endeavoured, like the true philosopher he was, to reconcile himself to his hope deferred. Few people were more easily susceptible of consolation than Lord Mauleverer.   He found an agreeable lady, of a face more unfaded than her reputation, to whom he intrusted the care of relieving his leisure moments from *ennui ;* and being a lively woman, the *confidante* discharged the trust with great satisfaction to Lord Mauleverer, for the space of a fortnight, so that he naturally began to feel his love for Lucy gradually wearing away, by absence and other ties ; but just as the triumph of time over passion was growing decisive, the lady left Bath in company with a tall guardsman, and Mauleverer received Brandon's letter. These two events recalled our excellent lover to a sense of his allegiance ; and there being now at Bath no particular attraction to counterbalance the ardour of his affection, Lord Mauleverer ordered the horses to his carriage, and attended only by his valet, set out for London.

Nothing, perhaps, could convey a better portrait of the world's spoiled darling than a sight of Lord Mauleverer's thin, fastidious features, peering forth through the closed window of his luxurious travelling chariot ; the rest of the outer man being carefully enveloped in furs, half-a-dozen novels strewing the seat of the carriage, and a lean French dog, exceedingly like its master, sniffing in vain for the fresh air, which, to the imagination of Mauleverer, was peopled with all sorts of asthmas and catarrhs ! Mauleverer got out of his carriage at Salisbury, to stretch his limbs, and to amuse himself with a cutlet. Our nobleman was well known on the roads ; and, as nobody could be more affable, he was equally popular. The officious landlord bustled into the room, to wait himself upon his lordship, and to tell all the news of the place.

"Well, Mr. Cheerly," said Mauleverer, bestowing a penetrating glance on his cutlet, "the bad times, I see, have not ruined your cook."

"Indeed, my lord, your lordship is very good, and the times, indeed, are very bad—very bad indeed. Is there enough gravy? Perhaps your lordship will try the pickled onions?"

"The what?—Onions!—oh!—ah! nothing can be better ; but I never touch them. So, are the roads good?"

"Your lordship has, I hope, found them good to Salisbury?"

"Ah! I believe so. Oh! to be sure, excellent to Salisbury. But how are they to London? We have had wet weather lately, I think!"

"No, my lord. *Here*, the weather has been as dry as a bone."

"Or a cutlet!" muttered Mauleverer, and the host continued,—

"As for the roads themselves, my lord—so far as the roads are concerned—they are pretty good, my lord ; but I can't say as how there is not something about them that might be mended."

"By no means improbable!—You mean the inns and the turnpikes?" rejoined Mauleverer.

"Your lordship is pleased to be facetious ;—no! I meant something worse than them."

"What! the cooks?"

"No, my lord,—the highwaymen!"

"The highwaymen!—indeed!" said Mauleverer anxiously ; for he had with him a case of diamonds, which at that time were, on grand occasions, often the ornaments of a gentleman's dress, in the shape of buttons, buckles, &c.; he had also a tolerably large sum of ready money about him, a blessing he had lately begun to find very rare:—"By the way, the rascals robbed me before on this very road. My pistols shall be *loaded* this time.—Mr. Cheerly, you had better order the horses; one may as well escape the night-fall."

"Certainly, my lord—certainly.—Jem, the horses immediately! —Your lordship will have another cutlet?"

"Not a morsel!"

"A tart?"

"A dev—! not for the world!"

"Bring the cheese, John!"

"Much obliged to you, Mr. Cheerly, but I have dined; and if I have not done justice to your good cheer, thank yourself and the highwaymen.—Where do these highwaymen attack one?"

"Why, my lord, the neighbourhood of Reading is, I believe, the worst part; but they are very troublesome all the way to Salthill."

"Damnation!—the very neighbourhood in which the knaves robbed me before!—You may well call them *troublesome!* Why the deuce don't the police clear the country of such a movable species of trouble?"

"Indeed, my lord, I don't know: but they say as how Captain Lovett, the famous robber, be one of the set; and nobody can catch him, I fear!"

"Because, I suppose, the dog has the sense to bribe as well as bully.—What is the general number of these ruffians?"

"Why, my lord, sometimes one, sometimes two, but seldom more than three."

Mauleverer drew himself up. "My dear diamonds, and my pretty purse!" thought he; "I may save you yet!"

"Have you been long plagued with the fellows?" he asked, after a pause, as he was paying his bill.

"Why, my lord, we have and we have not. I fancy as how they have a sort of haunt near Reading, for sometimes they are intolerable just about there, and sometimes they are quiet for months together! For instance, my lord, we thought them all gone some time ago; but lately they have regularly stopped every one, though I hear as how they have cleared no great booty as yet."

Here the waiter announced the horses, and Mauleverer slowly re-entered his carriage, among the bows and smiles of the charmed spirits of the hostelry.

During the daylight, Mauleverer, who was naturally of a gallant and fearless temper, thought no more of the highwaymen,—a species

of danger so common at that time, that men almost considered it
disgraceful to suffer the dread of it to be a cause of delay on the road.
Travellers seldom deemed it best to lose time in order to save money ;
and they carried with them a stout heart and a brace of pistols, instead of sleeping all night on the road.   Mauleverer, rather a *preux
chevalier*, was precisely of this order of wayfarers ; and a night at an
inn, when it was possible to avoid it, was to him, as to most rich
Englishmen, a tedious torture zealously to be shunned.   It never,
therefore, entered into the head of our excellent nobleman, despite
his experience, that his diamonds and his purse might be saved from
all danger, if he would consent to deposit them, with his own person,
at some place of hospitable reception ; nor, indeed, was it till he was
within a stage of Reading, and the twilight had entirely closed in,
that he troubled his head much on the matter.   But while the horses
were putting to, he summoned the postboys to him ; and, after regarding their countenances with the eye of a man accustomed to read
physiognomies, he thus eloquently addressed them :—

   "Gentlemen,—I am informed that there is some danger of being
robbed between this town and Salthill.   Now, I beg to inform you,
that I think it next to impossible for four horses, properly directed,
to be stopped by less than four men.   To that number I shall probably yield ; to a less number I shall most assuredly give nothing
but bullets.   You understand me?"

   The postboys grinned, touched their hats, and Mauleverer slowly
continued,—

   "If, therefore,—mark me !—one, two, or three men stop your
horses, and I find that the use of your whips and spurs are ineffectual in releasing the animals from the hold of the robbers,
I intend with these pistols—you observe them !—to shoot at the
gentlemen who detain you ; but as, though I am generally a dead
shot, my eyesight wavers a little in the dark, I think it very
possible that I may have the misfortune to shoot *you*, gentlemen,
instead of the robbers !   You see the rascals will be close by you,
sufficiently so to put you in jeopardy, unless, indeed, you knock
them down with the butt-end of your whips.   I merely mention
this, that you may be prepared.   Should such a mistake occur,
you need not be uneasy beforehand, for I will take every possible
care of your widows ; should it not, and should we reach Salthill
in safety, I intend to testify my sense of the excellence of your
driving by a present of ten guineas a-piece ' Gentlemen, I have
done with you.   I give you my honour, that I am serious in what
I have said to you.   Do me the favour to mount."

   Mauleverer than called his favourite servant, who sat in the
dickey in front (rumble-tumbles not being then in use).

"Smoothson," said he, "the last time we were attacked on this very road, you behaved damnably. See that you do better this time, or it may be the worse for you. *You* have pistols to-night about you, eh? Well! that's right! And you are sure they're loaded? Very well! Now, then, if we are stopped, don't lose a moment. Jump down, and fire one of your pistols at the first robber. Keep the other for a *sure* aim. One shot is to intimidate, the second to slay. You comprehend? *My* pistols are in excellent order, I suppose. Lend me the ramrod. So, so! No trick this time!"

"They would kill a fly, my lord, provided your lordship fired straight upon it."

"I do not doubt you," said Mauleverer; "light the lanterns, and tell the postboys to drive on."

It was a frosty and tolerably clear night. The dusk of the twilight had melted away beneath the moon which had just risen, and the hoary rime glittered from the bushes and the sward, breaking into a thousand diamonds as it caught the rays of the stars. On went the horses briskly, their breath steaming against the fresh air, and their hoofs sounding cheerily on the hard ground. The rapid motion of the carriage—the bracing coolness of the night—and the excitement occasioned by anxiety and the forethought of danger, all conspired to stir the languid blood of Lord Mauleverer into a vigorous and exhilarated sensation, natural in youth to his character, but utterly contrary to the nature he had imbibed from the customs of his manhood.

He felt his pistols, and his hands trembled a little as he did so :— not the least from fear, but from that restlessness and eagerness peculiar to nervous persons placed in a new situation.

"In this country," said he to himself, "I have been only once robbed in the course of my life. It was then a little my fault; for before I took to my pistols, I should have been certain they were loaded. To-night, I shall be sure to avoid a similar blunder; and my pistols have an eloquence in their barrels which is exceedingly moving. Humph, another milestone! These fellows drive well, but we are entering a pretty-looking spot for Messieurs the disciples of Robin Hood!"

It was, indeed, a picturesque spot by which the carriage was now rapidly whirling. A few miles from Maidenhead, on the Henley Road, our readers will probably remember a small tract of forest-like land, lying on either side of the road. To the left, the green waste bears away among trees and bushes; and one skilled in the country may pass from that spot, through a landscape as little tenanted as green Sherwood was formerly, into the chains of wild common and deep beech-woods which border a certain portion of

Oxfordshire, and contrast so beautifully the general characteristics of that county.

At the time we speak of, the country was even far wilder than it is now ; and just on that point where the Henley and the Reading roads unite was a spot (communicating then with the waste land we have described), than which, perhaps, few places could be more adapted to the purposes of such true men as have recourse to the primary law of nature. Certain it was that at this part of the road Mauleverer looked more anxiously from his window than he had hitherto done, and apparently the increased earnestness of his survey was not altogether without meeting its reward.

About a hundred yards to the left, three dark objects were just discernible in the shade ; a moment more, and the objects emerging grew into the forms of three men, well mounted, and riding at a brisk trot.

"*Only* three !" thought Mauleverer, " that is well," and leaning from the front-window with a pistol in either hand, Mauleverer cried out to the postboys in a stern tone, "Drive on, and recollect what I told you !—Remember !" he added to his servant. The postboys scarcely looked round ; but their spurs were buried in their horses, and the animals flew on like lightning.

The three strangers made a halt, as if in conference : their decision was prompt. Two wheeled round from their comrade, and darted at full gallop by the carriage. Mauleverer's pistol was already protruded from the front-window, when to his astonishment, and to the utter baffling of his ingenious admonition to his drivers, he beheld the two postboys knocked from their horses one after the other with a celerity that scarcely allowed him an exclamation ; and before he had recovered his self-possession, the horses taking fright (and their flight being skilfully taken advantage of by the highwaymen), the carriage was fairly whirled into a ditch on the right side of the road, and upset. Meanwhile, Smoothson had leaped from his station in the front ; and having fired, though without effect, at the third robber, who approached menacingly towards him, he gained the time to open the carriage door, and extricate his master.

The moment Mauleverer found himself on *terra firma*, he prepared his courage for offensive measures, and he and Smoothson standing side by side in front of the unfortunate vehicle, presented no unformidable aspect to the enemy. The two robbers who had so decisively rid themselves of the postboys acted with no less determination towards the horses. One of them dismounted, cut the traces, and suffered the plunging quadrupeds to go whither they listed. This measure was not, however, allowed to be taken with impunity ; a ball from Mauleverer's pistol passed through the

hat of the highwayman with an aim so slightly erring, that it whizzed
among the locks of the astounded hero with a sound that sent a terror
to his heart, no less from a love of his head than from anxiety for his
hair.   The shock staggered him for a moment ; and a second shot
from the hands of Mauleverer would have probably finished his
earthly career, had not the third robber, who had hitherto remained
almost inactive, thrown himself from his horse, which, tutored to
such docility, remained perfectly still, and advancing with a bold
step and a levelled pistol toward Mauleverer and his servant, said in
a resolute voice, " Gentlemen, it is useless to struggle ; we are well
armed, and resolved on effecting our purpose : your persons shall be
safe if you lay down your arms, and also such part of your property
as you may particularly wish to retain.   But if you resist, I cannot
answer for your lives ! "

Mauleverer had listened patiently to this speech in order that he
might have more time for adjusting his aim : his reply was a bullet,
which grazed the side of the speaker and tore away the skin, without
inflicting any more dangerous wound.   Muttering a curse upon the
error of his aim, and resolute to the last when his blood was once
up, Mauleverer backed one pace, drew his sword, and threw himself into the attitude of a champion well skilled in the use of the
instrument he wore.

But that incomparable personage was in a fair way of ascertaining
what happiness in the world to come is reserved for a man who has
spared no pains to make himself comfortable in this.   For the two
first and most active robbers having finished the achievement of
the horses, now approached Mauleverer, and the taller of them,
still indignant at the late peril to his hair, cried out in a stentorian
voice —

" By Jove ! you old fool, if you don't throw down your toasting-
fork, I'll be the death of you ! "

The speaker suited the action to the word, by cocking an immense pistol.   Mauleverer stood his ground ; but Smoothson
retreated, and stumbling against the wheel of the carriage fell backward ; the next instant, the second highwayman had possessed
himself of the valet's pistols, and, quietly seated on the fallen man's
stomach, amused himself by inspecting the contents of the domestic's
pockets   Mauleverer was now alone, and his stubbornness so
enraged the tall bully that his hand was already on his trigger, when
the third robber, whose side Mauleverer's bullet had grazed, thrust
himself between the two.—" Hold, Ned ! " said he, pushing back
his comrade's pistol.—" And you, my lord, whose rashness ought to
cost you your life, learn that men can rob generously."   So saying,
with one dexterous stroke from the robber's riding-whip, Mauleverer's

sword flew upwards, and alighted at the distance of ten yards from its owner.

"Approach now," said the victor to his comrades. "Rifle the carriage, and with all despatch!"

The tall highwaymen hastened to execute this order; and the lesser one having satisfactorily finished the inquisition into Mr. Smoothson's pockets, drew forth from his own pouch a tolerably thick rope; with this he tied the hands of the prostrate valet, moralising as he wound the rope round and round the wrists of the fallen man, in the following edifying strain:—

"Lie still, sir—lie still, I beseech you! All wise men are fatalists; and no proverb is more pithy than that which says, 'what can't be cured must be endured.' Lie still, I tell you! Little, perhaps, do you think that you are performing one of the noblest functions of humanity; yes, sir, you are filling the pockets of the destitute; and by my present action I am securing you from any weakness of the flesh likely to impede so praiseworthy an end, and so hazard the excellence of your action. There, sir, your hands are tight,—lie still and reflect."

As he said this, with three gentle applications of his feet, the moralist rolled Mr. Smoothson into the ditch, and hastened to join his lengthy comrade in his pleasing occupation.

In the interim, Mauleverer and the third robber (who, in the true spirit of government, remained dignified and inactive while his followers plundered what *he* certainly designed to share, if not to monopolise, stood within a few feet of each other, face to face.

Mauleverer had now convinced himself that all endeavour to save his property was hopeless, and he had also the consolation of thinking he had done his best to defend it. He, therefore, bade all thoughts return to the care of his person. He adjusted his fur collar around his neck with great *sang froid*, drew on his gloves, and, patting his terrified poodle, who sat shivering on its haunches with one paw raised and nervously trembling, he said,—

"You, sir, seem to be a civil person, and I really should have felt quite sorry if I had had the misfortune to wound you. You are not hurt, I trust. Pray, if I may inquire, how am I to proceed? My carriage is in the ditch, and my horses by this time are probably at the end of the world."

"As for that matter," said the robber, whose face, like those of his comrades, was closely masked in the approved fashion of highwaymen of that day, "I believe you will have to walk to Maidenhead—it is not far, and the night is fine!"

"A very trifling hardship, indeed!" said Mauleverer, ironically;

but his new acquaintance made no reply, nor did he appear at all desirous of entering into any further conversation with Mauleverer.

The earl, therefore, after watching the operations of the other robbers for some moments, turned on his heel, and remained humming an opera tune with dignified indifference until the pair had finished rifling the carriage, and, seizing Mauleverer, proceeded to rifle *him*.

With a curled lip and a raised brow, that supreme personage suffered himself to be, as the taller robber expressed it, "cleaned out." His watch, his rings, his purse, and his snuff-box, all went. It was long since the rascals had captured such a booty.

They had scarcely finished when the postboys, who had now begun to look about them, uttered a simultaneous cry, and at some distance a waggon was seen heavily approaching. Mauleverer really wanted his money, to say nothing of his diamonds; and so soon as he perceived assistance at hand, a new hope darted within him. His sword still lay on the ground; he sprang towards it— seized it, uttered a shout for help, and threw himself fiercely on the highwayman who had disarmed him; but the robber, warding off the blade with his whip, retreated to his saddle, which he managed, despite of Mauleverer's lunges, to regain with impunity.

The other two had already mounted, and within a minute afterwards not a vestige of the trio was visible. "This is what may fairly be called *single blessedness !*" said Mauleverer, as, dropping his useless sword, he thrust his hands into his pockets.

Leaving our peerless peer to find his way to Maidenhead on foot, accompanied (to say nothing of the poodle) by one waggoner, two postboys, and the released Mr. Smoothson, all four charming him with their condolences, we follow with our story the steps of the three *alieni appetentes.*

CHAPTER XXVI.

" The rogues were very merry on their booty. They said a thousand things that showed the wickedness of their morals."—GIL BLAS.

" They fixed on a spot where they made a cave, which was large enough to receive them and their horses This cave was enclosed within a sort of thicket of bushes and brambles. From this station they used to issue," &c —'MEMOIRS OF RICHARD TURPIN.'

IT was not for several minutes after their flight had com-menced that any conversation passed between the robbers. Their horses flew on like wind, and the country through which they rode presented to their speed no other obstacle than an occasional hedge, or a short cut through the thick-nesses of some leafless beechwood. The stars lent them a merry light, and the spirits of two of them at least were fully in sympathy with the exhilaration of the pace and the air. Perhaps, in the third, a certain presentiment that the present adventure would end less merrily than it had begun, conspired, with other causes of gloom, to check that exaltation of the blood which generally follows a success-ful exploit.

The path which the robbers took wound by the sides of long woods, or across large tracts of uncultivated land. Nor did they encounter anything living by the road, save now and then a solitary owl, wheeling its grey body around the skirts of the bare woods, or occasionally troops of conies, pursuing their sports and enjoying their midnight food in the fields.

"Heavens!" cried the tall robber, whose incognito we need no longer preserve, and who, as our readers are doubtless aware, answered to the name of Pepper,—"Heavens!" cried he, looking upward at the starry skies in a sort of ecstasy, "what a jolly life this is! Some fellows like hunting; d—— it! what hunting is like the road? If there be sport in hunting down a nasty fox, how much more is there in hunting down a nice clean nobleman's carriage! If there be joy in getting a brush, how much more is there in getting a purse! If it be pleasant to fly over a hedge in the broad daylight, hang me if it be not ten times finer sport to skim it by night,—here goes! Look how the hedges run away from us! and the silly old moon dances about, as if the sight of us put the good lady in spirits! Those old maids are always glad to have an eye upon such fine dashing young fellows."

"Ay," cried the more erudite and sententious Augustus Tomlinson, roused by success from his usual philosophical sobriety; "no work is so pleasant as night-work, and the witches our ancestors burnt were in the right to ride out on their broomsticks, with the owls and the stars. We are their successors *now*, Ned. We are your true fly-by-nights!"

"Only," quoth Ned, "we are a cursed deal more clever than they were; for they played their game without being a bit the richer for it, and we—I say, Tomlinson, where the devil did you put that red morocco case?"

"Experience never enlightens the foolish!" said Tomlinson; "or you would have known, without asking, that I had put it in the very safest pocket in my coat. 'Gad, how heavy it is!"

"Well!" cried Pepper, "I can't say I wish it were lighter! Only think of our robbing my lord twice, and on the same road too!"

"I say, Lovett," exclaimed Tomlinson, "was it not odd that we should have stumbled upon our Bath friend so unceremoniously? Lucky for us that we are so strict in robbing in masks! He would not have thought the better of Bath company if he had seen our faces."

Lovett, or rather Clifford, had hitherto been silent. He now turned slowly in his saddle, and said,—"As it was, the poor devil was very nearly despatched. Long Ned was making short work with him—if I had not interposed!"

"And why did you?" said Ned.

"Because I will have no killing · it is the curse of the noble art of our profession to have passionate professors like thee."

"Passionate!" repeated Ned: "well, I am a little choleric, I own it; but that is not so great a fault on the road as it would be in house-breaking. I don't know a thing that requires so much coolness and self-possession as cleaning out a house from top to bottom—quietly and civilly, mind you!"

"That is the reason, I suppose, then," said Augustus, "that you altogether renounced *that* career. Your first adventure was house-breaking, I think I have heard you say. I confess it was a vulgar *début*—not worthy of you!"

"No!—Harry Cook seduced me; but the specimen I saw that night disgusted me of picking locks; it brings one in contact with such low companions: only think, there was a merchant—a rag-merchant, one of the party!"

"Faugh!" said Tomlinson, in solemn disgust.

"Ay, you may well turn up your lip: I never broke into a house again."

"Who were your other companions?" asked Augustus.

"Only Harry Cook,[1] and a very singular woman——"

Here Ned's narrative was interrupted by a dark defile through a wood, allowing room for only one horseman at a time. They continued this gloomy path for several minutes, until at length it brought them to the brink of a large dell, overgrown with bushes, and spreading around somewhat in the form of a rude semicircle. Here the robbers dismounted, and led their reeking horses down the descent. Long Ned, who went first, paused at a cluster of bushes, which seemed so thick as to defy intrusion, but which yielding, on either side, to the experienced hand of the robber, presented what appeared the mouth of a cavern. A few steps along the passage of this gulf brought them to a door, which, even seen by torch-light, would have appeared so exactly similar in colour and material to the rude walls on either side, as to have deceived any unsuspecting eye, and which, in the customary darkness brooding over it, might have remained for centuries undiscovered. Touching a secret latch, the door opened, and the robbers were in the secure precincts of the "Red Cave!" It may be remembered that among the early studies of our exemplary hero, the memoirs of Richard Turpin had formed a conspicuous portion; and it may also be remembered that, in the miscellaneous adventures of that gentleman, nothing had more delighted the juvenile imagination of the student than the description of the forest cave in which the gallant Turpin had been accustomed to conceal himself, his friend, his horse,

"And that sweet saint who lay by Turpin's side,"

or, to speak more domestically, the respectable Mrs. Turpin. So strong a hold, indeed, had that early reminiscence fixed upon our hero's mind, that, no sooner had he risen to eminence among his friends, than he had put the project of his childhood into execution. He had selected for the scene of his ingenuity an admirable spot. In a thinly-peopled country, surrounded by commons and woods, and yet (as Mr. Robins would say, if he had to dispose of it by auction) "within an easy ride" of populous and well-frequented roads, it possessed all the advantages of secrecy for itself, and convenience for depredation. Very few of the gang, and those only who had been employed in its construction, were made acquainted with the secret of this cavern; and as our adventurers rarely visited it, and only on occasions of urgent want or secure concealment, it had continued for more than two years undiscovered and unsuspected.

The cavern, originally hollowed by nature, owed but little to the

_____
[1] A noted highwayman

decorations of art: nevertheless, the roughness of the walls was concealed by a rude but comfortable arras of matting: four or five of such seats as the robbers themselves could construct were drawn around a small but bright wood fire, which, as there was no chimney, spread a thin volume of smoke over the apartment. The height of the cave, added to the universal reconciler—custom—prevented, however, this evil from being seriously unpleasant; and, indeed, like the tenants of an Irish cabin, perhaps the inmates attached a degree of comfort to a circumstance which was coupled with their dearest household associations. A table, formed of a board coarsely planed, and supported by four legs of irregular size, made equal by the introduction of blocks or wedges between the legs and the floor, stood warming its uncouth self by the fire. At one corner, a covered cart made a conspicuous article of furniture, no doubt useful either in conveying plunder or provisions; beside the wheels were carelessly thrown two or three coarse carpenter's tools, and the more warlike utilities of a blunderbuss, a rifle, and two broad-swords. In the other corner was an open cupboard, containing rows of pewter platters, mugs, &c. Opposite the fire-place, which was to the left of the entrance, an excavation had been turned into a dormitory; and fronting the entrance was a pair of broad, strong, wooden steps, ascending to a large hollow about eight feet from the ground. This was the entrance to the stables; and as soon as their owners released the reins of the horses, the docile animals proceeded one by one leisurely up the steps, in the manner of quadrupeds educated at the public seminary of Astley's, and disappeared within the aperture.

These steps, when drawn up—which, however, from their extreme clumsiness, required the united strength of two ordinary men, and was not that instantaneous work which it should have been,—made the place above a tolerably strong hold, for the wall was perfectly perpendicular and level, and it was only by placing his hands upon the ledge, and so lifting himself gymnastically upward, that an active assailant could have reached the eminence: a work which defenders equally active, it may easily be supposed, would not be likely to allow.

This upper cave—for our robbers paid more attention to their horses than themselves, as the nobler animals of the two species— was evidently fitted up with some labour. The stalls were rudely divided, the litter of dry fern was clean, troughs were filled with oats, and a large tub had been supplied from a pond at a little distance. A cart-harness, and some old wagoners' frocks, were fixed on pegs to the wall. While at the far end of these singular stables was a door strongly barred, and only just large enough to admit the body of a man. The confederates had made it an express law never to enter their domain by this door, or to use it, except for the purpose of escape, should the cave ever be attacked ; in which case, while one or two defended the entrance from the inner cave, another might unbar the door, and as it opened upon the thickest part of the wood, through which with great ingenuity a labyrinthine path had been cut, not easily tracked by ignorant pursuers, these precautions of the highwaymen had provided a fair hope of at least a temporary escape from any invading enemies.

Such were the domestic arrangements of the Red Cave, and it will be conceded that at least some skill had been shown in the choice of the spot, if there were a lack of taste in its adornments.

While the horses were performing their nightly ascent, our three heroes, after securing the door, made at once to the fire. And there, O reader ! they were greeted in welcome by one,—an old and revered acquaintance of thine,—whom in such a scene it will equally astound and wound thee to re-behold.

Know, then,—but first we will describe to thee the occupation and the garb of the august personage to whom we allude. Bending over a large gridiron, daintily bespread with steaks of the fatted rump, the INDIVIDUAL stood ; with his right arm bared above the elbow, and his right hand grasping that mimic trident known unto gastronomers by the monosyllable "fork." His wigless head was adorned with a cotton night-cap. His upper vestment was discarded, and a whitish apron flowed gracefully down his middle man. His stockings were ungartered, and permitted between the knee and the calf interesting glances of the rude carnal. One list shoe and one of leathern manufacture cased his ample feet. Enterprise, or the noble glow of his present culinary profession, spread a yet rosier blush over a countenance early tinged by generous libations, and from beneath the curtain of his pallid eyelashes his large and rotund orbs gleamed dazzlingly on the new-comers. Such, O reader ! was the aspect and the occupation of the venerable man whom we have long since taught thee to admire ; such—alas for the mutabilities of earth !—was—a new chapter only can contain the name.

CHAPTER XXVII.

"CALIBAN.—*Hast thou not dropped from Heaven?*"—'TEMPEST.'

PETER MAC GRAWLER ! ' ! ! !
! ! ! ! ! ! ! !
! ' ! ' ! ' ! !
! ! ! ! ! ' ! !
! ! ' ' ' ! ! !
! ' ! ' ! ' ! !
! ! ! ' ! ' ! !
' ' ' ' ! ' ! !
! ! ! ' ! ' ! !
! ' ! ' ! ' ! !
! ! ! ! ! ' ! !

CHAPTER XXVIII.

"*God bless our King and Parliament,*
And send he may make such knaves repent!"
'LOYAL SONGS AGAINST THE RUMP PARLIAMENT.'

"*Ho, treachery! my guards, my cimeter!*"—BYRON.

WHEN the irreverent Mr. Pepper had warmed his hands sufficiently to be able to transfer them from the fire, he lifted the right palm, and, with an indecent jocularity of spirits, accosted the *ci-devant* ornament of "The Asinæum" with a sounding slap on his back—or some *such* part of his conformation.

"Ah, old boy!" said he, "is this the way you keep house for us? A fire not large enough to roast a nit, and a supper too small to fatten him beforehand! But how the deuce should you know how to provender for gentlemen? You thought you were in Scotland, I'll be bound!"

"Perhaps he did, when he looked upon you, Ned!" said Tomlinson, gravely; "'tis but rarely out of Scotland that a man can see so big a rogue in so little a compass!"

Mr. Mac Grawler, into whose eyes the palmistry of Long Ned had brought tears of sincere feeling, and who had hitherto been rubbing the afflicted part, now grumbled forth,—

"You may say what you please, Mr. Pepper, but it is not often in my country that men of genius are seen performing the part of cook to robbers!"

"No!" quoth Tomlinson, "they are performing the more profitable part of robbers to cooks, eh!"

"Dammee, you're out," cried Long Ned; "for in that country, there are either no robbers, because there is nothing to rob; or the inhabitants are all robbers, who have plundered one another, and made away with the booty!"

"May the de'il catch thee!" said Mac Grawler, stung to the quick,—for, like all Scots, he was a patriot; much on the same principle as a woman who has the worst children makes the best mother.

"The de'il!" said Ned, mimicking the "silver sound," as Sir W. Scott has been pleased facetiously to call the "mountain tongue,"—the Scots in general seem to think it *is* silver, they keep it so carefully. "The de'il—*Mac Deil*, you mean,—sure the gentleman must have been a Scotchman!"

The sage grinned in spite; but remembering the patience of Epictetus when a slave, and mindful also of the strong arm of Long Ned, he curbed his temper, and turned the beefsteaks with his fork.

"Well, Ned," said Augustus, throwing himself into a chair which he drew to the fire, while he gently patted the huge limbs of Mr. Pepper, as if to admonish him that they were not so transparent as glass—"let us look at the fire; and, by the by, it is your turn to see to the horses."

"Plague on it!" cried Ned, "it is always my turn, I think. Holla, you Scot of the pot! can't you prove that I groomed the beasts last? I'll give you a crown to do it."

The wise Mac Grawler pricked up his ears.

"A crown!" said he,—"a crown! do you mean to insult me, Mr. Pepper? But, to be sure, you did see to the horses last, and this worthy gentleman, Mr. Tomlinson, must remember it too."

"How, I!" cried Augustus; "you are mistaken, and I'll give you half a guinea to prove it."

Mac Grawler opened his eyes larger and larger, even as you may see a small circle in the water widen into enormity, if you disturb the equanimity of the surface by the obtrusion of a foreign substance.

"Half a guinea!" said he; "nay, nay, you joke: I'm not mercenary,—you think I am! Pooh, pooh! you are mistaken; I'm a man who means *weel*, a man of veracity, and will speak the truth in spite of all the half guineas in the world. But certainly, now I begin to think of it, Mr. Tomlinson did see to the creatures last,—and, Mr. Pepper, it *is* your turn."

"A very Daniel!" said Tomlinson, chuckling in his usual dry manner. "Ned, don't you hear the horses neigh?"

"Oh, hang the horses!" said the volatile Pepper, forgetting everything else, as he thrust his hands in his pockets, and felt the gains of the night; "let us first look to our winnings!"

So saying, he marched towards the table, and emptied his pockets thereon: Tomlinson, nothing loath, followed the example. Heavens! what exclamations of delight issued from the scoundrels' lips, as, one by one, they inspected their new acquisitions.

"Here's a magnificent creature!" cried Ned, handling that superb watch studded with jewels which the poor earl had once before unavailingly redeemed: "a repeater, by Jove!"

"I hope not," said the phlegmatic Augustus; "repeaters will not tell well for your conversation, Ned! But, powers that be! look at this ring,—a diamond of the first water!"

"Oh, the sparkler! it makes one's mouth water as much as itself. 'Sdeath, here's a precious box for a sneezer!—a picture inside, and rubies outside. The old fellow had excellent taste! it would charm him to see how pleased we are with his choice of jewellery!"

"Talking of jewellery," said Tomlinson, "I had almost forgotten the morocco case; between you and me, I imagine we have a prize there; it looks like a jewel casket!"

So saying, the robber opened that case which on many a gala day had lent lustre to the polished person of Mauleverer. O reader, the burst of rapture that ensued! imagine it! we cannot express it! Like the Grecian painter, we drop a veil over emotions too deep for words.

"But here," said Pepper, when they had almost exhausted their transports at sight of the diamonds, "here's a purse—fifty guineas! And what's this? notes, by Jupiter! We must change them to-morrow before they are stopped. Curse those fellows at the Bank! they are always imitating us; we stop their money, and they don't lose a moment in stopping it too. Three hundred pounds! Captain, what say you to our luck?"

Clifford had sat gloomily looking on, during the operations of the robbers; he now, assuming a correspondent cheerfulness of manner, made a suitable reply, and after some general conversation, the work of division took place.

"We are the best arithmeticians in the world!" said Augustus, as he pouched his share: "addition, subtraction, division, reduction,—

we have them all as pat as 'The Tutor's Assistant;' and, what is better, we make them all applicable to the *Rule of Three.*"

" You have left out multiplication!" said Clifford, smiling.

" Ah! because that works differently; the other rules apply to the species of the kingdom; but as for multiplication, we multiply, I fear, no species but our own!"

"Fie, gentlemen!" said Mac Grawler, austerely,—for there is a wonderful decorum in your true Scotsmen. Actions are trifles; nothing can be cleaner than their *words!*

" Oh, you thrust in *your* wisdom, do you?" said Ned. "I suppose you want your part of the booty!"

" Part!" said the subtilising Tomlinson. " He has nine times as many parts as we have already. Is he not a critic, and has he not the parts of speech at his fingers' end?"

"Nonsense!" said Mac Grawler, instinctively holding up his hands, with the fork dropping between the out-stretched fingers of the right palm.

" Nonsense yourself," cried Ned; "*you* have a share in what you never took! A pretty fellow, truly! Mind your business, Mr. Scot, and fork nothing but the beefsteaks?"

With this Ned turned to the stables, and soon disappeared among the horses; but Clifford, eyeing the disappointed and eager face of the culinary sage, took ten guineas from his own share, and pushed them towards his quondam tutor.

" There!" said he, emphatically.

"Nay, nay," grunted Mac Grawler; " I don't want the money,— it is my way to scorn such dross!" So saying, he pocketed the coins, and turned, muttering to himself, to the renewal of his festive preparations.

Meanwhile a whispered conversation took place between Augustus and the captain, and continued till Ned returned.

" And the night's viands smoked along the board!"

Souls of Don Raphael and Ambrose Lamela, what a charming thing it is to be a rogue for a little time! How merry men are when they have cheated their brethren! Your innocent milksops never made so jolly a supper as did our heroes of the way. Clifford, per-haps, acted a part, but the hilarity of his comrades was unfeigned. It was a delicious contrast,—the boisterous "ha, ha!" of Long Ned, and the secret, dry, calculating chuckle of Augustus Tomlinson. It was Rabelais against Voltaire. They united only in the objects of their jests, and foremost of those objects (wisdom is ever the butt of the frivolous!) was the great Peter Mac Grawler.

The graceless dogs were especially merry upon the subject of the sage's former occupation.

"Come, Mac, you carve this ham," said Ned ; "you have had practice in cutting up."

The learned man whose name was thus disrespectfully abbreviated proceeded to perform what he was bid. He was about to sit down for that purpose, when Tomlinson slily subtracted his chair, —the sage fell.

"No jests at Mac Grawler," said the malicious Augustus ; "whatever be his faults as a critic, you see that he is well grounded, and he gets at once to the bottom of a subject.—Mac, suppose your next work be entitled _a Tail_ of Woe !"

Men who have great minds are rarely flexible ; they do not take a jest readily ; so it was with Mac Grawler. He rose in a violent rage ; and had the robbers been more penetrating than they condescended to be, they might have noticed something dangerous in his eye. As it was, Clifford, who had often before been the protector of his tutor, interposed in his behalf, drew the sage a seat near to himself, and filled his plate for him. It was interesting to see this deference from Power to Learning ! It was Alexander doing homage to Aristotle !

"There is only one thing I regret," cried Ned, with his mouth full, "about the old lord,—it was a thousand pities we did not make him dance ! I remember the day, captain, when you would have insisted on it. What a merry fellow you were once ! Do you recollect, one bright moonlight night, just like the present, for instance, when we were doing duty near Staines, how you swore every person we stopped, above fifty years old, should dance a minuet with you ?"

"Ay ! " added Augustus, "and the first was a bishop in a white wig. Faith, how stiffly his lordship jigged it ! And how gravely Lovett bowed to him, with his hat off, when it was all over, and returned him his watch and ten guineas, —it was worth the sacrifice ! "

"And the next was an old maid of quality," said Ned, " as lean as a lawyer. Don't you remember how she curvetted ? "

" To be sure," said Tomlinson ; "and you very wittily called her a _hop_-pole ! "

"How delighted she was with the captain's suavity ! When he gave her back her earrings and _aigrette_, she bade him with a tender sigh keep them for her sake,—ha ! ha ! "

"And the third was a beau !" cried Augustus ; "and Lovett surrendered his right of partnership to me. Do you recollect how I danced his beauship into the ditch ?—Ah ! we were mad fellows then ; but we get sated—*blasés*, as the French say—as we grow older ! "

" We look only to the main chance now," said Ned.

" Avarice supersedes enterprise," added the sententious Augustus.

" And our captain takes to wine with an *h* after the *w !* " continued the metaphorical Ned.

" Come, we are melancholy," said Tomlinson, tossing off a bumper. " Methinks we are *really* growing old, we shall repent soon, and the next step will be—hanging ! "

" 'Fore Gad ! " said Ned, helping himself, "don't be so croaking. There are two classes of maligned gentry, who should always be particular to avoid certain colours in dressing : I hate to see a true boy in black, or a devil in blue. But here's my last glass tonight ! I am confoundedly sleepy, and we rise early to-morrow."

" Right, Ned," said Tomlinson ; "give us a song before you retire, and let it be that one which Lovett composed the last time we were here."

Ned, always pleased with an opportunity of displaying himself, cleared his voice and complied.

A DITTY FROM SHERWOOD.

I.

" Laugh with us at the prince and the palace,
   In the wild wood-life there is better cheer ;
Would you hoard your mirth from your neighbour's malice,
   Gather it up in our garners here.
Some kings their wealth from their subjects wring,
   While by their foes they the poorer wax ;
Free go the men of the wise wood-king,
   And it is only our foes we tax.
Leave the cheats of trade to the shrewd gude-wife .
   Let the old be knaves at ease ;
Away with the tide of that dashing life
   Which is stirred by a constant breeze !

II.

Laugh with us when you hear deceiving
   And solemn rogues tell you what knaves we be ,
Commerce and law have a method of thieving
   Worse than a stand at the outlaw's tree.
Say, will the maiden we love despise
   Gallants at least to each other true ?
I grant that we trample on legal ties,
   But I have heard that Love scorns them too
Courage, then,—courage, ye jolly boys,
   Whom the fool with the knavish rates :
Oh ! who that is loved by the world enjoys
   Half as much as the man it hates ? "

"Bravissimo, Ned!" cried Tomlinson, rapping the table; "bravissimo! your voice is superb to-night, and your song admirable. Really, Lovett, it does your poetical genius great credit; quite philosophical, upon my honour."

"Bravissimo!" said Mac Grawler, nodding his head awfully. "Mr. Pepper's voice is as sweet as a bagpipe!—Ah! such a song would have been invaluable to 'The Asinæum,' when I had the honour to——"

"Be Vicar of *Bray* to that establishment," interrupted Tomlinson. "Pray, Mac Grawler, why do they call Edinburgh the Modern Athens?"

"Because of the learned and great men it produces," returned Mac Grawler, with conscious pride.

"Pooh! pooh!—you are thinking of *ancient* Athens. Your city is called the *modern* Athens, because you are all so like the modern Athenians,—the greatest scoundrels imaginable, unless travellers belie them."

"Nay," interrupted Ned, who was softened by the applause of the critic, "Mac is a good fellow, spare him. Gentlemen, your health. I am going to bed, and I suppose you will not tarry long behind me."

"Trust us for that," answered Tomlinson; "the captain and I will consult on the business of the morrow, and join you in the twinkling of a bedpost, as it has been shrewdly expressed."

Ned yawned his last "good-night," and disappeared within the dormitory. Mac Grawler yawning also, but with a graver yawn, as became his wisdom, betook himself to the duty of removing the supper paraphernalia: after bustling soberly about for some minutes, he let down a press-bed in the corner of the cave (for he did not sleep in the robbers' apartment), and undressing himself, soon appeared buried in the bosom of Morpheus. But the chief and Tomlinson, drawing their seats nearer to the dying embers, defied the slothful god, and entered with low tones into a close and anxious commune

"So, then," said Augustus, "now that you have realised sufficient funds for your purpose, you will really desert us,—have you well weighed the *pros* and *cons?* Remember, that nothing is so dangerous to our state as reform; the moment a man grows honest, the gang forsake him; the magistrate misses his fee; the informer peaches; and the recusant hangs."

"I have well weighed all this," answered Clifford, "and have decided on my course. I have only tarried till my means could assist my will. With my share of our present and late booty, I shall betake myself to the Continent. Prussia gives easy trust, and ready promotion, to all who will enlist in her service. But this language, my dear friend, seems strange from your lips. Surely you will join me in my separation from the *corps?* What! you shake your head! Are you not the same Tomlinson who at Bath agreed with me that we were in danger from the envy of our comrades, and that retreat had become necessary to our safety? Nay, was not this your main argument for our matrimonial expedition?"

"Why, look you, dear Lovett," said Augustus, "we are all blocks of matter, formed from the atoms of custom;—in other words, we are a mechanism, to which habit is the spring. What could I do in an honest career? I am many years older than you. I have lived as a rogue till I have no other nature than roguery. I doubt if I should not be a coward were I to turn soldier. I am sure I should be the most consummate of rascals were I to affect to be honest. No : I mistook myself when I talked of separation. I must e'en jog on with my old comrades, and in my old ways, till I jog into the noose hempen—or, melancholy alternative, the noose matrimonial!"

"This is mere folly," said Clifford, from whose nervous and masculine mind habits were easily shaken. "We have not for so many years discarded all the servile laws of others, to be the abject slaves of our own weaknesses. Come, my dear fellow, rouse yourself. Heaven knows, were I to succumb to the feebleness of my own heart, I should be lost indeed. , And perhaps, wrestle I ever so stoutly, I do not wrestle away that which clings within me, and will kill me, though by inches. But let us not be cravens, and suffer fate to drown us rather than swim. In a word, fly with me ere it be too late. A smuggler's vessel waits me off the coast of Dorset : in three days from this I sail. Be my companion. We can both rein a fiery horse, and wield a good sword. As long as men make war one against another, those accomplishments will prevent their owner from starving, or——"

"If employed in the field, not the road," interrupted Tomlinson, with a smile,—"from hanging. But it cannot be! I wish you all joy—all success in your career : you are young, bold, and able ; and you always had a loftier spirit than I have! Knave I am, and knave I must be to the end of the chapter!"

"As you will," said Clifford, who was not a man of many words, but he spoke with reluctance : "if so, I must seek my fortune alone."

"When do you leave us?" asked Tomlinson.

"To-morrow, before noon. I shall visit London for a few hours, and then start at once for the coast!"

"London!" exclaimed Tomlinson ; "what, the very den of

danger?—Pooh! you do not know what you say : or, do you think
it filial to caress Mother Lobkins before you depart?"

"Not that," answered Clifford. "I have already ascertained
that she is above the reach of all want; and her days, poor soul!
cannot, I fear, be many. In all probability, she would scarcely
recognise me; for her habits cannot much have improved her
memory. Would I could say as much for her neighbours! Were I
to be seen in the purlieus of low thievery, you know, as well as I
do, that some stealer of kerchiefs would turn informer against the
notorious Captain Lovett."

"What, then, takes you to town? Ah!—you turn away your
face.—I guess! Well, Love has ruined many a hero before; may
you not be the worse for his godship!"

Clifford did not answer, and the conversation made a sudden and
long pause; Tomlinson broke it.

"Do you know, Lovett," said he, "though I have as little heart
as most men, yet I feel for you more than I could have thought it
possible. I would fain join you; there is devilish good tobacco in
Germany, I believe; and, after all, there is not so much difference
between the life of a thief and of a soldier!"

"Do profit by so sensible a remark," said Clifford. "Reflect
how certain of destruction is the path you now tread: the gallows
and the hulks are the only goals!"

"The prospects are not pleasing, I allow," said Tomlinson;
"nor is it desirable to be preserved for another century in the
immortality of a glass case in Surgeons' Hall, grinning from ear to
ear, as if one had made the merriest finale imaginable.—Well, I
will sleep on it, and you shall have my answer to-morrow;—but
poor Ned?"

"Would he not join us?"

"Certainly not · his neck is made for a rope, and his mind for
the Old Bailey. There is no hope for him; yet he is an excellent
fellow. We must not even tell him of our meditated desertion."

"By no means. I shall leave a letter to our London chief; it
will explain all. And now to bed;—I look to your companionship
as settled."

"Humph!" said Augustus Tomlinson.

So ended the conference of the robbers. About an hour after it
had ceased, and when no sound save the heavy breath of Long Ned
broke the stillness of the night, the intelligent countenance of Peter
Mac Grawler slowly elevated itself from the lonely pillow on which
it had reclined.

By degrees the back of the sage stiffened into perpendicularity,
and he sat for a few moments erect on his seat of honour, apparently

in listening deliberation. Satisfied with the deep silence that, save the solitary interruption we have specified, reigned around, the learned disciple of Vatel rose gently from the bed,—hurried on his clothes,—stole on tip-toe to the door,—unbarred it with a noiseless hand,—and vanished. Sweet reader! while thou art wondering at his absence, suppose we account for his appearance.

One evening, Clifford and his companion Augustus had been enjoying the rational amusement of Ranelagh, and were just leaving that celebrated place when they were arrested by a crowd at the entrance. That crowd was assembled round a pickpocket; and that pickpocket—O virtue!—O wisdom,—O Asinæum,—was Peter Mac Grawler! We have before said that Clifford was possessed of a good mien and an imposing manner, and these advantages were at that time especially effectual in preserving our Orbilius from the pump. No sooner did Clifford recognise the magisterial face of the sapient Scot, than he boldly thrust himself into the middle of the crowd, and collaring the enterprising citizen who had collared Mac Grawler, declared *himself* ready to vouch for the honesty of the very respectable person whose identity had evidently been so grossly mistaken. Augustus, probably foreseeing some ingenious *ruse* of his companion's, instantly seconded the defence. The mob, who never descry any difference between impudence and truth, gave way; a constable came up—took part with the friend of two gentlemen so unexceptionably dressed—our friends walked off—the crowd repented of their precipitation, and, by way of amends, ducked the gentleman whose pockets had been picked. It was in vain for him to defend himself, for he had an impediment in his speech; and Messieurs the mob, having ducked him once for his guilt, ducked him a second time for his embarrassment.

In the interim, Clifford had withdrawn his quondam Mentor to the asylum of a coffee-house; and while Mac Grawler's soul expanded itself by wine, he narrated the cause of his dilemma. It seems that that incomparable journal "The Asinæum," despite a series of most popular articles upon the writings of "Aulus Prudentius," to which were added an exquisite string of dialogues, written in a tone of broad humour, viz., broad Scotch (with Scotchmen it is all the same thing), despite these invaluable miscellanies, to say nothing of some glorious political articles, in which it was clearly proved to the satisfaction of the rich, that the less poor devils eat, the better for their constitutions,—despite, we say, these great acquisitions to British literature, "The Asinæum" tottered, fell, buried its bookseller, and crushed its author: Mac Grawler only—escaping, like Theodore from the enormous helmet of Otranto—Mac Grawler only survived. "Love," says Sir Philip Sidney, "makes a man see better than a pair of spectacles." Love of life has a very different effect on the optics,—it makes a man wofully dim of inspection, and sometimes causes him to see his own property in another man's purse! This *deceptio visûs*, did it impose upon Peter Mac Grawler? He went to Ranelagh. Reader, thou knowest the rest!

Wine and the ingenuity of the robbers having extorted this narrative from Mac Grawler, the barriers of superfluous delicacy were easily done away with.

Our heroes offered to the sage an introduction to their club ; the offer was accepted ; and Mac Grawler, having been first made drunk, was next made a robber. The gang engaged him in various little matters, in which we grieve to relate that, though his intentions were excellent, his success was so ill as thoroughly to enrage his employers ; nay, they were about at one time, when they wanted to propitiate justice, to hand him over to the secular power, when Clifford interposed in his behalf. From a robber the sage dwindled into a drudge ; menial offices (the robbers, the lying rascals, declared that such offices were best fitted to the genius of his country !) succeeded to noble exploits, and the worst of robbers became the best of cooks. How vain is all wisdom but that of long experience ! Though Clifford was a sensible and keen man,—though he knew our sage to be a knave, he never dreamed he could be a traitor. He thought him too indolent to be malicious, and—short-sighted humanity !— too silly to be dangerous. He trusted the sage with the secret of the cavern ; and Augustus, who was a bit of an epicure, submitted, though forebodingly, to the choice, because of the Scotchman's skill in broiling.

But Mac Grawler, like Brutus, concealed a scheming heart under a stolid guise ; the apprehension of the noted Lovett had become a matter of serious desire ; the police was no longer to *be* bribed : nay, they were now eager to bribe ;—Mac Grawler had watched his time —sold his chief, and was now on the road to Reading to meet and to guide to the cavern Mr. Nabbem of Bow Street and four of his attendants.

Having thus, as rapidly as we were able, traced the causes which brought so startlingly before your notice the most incomparable of critics, we now, reader, return to our robbers.

"Hist, Lovett!" said Tomlinson, half-asleep, "methought I heard something in the outer cave."

"It is the Scot, I suppose," answered Clifford : "you saw, of course, to the door?"

"To be sure !" muttered Tomlinson, and in two minutes more he was asleep.

Not so Clifford : many and anxious thoughts kept him waking. At one while, when he anticipated the opening to a new career, somewhat of the stirring and high spirit which still moved amidst the guilty and confused habits of his mind made his pulse feverish, and his limbs restless : at another time, an agonising remembrance— the remembrance of Lucy in all her charms, her beauty, her love, her tender and innocent heart,—Lucy all perfect, and lost to him for ever, banished every other reflection, and only left him the sick sensation of despondency and despair. "What avails my struggle for a better name !" he thought. "Whatever my future lot, *she* can never share it. My punishment is fixed,—it is worse than a death of shame ; it is a life without hope ! Every moment I feel, and shall feel to the last, the pressure of a chain that may never be broken or loosened ! And yet, fool that I am ! I cannot leave this country without seeing her again, without telling her that I have *really* looked my last. But have I not *twice* told her that ? Strange fatality ! But twice have I spoken to her of love, and each time it was to tear myself from her at the moment of my confession. And even now something that I have no power to resist compels me to the same idle and weak indulgence. Does destiny urge me ? Ay, perhaps to my destruction ! Every hour a thousand deaths encompass me. I have now obtained all for which I seemed to linger. I have won, by a new crime, enough to bear me to another land, and to provide me there a soldier's destiny. I should not lose an hour in flight, yet I rush into the nest of my enemies, only for one unavailing word with her ; and this, too, after I have already bade her farewell ! *Is* this fate ? if it be so, what matters it ? I no longer care for a life which, after all, I should reform in vain, if I could not reform it for her : yet—yet, selfish, and lost that I am ! will it be nothing to think hereafter that I have redeemed her from the disgrace of having loved an outcast and a felon ? If I can obtain honour, will it not, in my own heart at least,—will it not reflect, however dimly and distantly, upon her ? "

Such, bewildered, unsatisfactory, yet still steeped in the colours of that true love which raises even the lowest, were the midnight meditations of Clifford : they terminated, towards the morning, in an uneasy and fitful slumber. From this he was awakened by a loud yawn from the throat of Long Ned, who was always the earliest riser of his set.

"Holloa !" said he, "it is almost daybreak, and if we want to cash our notes, and to move the old lord's jewels, we should already be on the start."

"A plague on you !" said Tomlinson, from under cover of his woollen nightcap ; "it was but this instant that I was dreaming you were going to be hanged, and now you wake me in the pleasantest part of the dream ! "

" You be shot ! " said Ned, turning one leg out of bed ; " by the by, you took more than your share last night, for you owed me three guineas for our last game at cribbage ! You'll please to pay me before we part to-day : short accounts make long friends ' "

" However true that maxim may be," returned Tomlinson, " I know one much truer, namely—long friends will make short accounts ! You must ask Jack Ketch this day month if I'm wrong ! "

" That's what *you* call wit, I suppose ! " retorted Ned, as he now, struggling into his inexpressibles, felt his way into the outer cave.

" What, ho ! Mac ! " cried he, as he went, " stir those bobbins of thine, which thou art pleased to call legs ;—strike a light, and be d—d to you ! "

" A light for *you*," said Tomlinson, profanely, as he reluctantly left his couch, " will indeed be ' a light to lighten the Gentiles ! ' "

" Why, Mac—Mac ! " shouted Ned, " why don't you answer?—faith, I think the Scot's dead ! "

" Seize your men !—yield, sirs ! " cried a stern, sudden voice from the gloom ; and at that instant two dark lanterns were turned, and their light streamed full upon the astounded forms of Tomlinson and his gaunt comrade ! In the dark shade of the background four or five forms were also indistinctly visible ; and the ray of the lanterns glimmered on the blades of cutlasses and the barrels of weapons still less easily resisted.

Tomlinson was the first to recover his self-possession. The light just gleamed upon the first step of the stairs leading to the stables, leaving the rest in shadow. He made one stride to the place beside the cart, where, we have said, lay some of the robbers' weapons : he had been anticipated—the weapons were gone. The next moment Tomlinson had sprung up the steps.

" Lovett !—Lovett !—Lovett ! " shouted he.

The captain, who had followed his comrades into the cavern, was already in the grasp of two men. From few ordinary mortals, however, could any two be selected as fearful odds against such a man as Clifford ; a man in whom a much larger share of sinews and muscle than is usually the lot even of the strong had been hardened, by perpetual exercise, into a consistency and iron firmness which linked power and activity into a union scarcely less remarkable than that immortalised in the glorious beauty of the sculptured gladiator. His right hand is upon the throat of one assailant, his left locks, as in a vice, the wrist of the other ; you have scarcely time to breathe ! the former is on the ground—the pistol of the latter is wrenched from his gripe—Clifford is on the step—a ball—another—whizzes by him '—he is by the side of the faithful Augustus!

"Open the secret door!" whispered Clifford to his friend; "I will draw up the steps alone!"

Scarcely had he spoken, before the steps were already, but slowly, ascending beneath the desperate strength of the robber. Meanwhile, Ned was struggling, as he best might, with two sturdy officers, who appeared loath to use their weapons without an absolute necessity, and who endeavoured, by main strength, to capture and detain their antagonist.

"Look well to the door!" cried the voice of the principal officer, "and hang out more light!"

Two or three additional lanterns were speedily brought forward; and over the whole interior of the cavern a dim but sufficient light now rapidly circled, giving to the scene and to the combatants a picturesque and wild appearance!

The quick eye of the head-officer descried in an instant the rise of the steps, and the advantage the robbers were thereby acquiring. He and two of his men threw themselves forward, seized the ladder, if so it may be called, dragged it once more to the ground, and ascended. But Clifford, grasping with both hands the broken shaft of a cart that lay in reach, received the foremost invader with a salute that sent him prostrate and senseless back among his companions. The second shared the same fate; and the stout leader of the enemy, who, like a true general, had kept himself in the rear, paused now in the middle of the steps, dismayed alike by the reception of his friends and the athletic form towering above, with raised weapon and menacing attitude. Perhaps that moment seemed to the judicious Mr. Nabbem more favourable to parley than to conflict. He cleared his throat, and thus addressed the foe:—

"You, sir, Captain Lovett, alias Howard, alias Jackson, alias Cavendish, alias Solomons, alias Devil, for I knows you well, and could swear to you with half an eye, in your clothes or without: you lay down your club there, and let me come alongside of you, and you'll find me as gentle as a lamb; for I've been used to gemmen all my life, and I knows how to treat 'em when I has 'em '"

"But if I will not let you 'come alongside of me,'—what then?"

"Why, I must send one of these here pops through your skull, that's all!"

"Nay, Mr. Nabbem, that would be too cruel! You surely would not harm one who has such an esteem for you? Don't you remember the manner in which I brought you off from Justice Burnflat, when you were accused, you know whether justly or——"

"You're a liar, captain !" cried Nabbem, furiously, fearful that something not meet for the ears of his companions should transpire. "You knows you are ! Come down, or let me mount ; otherwise I won't be 'sponsible for the consequences !"

Clifford cast a look over his shoulder. A gleam of the grey day-light already glimmered through a chink in the secret door, which Tomlinson had now unbarred, and was about to open.

"Listen to me, Mr. Nabbem," said he, "and perhaps I may grant what you require ! What would you do with me if you had me ?"

"You speaks like a sinsible man, now," answered Nabbem, "and that's after my own heart. Why, you sees, captain, your time is come, and you can't shilly-shally any longer. You have had your full swing ; your years are up, and you must die like a man ! But I gives you my honour, as a gemman, that if you surrenders, I'll take you to the justice folks as tenderly as if you were made of cotton."

"Give way one moment," said Clifford, "that I may plant the steps firmer for you."

Nabbem retreated to the ground, and Clifford, who had, good-naturedly enough, been unwilling unnecessarily to damage so valu-able a functionary, lost not the opportunity now afforded him. Down thundered the steps, clattering heavily among the other officers, and falling like an avalanche on the shoulder of one of the arresters of Long Ned.

Meanwhile, Clifford sprang after Tomlinson through the aperture, and found himself—in the presence of four officers, conducted by the shrewd MacGrawler. A blow from a bludgeon on the right cheek and temple of Augustus felled that hero. But Clifford bounded over his comrade's body, dodged from the stroke aimed at himself, caught the blow aimed by another assailant in his open hand, wrested the bludgeon from the officer, struck him to the ground with his own weapon, and darting onward through the labyrinth of the wood, commenced his escape with a step too fleet to allow the hope of a successful pursuit.

CHAPTER XXIX.

"' In short, Isabella, I offer you myself !'
' Heavens !' cried Isabella, ' what do I hear ?   You, my lord ?' "
                                        'CASTLE OF OTRANTO.'

 NOVEL is like a weatherglass, where the man appears out at one time, the woman at another.   Variable as the atmosphere, the changes of our story now re-present Lucy to the reader.

That charming young person—who, it may be remarked, is (her father excepted) the only unsophisticated and unsullied character in the pages of a story in some measure designed to show, in the depravities of character, the depravities of that social state wherein characters are formed—was sitting alone in her apartment at the period in which we return to her.   As time, and that innate and insensible fund of *healing*, which Nature has placed in the bosoms of the young, in order that her great law, the passing away of the old, may not leave too lasting and keen a wound, had softened her first anguish at her father's death, the remembrance of Clifford again resumed its ancient sway in her heart.   The loneliness of her life,—the absence of amusement, — even the sensitiveness and languor which succeed to grief, conspired to invest the image of her lover in a tenderer and more impressive guise.   She recalled his words, his actions, his letters, and employed herself whole hours, whole days and nights, in endeavouring to decipher their mystery. Who that has been loved will not acknowledge the singular and mighty force with which a girl, innocent herself, clings to the belief of innocence in her lover?   In breasts young and unacquainted with the world, there is so pure a credulity in the existence of unmixed good, so firm a reluctance to think that where we love there can be that which we would not esteem, or where we admire there can be that which we ought to blame, that one may almost deem it an argument in favour of our *natural* power to attain a greater eminence in virtue, than the habits and arts of the existing world will allow us to reach.   Perhaps it is not paradoxical to say that we could scarcely believe perfection in others, were not the germ of perfectibility in our own minds !   When a man has lived some years among the actual contests of faction, without imbibing the prejudice as well as the experience, how wonderingly he smiles at his worship of former idols !—how different a colour does history wear to him !—how cautious is he now to praise !—how slow to admire !—how prone to cavil ! Human nature has become the human nature of art ; and he estimates it not from what it may be, but fiom what, in the corruptions of a semi-civilisation, it is ! But in the same manner as the young student clings to the belief that the sage or the minstrel, who has enlightened his reason or chained his imagination, is in character as in genius elevated above the ordinary herd, free from the passions, the frivolities, the little mean-nesses, and the darkening vices which ordinary flesh is heir to, does a woman, who loves for the first time, cling to the imagined excel-lence of him she loves ! When Evelina is so shocked at the idea of an occasional fit of intoxication in her "noble, her unrivalled" lover, who does not acknowledge how natural were her feelings ? Had Evelina been married six years, and the same lover, *then her husband*, been really guilty of what she suspected, who does not feel that it would have been very unnatural to have been shocked in the least at the occurrence? She would not have loved him less, nor admired him less, nor would he have been less "the noble and the unrivalled,"—he would have taken his glass too much, have joked the next morning on the event, and the gentle Evelina would have made him a cup of tea but that which would have been a matter of pleasantry in the husband would have been matter of damnation in the lover.—But to return to Lucy.

If it be so hard, so repellant to believe a lover guilty even of a trivial error, we may readily suppose that Lucy never for a moment admitted the supposition that Clifford had been really guilty of gross error or wilful crime. True, that expressions in his letter were more than suspicious ; but there is always a charm in the candour of self-condemnation. As it is difficult to believe the excellence of those who praise themselves, so it is difficult to fancy those criminal who condemn ! What, too, is the process of a woman's reasoning? Alas ! she is too credulous a physiognomist. The turn of a throat, with her, is the unerring token of nobleness of mind ; and no one can be guilty of a sin who is blest with a beautiful forehead ! How fondly, how fanatically Lucy loved ! She had gathered together a precious and secret hoard ;—a glove— a pen—a book—a withered rose-leaf ;—treasures rendered inestim-able because *he* had touched them : but more than all, had she the series of his letters, from the first formal note written to her father, meant for her, in which he answered an invitation, and requested Miss Brandon's acceptance of the music she had wished to have, to the last wild and, to her, inexplicable letter in which he had resigned her for ever. On these relics her eyes fed for hours ; and as she pored over them, and over thoughts too deep not only for tears, but for all utterance or conveyance, you might have almost literally watched the fading of her rich cheek, and the pining away of her rounded and elastic form.

It was just in such a mood that she was buried when her uncle knocked at her door for admittance : she hurried away her treasures, and hastened to admit and greet him. "I have come," said he, smiling, "to beg the pleasure of your company for an old friend who dines with us to-day.—But stay, Lucy, your hair is ill-arranged. Do not let me disturb so important an occupation as your toilette : dress yourself, my love, and join us."

Lucy turned, with a suppressed sigh, to the glass. The uncle lingered for a few moments, surveying her with mingled pride and doubt ; he then slowly left the chamber.

Lucy soon afterwards descended to the drawing-room, and beheld, with a little surprise (for she had not had sufficient curiosity to inquire the name of the guest), the slender form and comely features of Lord Mauleverer. The earl approached with the same grace which had, in his earlier youth, rendered him almost irresistible, but which now, from the contrast of years with manner, contained a *slight* mixture of the comic. He paid his compliments, and in paying them, declared that he must leave it to his friend, Sir William, to explain *all* the danger he had dared, for the sake of satisfying himself that Miss Brandon was no less lovely than when he had last beheld her.

"Yes, indeed," said Brandon, with a scarcely perceptible sneer, "Lord Mauleverer has literally endured the moving accidents of flood and field—for he was nearly exterminated by a highwayman, and all but drowned in a ditch !"

"Commend me to a friend for setting one off to the best advantage," said Mauleverer, gaily. "Instead of attracting your sympathy, you see, Brandon would expose me to your ridicule : judge for yourself whether I deserve it ;"—and Mauleverer proceeded to give, with all the animation which belonged to his character, the particulars of that adventure with which the reader is so well acquainted. He did not, we may be sure, feel any scruple in representing himself and his prowess in the most favourable colours.

The story was scarcely ended when dinner was announced. During that meal, Mauleverer exerted himself to be amiable with infinite address. Suiting his conversation, more than he had hitherto deigned to do, to the temper of Lucy, and more anxious to soften than to dazzle, he certainly never before appeared to her so attractive. We are bound to add, that the point of attraction

did not reach beyond the confession that he was a very agreeable
old man.

Perhaps, if there had not been a certain half-melancholy vein in
his conversation, possibly less uncongenial to his lordship from the
remembrance of his lost diamonds, and the impression that Sir
William Brandon's cook was considerably worse than his own, he
might not have been so successful in pleasing Lucy. As for himself, all the previous impressions she had made on him returned in
colours yet more vivid; even the delicate and subdued cast of
beauty which had succeeded to her earlier brilliancy, was far more
charming to his fastidious and courtly taste than her former glow
of spirits and health. He felt himself very much in love during
dinner; and after it was over, and Lucy had retired, he told
Brandon with a passionate air, "that he *adored* his niece to
distraction!"

The wily judge affected to receive the intimation with indifference; but knowing that too long an absence is injurious to a *grande
passion*, he did not keep Mauleverer very late over his wine.

The earl returned rapturously to the drawing-room, and besought
Lucy, in a voice in which affectation seemed swooning with delight,
to indulge him with a song. More and more enchanted by her
assent, he drew the music-stool to the harpsichord, placed a chair
beside her, and presently appeared lost in transport. Meanwhile
Brandon, with his back to the pair, covered his face with his
handkerchief, and, to all appearance, yielded to the voluptuousness
of an after-dinner repose.

Lucy's song-book opened accidentally at a song which had been
praised by Clifford; and as she sang, her voice took a richer and
more tender tone than in Mauleverer's presence it had ever before
assumed.

THE COMPLAINT OF THE VIOLETS WHICH LOSE THEIR SCENT IN MAY.

I.

"In the shadow that falls from the silent hill
    We slept, in our green retreats.
And the April showers were wont to fill
    Our hearts with sweets

II.

And though we lay in a lowly bower
    Yet all things loved us well,
And the waking bee left her fairest flower,
    With us to dwell

III.

But the warm May came in his pride to woo
  The wealth of our honied store ;
And our hearts just felt his breath, and knew
  Their sweets no more !

IV.

And the summer reigns on the quiet spot
  Where we dwell, and its suns and showers
Bring balm to *our sisters'* hearts, but not—
  Ah ! not to *ours*.

V

We live, we bloom, but for ever o'er
  Is the charm of the earth and sky ;
To our life, ye heavens, that balm restore,
  Or—bid us die ! "

As with eyes suffused with many recollections, and a voice which melted away in an indescribable and thrilling pathos, Lucy ceased her song, Mauleverer, charmed out of himself, gently took her hand, and, holding the soft treasure in his own, scarcely less soft, he murmured,—

"Angel! sing on. Life would be like your own music, if I could breathe it away at your feet !"

There had been a time when Lucy would have laughed outright at this declaration ; and even as it was, a suppressed and half-arch smile played in the dimples of her beautiful mouth, and bewitchingly contrasted the swimming softness of her eyes.

Drawing rather an erroneous omen from the smile, Mauleverer rapturously continued, still detaining the hand which Lucy endeavoured to extricate.

"Yes, enchanting Miss Brandon ! I who have for so many years boasted of my invulnerable heart, am subdued at last. I have long, very long, struggled against my attachment to you. Alas ! it is in vain ; and you behold me now utterly at your mercy. Make me the most miserable of men, or the most enviable. Enchantress, speak !"

"Really, my lord," said Lucy, hesitating, yet rising, and freeing herself from his hand, "I feel it difficult to suppose you serious ; and, perhaps, this is merely a gallantry to me, by way of practice on others."

"Sweet Lucy, if I may so call you," answered Mauleverer, with an ardent gaze, "do not, I implore you, even for a moment, affect to mistake me ! do not for a moment jest at what, to me, is the bane or bliss of life ! Dare I hope that my hand and heart, which I now offer you, are not deserving of your derision ?"

Lucy gazed on her adorer with a look of serious inquiry; Brandon still appeared to sleep.

"If you are in earnest, my lord," said Lucy, after a pause, "I am truly and deeply sorry; for the friend of my uncle I shall always have esteem: believe that I am truly sensible of the honour you render me, when I add my regret, that I can have no *other* sentiment than esteem."

A blank and puzzled bewilderment, for a moment, clouded the expressive features of Mauleverer—it passed away.

"How sweet is your rebuke!" said he. "Yes! I do not yet deserve any other sentiment than esteem: you are not to be won precipitately; a long trial,—a long course of attentions,—a long knowledge of my devoted and ardent love, alone will entitle me to hope for a warmer feeling in your breast. Fix then your own time of courtship, angelic Lucy! a week,—nay, a month!—till then, I will not even press you to appoint that day, which to me will be the whitest of my life!"

"My lord!" said Lucy, smiling now no longer *half* archly, "you must pardon me for believing your proposal can be nothing but a jest; but here, I beseech you, let it rest for ever: do not mention this subject to me again."

"By heavens!" cried Mauleverer, "this is too cruel.—Brandon, intercede for me with your niece."

Sir William started, naturally enough, from his slumber, and Mauleverer continued,—

"Yes, intercede for me; you, my oldest friend, be my greatest benefactor! I sue to your niece,—she affects to disbelieve,—will you convince her of my truth, my devotion, my worship?"

"Disbelieve you!" said the bland judge, with the same secret sneer that usually lurked in the corners of his mouth. "I do not wonder that she is slow to credit the honour you have done her, and for which the noblest damsels in England have sighed in vain. Lucy, will you be cruel to Lord Mauleverer? Believe me, he has often confided to me his love for you; and if the experience of some years avails, there is not a question of his honour and his truth: I leave his fate in your hands."

Brandon turned to the door.

"Stay, dear sir," said Lucy, "and, instead of interceding for Lord Mauleverer, intercede for me." Her look now settled into a calm and decided seriousness of expression. "I feel highly flattered by his lordship's proposal, which, as you say, I might well doubt to be gravely meant. I wish him all happiness with a lady of higher deserts; but I speak from an unalterable determination, when I say, that I can never accept the dignity with which he would invest me."

So saying, Lucy walked quickly to the door, and vanished, leaving the two friends to comment as they would, upon her conduct.

"You have spoilt all with your precipitation," said the uncle.

"Precipitation! d—n it, what would you have? I have been fifty years making up my mind to marry; and now, when I have not a day to lose, you talk of precipitation!" answered the lover, throwing himself into an easy chair.

"But you have not been fifty years making up your mind to marry my niece," said Brandon, dryly.

"To be refused—positively refused, by a country girl!" continued Mauleverer, soliloquising aloud; "and that too at my age, and with all my experience!—a country girl without rank, *ton*, accomplishments! By heavens! I don't care if all the world heard it,—for not a soul in the world would ever believe it."

Brandon sat speechless, eyeing the mortified face of the courtier with a malicious complacency, and there was a pause of several minutes. Sir William then mastering the strange feeling which made him almost rejoice in whatever threw ridicule on his *friend*, approached, laid his hand kindly on Mauleverer's shoulder, and talked to him of comfort and of encouragement. The reader will believe, that Mauleverer was not a man whom it was impossible to encourage.

CHAPTER XXX.

" Before he came, everything loved me, and I had more things to love than I could reckon by the hairs of my head. Now, I feel I can love but one, and that one has deserted me.

        *   *   *   *   *

        *   *   *   *   *

Well, be it so—let her perish, let her be anything but mine."
                          'MELMOTH.'

EARLY the next morning, Sir William Brandon was closeted for a long time with his niece, previous to his departure to the duties of his office. Anxious and alarmed for the success of one of the darling projects of his ambition, he spared no art in his conversation with Lucy, that his great ingenuity of eloquence and wonderful insight into human nature could suggest, in order to gain at least a foundation for the raising of his scheme. Among other resources of his worldly tact, he hinted at Lucy's love for Clifford ; and (though darkly and subtly, as befitting the purity of the one he addressed) this abandoned and wily person did not scruple to hint also at the possibility of indulging that love *after* marriage ; though he denounced, as the last of indecorums, the crime of encouraging it *before*. This hint, however, fell harmless upon the innocent ear of Lucy. She did not, in the remotest degree, comprehend its meaning ; she only, with a glowing cheek and a pouting lip, resented the allusion to a love which she thought it insolent in any one even to suspect.

When Brandon left the apartment, his brow was clouded, and his eye absent and thoughtful : it was evident that there had been little in the conference with his niece to please or content him. Miss Brandon herself was greatly agitated · for there was in her uncle's nature that silent and impressive secret of influencing or command-ing others, which almost so invariably, and yet so quietly, attains the wishes of its owner ; and Lucy, who loved and admired him sin-cerely—not the less, perhaps, for a certain modicum of fear—was greatly grieved at perceiving how rooted in him was the desire of that marriage which she felt was a moral impossibility. But if Brandon possessed the secret of sway, Lucy was scarcely less singu-larly endowed with the secret of resistance. It may be remembered, in describing her character, that we spoke of her as one who seemed, to the superficial, as of too yielding and soft a temper. But circum-stances gave the lie to manner, and proved that she eminently possessed a quiet firmness and latent resolution, which gave to her mind a nobleness and *trustworthy* power, that never would have been suspected by those who met her among the ordinary paths of life.

Brandon had not been long gone, when Lucy's maid came to inform her that a gentleman, who expressed himself very desirous of seeing her, waited below. The blood rushed from Lucy's cheek at this announcement, simple as it seemed. "What gentleman *could* be desirous of seeing her ? Was it—was it Clifford ?" She remained for some moments motionless, and literally unable to move ; at length she summoned courage, and smiling with self-contempt at a notion which appeared to her *after* thoughts utterly absurd, she descended to the drawing-room. The first glance she directed towards the stranger, who stood by the fireplace with folded arms, was sufficient,—it was impossible to mistake, though the face was averted, the unequalled form of her lover. She advanced eagerly with a faint cry, checked herself, and sank upon the sofa.

Clifford turned towards her, and fixed his eyes upon her coun-tenance with an intense and melancholy gaze, but he did not utter a syllable ; and Lucy, after pausing in expectation of his voice, looked up, and caught, in alarm, the strange and peculiar aspect of his features. He approached her slowly, and still silent; but his gaze seemed to grow more earnest and mournful as he advanced.

"Yes," said he at last, in a broken and indistinct voice, "I see you once more, after all my promises to quit you for ever,—after my solemn farewell, after all that I have cost you ;—for, Lucy, you love me,—you love me,—and I shudder while I feel it ; after all I myself have borne and resisted, I once more come wilfully into your presence ! How have I burnt and sickened for this moment ! How have I said, 'Let me behold her once more—only once more, and Fate may then do her worst !' Lucy ! dear, dear Lucy ! forgive me for my weakness. It is now in bitter and stern reality the very last I can be guilty of !"

As he spoke, Clifford sank beside her. He took both her hands in his, and holding them, though without pressure, again looked passionately upon her innocent yet eloquent face. It seemed as if he were moved beyond all the ordinary feelings of reunion and of love. He did not attempt to kiss the hands he held ; and though the touch thrilled through every vein and fibre of his frame, his clasp was as light as that in which the first timidity of a boy's love ventures to stamp itself !

"You are pale, Lucy," said he, mournfully, "and your cheek is much thinner than it was when I first saw you ! Ah ! would for your sake that that had never been ! Your spirits were light then, Lucy. Your laugh came from the heart,—your step spurned the earth. Joy broke from your eyes, everything that breathed around you seemed full of happiness and mirth ! and now, look upon me, Lucy ; lift those soft eyes, and teach them to flash upon me indignation and contempt ! Oh, not thus, not thus ! I could leave you happy,—yes, literally blest,—if I could fancy you less forgiving, less gentle, less angelic !"

"What have I to forgive ?" said Lucy, tenderly.

"What ! everything for which one human being can pardon another. Have not deceit and injury been my crimes against you ? Your peace of mind, your serenity of heart, your buoyancy of temper, have I marred *these* or not ?"

"Oh, Clifford !" said Lucy, rising from herself and from all selfish thoughts, "why,—why will you not trust me ? You do not know me, indeed you do not—you are ignorant even of the very nature of a woman, if you think me unworthy of your confidence ! Do you believe I could betray it ? or, do you think, that if you had done that for which all the world forsook you, *I* could forsake ?"

Lucy's voice faltered at the last words ; but it sank as a stone sinks into deep waters, to the very core of Clifford's heart. Transported from all resolution and all forbearance, he wound his arms around her in one long and impassioned caress ; and Lucy, as her breath mingled with his, and her cheek drooped upon his bosom, did indeed feel as if the past could contain no secret powerful enough even to weaken the affection with which her heart clung to his. She was the first to extricate herself from their embrace. She drew back her face from his, and smiling on him through her tears, with a brightness that the smiles of her earliest youth had never surpassed, she said,—

"Listen to me. Tell me your history or not, as you will. But believe me, a woman's wit is often no despicable counsellor. They who accuse themselves the most bitterly, are not often those whom it is most difficult to forgive ; and you must pardon me, if I doubt the extent of the blame you would so lavishly impute to yourself. I am now alone in the world (here the smile withered from Lucy's lips).—My poor father is dead. I can injure no one by my conduct ; is there no one on earth to whom I am bound by duty. I am independent, I am rich. You *profess* to love me. I am foolish and vain, and I believe you. Perhaps, also, I have the fond hope which so often makes dupes of women—the hope, that, if you have erred, I may reclaim you ; if you have been unfortunate, I may con- sole you ! I know, Mr. Clifford, that I am saying that for which many would despise me, and for which, perhaps, I ought to despise myself ; but there are times when we speak only as if some power at our hearts constrained us, despite ourselves,—and it is thus that I have now spoken to you."

It was with an air very unwonted to herself that Lucy had con- cluded her address, for her usual characteristic was rather softness than dignity · but, as if to correct the meaning of her words, which might otherwise appear unmaidenly, there was a chaste, a proud, yet not the less a tender and sweet propriety and dignified frankness in her look and manner ; so that it would have been utterly impossible for one who heard her not to have done justice to the nobleness of her motives, or not to have felt both touched and penetrated, as much by respect as by any warmer or more familiar feeling.

Clifford, who had risen while she was speaking, listened with a countenance that varied at every word she uttered :—now all hope —now all despondency. As she ceased, the expression hardened into a settled and compulsive resolution.

"It is well ! " said he, mutteringly. " I am worthy of this—very —very worthy ! Generous, noble girl !—had I been an emperor, I would have bowed down to you in worship ; but to debase, to degrade you—no ! no ! "

" Is there debasement in love ? " murmured Lucy.

Clifford gazed upon her with a sort of enthusiastic and self-congratulatory pride ; perhaps he felt to be thus loved, and by such a creature, *was* matter of pride, even in the lowest circumstances to which he could ever be exposed. He drew his breath hard, set his teeth, and answered,—

" You could love, then, an outcast, without birth, fortune, or character ?—No ! you believe this now, but you could not. Could you desert your country, your friends, and your home—all that you are born and fitted for ?—Could you attend one over whom the sword hangs, through a life subjected every hour to discovery and disgrace?—Could you be subjected yourself to the moodiness of an evil memory, and the gloomy silence of remorse?—Could you be the victim of one who has no merit but his love for you, and who, if that love destroy you, becomes utterly redeemed ? Yes, Lucy, I was wrong—I will do you justice : all this, nay more, you *could* bear, and your generous nature would disdain the sacrifice ? But am *I* to be all selfish, and *you* all devoted? Are *you* to yield everything to me, and *I* to accept everything and yield none ?—Alas ! I have but one good, one blessing to yield, and that is yourself. Lucy, I deserve you ; I outdo you in generosity : all that you would desert for me is nothing—O God !—nothing to the sacrifice I make to you ! —And now, Lucy, I have seen you, and I must once more bid you farewell : I am on the eve of quitting this country for ever. I shall enlist in a foreign service. Perhaps—(and Clifford's dark eyes flashed with fire)—you will yet hear of me, and not blush when you hear ! But—(and his voice faltered, for Lucy, hiding her face with both hands, gave way to her tears and agitation)—but, in one respect, you have conquered. I had believed that you could never be mine —that my past life had *for ever* deprived me of that hope ! I now begin, with a rapture that can bear me through all ordeals, to form a more daring vision. A soil may be effaced—an evil name may be redeemed—the past is not set and sealed, without the power of revoking what has been written. If I can win the right of meriting your mercy, I will throw myself on it without reserve ; till then, or till death, you will see me no more ! "

He dropped on his knee, left his kiss and his tears upon Lucy's cold hand ; the next moment she heard his step on the stairs,—the door closed heavily and jarringly upon him,—and Lucy felt one bitter pang, and, for some time at least, she felt no more !

CHAPTER XXXI.

"*Many things fall between the cup and the lip!*
Your man does please me
With his conceit.

* * * * *

Comes Chanon Hugh accoutred as you see
Disguised!
And thus am I to gull the constable?
Now have among you for a man at arms.

* * * * *

High-constable was more, though
He laid Dick Tator by the heels."

BEN JONSON : 'Tale of a Tub.'

MEANWHILE, Clifford strode rapidly through the streets which surrounded the judge's house, and, turning to an obscurer *quartier* of the town, entered a gloomy lane or alley. Here he was abruptly accosted by a man wrapped in a shaggy great-coat, and of somewhat a suspicious appearance :—

"Aha, captain!" said he, "you are beyond your time, but all's well!"

Attempting, with indifferent success, the easy self-possession which generally marked his address to his companions, Clifford, repeating the stranger's words, replied,—

"All's well!—what! are the prisoners released?"

"No, faith!" answered the man, with a rough laugh, "not yet; but all in good time; it is a little too much to expect the justices to do our work, though, by the Lord Harry, we often do theirs!"

"What then?" asked Clifford, impatiently.

"Why, the poor fellows had been carried to the town of ——, and brought before the queer cuffin [1] ere I arrived, though I set off the moment you told me, and did the journey in four hours. The examination lasted all yesterday, and they were remanded till to-day ; —let's see, it is not yet noon , we may be there before it's over."

"And this is what you call well!" said Clifford, angrily.

"No, captain, don't be glimflashey! you have not heard all yet! —It seems that the only thing buffed hard against them was by a stout grazier, who was cried 'Stand!' to. some fifty miles off the town ; so the queer cuffin thinks of sending the poor fellows to the gaol of the county where they did the business!"

[1] Magistrate.

"Ah! that may leave some hopes for them!—We must look sharp to their journey; if they once get to prison, their only chances are the file and the bribe. Unhappily, neither of them is so lucky as myself at that trade!"

"No, indeed, there is not a stone wall in England that the great Captain Lovett could not creep through, I'll swear!" said the admiring satellite.

"Saddle the horses and load the pistols!—I will join you in ten minutes. Have my farmer's dress ready, the false hair, &c. Choose your own trim. Make haste;—the Three Feathers is the house of meeting."

"And in ten minutes only, captain?"

"Punctually!"

The stranger turned a corner, and was out of sight. Clifford, muttering—"Yes, I was the cause of their apprehension; it was I who was sought; it is but fair that I should strike a blow for their escape, before I attempt my own,"—continued his course till he came to the door of a public-house. The sign of a seaman swung aloft, portraying the jolly tar with a fine pewter pot in his hand, considerably huger than his own circumference. An immense pug sat at the door, lolling its tongue out, as if, having stuffed itself *to* the tongue, it was forced to turn that useful member out of its proper place. The shutters were half closed, but the sounds of coarse merriment issued jovially forth.

Clifford disconcerted the pug; and, crossing the threshold, cried, in a loud tone, "Janseen!"—"Here!" answered a gruff voice; and Clifford, passing on, came to a small parlour adjoining the tap. There, seated by a round oak-table, he found mine host, a red, fierce, weather-beaten, but bloated-looking personage, like Dirk Hatteraick in a dropsy.

"How now, captain!" cried he, in a guttural accent, and interlarding his discourse with certain Dutch graces, which, with our reader's leave, we will omit, as being unable to spell them: "how now!—not gone yet!"

"No!—I start for the coast to-morrow; business keeps me to-day. I came to ask if Mellon may be fully depended on?"

"Ay—honest to the back-bone."

"And you are sure that, in spite of my late delays, he will not have left the village?"

"Sure!—what else can I be?—don't I know Jack Mellon these twenty years! He would lie like a log in a calm for ten months together, without moving a hair's breadth, if he was under orders."

"And his vessel is swift and well manned, in case of an officer's chase?"

"The Black Molly swift?—Ask your grandmother. The Black Molly would outstrip a shark."

"Then good-bye, Janseen; there is something to keep your pipe alight: we shall not meet within the three seas again, I think. England is as much too hot for me as Holland for you!"

"You are a capital fellow!" cried mine host, shaking Clifford by the hand; "and when the lads come to know their loss, they will know they have lost the bravest and truest gill that ever took to the toby: so, good-bye, and be d—d to you!"

With this valedictory benediction, mine host released Clifford; and the robber hastened to his appointment at the Three Feathers.

He found all prepared. He hastily put on his disguise, and his follower led out his horse, a noble animal of the grand Irish breed, of remarkable strength and bone, and, save only that it was somewhat *sharp* in the quarters (a fault which they who look for speed as well as grace will easily forgive), of almost unequalled beauty in its symmetry and proportions. Well did the courser know, and proudly did it render obeisance to, its master; snorting impatiently, and rearing from the hand of the attendant robber, the sagacious animal freed itself from the rein, and, as it tossed its long mane in the breeze of the fresh air, came trotting to the place where Clifford stood.

"So ho, Robin!—so ho!—what, thou chafest that I have left thy fellow behind at the Red Cave. Him we may never see more. But, while I have life, I will not leave *thee*, Robin!"

With these words, the robber fondly stroked the shining neck of his favourite steed; and as the animal returned the caress, by rubbing his head against the hands and the athletic breast of its master, Clifford felt at his heart somewhat of that old racy stir of the blood which had been once to him the chief charm of his criminal profession, and which, in the late change of his feelings, he had almost forgotten.

"Well, Robin, well," he renewed, as he kissed the face of his steed;—"well, we will have some days like our old ones yet; thou shalt say, ha! ha! to the trumpet, and bear thy master along on more glorious enterprises than he has yet thanked thee for sharing. Thou wilt now be my only familiar,—my only friend, Robin; we two shall be strangers in a foreign land. But thou wilt make thyself welcome easier than thy lord, Robin; and *thou* wilt forget the old days, and thine old comrades, and thine old loves, when—ha!" and Clifford turned abruptly to his attendant, who addressed him, "It is late, you say; true! look you, it will be unwise for us both to quit London together; you know the sixth milestone, join me there, and we can proceed in company!"

Not unwilling to linger for a parting-cup, the comrade assented to the prudence of the plan proposed ; and, after one or two additional words of caution and advice, Clifford mounted and rode from the yard of the inn. As he passed through the tall wooden gates into the street, the imperfect gleam of the wintry sun falling over himself and his steed, it was scarcely possible, even in spite of his disguise and rude garb, to conceive a more gallant and striking specimen of the lawless and daring tribe to which he belonged ; the height, strength, beauty, and exquisite *grooming* visible in the steed ; the sparkling eye, the bold profile, the sinewy chest, the graceful limbs, and the careless and practised horsemanship of the rider.

Looking after his chief with a long and an admiring gaze, the robber said to the ostler of the inn, an aged and withered man, who had seen nine generations of highwaymen rise and vanish,—

" There, Joe, when did you ever look on a hero like that? The bravest heart, the frankest hand, the best judge of a horse, and the handsomest man that ever did honour to Hounslow ! "

" For all that," returned the ostler, shaking his palsied head, and turning back to the tap-room,—" For all that, master, his time be up. Mark my whids, Captain Lovett will not be over the year,— no ! nor mayhap the month ! "

" Why, you old rascal, what makes you so wise? You will not peach, I suppose ! "

" I peach ! devil a bit ! But there never was the gemmen of the road, great or small, knowing or stupid, as outlived his seventh year. And this will be the captain's seventh, come the 21st of next month ; but he be a fine chap, and I'll go to his hanging ! "

" Pish ! " said the robber, peevishly,—he himself was verging towards the end of his sixth year,—" pish ! "

" Mind, I tells it you, master ; and somehow or other I thinks,— and I has experience in these things—by the *fey* [1] of his eye, and the drop of his lip, that the captain's time will be up *to-day !* "

Here the robber lost all patience, and pushing the hoary boder of evil against the wall, he turned on his heel, and sought some more agreeable companion to share his stirrup-cup.

It was in the morning of the day following that in which the above conversations occurred, that the sagacious Augustus Tomlinson and the valorous Edward Pepper, handcuffed and fettered, were jogging along the road in a postchaise, with Mr. Nabbem squeezed in by the side of the former, and two other gentlemen in Mr. Nabbem's confidence mounted on the box of the chaise,

[1] A word difficult to translate : but the closest interpretation of which is, perhaps, " *the ill omen* "

T

and interfering sadly, as Long Ned growlingly remarked, with "the beauty of the prospect"

"Ah, well!" quoth Nabbem, unavoidably thrusting his elbow into Tomlinson's side, while he drew out his snuff-box, and helped himself largely to the intoxicating dust. "You had best prepare yourself, Mr. Pepper, for *a change* of prospects. I believes as how there is little to please you in *quod* (prison)."

"Nothing makes men so facetious as misfortune to others !" said Augustus, moralising, and turning himself, as well as he was able, in order to deliver his body from the pointed elbow of Mr. Nabbem. "When a man is down in the world, all the bystanders, very dull fellows before, suddenly become wits !"

"You reflects on I," said Mr. Nabbem : "well, it does not sinnify a pin, for directly we does our duty, you chaps become howdaciously ungrateful !"

"Ungrateful !" said Pepper : "what a plague have we got to be grateful for ? I suppose you think we ought to tell you, you are the best friend we have, because you have *scrouged* us, neck and crop, into this horrible hole, like turkeys fatted for Christmas. 'Sdeath ! one's hair is flatted down like a pancake ; and as for one's legs, you had better cut them off at once than tuck them up in a place a foot square,—to say nothing of these blackguardly irons !"

"The only irons pardonable in your eyes, Ned," said Tomlinson, "are the curling-irons, eh ?"

"Now if this is not too much !" cried Nabbem, crossly ; "you objects to go in a cart like the rest of your profession ; and when I puts myself out of the way to obleedge you with a shay, you slangs I for it !"

"Peace, good Nabbem !" said Augustus, with a sage's dignity ; "you must allow a little bad humour in men so unhappily situated as we are."

The soft answer turneth away wrath. Tomlinson's answer softened Nabbem ; and, by way of conciliation, he held his snuff-box to the nose of his unfortunate prisoner. Shutting his eyes, Tomlinson long and earnestly sniffed up the luxury, and as soon as, with his own kerchief of spotted yellow, the officer had wiped from his proboscis some lingering grains, Tomlinson thus spoke :—

"You see us now, Mr. Nabbem, in a state of broken-down opposition ; but our spirits are not broken too. In our time we have had something to do with the administration ; and our comfort at present, is the comfort of fallen ministers !"

"Oho ! you were in the Methodist line before you took to the road ?" said Nabbem.

"Not so !" answered Augustus, gravely. "We were the

Methodists of politics, not of the church, viz., we lived upon our flock without a legal authority to do so, and that which the law withheld from us, our wits gave. But tell me, Mr. Nabbem, are you addicted to politics?"

"Why, they says I be," said Mr. Nabbem, with a grin; "and for my part, I thinks all who sarves the King should stand up for him, and take care of their little families!"

"You *speak* what others *think!*" answered Tomlinson, smiling also. "And I will now, since you like politics, point out to you what I dare say you have not observed before."

"What be that?" said Nabbem.

"A wonderful likeness between the life of the gentlemen adorning his Majesty's senate and the life of the gentlemen whom you are conducting to his Majesty's gaol."

THE LIBELLOUS PARALLEL OF AUGUSTUS TOMLINSON.

"We enter our career, Mr. Nabbem, as your embryo ministers enter parliament,—by bribery and corruption. There is this difference, indeed, between the two cases:—*we* are enticed to enter by the bribery and corruption of *others,—they* enter spontaneously by dint of their *own.* At first, deluded by romantic visions, we like the glory of our career better than the profit, and in our youthful generosity we profess to attack the rich solely from consideration for the poor! By and by, as we grow more hardened, we laugh at these boyish dreams,—peasant or prince fares equally at our impartial hands; we grasp at the bucket, but we scorn not the thimbleful; we use the word glory only as a trap for proselytes and apprentices; our fingers, like an office-door, are open for all that can possibly come into them: we consider the wealthy as our salary, the poor as our perquisites. What is this, but a picture of your member of parliament ripening into a minister,—your patriot mellowing into your placeman? And mark me, Mr. Nabbem! is not the very language of both as similar as the deeds? What is the phrase either of us loves to employ?—'To deliver.' What?—'The Public.' And do we not both invariably deliver it of the same thing?—viz., its *purse?* Do we want an excuse for sharing the gold of our neighbours, or abusing them if they resist? Is not our mutual —our pithiest plea—'Distress?' True, your patriot calls it 'distress of the country;' but does he ever, a whit more than we do, mean any distress but his own? When we are brought low, and our coats are shabby, do we not both shake our heads and talk of 'reform?' And when—oh! when we are up in the world, do we not both kick 'reform' to the devil? How often your parliament

man 'vacates his seat,' only for the purpose of resuming it with a
weightier purse!   How often, dear Ned, have our seats been vacated
for the same end !   Sometimes, indeed, he *really* finishes his career
by accepting the hundreds,—it is by 'accepting the hundreds' that
ours may be finished too !—(Ned drew a long sigh.)—Note us now,
Mr. Nabbem, in the zenith of our prosperity—we have filled our
pockets, we have become great in the mouths of our party.   Our
pals admire us, and our blowens adore !   What do we in this short-
lived summer !   Save and be thrifty ?   Ah, no ! we must give our
dinners, and make light of our lush.   We sport horses on the race-
course, and look big at the multitude we have bubbled.   Is not this
your minister come into office ?   Does not this remind you of *his*
equipage, *his* palace, *his* plate ?   In both cases lightly won, lavishly
wasted ; and the public, whose cash we have fingered, may at least
have the pleasure of gaping at the figure we make with it !   This,
then, is our harvest of happiness ; our foes, our friends, are ready
to eat us with envy—yet what is so little enviable as our station?
Have we not both our common vexations and our mutual dis-
quietudes?   Do we not both bribe—(Nabbem shook his head and
buttoned his waistcoat)—our enemies, cajole our partisans, bully our
dependents, and quarrel with our only friends, viz., ourselves ?   Is
not the secret question with each—'It is all confoundedly fine ; but
how long will it last ?'   Now, Mr. Nabbem, note me,—reverse the
portrait : we are fallen, our career is over—the road is shut to us,
and new plunderers are robbing the carriages that once we robbed.
Is not this the lot of—no, no ! I deceive myself!   Your ministers,
your jobmen, for the most part milk the popular cow, while there's
a drop in the udder.   Your chancellor declines on a pension,—your
minister attenuates on a grant,—the feet of your great rogues may
be gone from the treasury benches, but they have their little fingers
in the treasury.   Their past services are remembered by his Majesty,
—ours only noted by the Recorder : they save themselves, for they
hang by one another ; we go to the devil, for we hang by ourselves
we have our little day of the public, and all is over ; but it is *never*
over with them.   We both hunt the same fox : but we are your fair
riders : they are your knowing ones—we take the leap, and our
necks are broken : they sneak through the gates, and keep it up
to the last ! "

As he concluded, Tomlinson's head drooped on his bosom, and it
was easy to see that painful comparisons, mingled perhaps with
secret murmurs at the injustice of fortune, were rankling in his
breast.   Long Ned sat in gloomy silence ; and even the hard
heart of the severe Mr. Nabbem was softened by the affecting
parallel to which he had listened.   They had proceeded without

speaking for two or three miles, when Long Ned, fixing his eyes
on Tomlinson, exclaimed,—

"Do you know, Tomlinson, I think it was a burning shame in
Lovett to suffer us to be carried off like muttons, without attempting
to rescue us by the way! It is all his fault that we are here! for it
was he whom Nabbem wanted, not us!"

"Very true," said the cunning policeman; "and if I were you,
Mr. Pepper, hang me if I would not behave like a man of spirit, and
shew as little consarn for him as he shews for you! Why, Lord
now, I doesn't want to 'tice you; but this I *does* know, the justices
are very anxious to catch Lovett; and one who gives him up, and
says a word or two about his cracter, so as to make conviction
sartain, may himself be sartain of a free pardon for all little sprees
and so forth!"

"Ah!" said Long Ned, with a sigh, "that is all very well, Mr.
Nabbem, but I'll go to the crap like a gentleman, and not peach of
my comrades; and now I think of it, Lovett could scarcely have assisted us. One man alone, even Lovett, clever as he is, could not
have forced us out of the clutches of you and your myrmidons, Mr.
Nabbem! And when we were once at ——, they took excellent
care of us. But tell me now, my dear Nabbem," and Long Ned's
voice wheedled itself into something like softness;—"tell me, do
you think the grazier will buff it home?"

"No doubt of that," said the unmoved Nabbem. Long Ned's
face fell. "And what if he does?" said he; "they can but
transport us!"

"Don't desave yourself, Master Pepper!" said Nabbem: "you're
too old a hand for the herring-pond. They're resolved to make
gallows *apples* of all such numprels (*Nonpareils*) as you!"

Ned cast a sullen look at the officer.

"A pretty comforter you are!" said he. "I have been in a
postchaise with a pleasanter fellow, I'll swear! You may call me
an apple if you will, but, I take it, I am not an apple you'd like to
see *peeled*."

With this pugilistic and menacing pun, the lengthy hero relapsed
into meditative silence.

Our travellers were now entering a road skirted on one side by
a common of some extent, and on the other by a thick hedgerow,
which through its breaks gave occasional glimpses of woodland and
fallow, interspersed with cross-roads and tiny brooklets.

"There goes a jolly fellow!" said Nabbem, pointing to an
athletic-looking man, riding before the carriage, dressed in a
farmer's garb, and mounted on a large and powerful horse of the
Irish breed. "I dare say he is well acquainted with *your* grazier,

Mr. Tomlinson ; he looks mortal like one of the same kidney ; and here comes another chap,"—(as the stranger was joined by a short, stout, ruddy man in a carter's frock, riding on a horse less showy than his comrade's, but of the lengthy, reedy, lank, yet muscular race, which a knowing jockey would like to bet on).—" Now that's what I calls a comely lad !" continued Nabbem, pointing to the latter horseman ; "none of your thin-faced, dark, strapping fellows like that Captain Lovett, as the blowens raves about, but a nice, tight, little body, with a face like a carrot ! That's a beauty for my money ! honesty's stamped on his face, Mr. Tomlinson ! I dare says —(and the officer grinned, for he had been a lad of the cross in his own day)—I dare says, poor innocent booby, he knows none of the ways of Lunnon town ; and if he has not as merry a life as some folks, mayhap he may have a longer. But a merry one for ever, for such lads as us, Mr. Pepper ! I say, has you heard as how Bill Fang went to Scratchland (Scotland) and was stretched for smash-ing queer screens? (*i e*, hung for uttering forged notes) He died 'nation game ; for when his father, who was a grey-headed parson, came to see him after the sentence, he says to the governor, says he, ' Give us a tip, old 'un, to pay the expenses, and die dacently.' The parson forks him out ten shiners, preaching all the while like winkey. Bob drops one of the guineas between his fingers, and says, ' Holla, dad, you have only tipped us nine of the yellow boys ! just now you said as how it was ten !' On this the parish-bull, who was as poor as if he had been a mouse of the church instead of the curate, lugs out another ; and Bob, turning round to the gaoler, cries, ' Flung the governor out of a guinea, by G—d !' ¹ Now, that's what I calls keeping it up to the last !"

Mr. Nabbem had scarcely finished this anecdote, when the farmer-like stranger who had kept up by the side of the chaise, suddenly rode to the window, and touching his hat, said in a Norfolk accent, " Were the gentlemen we met on the road belonging to your party? They were asking after a chaise and pair."

" No !" said Nabbem, "there be no gentlemen as belongs to our party !" So, saying, he tipped a knowing wink at the farmer, and glanced over his shoulder at the prisoners.

" What ! you are going all alone ?" said the farmer

" Ay, to be sure," answered Nabbem ; "not much danger, I think, in the day-time, with the sun out as big as a sixpence, which is as big as ever I see'd him in this country !"

At that moment, the shorter stranger, whose appearance had at-tracted the praise of Mr. Nabbem (that personage was himself very short and ruddy), and who had hitherto been riding close to the post-horses, and talking to the officers on the box, suddenly threw himself from his steed, and in the same instant that he arrested the horses of the chaise, struck the postilion to the ground with a short heavy bludgeon which he drew from his frock. A whistle was heard and answered, as if by a signal : three fellows, armed with bludgeons, leaped from the hedge ; and in the interim the pretended farmer, dismounting, flung open the door of the chaise, and seizing Mr. Nabbem by the collar, swung him to the ground with a celerity that became the circular rotundity of the policeman's figure, rather than the deliberate gravity of his dignified office.

Rapid and instantaneous as had been this work, it was not without a check. Although the policemen had not dreamed of a rescue in the very face of the day, and on the high road, their profession was not that which suffered them easily to be surprised The two guardians of the dicky leaped nimbly to the ground ; but before they had time to use their fire-arms, two of the new aggressors, who had appeared from the hedge, closed upon them, and bore them to the ground : while this scuffle took place, the farmer had disarmed the prostrate Nabbem, and giving him in charge to the remaining confederate, extricated Tomlinson and his comrade from the chaise.

"Hist !" said he in a whisper, "beware my name ; my disguise hides me at present—lean on me—only through the hedge, a cart waits there, and you are safe ! "

With these broken words he assisted the robbers, as well as he could, in spite of their manacles, through the same part of the hedge from which the three allies had sprung. They were already through the barrier ; only the long legs of Ned Pepper lingered behind ; when at the far end of the road, which was perfectly straight, a gentleman's carriage became visible. A strong hand from the interior of the hedge seizing Pepper dragged him through, and Clifford—for the reader need not be told who was the farmer— perceiving the approaching reinforcement, shouted at once for flight. The robber who had guarded Nabbem, and who indeed was no other than Old Bags, slow as he habitually was, lost not an instant in providing for himself ; before you could say "Laudamus," he was on the other side of the hedge : the two men engaged with the police-officers were not capable of any equal celerity ; but Clifford, throwing himself into the contest and engaging the policemen, gave the robbers the opportunity of escape. They scrambled through the fence, the officers, tough fellows and keen, clinging lustily to them, till one was felled by Clifford, and the other, catching against a stump, was forced to relinquish his hold ; he then sprang back into the road and prepared for Clifford, who now, however, occupied himself rather in fugitive than warlike measures. Meanwhile, the moment the other rescuers had passed the Rubicon of the hedge, their flight, and that of the gentlemen who had passed before them, commenced. On this mystic side of the hedge was a cross-road, striking at once through an intricate and wooded part of the country, which allowed speedy and ample opportunities of dispersion. Here a light cart, drawn by two swift horses, in a tandem fashion, awaited the fugitives. Long Ned and Augustus were stowed down at the bottom of this vehicle ; three fellows filed away at their irons, and a fourth, who had hitherto remained inglorious with the cart, gave the lash—and he gave it handsomely—to the coursers. Away rattled the equipage ; and thus was achieved a flight, still memorable in the annals of the elect, and long quoted as one of the boldest and most daring exploits that illicit enterprise ever accomplished.

Clifford and his equestrian comrade only remained in the field, or rather the road ; the former sprang at once on his horse,—the latter was not long in following the example. But the policeman, who, it has been said, baffled in detaining the fugitives of the hedge, had leaped back into the road, was not idle in the meanwhile. When he saw Clifford about to mount, instead of attempting to seize the enemy, he recurred to his pistol, which in the late struggle hand to hand he had been unable to use, and taking sure aim at Clifford, whom he judged at once to be the leader of the rescue, he lodged a ball in the right side of the robber, at the very moment he had set spurs in his horse and turned to fly. Clifford's head drooped to the saddle bow. Fiercely the horse sprang on ; the robber endeavoured, despite his reeling senses, to retain his seat—once he raised his head—once he nerved his slackened and listless limbs—and then, with a faint groan, he fell to the earth. The horse bounded but one step more, and, true to the tutorship it had received, stopped abruptly. Clifford raised himself with great difficulty on one arm ; with the other hand he drew forth a pistol ; he pointed it deliberately towards the officer that wounded him ; the man stood motionless, cowering and spell-bound, beneath the dilating eye of the robber It was but for a moment that the man had cause for dread ; for muttering between his ground teeth, "Why waste it on *an enemy* ?" Clifford turned the muzzle towards the head of the unconscious steed, which seemed sorrowfully and wistfully to incline towards him. "Thou," he said, "whom I have fed and loved shall never know hardship from another !" and with a merciful cruelty he dragged himself one pace nearer to his beloved steed, uttered a well-known word, which brought the docile creature to his side, and placing the muzzle of the pistol close to his ear he fired, and fell back senseless at the exertion. The animal staggered, and dropped down dead

Meanwhile Clifford's comrade, profiting by the surprise and sudden panic of the officer, was already out of reach, and darting across the common, he and his ragged courser speedily vanished.

CHAPTER XXXII.

" *Lose I not*
With him what fortune could in life allot?
Lose I not hope, life's cordial!

* * * * *

In fact, the lessons he from prudence took
Were written in his mind as in a book.
There what to do he read, and what to shun,
And all commanded was with promptness done:
He seemed without a passion to proceed,

* * * * *

Yet some believed those passions only slept! '

      CRABBE.

* * * * *
* * * * *

" *Relics of love, and life's enchanted spring!*"
   A. WATTS, 'on burning a Packet of Letters.'

* * * * *
* * * * *

" *Many and sad and deep*
Were the thoughts folded in thy silent breast!
Thou, too, couldst watch and weep! "

     MRS. HEMANS.

WHILE Sir William Brandon was pursuing his ambitious schemes, and, notwithstanding Lucy's firm and steady refusal of Lord Mauleverer, was still determined on that ill-assorted marriage; while Mauleverer himself, day after day, attended at the judge's house, and, though he spoke not of love, looked it with all his might; it became obvious to every one but the lover and the guardian, that Lucy herself was rapidly declining in appearance and health. Ever since the day she had last seen Clifford, her spirit, before greatly shattered, had refused to regain even a likeness to their naturally cheerful and happy tone. She became silent and abstracted; even her gentleness of temper altered at times into a moody and fretful humour. Neither to books nor music, nor any art by which time is beguiled, she recurred for a momentary alleviation of the bitter feelings at her heart, or for a transient forgetfulness of their sting. The whole world of her mind had been

I 2

shaken. Her pride was wounded; her love galled; her faith in
Clifford gave way at length to gloomy and dark suspicion. Nothing,
she now felt, but a name as well as fortunes utterly abandoned, could
have justified him for the stubbornness of heart in which he had fled
and deserted her. Her own self-acquittal no longer consoled her in
affliction. She condemned herself for her weakness, from the birth
of her ill-starred affection to the crisis it had now acquired. "Why
did I not wrestle with it at first?" she said bitterly. "Why did I
allow myself so easily to love one unknown to me, and equivocal in
station, despite the cautions of my uncle and the whispers of the
world?" Alas! Lucy did not remember, that at the time she was
guilty of this weakness, she had not learned to reason as she since
reasoned. Her faculties were but imperfectly awakened; her experience of the world was utter ignorance. She scarcely knew that
she loved, and she knew not at all that the delicious and excited
sentiment which filled her being, could ever become as productive of
evil and peril as it had done now; and even *had* her reason been
more developed, and her resolutions more strong, does the exertion
of reason and resolution always avail against the master passion?
Love, it is true, is *not* unconquerable; but how few have ever, mind
and soul, coveted the conquest! Disappointment makes a vow,
but the heart records it not. Or in the noble image of one who has
so tenderly and so truly portrayed the feelings of her own sex,—

> ———"We make
> A ladder of our thoughts where angels step,
> But sleep ourselves at the foot!"[1]

Before Clifford had last seen her, we have observed that Lucy
had (and it was a consolation) clung to the belief that, despite of
appearances and his own confession, his past life had not been such
as to place him without the pale of her just affections; and there
were frequent moments when, remembering that the death of her
father had removed the only being who could assert an unanswer-
able claim to the dictation of her actions, she thought that Clifford,
hearing her hand was utterly at her own disposal, might again
appear, and again urge a suit which she felt so few circumstances
could induce her to deny. All this half-acknowledged, yet earnest
train of reasoning and hope vanished from the moment he had
quitted her uncle's house. His words bore no misinterpretation.
He had not yielded even to her own condescension, and her cheek
burnt as she recalled it. Yet he loved her. She saw, she knew it
in his every word and look! Bitter, then, and dark must be that
remorse which could have conquered every argument but that which

[1] "The History of the Lyre," by L. E. L.

urged him to leave her, when he might have claimed her for ever. True, that when his letter formerly bade her farewell, the same self-accusing language was recurred to, the same dark hints and allusions to infamy or guilt; yet never till now had she interpreted them rigidly, and never till now had she dreamed how far their meaning could extend. Still, what crimes could he have committed? The true ones never occurred to Lucy. She shuddered to ask herself, and hushed her doubts in a gloomy and torpid silence! But through all her accusations against herself, and through all her awakened suspicions against Clifford, she could not but acknowledge that something noble and not unworthy of her mingled in his conduct, and occasioned his resistance to her and to himself; and this belief, perhaps, irritated even while it touched her, and kept her feelings in a perpetual struggle and conflict, which her delicate frame and soft mind were little able to endure. When the nerves once break, how breaks the character with them! How many ascetics, withered and soured, do we meet in the world, who but for one shock to the heart and form might have erred on the side of meekness! Whether it come from woe or disease, the stroke which mars a single fibre plays strange havoc with the mind. Slaves we are to our muscles, and puppets to the spring of the capricious blood; and the great soul, with all its capacities, its solemn attributes, and sounding claims, is, while on earth, but a jest to this mountebank—the body—from the dream which toys with it for an hour, to the lunacy which shivers it into a driveller, laughing as it plays with its own fragments, and reeling benighted and blinded to the grave!

We have before said, that Lucy was fond both of her uncle and his society; and still, whenever the subject of Lord Mauleverer and his suit was left untouched, there was that in the conversation of Sir William Brandon which aroused an interest in her mind, engrossed and self-consuming as it had become. Sorrow, indeed, and sorrow's companion, reflection, made her more and more capable of comprehending a very subtle and intricate character. There is no secret for discovering the human heart like affliction— especially the affliction which springs from passion. Does a writer startle you with his insight into your nature, be sure that he has mourned: such lore is the alchymy of tears. Hence the insensible and almost universal confusion of idea which confounds melancholy with depth, and finds but hollow inanity in the symbol of a laugh. Pitiable error! Reflection first leads us to gloom, but its next stage is to brightness. The Laughing Philosopher has reached the goal of Wisdom: Heraclitus whimpered at the starting-post. But enough for Lucy to gain even the vestibule of philosophy.

Notwithstanding the soreness we naturally experience towards all who pertinaciously arouse an unpleasant subject, and in spite therefore of Brandon's furtherance of Mauleverer's courtship, Lucy felt herself incline strangely, and with something of a daughter's affection, towards this enigmatical being; in spite, too, of all the cold and measured vice of his character,—the hard and wintry greyness of heart with which he regarded the welfare of others, or the substances of Truth, Honour, and Virtue,—the callousness of his fossilised affections, which no human being softened but for a moment, and no warm and healthful impulse struck, save into an evanescent and idle flash; in spite of this consummate obduracy and worldliness of temperament, it is not paradoxical to say that there was something in the man which Lucy found at times analogous to her own vivid and generous self. This was, however, only noticeable when she led him to talk over earlier days, and when by degrees the sarcastic lawyer forgot the present, and grew eloquent, not over the actions but the feelings of the past. He would speak to her for hours of his youthful dreams, his occupations, or his projects, as a boy. Above all, he loved to converse with her upon Warlock, its remains of ancient magnificence, the green banks of the placid river that enriched its domains, and the summer pomp of wood and heath-land, amidst which his noon-day visions had been nursed.

When he spoke of these scenes and days, his countenance softened, and something in its expression, recalling to Lucy the image of one still dearer, made her yearn to him the more. An ice seemed broken from his mind, and streams of released and gentle feelings, mingled with kindly and generous sentiment, flowed forth. Suddenly, a thought, a word, brought him back to the present—his features withered abruptly into their cold placidity or latent sneer · the seal closed suddenly on the broken spell, and, like the victim of a fairy-tale, condemned at a stated hour, to assume another shape, the very being you had listened to seemed vanished, and replaced by one whom you startled to behold. But there was one epoch of his life on which he was always silent, and that was, his first onset into the actual world—the period of his early struggle into wealth and fame. All *that* space of time seemed as a dark gulf, over which he had passed, and become changed at once—as a traveller landing on a strange climate may adopt, the moment he touches its shore, its costume and its language.

All *men*—the most modest—have a common failing, but it is one which often assumes the domino and mask—*pride!* Brandon was, however, proud to a degree very rare in men who have risen and flourished in the world. Out of the wrecks of all other feelings, this imperial survivor made one great palace for its residence, and called the fabric "Disdain." Scorn was the real essence of Brandon's nature : even in the blandest disguises, the smoothness of his voice, the insinuation of his smile, the popular and supple graces of his manners, an oily derision floated, rarely discernible, it is true, but proportioning its strength and quantum to the calm it produced.

In the interim, while his character thus displayed and contradicted itself in private life, his fame was rapidly rising in public estimation. Unlike many of his brethren, the brilliant lawyer had exceeded expectation, and shown even yet more conspicuously in the less adventitiously aided duties of the judge. Envy itself,—and Brandon's political virulence had, despite his personal affability, made him many foes,—was driven into acknowledging the profundity of his legal knowledge, and in admiring the manner in which the peculiar functions of his novel dignity were discharged. No juvenile lawyer browbeat, no hackneyed casuist puzzled, him ; even his attention never wandered from the dullest case subjected to his tribunal. A painter, desirous of stamping on his canvas the portrait of an upright judge, could scarcely have found a finer realisation for his *beau idéal* than the austere, collected, keen, yet majestic countenance of Sir William Brandon, such as it seemed in the trappings of office and from the seat of justice.

The newspapers were not slow in recording the singular capture of the notorious Lovett. The boldness with which he had planned and executed the rescue of his comrades, joined to the suspense in which his wound for some time kept the public, as to his escape from one death by the postern gate of another, caused a very considerable ferment and excitation in the popular mind : and, to feed the impulse, the journalists were little slothful in retailing every anecdote, true or false, which they could collect, touching the past adventures of the daring highwayman. Many a good story then came to light, which partook as much of the comic as the tragic ; for not a single one of the robber's adventures was noted for cruelty or bloodshed ; many of them betokened rather an hilarious and jovial spirit of mirthful enterprise. It seemed as if he had thought the highway a capital arena for jokes, and only robbed for the sake of venting a redundant affection for jesting. Persons felt it rather a sin to be severe with a man of so merry a disposition ; and it was especially observable that not one of the ladies who had been despoiled by the robber could be prevailed on to prosecute : on the contrary, they always talked of the event as one of the most agreeable remembrances in their lives, and seemed to bear a provoking gratitude to the comely offender, rather than resentment.

All the gentlemen were not, however, of so placable a temper ; and
two sturdy farmers, with a grazier to boot, were ready to swear,
"through thick and thin," to the identity of the prisoner with a
horseman who had civilly borne each of them company for an hour
in their several homeward rides from certain fairs, and had carried
the pleasure of his society, they very gravely asserted, considerably
beyond a joke ; so that the state of the prisoner's affairs took a very
sombre aspect, and the counsel—an old hand—intrusted with his
cause, declared confidentially that there was not a chance. But a
yet more weighty accusation, because it came from a much nobler
quarter, awaited Clifford. In the robbers' cavern were found several
articles answering exactly to the description of those valuables
feloniously abstracted from the person of Lord Mauleverer. That
nobleman attended to inspect the articles, and to view the prisoner.
The former he found himself able to swear to, with a very tranquil-
lised conscience ; the latter he beheld feverish, attenuated, and in a
moment of delirium, on the sick-bed to which his wound had brought
him. He was at no loss, however, to recognise in the imprisoned
felon the gay and conquering Clifford, whom he had once even
honoured with his envy. Although his former dim and vague suspicions of Clifford were thus confirmed, the good-natured peer felt
some slight compunction at appearing as his prosecutor : this compunction, however, vanished the moment he left the sick man's
apartment ; and, after a little patriotic conversation with the magistrates about the necessity of public duty—a theme which brought
virtuous tears into the eyes of those respectable functionaries—he
re-entered his carriage, returned to town, and, after a lively dinner
tête-à-tête with an old *chère amie*, who, of all her charms, had preserved only the attraction of conversation and the capacity of relishing
a *salmi*, Mauleverer, the very evening of his return, betook himself
to the house of Sir William Brandon.

When he entered the hall, Barlow, the judge's favourite servant,
met him, with rather a confused and mysterious air, and arresting
him as he was sauntering into Brandon's library, informed him that
Sir William was particularly engaged, but would join his lordship in
the drawing-room. While Barlow was yet speaking, and Mauleverer
was bending his right ear (with which he heard the best) towards
him, the library-door opened, and a man in a very coarse and ruffianly
garb awkwardly bowed himself out. "So this is the particular
engagement," thought Mauleverer ; "a strange Sir Pandarus : but
those *old* fellows have droll tastes."

"I may go in now, my good fellow, I suppose?" said his lordship to Barlow ; and, without waiting an answer, he entered the
library. He found Brandon alone, and bending earnestly over some

letters which strewed his table. Mauleverer carelessly approached, and threw himself into an opposite chair. Sir William lifted his head, as he heard the movement, and Mauleverer (reckless as was that personage) was chilled and almost awed by the expression of his friend's countenance. Brandon's face was one which, however pliant, nearly always wore one pervading character—*calmness :* whether in the smoothness of social courtesy, or the austerity of his official station, or the bitter sarcasm which escaped him at no unfrequent intervals ; still a certain hard and inflexible dryness stamped both his features and his air. But at this time a variety of feelings not ordinarily eloquent in the outward man struggled in his dark face, expressive of all the energy and passion of his powerful and masculine nature ; there seemed to speak from his features and eyes something of shame, and anger, and triumph, and regret, and scorn. All these various emotions, which, it appears almost a paradox to assert, met in the same expression, nevertheless, were so individually and almost fearfully stamped, as to convey at once their signification to the mind of Mauleverer. He glanced towards the letters, in which the writing seemed faint and discoloured by time or damp ; and then once more regarding the face of Brandon, said in rather an anxious and subdued tone,—

"Heavens, Brandon ! are you ill? or has anything happened ?— you alarm me ! "

" Do you recognise these locks ? " said Brandon in a hollow voice ; and from under the letters he drew some ringlets of an auburn hue, and pushed them with an averted face towards Mauleverer.

The earl took them up — regarded them for a few moments— changed colour, but shook his head with a negative gesture, as he laid them once more on the table.

" This handwriting, then ? " renewed the judge in a yet more impressive and painful voice ; and he pointed to the letters.

Mauleverer raised one of them, and held it between his face and the lamp, so that whatever his features might have betrayed was hidden from his companion. At length he dropped the letter with an affected *nonchalance* and said,—

" Ah, I know the writing even at this distance of time ; this letter is directed to you ! "

" It is,—so are all these," said Brandon, with the same voice of preternatural and strained composure. " They have come back to me after an absence of nearly twenty-five years ; they are the letters she wrote to me in the days of our courtship—(here Brandon laughed scornfully)—she carried them away with her, you know when ; and (a pretty clod of consistency is woman !) she kept them, it seems, to her dying day ! "

The subject in discussion, whatever it might be, appeared a sore one to Mauleverer; he turned uneasily on his chair, and said at length,—

"Well, poor creature! these are painful remembrances, since it turned out so unhappily; but it was not our fault, dear Brandon: we were men of the world,—we knew the value of—of—women, and treated them accordingly!"

"Right! right! right!" cried Brandon, vehemently, laughing in a wild and loud disdain; the intense force of which it would be in vain to attempt expressing. "Right! and faith, my lord, I repine not, nor repent."

"So, so, that's well!" said Mauleverer, still not at his ease, and hastening to change the conversation. "But, my dear Brandon, I have strange news for you! You remember that fellow Clifford, who had the insolence to address himself to your adorable niece? I told you I suspected that long friend of his of having made my acquaintance somewhat unpleasantly, and I therefore doubted of Clifford himself. Well, my dear friend, this Clifford is—whom do you think?—no other than Mr. Lovett, of Newgate celebrity!"

"You do not say so!" rejoined Brandon, apathetically, as he slowly gathered his papers together, and deposited them in a drawer.

"Indeed it is true; and what is more, Brandon, this fellow is one of the very identical highwaymen who robbed me on my road from Bath. No doubt he did me the same kind office on my road to Mauleverer Park."

. "Possibly," said Brandon, who appeared absorbed in a reverie.

"Ay!" answered Mauleverer, piqued at this indifference. "But do you not see the consequences to your niece?"

"My niece!" repeated Brandon, rousing himself.

"Certainly. I grieve to say it, my dear friend,—but she was young, very young, when at Bath. She suffered this fellow to address her too openly. Nay,—for I will be frank,—she was suspected of being in love with him!"

"She *was* in love with him," said Brandon dryly, and fixing the malignant coldness of his eye upon the suitor. "And, for aught I know," added he, "she is so at this moment."

"You are cruel!" said Mauleverer, disconcerted. "I trust not, for the sake of my continued addresses."

"My dear lord," said Brandon, urbanely taking the courtier's hand, while the *anguis in herbâ* of his sneer played around his compressed lips,—"my dear lord, we are old friends, and need not deceive each other. You wish to marry my niece, because she is an heiress of great fortune, and you suppose that my wealth will in all probability swell her own. Moreover, she is more beautiful than any other young lady of your acquaintance; and, polished by your example, may do honour to your taste as well as your prudence. Under these circumstances you will, I am quite sure, look with lenity on her girlish errors, and not love her the less because her foolish fancy persuades her that she is in love with another."

"Ahem!" said Mauleverer, "you view the matter with more sense than sentiment; but look you, Brandon, we must try, for both our sakes, if possible, to keep the identity of Lovett with Clifford from being known. I do not see why it should be. No doubt he was on his guard while playing the gallant, and committed no atrocity at Bath. The name of Clifford is hitherto perfectly unsullied. No fraud, no violence are attached to the appellation; and if the rogue will but keep his own counsel, we may hang him out of the way without the secret transpiring."

"But, if I remember right," said Brandon, "the newspapers say that this Lovett will be tried some seventy or eighty miles only from Bath, and that gives a chance of recognition."

"Ay, but he will be devilishly altered, I imagine; for his wound has already been but a bad beautifier to his face: moreover, if the dog has any delicacy, he will naturally dislike to be known as the gallant of that gay city, where he shone so successfully, and will disguise himself as well as he is able. I hear wonders of his powers of self-transformation."

"But he may commit himself on the point between this and his trial," said Brandon.

"I think of ascertaining how far that is likely, by sending my valet down to him (you know one treats these gentlemen highwaymen with a certain consideration, and hangs them with all due respect to their feelings), to hint that it will be doubtless very unpleasant to him, under his 'present unfortunate circumstances' (is not that the phrase?), to be known as the gentleman who enjoyed so deserved a popularity at Bath, and that, though 'the laws of my country compel me' to prosecute him, yet, should he desire it, he may be certain that I will preserve his secret.—Come, Brandon, what say you to that manœuvre? it will answer my purpose, and make the gentleman—for doubtless he is all sensibility—shed tears at my generous forbearance!"

"It is no bad idea," said Brandon. "I commend you for it. At all events, it is necessary that my niece should not know the situation of her lover. She is a girl of a singular turn of mind, and fortune has made her independent. Who knows but what she might commit some folly or another, write petitions to the King, and beg me to present them, or go—for she has a world of romance in her

—to prison, to console him ; or, at all events, she would beg my kind offices on his behalf—a request peculiarly awkward, as in all probability I shall have the honour of trying him."

"Ay, by the by, so you will. And I fancy the poor rogue's audacity will not cause you to be less severe than you usually are. They say you promise to make more human pendulums than any of your brethren."

"They do say that, do they?" said Brandon. "Well, I own I have a bile against my species ; I loathe their folly and their half vices. '*Ridet et odit*'[1] is my motto ; and I allow, that it is not the philosophy that makes men merciful !"

"Well, Juvenal's wisdom be yours!—mine be Horace's!" rejoined Mauleverer, as he picked his teeth ; "but I am glad you see the absolute necessity of keeping this secret from Lucy's suspicion. She never reads the papers, I suppose?—Girls never do !"

"No ! and I will take care not to have them thrown in her way ; and as, in consequence of my poor brother's recent death, she sees nobody but us, there is little chance, should Lovett's right to the name of Clifford be discovered, that it should reach her ears !"

"But those confounded servants?"

"True enough ! but consider, that before *they* know it, the newspapers will ; so that, should it be needful, we shall have our own time to caution them. I need only say to Lucy's woman, 'A poor gentleman, a friend of the late squire's, whom your mistress used to dance with, and you must have seen—Captain Clifford—is to be tried for his life : it will shock her, poor thing ! in her present state of health, to tell her of so sad an event to her father's friend ; therefore be silent, as you value your place and ten guineas,'—and I may be tolerably sure of caution !"

"You ought to be chairman to the 'ways and means' committee !" cried Mauleverer. "My mind is now easy ; and when once poor Clifford is gone—'*fallen from a high estate*,'—we may break the matter gently to her ; and, as I intend thereon to be very respectful, very delicate, &c., she cannot but be sensible of my kindness and real affection !"

"And if a live dog be better than a dead lion," added Brandon, "surely a lord in existence will be better than a highwayman hanged !"

"According to ordinary logic," rejoined Mauleverer, "that syllogism is clear enough ; and though I believe a girl may cling, now and then, to the memory of a departed lover, I do not think she will when the memory is allied with shame. Love is nothing more than vanity pleased ; wound the vanity, and you destroy the love ! Lucy

---

[1] "*He laughs and hates*"

will be forced, after having made so bad a choice of a lover, to make a good one in a husband,—in order to recover her self-esteem!"

"And therefore *you* are certain of her!" said Brandon, ironically.

"Thanks to my star—my garter—my ancestor, the first baron, and myself, the first earl—I hope I am," said Mauleverer, and the conversation turned. Mauleverer did not stay much longer with the judge; and Brandon, left alone, recurred once more to the perusal of his letters.

We scarcely know what sensations it would have occasioned in one who had known Brandon only in his later years, could he have read those letters, referring to so much earlier a date. There was in the keen and arid character of the man, so little that recalled any idea of courtship or youthful gallantry, that a correspondence of that nature would have appeared almost as unnatural as the loves of plants, or the amatory softenings of a mineral. The correspondence now before Brandon was descriptive of various feelings, but all appertaining to the same class: most of them were apparent answers to letters from him. One while they replied tenderly to expressions of tenderness, but intimated a doubt whether the writer would be able to constitute his future happiness, and atone for certain sacrifices of birth and fortune, and ambitious prospects, to which she alluded: at other times, a vein of latent coquetry seemed to pervade the style—an indescribable air of coolness and reserve contrasted former passages in the correspondence, and was calculated to convey to the reader an impression that the feelings of the lover were not altogether adequately returned. Frequently the writer, as if Brandon had expressed himself sensible of this conviction, reproached him for unjust jealousy and unworthy suspicion. And the tone of the reproach varied in each letter: sometimes it was gay and satirising; at others, soft and expostulatory; at others, gravely reasoning; and often, haughtily indignant. Still, throughout the whole correspondence, on the part of the mistress, there was a sufficient stamp of individuality to give a shrewd examiner some probable guess at the writer's character. He would have judged her, perhaps, capable of strong and ardent feeling, but ordinarily of a light and capricious turn, and seemingly prone to imagine and to resent offence. With these letters were mingled others in Brandon's writing—of how different, of how impassioned a description! All that a deep, proud, meditative, exacting character could dream of love given, or require of love returned, was poured burningly over the pages; yet they were full of reproach, of jealousy, of a nice and torturing observation, as calculated to wound as the ardour might be fitted to charm; and often the bitter tendency to disdain that distinguished his temperament broke through the fondest enthusiasm of courtship, or the softest outpourings of love. '' You saw me not yesterday," he wrote in one letter, "but I saw you ; all day I was by you ; you gave not a look which passed me unnoticed ; you made not a movement which I did not chronicle in my memory. Julia, do you tremble when I tell you this? Yes, if you have a heart, *I know* these words would stab it to the core! You may affect to answer me indignantly! Wise dissembler!—it is very skilful—very, to assume anger when you have no reply. I repeat, during the whole of that party of pleasure—(pleasure ! well, your tastes, it must be acknowledged, are exquisite !) which you enjoyed yesterday, and which you so faintly asked me to share, my eye was on you. You did not know that I was in the wood when you took the arm of the incomparable Digby, with so pretty a semblance of alarm at the moment the snake, which my foot disturbed, glided across your path. You did not know I was within hearing of the tent where you made so agreeable a repast, and from which your laughter sent peals so merry and so numerous. Laughter! O, Julia, *can* you tell me that you love, and yet be happy, even to mirth, when I am away? Love! O God, how different a sensation is mine! Mine makes my whole principle of life! Yours ! I tell you, that I think, at moments, I would rather have your hate than the lukewarm sentiment you bear to me, and honour by the name of 'affection.' Pretty phrase! I have *no affection* for you! Give me not that sickly word ; but try with me, Julia, to invent some expression that has never filtered a paltry meaning through the lips of another ! Affection ! why that is a sister's word—a girl's word to her pet squirrel ! never was it made for that ruby and most ripe mouth ! Shall I come to your house this evening? Your mother has asked me, and you—*you* heard her, and said nothing. Oh ! but that was maiden reserve—was it? and maiden reserve caused you to take up a book the moment I left you, as if my company made but an ordinary amusement instantly to be replaced by another ! When *I* have seen you, society, books, food, all are hateful to me ; but *you*, sweet Julia, *you* can read, can you? Why, when *I* left you, I lingered by the parlour window for hours, till dusk, and you never once lifted your eyes, nor saw me pass and repass. At least, I thought you would have watched my steps when I left the house, but I err, charming moralist ! According to you, that vigilance would have been meanness."

In another part of the correspondence, a more grave, if not a deeper, gush of feeling struggled for expression.

"You say, Julia, that were you to marry one who thinks so much of what he surrenders for you, and who requires from yourself so vast a return of love, you should tremble for the future happiness of both of us. Julia, the triteness of that fear proves that you love not at all. I do not tremble for our future happiness; on the contrary, the intensity of my passion for you makes me *know* that we never can be happy! never beyond the first rapture of our union. Happiness is a quiet and tranquil feeling. No feeling that I can possibly bear to you will ever receive those epithets,—I know that I shall be wretched and accursed when I am united to you. Start not ; I will presently tell you why. But I do not dream of happiness, neither (could you fathom one drop of the dark and limitless ocean of my emotions) would you name to me that word. It is not the mercantile and callous calculation of chances for 'future felicity' (what homily supplied you with so choice a term ?) that enters into the heart that cherishes an all-pervading love. Passion looks only to one object, to nothing beyond,—I thirst, I consume, not for happiness, but *you*. Were your possession inevitably to lead me to a gulf of anguish and shame, think you I should covet it one jot the less ? If you carry one thought, one hope, one dim fancy, beyond the event that makes you mine, you may be more worthy of the esteem of others ; but you are utterly undeserving of *my love*.

* * * * *

* * * * *

" I will tell you now why I know we cannot be happy. In the first place, when you say that I am proud of birth, that I am morbidly ambitious, that I am anxious to shine in the great world, and that after the first intoxication of love has passed away I shall feel bitterness against one who has so humbled my pride and darkened my prospects, I am not sure that you wholly err. But I *am* sure that the instant remedy is in your power. Have you patience, Julia, to listen to a kind of history of myself, or rather of my feelings? if so, perhaps it may be the best method of explaining all that I would convey. You will see, then, that my family pride and my worldly ambition are not founded altogether on those basements which move my laughter in another :—if my feelings thereon are really, however, as you would insinuate, equal matter for derision, behold, my Julia, I can laugh equally at them ! So pleasant a thing to me is scorn, that I would rather despise myself than have no one to despise ;—but to my narrative ! You must know that there are but two of us, sons of a country squire, of old family, which once possessed large possessions and something of historical renown. We lived in an old country place ; my father was a convivial dog, a fox-hunter, a drunkard, yet in his way a fine gentleman,—and a very disreputable member of society. The first feelings towards him that I can remember were those of shame. Not much matter of family pride here, you will say ! True, and that is exactly the reason which made me cherish family pride elsewhere. My father's house was filled with guests, some high and some low,—they all united in ridicule of the host   I soon detected the laughter, and you may imagine that it did not please me.   Meanwhile the old huntsman, whose family was about as ancient as ours, and whose ancestors had officiated in his capacity for the ancestors of his master time out of mind, told me story after story about the Brandons of yore.   I turned from the stories to more legitimate history, and found the legends were tolerably true.   I learned to glow at this discovery : the pride—humbled when I remembered my sire—revived when I remembered my ancestors; I became resolved to emulate them, to restore a sunken name, and vowed a world of nonsense on the subject. The habit of brooding over these ideas grew on me ; I never heard a jest broken on my paternal guardian—I never caught the maudlin look of his reeling eyes, nor listened to some exquisite inanity from his besotted lips, but what my thoughts flew instantly back to the Sir Charleses and the Sir Roberts of my race, and I comforted myself with the hope that the present degeneracy should pass away. Hence, Julia, my family pride ; hence, too, another feeling you dislike in me—disdain !   I first learned to despise my father, the host, and I then despised my acquaintances, his guests ; for I saw, while they laughed at him, that they flattered, and that their meriment was not the only thing suffered to feed at his expense.   Thus contempt grew up with me, and I had nothing to check it ; for when I looked around I saw not one living thing that I could respect. This father of mine had the sense to think I was no idiot.   He was proud (poor man !) of 'my talents,' viz., of prizes won at school, and congratulatory letters from my masters.   He sent me to college : my mind took a leap there : I will tell you, prettiest, what it was ! Before I went thither I had some fine vague visions about virtue.   I thought to revive my ancestral honours by being good ; in short, I was an embryo King Pepin.   I awoke from this dream at the university.   There, for the first time, I perceived the real consequence of rank.

"At school, you know, Julia, boys care nothing for a lord.   A good cricketer, an excellent fellow, is worth all the earls in the peerage.   But at college all *that* ceases : bats and balls sink into the nothingness in which corals and bells had sunk before.   One grows manly, and worships coronets and carriages.   I saw it was a fine thing to get a prize, but it was ten times a finer thing to get drunk with a peer.   So, when I had done the first, my resolve to be worthy of my sires made me do the second—not, indeed, exactly ; I never got *drunk;* my father disgusted me with that vice betimes. To his gluttony I owe my vegetable diet, and to his inebriety my addiction to water. No; I did not get drunk with peers: but I was just as agreeable to them as if I had been equally embruted. I knew intimately all the 'Hats'[1] in the university, and I was henceforth looked up to by the 'Caps,' as if my head had gained the height of every hat that I knew. But I did not do this immediately. I must tell you two little anecdotes, that first initiated me into the secret of real greatness. The first was this: I was sitting at dinner with some fellows of a college, grave men and clever; two of them, not knowing me, were conversing about me: they heard, they said, that I should never be so good a fellow as my father,—have such a cellar, or keep such a house.

" 'I have met six earls there and a marquess,' quoth the other senior.

" 'And his son,' returned the first don, 'only keeps company with sizars, I believe.'

" 'So then,' said I to myself, 'to deserve the praise even of clever men, one must have good wines, know plenty of earls, and forswear sizars.'

"Nothing could be truer than my conclusion.

"Anecdote the second is this:—On the day I gained a high university prize, I invited my friends to dine with me: four of them refused because they were engaged (they had been asked *since* I asked them)—to whom? the richest man at the university. These occurrences happening at the same time, threw me into a profound reverie: I awoke, and became a man of the world. I no longer resolved to be virtuous, and to hunt after the glory of your Romans and your Athenians—I resolved to become rich, powerful, and of worldly repute.

"I abjured my honest sizars, and as I said before, I courted some rich 'Hats.' Behold my first grand step in the world! I became the parasite and the flatterer. What! would my pride suffer this? Verily yes, my pride delighted in it; for it soothed my spirit of contempt to put these fine fellows to my use! it soothed me to see how easily I could cajole them, and to what a variety of purposes I could apply even the wearisome disgust of their acquaintance. Nothing is so foolish as to say the idle great are of no use; they can be put to any use whatsoever that a wise man is inclined to make of them! Well, Julia, lo! my character already formed; family pride, disdain, and worldly ambition,—there it is for you; after circumstances only strengthened the impression already made. I desired, on leaving college, to go abroad; my father had no money to give me. What signified that? I looked carelessly round for some wealthier convenience than the paternal hoard; I found it in a Lord Mauleverer;

[1] At Cambridge the sons of noblemen, and the eldest sons of baronets, are allowed to wear hats instead of the academical cap.

he had been at college with me, and I endured him easily as a companion,—for he had accomplishments, wit, and good nature; I made him wish to go abroad, and I made him think he should die of *ennui* if I did not accompany him. To his request to that effect, I *reluctantly* agreed, and saw everything in Europe, which he neglected to see, at his expense. What amused me the most was the perception that I, the parasite, was respected by him; and he, the patron, was ridiculed by me! It would not have been so if I had depended on 'my virtue.' Well, sweetest Julia, the world, as I have said, gave to my college experience a sacred authority. I returned to England, and my father died, leaving to me not a sixpence, and to my brother an estate so mortgaged that he could not enjoy it, and so restricted that he could not sell it. It was now the time for me to profit by the experience I boasted of. I saw that it was necessary I should take some profession. Professions are the masks to your pauper-rogue; they give respectability to cheating, and a diploma to feed upon others. I analysed my talents, and looked to the customs of my country: the result was my resolution to take to the bar. I had an inexhaustible power of application; I was keen, shrewd, and audacious. All these qualities 'tell' at the courts of justice. I kept my legitimate number of terms,—I was called,—I went the circuit,—I obtained not a brief—not a brief, Julia! My health, never robust, gave way beneath study and irritation. I was ordered to betake myself to the country; I came to this village, as one both salubrious and obscure. I lodged in the house of your aunt, —you came thither daily,—I saw you,—you know the rest. But where, all this time, were my noble friends, you will say? 'Sdeath, since we had left college, they had learned a little of the wisdom I had *then* possessed; they were not disposed to give something for nothing; they had younger brothers, and cousins and mistresses, and, for aught I know, children to provide for. Besides, they had their own expenses: the richer a man is, the less he has to give. One of them would have bestowed on me a living, if I had gone into the church; another, a commission if I had joined his regiment. But I knew the day was past both for priest and soldier; and it was not merely to live, no, nor to live comfortably, but to enjoy power, that I desired; so I declined these offers. Others of my friends would have been delighted to have kept me in their house, feasted me, joked with me, rode with me, and nothing more! But I had already the sense to see, that if a man dances himself into distinction, it is never by the steps of attendance. One must receive favours and court patronage, but it must be with the air of an independent man. My old friends thus rendered useless, my legal studies forbade me to make new, nay, they even estranged me from

the old ; for people may say what they please about a similarity of
opinions being necessary to friendship,—a similarity of habits is
much more so.   It is the man you dine, breakfast, and lodge with,
walk, ride, gamble, or thieve with, that is your friend ; not the man
who likes Virgil as well as you do, and agrees with you in an
admiration of Handel. Meanwhile, my chief prey, Lord Mauleverer,
was gone ; he had taken another man's dulcinea, and sought out
a bower in Italy ; from that time to this I have never heard of him
nor seen him ; I know not even his address.   With the exception of
a few stray gleanings from my brother, who, good easy man ! I could
plunder more, were I not resolved not to ruin the family stock, I have
been thrown on myself; the result is, that, though as clever as my
fellows, I have narrowly shunned starvation : had my wants been
less simple, there would have been no shunning in the case.   But a
man is not easily starved who drinks water, and eats by the ounce.
A more effectual fate might have befallen me : disappointment,
wrath, baffled hope, mortified pride, all these, which gnawed at my
heart, might have consumed it long ago ; I might have fretted away
as a garment which the moth eateth, had it not been for that fund
of obstinate and iron hardness, which nature,—I beg pardon, there
is no nature,—*circumstance* bestowed upon me.   This has borne me
up, and will bear me yet through time, and shame, and bodily weakness, and mental fever, until my ambition has won a certain height,
and my disdain of human pettiness rioted in the external sources of
fortune, as well as an inward fountain of bitter and self-fed consolation.   Yet, oh, Julia ! I know not if even this would have supported
me, if at that epoch of life, when I was most wounded, most stricken
in body, most soured in mind, my heart had not met and fastened
itself to yours : I saw you, loved you, and life became to me a new
object.   Even now, as I write to you, all my bitterness, my pride,
vanish ; everything I have longed for disappears ; my very ambition
is gone.   I have no hope but for you, Julia ; beautiful, adored
Julia !—when I love you, I love even my kind.   Oh, you know
not the power you possess over me !   Do not betray it : you can
yet make me all that my boyhood once dreamed ; or you can harden
every thought, feeling, sensation, into stone.

     *   *   *   *   *   *   *

     *   *   *   *   *   *   *

"I was to tell you why I look not for happiness in our union.
You have now seen my nature.   You have traced the history of my
life, by tracing the history of my character.   You see what I surrender in gaining you.   I do not deny the sacrifice.   I surrender
the very essentials of my present mind and soul.   I cease to be
worldly.   I cannot raise myself, I cannot revive my ancestral name :

nay, I shall relinquish it for ever. I shall adopt a disguised appellation. I shall sink into another grade of life. In some remote
village, by means of some humbler profession than that I now follow,
we must earn our subsistence, and smile at ambition. I tell you
frankly, Julia, when I close the eyes of my heart,—when I shut
you from my gaze, this sacrifice appals me. But even then you
force yourself before me, and I feel that one glance from your eye is
more to me than all. If you could bear with me,—if you could
soothe me,—if when a cloud is on me you could suffer it to pass
away unnoticed, and smile on me the moment it is gone, oh, Julia!
there would be then no extreme of poverty,—no abasement of fortune,
—no abandonment of early dreams which would not seem to me
rapture if coupled with the bliss of knowing that you are mine. Never
should my lip—never should my eye tell you that there is that thing
on earth for which I repine, or which I could desire. No, Julia,
could I flatter my heart with this hope you would not find me dream
of unhappiness and you united. But I tremble, Julia, when I think of
your temper and my own : you will conceive a gloomy look from one
never mirthful is an insult ; and you will feel every vent of passion
on Fortune or on others as a reproach to you. Then, too, you
cannot enter into my nature ; you cannot descend into its caverns ;
you cannot behold, much less can you deign to lull, the exacting
and lynx-eyed jealousy that dwells there. Sweetest Julia! every
breath of yours, every touch of yours, every look of yours I yearn
for beyond all a mother's longing for the child that has been torn
from her for years. Your head leaned upon an old tree (do you
remember it, near * * *?), and I went every day, after seeing you,
to kiss it. Do you wonder that I am jealous? How can I love
you as I do and be otherwise? My whole being is intoxicated with
you!"

  * * * * * * *
  * * * * * * *

"This, then, your pride and mine, your pleasure in the admiration of others, your lightness, Julia, make me foresee an eternal
and gushing source of torture to my mind. I care not ;—I care for
nothing so that you are mine, if but for one hour."

It seems that, despite the strange, sometimes the unloverlike and
fiercely selfish nature of these letters from Brandon, something of
a genuine tone of passion,—perhaps their originality,—aided, no
doubt, by some *uttered* eloquence of the writer, and some treacherous
inclination on the part of the mistress, ultimately conquered ; and
that a union so little likely to receive the smile of a prosperous star
was at length concluded. The letter which terminated the correspondence was from Brandon : it was written on the evening before

the marriage, which, it appeared by the same letter, was to be private and concealed. After a rapturous burst of hope and joy, it continued thus :—

"Yes, Julia, I recant my words : I have no belief that you or I shall ever have cause hereafter for unhappiness. Those eyes that dwelt so tenderly on mine ; that hand whose presence lingers yet in every nerve of my frame; those lips turned so coyly, yet, shall I say, reluctantly ? from me ; all tell me that you love me ; and my fears are banished. Love, which conquered my nature, will conquer the only thing I would desire to see altered in yours. Nothing could ever make *me* adore you less, though you affect to dread it ; nothing but a knowledge that you are unworthy of me, that you have a thought for another,—then I should not hate you. No : the privilege of my past existence would revive ; I should revel in a luxury of contempt, I should despise you, I should mock you, and I should be once more what I was before I knew you. But why do I talk thus ? My bride, my blessing, forgive me !"

    *   *   *   *   *   *   *

In concluding our extracts from this correspondence, we wish the reader to note, first, that the love professed by Brandon seems of that vehement and corporeal nature which, while it is often the least durable, is also the most susceptible of the fiercest extremes of hatred, or even of disgust. Secondly, that the character opened by this sarcastic candour evidently required in a mistress either an utter devotion or a skilful address. And thirdly, that we have hinted at such qualities in the fair correspondent as did not seem sanguinely to promise either of those essentials.

While with a curled, yet often with a quivering, lip the austere and sarcastic Brandon slowly compelled himself to the task of proceeding through these monuments of former folly and youthful emotion, the further elucidation of those events, now rapidly urging on a fatal and dread catastrophe, spreads before us a narrative occurring many years prior to the time at which we are at present arrived.

CHAPTER XXXIII.

"CLEM. *Lift the dark veil of years !—behind—what waits ?*
A human heart. Vast city, where reside
All glories and all vilenesses !—while foul,
Yet silent, through the roar of passions rolls
The river of the Darling Sin—and bears
A life and yet a poison on its tide.

*   *   *   *   *

' CLEM *Thy wife ?—*
VICT   *Avaunt ! I've changed that word to ' scorn ''*
CLEM. *Thy child ?—*
VICT   *Ay, that strikes home—my child—my child !'*

' LOVE AND HATRED,' BY ——

O an obscure town in * * * * shire, there came to reside a
young couple, whose appearance and habits drew towards
them from the neighbouring gossips a more than ordinary
attention. They bore the name of *Welford.* The man
assumed the profession of a solicitor. He came without introduction or recommendation ; his manner of life bespoke poverty ;
his address was reserved, and even sour ; and despite the notice
and scrutiny with which he was regarded, he gained no clients, and
made no lawsuits. The want of all those decent *charlatanisms*
which men of every profession are almost necessitated to employ, and
the sudden and unushered nature of his coming were, perhaps, the
cause of this ill-success. "His house was too small," people said,
"for respectability." And little good could be got from a solicitor,
the very rails round whose door were so sadly in want of re-
painting ! Then, too, Mrs. Welford made a vast number of enemies.
She was, beyond all expression, beautiful ; and there was a certain coquetry in her manner which showed she was aware of her
attractions. All the ladies of * * * * hated her. A few people
called on the young couple. Welford received them coldly ; their
invitations were unaccepted, and, what was worse, they were never
returned. The devil himself could not have supported an attorney
under such circumstances. Reserved—shabby—poor—rude—intro-
ductionless—a bad house—an unpainted railing—and a beautiful
wife ! Nevertheless, though Welford was not employed, he was,
as we have said, watched. On their first arrival, which was in
summer, the young pair were often seen walking together in the
fields or groves which surrounded their home. Sometimes they

walked affectionately together, and it was observed with what care Welford adjusted his wife's cloak or shawl around her slender shape, as the cool of the evening increased. But often his arm was withdrawn,—he lingered behind, and they continued their walk or returned homeward in silence and apart. By degrees whispers circulated throughout the town that the new-married couple lived by no means happily. The men laid the fault on the stern-looking husband; the women, on the minx of a wife. However, the solitary servant whom they kept declared, that though Mr. Welford did sometimes frown, and Mrs. Welford did sometimes weep, they were extremely attached to each other, and only quarrelled through love. The maid had had four lovers herself, and was possibly experienced in such matters. They received no visitors, near or from a distance; and the postman declared he had never seen a letter directed to either. Thus a kind of mystery hung over the pair, and made them still more gazed on and still more disliked—which is saying a great deal—than they would have otherwise been. Poor as Welford was, his air and walk eminently bespoke what common persons term *gentility*. And in this he had greatly the advantage of his beautiful wife, who, though there was certainly nothing vulgar or plebeian in her aspect, altogether wanted the refinement of manner, look, and phrase, which characterised Welford. For about two years they lived in this manner, and so frugally and tranquilly, that though Welford had not any visible means of subsistence, no one could well wonder in what manner they *did* subsist. About the end of that time, Welford suddenly embarked a small sum in a county speculation. In the course of this adventure, to the great surprise of his neighbours, he evinced an extraordinary turn for calculation, and his habits plainly bespoke a man both of business and ability. This disposal of capital brought a sufficient return to support the Welfords, if they had been so disposed, in rather a better style than heretofore. They remained, however, in much the same state; and the only difference that the event produced was the retirement of Mr. Welford from the profession he had embraced. He was no longer a solicitor! It must be allowed that he resigned no great advantages in this retirement. About this time some officers were quartered at * * * *; and one of them, a handsome lieutenant, was so struck with the charms of Mrs. Welford, whom he saw at church, that he lost no opportunity of testifying his admiration. It was maliciously, yet not unfoundedly, remarked, that though no absolute impropriety could be detected in the manner of Mrs. Welford, she certainly seemed far from displeased with the evident homage of the young lieutenant. A blush tinged her cheek when she saw him; and the gallant coxcomb asserted that the blush was not always without a smile. Emboldened by the interpretations of his vanity, and contrasting, as every one else did, his own animated face and glittering garb with the ascetic and gloomy countenance, the unstudied dress, and austere gait, which destroyed in Welford the effect of a really handsome person, our lieutenant thought fit to express his passion by a letter, which he conveyed to Mrs. Welford's pew. Mrs. Welford went not to church that day ; the letter was found by a good-natured neighbour, and enclosed anonymously to the husband.

Whatever, in the secrecy of domestic intercourse, took place on this event was necessarily unknown ; but the next Sunday the face of Mr. Welford, which had never before appeared at church, was discerned by one vigilant neighbour — probably the anonymous friend,—not in the same pew with his wife, but in a remote corner of the sacred house. And once, when the lieutenant was watching to read in Mrs. Welford's face some answer to his epistle, the same obliging spectator declared that Welford's countenance assumed a sardonic and withering sneer that made his very blood to creep. However this be, the lieutenant left his quarters, and Mrs. Welford's reputation remained dissatisfactorily untarnished. Shortly after this the county speculation failed, and it was understood that the Welfords were about to leave the town, whither none knew,— some said to gaol ; but then, unhappily, no debts could be dis- covered. Their bills had been "next to nothing;" but, at least, they had been regularly paid. However, before the rumoured emigration took place, a circumstance equally wonderful to the good people of * * * * occurred. One bright spring morning, a party of pleasure from a great house in the vicinity passed through that town. Most conspicuous of these was a young horseman, richly dressed, and of a remarkably showy and handsome appearance. Not a little sensible of the sensation he created, this cavalier lingered behind his companions in order to eye more deliberately certain damsels stationed in a window, and who were quite ready to return his glances with interest. At this moment the horse, which was fretting itself fiercely against the rein that restrained it from its fellows, took fright at a knife-grinder, started violently to one side, and the graceful cavalier, who had been thinking, not of the attitude best adapted to preserve his equilibrium, but to display his figure, was thrown with some force upon a heap of bricks and rubbish which had long, to the scandal of the neighbourhood, stood before the paintless railings around Mr. Welford's house. Welford him- self came out at the time, and felt compelled, for he was by no means one whose sympathetic emotions flowed easily, to give a glance to the condition of a man who lay motionless before his very

door. The horseman quickly recovered his senses, but found himself unable to rise ; one of his legs was broken. Supported in the
arms of his groom he looked around, and his eye met Welford's.
An instant recognition gave life to the face of the former, and threw
a dark blush over the sullen features of the latter. "Heavens!"
said the cavalier, "is that——"

"Hist, my lord!" cried Welford, quickly interrupting him, and
glancing round. "But you are hurt,—will you enter my house?"

The horseman signified his assent, and, between the groom and
Welford, was borne within the shabby door of the ex-solicitor. The
groom was then despatched with an excuse to the party, many of
whom were already hastening around the house ; and though one or
two did force themselves across the inhospitable threshold, yet so
soon as they had uttered a few expletives, and felt their stare sink
beneath the sullen and chilling asperity of the host, they satisfied
themselves, that though it was d——d unlucky for their friend, yet
they could do nothing for him at present ; and promising to send to
inquire after him the next day, they remounted and rode homeward,
with an eye more attentive than usual to the motion of their steeds.
They did not, however, depart till the surgeon of the town had
made his appearance, and declared that the patient must not on
any account be moved. A lord's leg was a windfall that did not
happen every day to the surgeon of * * * *. All this while we
may imagine the state of anxiety experienced in the town, and the
agonised endurance of those rural nerves which are produced in
scanty populations, and have so *Taliacotian* a sympathy with the
affairs of other people. One day—two days—three days—a week—
a fortnight, nay, a month, passed, and the lord was still the inmate of
Mr. Welford's abode. Leaving the gossips to feed on their curiosity,
—"Cannibals of their own hearts,"—we must give a glance
towards the interior of the inhospitable mansion of the ex-solicitor.

It was towards evening, the sufferer was supported on a sofa, and
the beautiful Mrs. Welford, who had officiated as his nurse, was
placing the pillow under the shattered limb. He himself was
attempting to seize her hand, which she coyly drew back, and
uttering things sweeter and more polished than she had ever listened
to before. At this moment Welford softly entered ; he was unnoticed by either ; and he stood at the door contemplating them with
a smile of calm and self-hugging derision. The face of Mephistopheles regarding Margaret and Faust might suggest some idea
of the picture we design to paint ; but the countenance of Welford
was more lofty, as well as comelier, in character, though not less
malignant in expression, than that which the incomparable Retsch
has given to the mocking fiend. So utter, so congratulatory, so

lordly was the contempt on Welford's dark and striking features,
that though he was in that situation in which ridicule usually attaches
itself to the husband, it was the gallant and the wife that would
have appeared to the beholder in a humiliating and unenviable light.

After a momentary pause, Welford approached with a heavy step,
—the wife started ;—but, with a bland and smooth expression,
which, since his sojourn in the town of * * * *, had been rarely
visible in his aspect, the host joined the pair, smiled on the nurse,
and congratulated the patient on his progress towards recovery.
The nobleman, well learned in the usages of the world, replied
easily and gaily ; and the conversation flowed on cheerful enough
till the wife, who had sat abstracted and apart, stealing ever and
anon timid glances towards her husband, and looks of a softer
meaning towards the patient, retired from the room.   Welford then
gave a turn to the conversation : he reminded the nobleman of the
pleasant days they had passed in Italy,—of the adventures they had
shared, and the intrigues they had enjoyed ; as the conversation
warmed it assumed a more free and licentious turn ; and not a little,
we ween, would the good folks of * * * * have been amazed could
they have listened to the gay jests and the libertine maxims which
flowed from the thin lips of that cold and severe Welford, whose
countenance gave the lie to mirth.   Of women in general they spoke
with that lively contempt which is the customary tone with men of
the world,—only in Welford it assumed a bitterer, a deeper, and
a more philosophical cast, than it did in his more animated yet less
energetic guest.

The nobleman seemed charmed with his friend ; the conversation
was just to his taste ; and when Welford had supported him up to
bed, he shook that person cordially by the hand, and hoped he
should soon see him in very different circumstances.   When the
peer's door was closed on Welford, he stood motionless for some
moments ; he then with a soft step ascended to his own chamber.
His wife slept soundly ; beside the bed was the infant's cradle.   As
his eyes fell on the latter, the rigid irony, now habitual to his
features, relaxed ; he bent over the cradle long, and in deep silence.
The mother's face, blended with the sire's, was stamped on the
sleeping and cherub countenance before him ; and as at length,
rousing from his reverie, he kissed it gently, he murmured,—

" When I look on you I will believe that she once loved me,—
Pah ! " he said abruptly, and rising,—" this fatherly sentiment for
a ——'s offering is exquisite in *me!* "   So saying, without glancing
towards his wife, who, disturbed by the loudness of his last words,
stirred uneasily, he left the room, and descended into that where he
had conversed with his guest.   He shut the door with caution, and

striding to and fio the humble apartment, gave vent to thoughts marshalled somewhat in the broken airay in which they now appear to the reader.

"Ay, ay, she has been my ruin! and if I were one of your weak fools who make a gospel of the silliest and most mawkish follies of this social state, she would now be my disgrace; but, instead of my disgrace, I will make her my footstool to honour and wealth. And, then, to the devil with the footstool! Yes! two years I have borne what was enough to turn my whole blood into gall: inactivity, hopelessness—a wasted heart and life in myself, contumely from the world, coldness, bickering, ingratitude, from the one for whom—oh, ass that I was!—I gave up the most cherished part of my nature— rather my nature itself! Two years I have borne this, and now will I have my revenge;—I will sell her—sell her! God! I will sell her like the commonest beast of a market! And this paltry piece of false coin shall buy me—my world! Other men's vengeance comes from hatred—a base, rash, unphilosophical sentiment! mine comes from scorn—the only wise state for the reason to rest in. Other men's vengeance ruins themselves—mine shall save me! Hah!—how my soul chuckles when I look at this pitiful pair, who think I see them not, and know that every movement they make is on a mesh of my web! Yet," and Welford paused slowly,—"yet I cannot but mock myself when I think of the arch gull that this boy's madness, love,—love, indeed!—the very word turns me sick with loathing,—made of me. Had that woman, silly, weak, auto-matal as she is, really loved me,—had she been sensible of the unspeakable sacrifice I had made to her (Antony's was nothing to it —he lost a real world only; mine was the world of imagination),— had she but condescended to learn my nature, to subdue the woman's devil at her own, I could have lived on in this babbling hermitage for ever, and fancied myself happy and resigned—I could have become a different being. I fancy I could have become what your moralists (quacks!) call 'good.' But this fretting frivolity of heart, —this lust of fool's praise,—this peevishness of temper,—this sullen-ness in answer to the moody thought, which in me she neither fathomed nor forgave,—this vulgar, daily, hourly pining at the paltry pinches of the body's poverty, the domestic whine, the house-hold complaint,—when I—I have not a thought for such pitiful trials of affection; and all this while my curses, my buried hope, and disguised spirit, and sunken name not thought of; the magnitude of my surrender to her not even comprehended; nay, her 'incon-veniences,'—a dim hearth, I suppose, or a dauntless table,—com-pared, ay, absolutely, compared with all which I abandoned for her sake! As if it were not enough,—had I been a fool, an ambitionless,

M

soulless fool,—the mere thought that I had linked my name to that
of a tradesman—I beg pardon, a *retired* tradesman!—as if that
knowledge—a knowledge I would strangle my whole race, every one
who has ever met, seen me, rather than they should penetrate—were
not enough when she talks of 'comparing,'—to make me gnaw the
very flesh from my bones! No, no, no! Never was there so bright
a turn in my fate as when this titled coxcomb, with his smooth voice
and gaudy fripperies, came hither! I will make her a tool to carve
my escape from this cavern wherein she has plunged me. I will
foment 'my lord's' passion, till 'my lord' thinks 'the passion' (a
butterfly's passion!) worth any price. I will then make my own
terms, bind 'my lord' to secresy, and get rid of my wife, my shame,
and the obscurity of Mr. Welford, for ever. Bright, bright prospects! let me shut my eyes to enjoy you! But softly,—my noble
friend calls himself a man of the world, skilled in human nature,
and a derider of its prejudices ; true enough, in his own little way
—thanks not to enlarged views but a vicious experience—so he is!
The book of the world is a vast miscellany ; he is perfectly well
acquainted, doubtless, with those pages that treat of the fashions,—
profoundly versed, I warrant, in the *Magasin des Modes* tacked to
the end of the index. But shall I, even with all the mastership
which my mind *must* exercise over his,—shall I be able utterly to
free myself in this 'peer of the world's' mind from a degrading
remembrance? Cuckold! cuckold! 'tis an ugly word ; a convenient,
willing cuckold, humph!—there is no grandeur, no philosophical
varnish in the phrase. Let me see—yes! I have a remedy for
all that. I was married privately,—well! under disguised names,
—well! It was a stolen marriage, far from her town,—well!
witnesses unknown to her,—well! proofs easily secured to my
possession,—excellent! the fool shall believe it a forged marriage,
an ingenious gallantry of mine ; I will wash out the stain cuckold
with the water of another word ; I will make market of a mistress,
not a *wife*. I will warn him not to acquaint *her* with this secret ;
let me consider for what reason,—oh! my son's legitimacy *may* be
convenient to me hereafter. He will understand that reason, and I
will have his 'honour' thereon. And by the way, I do care for
that legitimacy, and will guard the proofs ; I love my child,—ambitious men do love their children ; I may become a lord myself,
and may wish for a lord to succeed me ; and that son *is* mine ;
thank Heaven! I am sure on that point,—the only child, too, that
ever shall arise to me Never, I swear, will I again put myself
beyond my own power! All my nature, save one passion, I have
hitherto mastered ; that passion shall henceforth be my slave, my
only t'   · · · · · · · · · · · · · · · be the world!"

As thus terminated the reverie of a man whom the social circumstances of the world were calculated, as if by system, to render
eminently and basely wicked, Welford slowly ascended the stairs, and
re-entered his chamber. his wife was still sleeping ; her beauty was
of the fair, and girlish, and harmonised order, which lovers and poets
would express by the word "angelic ;" and as Welford looked upon
her face, hushed and almost hallowed by slumber, a certain weakness
and irresolution might have been discernible in the strong lines of
his haughty features. At that moment, as if for ever to destroy the
return of hope or virtue to either, her lips moved, they uttered one
word,—it was the name of Welford's courtly guest.

About three weeks from that evening, Mrs. Welford eloped with
the young nobleman, and on the morning following that event, the
distracted husband with his child disappeared for ever from the town
of * * * * From that day no tidings whatsoever respecting him
ever reached the titillated ears of his anxious neighbours ; and doubt,
curiosity, discussion, gradually settled into the belief that his despair
had hurried him into suicide.

Although the unfortunate Mrs. Welford was in reality of a light
and frivolous turn, and, above all, susceptible to personal vanity,
she was not without ardent affections and keen sensibilities. Her
marriage had been one of love, that is to say, on her part, the
ordinary love of girls, who love not through actual and natural
feeling so much as forced predisposition. Her choice had fallen
on one superior to herself in birth, and far above all, in person
and address, whom she had habitually met. Thus her vanity had
assisted her affection, and something strange and eccentric in the
temper and mind of Welford had, though at times it aroused her
fear, greatly contributed to inflame her imagination. Then, too,
though an uncourtly, he had been a passionate and a romantic
lover. She was sensible that he gave up for her much that he had
previously conceived necessary to his existence ; and she stopped
not to inquire how far this devotion was likely to last, or what
conduct on her part might best perpetuate the feelings from which
it sprung. She had eloped with him. She had consented to a
private marriage. She had passed one happy month, and then
delusion vanished ! Mrs. Welford was not a woman who could
give to reality, or find in it, the charm equal to delusion. She was
perfectly unable to comprehend the intricate and dangerous character of her husband. She had not the key to his virtues, nor
the spell for his vices. Neither was the state to which poverty
compelled them one well calculated for that tender meditation,
heightened by absence, and cherished in indolence, which so often
supplies one who loves with the secret to the nature of the one

beloved. Though not equal to her husband in birth or early prospects, Mrs. Welford had been accustomed to certain comforts, often more felt by those who belong to the inferior classes than by those appertaining to the more elevated, who, in losing one luxury, will often cheerfully surrender all. A fine lady can submit to more hardships than her woman; and every gentleman who travels smiles at the privations which agonise his valet. Poverty and its grim comrades made way for a whole host of petty irritations and peevish complaints; and as no guest or visitor ever relieved the domestic discontent, or broke on the domestic bickering, they generally ended in that moody sullenness which so often finds love a grave in repentance. Nothing makes people tire of each other like a familiarity that admits of carelessness in quarrelling and coarseness in complaining. The biting sneer of Welford gave acrimony to the murmur of his wife; and when once each conceived the other the injurer, or him or herself the wronged, it was vain to hope that one would be more wary, or the other more indulgent. They both exacted too much, and the wife in especial conceded too little. Mrs. Welford was altogether and emphatically what a libertine calls "a woman,"—*such as a frivolous education makes a woman,*—generous in great things, petty in small; vain, irritable, full of the littleness of herself and her complaints, ready to plunge into an abyss with her lover, but equally ready to fret away all love with reproaches when the plunge had been made. Of all men, Welford could bear this the least. A woman of a larger heart, a more settled experience, and an intellect capable of appreciating his character, and sounding all his qualities, might have made him perhaps an useful and a great man; and, at least, *her* lover for life. Amidst a harvest of evil feelings, the mere strength of his nature rendered him especially capable of intense feeling and generous emotion. One who relied on him was safe,—one who rebelled against him trusted only to the caprice of his scorn. Still, however, for two years, love, though weakening with each hour, fought on in either breast, and could scarcely be said to be entirely vanquished in the *wife*, even when she eloped with her handsome seducer. A French writer has said, pithily enough, "Compare for a moment the apathy of a husband with the attention, the gallantry, the adoration of a lover, and *can* you ask the result?" He was a *French* writer; but Mrs. Welford had in her temper much of the Frenchwoman. A suffering patient, young, handsome, well versed in the arts of intrigue, contrasted with a gloomy husband whom she had never comprehended, long feared, and had lately doubted if she disliked,—ah! a much weaker contrast has made many a much better woman food for the lawyers!

Mrs. Welford eloped; but she felt a revived tenderness for her husband on the very morning that she did so. She carried away with her his letters of love as well as her own, which when they first married she had in an hour of fondness collected together,—*then* an inestimable hoard! and never did her new lover receive from her beautiful lips half so passionate a kiss as she left on the cheek of her infant. For some months she enjoyed with her paramour all for which she had sighed in her home. The one for whom she had forsaken her legitimate ties was a person so habitually cheerful, courteous, and what is ordinarily termed good-natured (though he had in him as much of the essence of selfishness as any nobleman can decently have), that he continued gallant to her without an effort long after he had begun to think it possible to tire even of so lovely a face. Yet there were moments when the fickle wife recalled her husband with regret; and, contrasting him with her seducer, did not find all the colourings of the contrast flattering to the latter. There is something in a powerful and marked character which women, and all weak natures, feel themselves constrained to respect; and Welford's character thus stood in bold, and therefore advantageous though gloomy, relief when opposed to the levities and foibles of this guilty woman's present adorer. However this be, the die was cast; and it would have been policy for the lady to have made the best of her present game. But she who had murmured as a wife was not complaisant as a mistress. Reproaches made an interlude to caresses, which the noble lover by no means admired. He was not a man to retort, he was too indolent; but neither was he one to forbear. "My charming friend," said he one day, after a scene, "you weary of me,—nothing more natural! Why torment each other? You say I have ruined you; my sweet friend, let me make you reparation —become independent; I will settle an annuity upon you, fly me—seek happiness elsewhere, and leave your unfortunate, your despairing lover to his fate."

"Do you taunt me, my lord?" cried the angry fair; "or do you believe that money can replace the rights of which you have robbed me? Can you make me again a wife—a happy, a respected wife? Do this, my lord, and you atone to me!"

The nobleman smiled, and shrugged his shoulders. The lady yet more angrily repeated her question. The lover answered by an innuendo, which at once astonished and doubly enraged her. She eagerly demanded explanation; and his lordship, who had gone farther than he intended, left the room. But his words had sunk deep into the breast of this unhappy woman, and she resolved to procure an elucidation. Agreeably to the policy which stripped the fabled traveller of his cloak, she laid aside the storm, and preferred the sunshine: she watched a moment of tenderness, turned the opportunity to advantage, and, by little and little, she possessed herself of a secret which sickened her with shame, disgust, and dismay. Sold! bartered! the object of a contemptuous huxtering to the purchaser and the seller; sold, too, with a lie that debased her at once into an object for whom even pity was mixed with scorn. Robbed already of the name and honour of a wife, and transferred as a harlot, from the wearied arms of one leman to the capricious caresses of another. Such was the image that rose before her; and while it roused at one moment all her fiercer passions into madness, humbled, with the next, her vanity into the dust. She, who knew the ruling passion of Welford, saw, at a glance, the object of scorn and derision which she had become to him. While she imagined herself the betrayer, she had been the betrayed; she saw vividly before her (and shuddered as she saw) her husband's icy smile—his serpent eye—his features steeped in sarcasm, and all his mocking soul stamped upon the countenance, whose lightest derision was so galling. She turned from this picture, and saw the courtly face of the purchaser—his subdued smile at her reproaches—his latent sneer at her claims to a station which he had been taught, by the arch plotter, to believe she had never possessed. She saw his early weariness of her attractions, expressed with respect indeed—an insulting respect,—but felt without a scruple of remorse. She saw in either—as around—only a reciprocation of contempt. She was in a web of profound abasement. Even that haughty grief of conscience for crime committed to another, which if it stings, humbles not, was swallowed up in a far more agonising sensation, to one so vain as the adultress—the burning sense of shame at having herself, while sinning, been the duped and deceived. Her very soul was appalled with her humiliation. The curse of Welford's vengeance was on her—and it was wreaked to the last! Whatever kindly sentiment she might have experienced towards her protector, was swallowed up at once by this discovery. She could not endure the thought of meeting the eye of one who had been the gainer by this ignominious barter, the foibles and weaknesses of the lover assumed a despicable as well as hateful dye. And in feeling *herself* degraded, she loathed *him.* The day after she had made the discovery we have referred to. Mrs. Welford left the house of her protector, none knew whither. For two years from that date, all trace of her history was lost. At the end of that time, what was Welford?—A man rapidly rising in the world, distinguished at the bar, where his first brief had lifted him into notice, commencing a flattering career in the senate, holding lucrative and honourable offices, esteemed for the austere rectitude of his moral character, gathering the golden opinions of all men, as he strode onward to public reputation. He had re-assumed his hereditary name; his early history was unknown; and no one in the obscure and distant town of * * * * had ever guessed that the humble Welford was the William Brandon whose praise was echoed in so many journals, and whose rising genius was acknowledged by all. That asperity, roughness, and gloom which had noted him at * * * * and which, being natural to him, he deigned not to disguise in a station ungenial to his talents and below his hopes, were now glitteringly varnished over by an hypocrisy well calculated to aid his ambition. So learnedly could this singular man fit himself to others, that few among the great met him as a companion, nor left him without the temper to become his friend. Through his noble rival, that is (to make our reader's "surety doubly sure") through Lord Mauleverer, he had acquired his first lucrative office, a certain patronage from government, and his seat in parliament. If he had persevered at the bar, rather than given himself entirely to state intrigues, it was only because his talents were eminently more calculated to advance him in the former path to honour, than in the latter. So devoted was he become to public life, that he had only permitted himself to cherish one private source of enjoyment,—his son. As no one, not even his brother, knew he had been married—(during the two years of his disguised name, he had been supposed abroad,)—the appearance of this son made the only piece of scandal whispered against the rigid morality of his fair fame; but he himself, waiting his own time for avowing a legitimate heir, gave out that it was the orphan child of a dear friend whom he had known abroad; and the puritan demureness not only of life, but manner, which he assumed, gained a pretty large belief to the statement. This son Brandon idolised. As we have represented himself to say,—ambitious men are commonly fond of their children, beyond the fondness of other sires. The perpetual reference which the ambitious make to posterity, is perhaps the main reason. But Brandon was also fond of children generally; philoprogenitiveness was a marked trait in his character, and would seem to belie the hardness and artifice belonging to that character, were not the same love so frequently noticeable in the harsh and the artificial. It seems as if a half-conscious but pleasing feeling, that *they* too were once gentle and innocent, makes them delight in reviving any sympathy with their early state.

Often after the applause and labour of the day, Brandon would repair to his son's chamber, and watch his slumber for hours; often before his morning toil commenced, he would nurse the infant in his arms with all a woman's natural tenderness and gushing joy. And often, as a graver and more characteristic sentiment stole over him, he would mentally say,—"You shall build up our broken name on a better foundation than your sire I begin too late in life, and I labour up a painful and stony road; but I shall make the journey to Fame smooth and accessible for you. Never, too, while *you* aspire to honour, shall you steel your heart to tranquillity. For you, my child, shall be the joys of home and love, and a mind that does not sicken at the past, and strain, through mere fretfulness, towards a solitary and barren distinction for the future. Not only what your father gains you shall enjoy, but what has cursed him, his vigilance shall lead you to shun!"

It was thus not only that his softer feelings, but all the better and nobler ones, which even in the worst and hardest bosom, find some root, turned towards his child; and that the hollow and vicious man promised to become the affectionate and perhaps the wise parent.

One night, Brandon was returning home, on foot, from a ministerial dinner. The night was frosty and clear, the hour was late, and his way lay through the longest and best-lighted streets of the metropolis. He was, as usual, buried in thought, when he was suddenly aroused from his reverie by a light touch laid on his arm. He turned, and saw one of the unhappy persons who haunt the midnight streets of cities, standing right before his path. The gaze of each fell upon the other; and it was thus, for the first time since they laid their heads on the same pillow, that the husband met the wife. The skies were intensely clear, and the lamplight was bright and calm upon the faces of both. There was no doubt in the mind of either. Suddenly, and with a startled and ghastly consciousness, they recognised each other. The wife staggered, and clung to a post for support. Brandon's look was calm and unmoved. The hour that his bitter and malignant spirit had yearned for was come · his nerves expanded in a voluptuous calmness, as if to give him a deliberate enjoyment of his hope fulfilled. Whatever the words that, in that unwitnessed and almost awful interview, passed between them, we may be sure that Brandon spared not one atom of his power. The lost and abandoned wife returned home, and all her nature, embruted as it had become by guilt and vile habits, hardened into revenge,—that preternatural feeling which may be termed the hope of despair.

Three nights from that meeting, Brandon's house was broken into. Like the houses of many legal men, it lay in a dangerous and thinly-populated outskirt of the town, and was easily accessible to robbery. He was awakened by a noise: he started, and found himself in the grasp of two men. At the foot of the bed stood a female, raising a light, and her face, haggard with searing passions, and ghastly with the leprous whiteness of disease and approaching death, glared full upon him.

"It is now *my* turn," said the female, with a grin of scorn which Brandon himself might have envied; "you have cursed me, and I return the curse! You have told me that my child shall never name me but to blush. Fool! I triumph over you: *you* he shall never know to his dying day! You have told me, that to my child and my child's child (a long transmission of execration), my name—the name of the wife you basely sold to ruin and to hell, should be left as a legacy of odium and shame! Man, you shall teach that child no farther lesson whatever: you shall know not whether he live or die, or have children to carry on your boasted race; or whether, if he have, those children be not outcasts of the earth—the accursed of man and God—the fit offspring of the thing you have made me. Wretch! I hurl back on you the denunciation with which, when we met three nights since, you would have crushed the victim of your own perfidy. You shall tread the path of your ambition childless, and objectless, and hopeless. Disease shall set her stamp upon your frame. The worm shall batten upon your heart. You shall have honours and enjoy them not: you shall gain your ambition, and despair: you shall pine for your son, and find him not; or, if you find him, you shall curse the hour in which he was born. Mark me, man—I am dying while I speak—I know that I am a prophet in my curse. From this hour I am avenged, and *you* are my scorn!"

As the hardest natures sink appalled before the stony eye of the maniac, so, in the dead of the night, pinioned by ruffians, the wild and solemn voice (sharpened by passion and partial madness) of the ghastly figure before him curdling through his veins, even the haughty and daring character of William Brandon quailed! He uttered not a word. He was found the next morning, bound by strong cords to his bed. He spoke not when he was released, but went in silence to his child's chamber :—the child was gone! Several articles of property were also stolen: the desperate tools the mother had employed worked not perhaps without their own reward.

We need scarcely add, that Brandon set every engine and channel of justice in motion for the discovery of his son. All the especial shrewdness and keenness of his own character, aided by his professional experience, he employed for years in the same pursuit. Every research was wholly in vain: not the remotest vestige towards discovery could be traced, until were found (we have recorded when) some of the articles that had been stolen. Fate treasured in her gloomy womb, altogether undescribed by man, the hour and the scene in which the most ardent wish of William Brandon was to be realised.

CHAPTER XXXIV.

" O Fortuna, viris invida fortibus
Quam non æqua bonis præmia dividis."
                                                SENECA.

      *   *   *   *   *

" And as a hare, whom hounds and horns pursue,
Pants to the place from whence at first he flew."

      *   *   *   *   *

" Here, to the houseless child of want,
My door is open still."
                                                GOLDSMITH.

SLOWLY for Lucy waned the weeks of a winter, which, to her, was the most dreary portion of life she had ever passed. It became the time for the judge to attend his periodical visitations so fraught with dread and dismay to the miserable inmates of the dark abodes which the complex laws of this country so bounteously supply—those times of great hilarity and eating to the legal gentry,

" Who feed on crimes and fatten on distress,
And wring vile mirth from suffering's last excess "

Ah ! excellent order of the world, which it is so wicked to disturb ! How miraculously beautiful must be that system which makes wine out of the scorching tears of guilt ; and from the suffocating suspense, the agonised fear, the compelled and self-mocking bravery, the awful sentence, the despairing death-pang of one man, furnishes the smirking expectation of fees, the jovial meeting, and the mercenary holiday to another ! "Of Law, nothing less can be said, than that her seat is the bosom of God." [1] To be sure not ; Richard Hooker, you are perfectly right. The divinity of a sessions, and the inspiration of the Old Bailey, are undeniable !

The care of Sir William Brandon had effectually kept from Lucy's ears the knowledge of her lover's ignominious situation. Indeed, in her delicate health, even the hard eye of Brandon, and the thoughtless glance of Mauleverer, perceived the danger of such a discovery. The earl now waiting the main attack on Lucy, till the curtain had for ever dropped on Clifford, proceeded with great caution and delicacy in his suit to his purposed bride. He waited with the more patience, inasmuch as he had drawn in advance on his friend Sir William for

[1] Hooker's *Ecclesiastical Polity*

some portion of the heiress's fortune ; and he readily allowed that he could not, in the meanwhile, have a better advocate than he found in Brandon. So persuasive, indeed, and so subtle was the eloquence of this able sophist, that often, in his artful conversations with his niece, he left even on the unvitiated, and strong though simple mind of Lucy an uneasy and restless impression, which time might have ripened into an inclination towards the worldly advantages of the marriage at her command. Brandon was no bungling mediator or violent persecutor. He seemed to acquiesce in her rejection of Mauleverer. He scarcely recurred to the event. He rarely praised the earl himself, save for the obvious qualities of liveliness and good-nature. But he spoke, with all the vivid colours he could infuse at will into his words, of the pleasures and the duties of rank and wealth. Well could he appeal alike to all the prejudices and all the foibles of the human breast, and govern virtue through its weaknesses. Lucy had been brought up, like the daughters of most country gentlemen of ancient family, in an undue and idle consciousness of superior birth ; and she was far from inaccessible to the warmth and even feeling (for *here* Brandon was sincere) with which her uncle spoke of the duty of raising a gallant name sunk into disrepute, and sacrificing our own inclination, for the redecorating the mouldered splendour of those who have gone before us. If the confusion of idea occasioned by a vague pomposity of phrase, or the infant inculcation of a sentiment that is mistaken for a virtue, so often makes fools of the wise on the subject of ancestry ; if it clouded even the sarcastic and keen sense of Brandon himself, we may forgive its influence over a girl so little versed in the arts of sound reasoning as poor Lucy, who, it may be said, had never learnt to think until she had learnt to love. However, the impression made by Brandon, in his happiest moments of persuasion, was as yet, only transient ; it vanished before the first thought of Clifford, and never suggested to her even a doubt as to the suit of Mauleverer.

When the day arrived for Sir William Brandon to set out on the circuit, he called Barlow, and enjoined that acute and intelligent servant the strictest caution with respect to Lucy. He bade him deny her to every one, of whatever rank, and carefully to look into every newspaper that was brought to her, as well as to withhold every letter, save such as were addressed to her in the judge's own hand-writing. Lucy's maid Brandon had already won over to silence ; and the uncle now pleased himself with thinking that he had put an effectual guard to every chance of discovery. The identity of Lovett with Clifford had not yet even been rumoured, and Mauleverer had rightly judged of Clifford, when he believed the prisoner would himself take every precaution against the detection

of that fact. Clifford answered the earl's note and promise, in a
letter couched in so affecting yet so manly a tone of gratitude, that
even Brandon was touched when he read it. And since his confinement and partial recovery of health, the prisoner had kept himself
closely secluded, and refused all visitors. Encouraged by this reflection, and the belief in the safety of his precautions, Brandon took
leave of Lucy. "Farewell!" said he, as he embraced her affectionately. "Be sure that you write to me, and forgive me if I do
not answer you punctually. Take care of yourself, my sweet niece,
and let me see a fresher colour on that soft cheek when I return!"

"Take care of yourself rather, my dear, dear uncle," said Lucy,
clinging to him and weeping, as of late her weakened nerves caused
her to do at the least agitation. "Why may I not go with you?
You have seemed to me paler than usual the last three or four days,
and you complained yesterday. Do let me go with you; I will be
no trouble, none at all; but I am sure you require a nurse."

"You want to frighten me, my pretty Lucy," said Brandon,
shaking his head with a smile. "I am well, very well: I felt a
strange rush of blood towards the head yesterday, it is true; but
I feel to-day stronger and lighter than I have done for years. Once
more, God bless you, my child!"

And Brandon tore himself away, and commenced his journey.

The wandering and dramatic course of our story now conducts us
to an obscure lane in the metropolis, leading to the Thames, and
makes us spectators of an affecting farewell between two persons,
whom the injustice of fate, and the persecutions of men, were about
perhaps for ever to divide.

"Adieu, my friend!" said Augustus Tomlinson, as he stood looking full on that segment of the face of Edward Pepper which was
left unconcealed by a huge hat and a red belcher handkerchief.
Tomlinson himself was attired in the full costume of a dignified
clergyman. "Adieu, my friend, since you *will* remain in England,—
adieu! I am, I exult to say, no less sincere a patriot than you. Heaven
be my witness, how long I looked repugnantly on poor Lovett's proposal to quit my beloved country. But all hope of life *here* is now
over: and really, during the last ten days, I have been so hunted
from corner to corner, so plagued with polite invitations, similar to
those given by a farmer's wife to her ducks, 'Dilly, dilly, dilly,
come and be killed!' that my patriotism has been prodigiously
cooled, and I no longer recoil from thoughts of self-banishment.
'The earth,' my dear Ned, as a Greek sage has very well observed,
—'the earth is the same everywhere!' and if I am asked for my
home, I can point, like Anaxagoras, to heaven!"

"'Pon my soul, you affect me!" said Ned, speaking thick, either

from grief or the pressure of the belcher handkerchief on his mouth ;
" it is quite beautiful to hear you talk ! "

" Bear up, my dear friend," continued Tomlinson ; " bear up
against your present afflictions. What, to a man who fortifies himself by reason and by reflection on the shortness of life, are the
little calamities of the body ! What is imprisonment, or persecution,
or cold, or hunger ?—By-the-by, you did not forget to put the sand-
wiches into my coat-pocket ! "

" Hush ! " whispered Ned, and he moved on involuntarily ; " I
see a man at the other end of the street."

" Let us quicken our pace," said Tomlinson ; and the pair proceeded towards the river.

" And now," began Ned, who thought he might as well say something about himself, for hitherto Augustus, in the ardour of his
friendship, had been only discussing his own plans ;—"and now,—
that is to say, when I leave you,—I shall hasten to dive for shelter,
until the storm blows over. I don't much like living in a cellar,
and wearing a smock frock,—but those concealments have something interesting in them, after all ! The safest and snuggest place
I know of is the *Pays Bas*, about Thames Court ; so I think of hiring
an apartment underground, and taking my meals at poor Lovett's
old quarters, the Mug,—the police will never dream of looking in
those vulgar haunts for a man of my fashion."

" You cannot then tear yourself from England ?" said Tomlinson.

" No, hang it ! the fellows are so cursed unmanly on the other
side of the water. I hate their wine and their *parley woo*. Besides,
there is no fun there."

Tomlinson, who was absorbed in his own thoughts, made no
comment on his friend's excellent reasons against travel, and the
pair now approached the brink of the river. A boat was in waiting
to receive and conduct to the vessel in which he had taken his place
for Calais, the illustrious emigrant. But as Tomlinson's eye fell
suddenly on the rude boatman and the little boat which were to bear
him away from his native land ; as he glanced too, across the blue
waters, which a brisk wind wildly agitated, and thought how much
rougher it would be at sea, where " his soul " invariably " sickened
at the heaving wave," a whole tide of deep and sorrowful emotions
rushed upon him.

He turned away —the spot on which he stood was a piece of
ground to be let (as a board proclaimed) upon a building lease ;
below, descended the steps which were to conduct him to the boat ;
around, the desolate space allowed him to see in far and broad
extent the spires and domes, and chimneys of the great city whose
inhabitants he might never plunder more. As he looked and

looked, the tears started to his eyes, and with a gust of enthusiasm little consonant with his temperate and philosophical character, he lifted his right hand from his black breeches-pocket, and burst into the following farewell to the metropolis of his native shores :—

"Farewell, my beloved London, farewell! Where shall I ever find a city like you? Never, till now, did I feel how inexpressibly dear you were to me. You have been my father, and my brother, and my mistress, and my tailor, and my shoemaker, and my hatter, and my cook, and my wine-merchant! You and I never misunderstood each other. I did not grumble when I saw what fine houses and good strong boxes you gave to other men. No! I rejoiced at their prosperity. I delighted to see a rich man—my only disappointment was in stumbling on a poor one. You gave riches to my neighbours ; but, O generous London, you gave those neighbours to me! Magnificent streets, all Christian virtues abide within you! Charity is as common as smoke! Where, in what corner of the habitable world, shall I find human beings with so many superfluities? Where shall I so easily decoy, from benevolent credulity, those superfluities to myself? Heaven only knows, my dear, dear, darling London, what I lose in you! O public charities!—O public institutions!—O banks that belie mathematical axioms and make lots out of nothing !—O ancient constitution always to be questioned [1]— O modern improvements that never answer !—O speculations !— O companies !—O usury laws which guard against usurers, by making as many as possible !—O churches in which no one profits, save the parson, and the old women that let pews of an evening !—O superb theatres, too small for parks, too enormous for houses, which exclude comedy and comfort, and have a monopoly for performing nonsense gigantically !—O houses of plaster built in a day !—O palaces four yards high, with a dome in the middle, meant to be invisible ! [1]—O shops worth thousands, and O shopkeepers not worth a shilling !— O system of credit by which beggars are princes, and princes are beggars !—O imprisonment for debt, which lets the mare be stolen, and then locks up the bridle ! O sharpers, bubbles, senators, beaux, taverns, brothels, clubs, houses private and public !—O LONDON, in a word, receive my last adieu ! Long may you flourish in peace and plenteousness ! May your knaves be witty, and your fools be rich ! May you alter only two things—your damnable tricks of transport-

---

[1] We must not suppose this apostrophe to be an anachronism ! Tomlinson, of course, refers to some palace of *his* day ; one of the boxes—Christmas boxes— given to the King by his economical nation of shopkeepers We suppose it is either pulled down or blown down long ago it is doubtless forgotten by this time, except by antiquaries Nothing is so ephemeral as great houses built by the people. Your kings play the deuce with their playthings !

ation and hanging! Those are your sole faults; but for those I would never desert you.—Adieu!"

Here Tomlinson averted his head, and then hastily shaking the hand of Long Ned with a tremulous and warm grasp, he hurried down the stairs and entered the boat. Ned remained motionless for some moments, following him with his eyes as he sat at the end of the boat, waving a white pocket handkerchief. At length, a line of barges snatched him from the sight of the lingerer, and Ned slowly turning away, muttered—"Yes, I have always heard that Dame Lobkins's was the safest asylum for misfortune like mine. I will go forthwith in search of a lodging, and to-morrow I will make my breakfast at the Mug!"

Be it our pleasing task, dear reader, to *forestall* the good robber, and return, at the hour of sunrise on the day following Tomlinson's departure, to the scene at which our story commenced. We are now once more at the house of Mrs. Margery Lobkins.

The room which served so many purposes was still the same as when Paul turned it into the arena of his mischievous pranks. The dresser, with its shelves of mingled delf and pewter, occupied its ancient and important station. Only it might be noticed that the pewter was more dull than of yore, and that sundry cracks made their erratic wanderings over the yellow surface of the delf. The eye of the mistress had become less keen than heretofore, and the care of the handmaid had, of necessity, relaxed. The tall clock still ticked in monotonous warning; the blanket-screen, haply innocent of soap since last we described it, many-storied and poly-balladed, still unfolded its ample leaves " rich with the spoils of time." The spit and the musket yet hung from the wall in amicable proximation. And the long smooth form, "with many a holy text *thereon bestrewn*," still afforded rest to the weary traveller, and an object to the vacant stare of Mrs. Margery Lobkins, as she lolled in her opposite seat and forgot the world. But poor Piggy Lobb! *there* was the alteration! The soul of the woman was gone! The spirit had evaporated from the human bottle! She sat with open mouth and glassy eye in her chair, sidling herself to and fro, with the low, peevish sound of fretful age and bodily pain; sometimes this querulous murmur sharpened into a shrill but unmeaning scold. "There now, you gallows bird! you has taken the swipes without chalking; you wants to cheat the poor widow: but I sees you, I does! Providence protects the aged and the innocent—oh, oh! these twinges will be the death o' me. Where's Martha? You jade, you! you wiperous hussy, bring the tape here: doesn't you see how I suffers? Has you no bowels, to let a poor Christin cretur perish for want o' help! That's the way with 'em, that's the way ! No one cares for I now—no one has respect for the grey 'airs of the old!" And then the voice dwindled into the whimpering "tenor of its way." Martha, a strapping wench with red hair streaming over her "hills of snow," was not, however, inattentive to the wants of her mistress. "Who knows," said she to a man who sat by the hearth, drinking tea out of a blue mug, and toasting with great care two or three huge rounds of bread, for his own private and especial nutriment—"who knows," said she, "what we may come to ourselves?" And, so saying, she placed a glowing tumbler by her mistress's elbow. But in the sunken prostration of her intellect, the old woman was insensible even to her consolation · she sipped and drank, it is true ; but as if the stream warmed not the benumbed region through which it passed, she continued muttering in a crazed and groaning key, "Is this your gratitude, you serpent ! why does not you bring the tape, I tells you ? Am I of a age to drink water like a oss, you nasty thing ! Oh, to think as ever I should live to be desarted !"

Inattentive to these murmurs, which she felt unreasonable, the bouncing Martha now quitted the room, to repair to her "upper household" avocations. The man at the hearth was the only companion left to the widow. Gazing at her for a moment, as she sat whining, with a rude compassion in his eye, and slowly munching his toast which he had now buttered, and placed in a delf plate on the hob, this person thus soothingly began :—

"Ah, Dame Lobkins, if so be as ow little Paul vas a vith you, it would be a gallows comfort to you in your latter hend !"

The name of Paul made the good woman incline her head towards the speaker ; a ray of consciousness shot through her bedulled brain

"Little Paul, eh, sirs! where is Paul? Paul. I say, my ben-cull. Alack ! he's gone—left his poor old nurse to die like a cat in a cellar. Oh, Dummie, never live to be old, man ! They leaves us to oursels, and then takes away all the lush with 'em ! I has not a drop o' comfort in the varsal world !"

Dummie, who at this moment had his own reasons for soothing the dame, and was anxious to make the most of the opportunity of a conversation as unwitnessed as the present, replied tenderly ; and with a cunning likely to promote his end, reproached Paul bitterly for never having informed the dame of his whereabout and his proceedings. "But come, dame," he wound up, "come, I guess as how he is better nor all that, and that you need not beat your hold brains to think where he lies, or vot he's a doing. Blow me tight, mother Lob,—I ax pardon, Mrs. Margery, I should say,—if I vould not give five bob, ay, and five to the tail o' that, to know what the poor lad is about ; I takes a mortal hinterest in that 'ere chap !"

"Oh! oh!" groaned the old woman, on whose palsied sense the astute inquiries of Dummie Dunnaker fell harmless; "my poor sinful carcass! what a way it be in!"

Artfully again did Dummie Dunnaker, nothing defeated, renew his attack; but fortune does not always favour the wise, and it failed Dummie now, for a twofold reason; first, because it was not possible for the dame to comprehend him; secondly, because even if it had been, she had nothing to reveal. *Some* of Clifford's pecuniary gifts had been conveyed anonymously, *all* without direction or date; and, for the most part, they had been appropriated by the sage Martha, into whose hands they fell, to her own private uses. Nor did the dame require Clifford's grateful charity; for she was a woman tolerably well off in this world, considering how near she was waxing to another. Longer, however, might Dummie have tried his unavailing way, had not the door of the inn creaked on its hinges, and the bulky form of a tall man in a smock-frock, but with a remarkably fine head of hair, darkened the threshold. He honoured the dame, who cast on him a lack-lustre eye, with a sulky, yet ambrosial nod, seized a bottle of spirits and a tumbler, lighted a candle, drew a small German pipe and a tobacco-box from his pouch, placed these several luxuries on a small table, wheeled it to a far corner of the room, and throwing himself into one chair, and his legs into another, he enjoyed the result of his pains in a moody and supercilious silence. Long and earnestly did the meek Dummie gaze on the face of the gentleman before him. It had been some years since he had last beheld it; but it was one which did not easily escape the memory; and although its proprietor was a man who had risen in the world, and had gained the height of his profession (a station far beyond the diurnal sphere of Dummie Dunnaker), and the humble purloiner was, therefore, astonished to encounter him in these lower regions; yet Dummie's recollection carried him back to a day when they had gone shares together without respect of persons, and been right jolly partners in the practical game of beggar my neighbour. While, however, Dummie Dunnaker, who was a little inclined to be shy, deliberated as to the propriety of claiming acquaintanceship, a dirty boy, with a face which betokened the frost, as Dummie himself said, like a plum dying of the scarlet fever, entered the room, with a newspaper in his dexter paw. "Great news!—great news!" cried the urchin, imitating his vociferous originals in the street; "all about the famous Captain Lovett, as large as life!"

"Old your blarney, you blattergowl!" said Dummie, rebukingly, and seizing the journal.

"Master says as how he must have it to send to Clapham, and can't spare it for more than a 'our!" said the boy, as he withdrew.

"*I*'members the day," said Dummie, with the zeal of a clansman, "when the Mug took a paper all to itsel instead o' 'iring it by the job like!"

Thereon he opened the paper with a fillip, and gave himself up to the lecture. But the tall stranger, half rising with a start, exclaimed, "Can't you have the manners to be communicative?—do you think nobody cares about Captain Lovett but yourself?"

On this, Dummie turned round on his chair, and, with a "blow me tight, you're welcome, I'm sure;" began as follows:—(we copy the paper, not the diction of the reader.)

"The trial of the notorious Lovett commences this day. Great exertions have been made by people of all classes to procure seats in the Town Hall, which will be full to a degree never before known in this peaceful province. No less than seven indictments are said to await the prisoner; it has been agreed that the robbery of Lord Mauleverer should be the first to come on. The principal witness in this case against the prisoner is understood to be the king's evidence, Mac Grawler. No news, as yet, have been circulated concerning the suspected accomplices, Augustus Tomlinson and Edward Pepper. It is believed that the former has left the country, and that the latter is lurking among the low refuges of guilt with which the heart of the metropolis abounds. Report speaks highly of the person and manners of Lovett. He is also supposed to be a man of some talent, and was formerly engaged in an obscure periodical edited by Mac Grawler, and termed the Altenæum, or Asinæum. Nevertheless, we apprehend that his origin is remarkably low, and suitable to the nature of his pursuits. The prisoner will be most fortunate in a judge. Never did any one holding the same high office as Sir William Brandon earn an equal reputation in so short a time. The Whigs are accustomed to sneer at us, when we insist on the *private* virtues of our public men. Let them look at Sir William Brandon, and confess that the austerest morals may be linked with the soundest knowledge and the most brilliant genius. The opening address of the learned judge to the jury at * * * is perhaps the most impressive and solemn piece of eloquence in the English language!" A cause for this eulogium might haply be found in another part of the paper, in which it was said, "Among the higher circles, we understand, the rumour has gone forth, that Sir William Brandon is to be recalled to his old parliamentary career in a more elevated scene. So highly are this gentleman's talents respected by his Majesty and the ministers, that they are, it is reported, anxious to secure his assistance in the House of Lords!"

When Dummie had spent his "toilsome march" through the first of the above extracts, he turned round to the tall stranger, and eyeing him with a sort of winking significance, said,—

"So Mac Grawler peaches! blows the gaff on his pals, eh! Vel now, I always suspected that 'ere son of a gun! Do you know, he used to be at the Mug many's a day, a teaching our little Paul, and says I to Piggy Lobb, says I, 'Blow me tight, but that cove is a queer one! and if he does not come to be scragged,' says I, 'it vill only be because he'll turn a rusty, and scrag one of his pals!' So you sees—(here Dummie looked round, and his voice sank into a whisper)—so you sees, *Meester Pepper*, I vas no fool there!"

Long Ned dropped his pipe, and said sourly, with a suspicious frown, "What! you know me?"

"To be sure and sartain I does," answered little Dummie, walking to the table where the robber sat. "Does not you know I?"

Ned regarded the interrogator with a sullen glance, which gradually brightened into knowledge. "Ah!" said he, with the air of a Brummel, "Mr. Bummie, or Dummie, I think, eh! Shake a paw —I'm glad to see you.—Recollect the last time I saw you, you rather affronted me. Never mind. I dare say you did not mean it." Encouraged by this affable reception from the highwayman, though a little embarrassed by Ned's allusion to former conduct on his part, which he felt was just, Dummie grinned, pushed a stool near Ned, sat himself down, and carefully avoiding any immediate answer to Ned's complaint, he rejoined.—

"Do you know, Meester Pepper, you struck I all of a heep. I could not have sposed as how you'd condescend nowadays to come to the Mug, vhere I never seed you but once afore. Lord love ye, they says as 'ow you go to all the fine places in ruffles with a pair of silver pops in your vaistcoat pocket! Vy, the boys hereabouts say that you and Meester Tomlinson, and this 'ere poor devil in quod, vere the finest gemmen in town; and, Lord, for to think of your civility to a pitiful rag-merchant, like I!"

"Ah!" said Ned, gravely, "there are sad principles afloat now. They want to do away with all distinctions in ranks,—to make a duke no better than his valet, and a gentleman highwayman class with a filcher of fogles.[1] But, dammee, if I don't think misfortune levels us all quite enough; and misfortune brings me here, little Dummie."

"Ah! you vants to keep out of the vay of the bulkies!"

"Right. Since poor Lovett was laid by the heels, which I must say was the fault of his own deuced gentlemanlike behaviour to me and Augustus (you've heard of Guz, you say), the knot of us seems quite broken. One's own friends look inclined to play one false; and really, the queer cuffins hover so sharply upon us, that I thought

1 Pickpocket.

it safe to duck for a time. So I have taken a lodging in a cellar, and I intend for the next three months to board at the Mug. I have heard that I may be sure of lying snug here ;—Dummie, your health! Give us the baccy!"

"I say, Meester Pepper," said Dummie, clearing his throat, when he had obeyed the request, "can you tell I, if so be you as met in your travels our little Paul? Poor chap! You knows as ow and vy he vas sent to *quod* by Justice Burnflat. Vel, ven he got out, he vent to the devil, or summut like it, and ve have not eard a vord of him since. You 'members the lad—a 'nation fine cull, tall and straight as a harrow!"

"Why, you fool," said Ned, "don't you know,"—then checking himself suddenly,—"ah! by-the-by, that rigmarole oath!—I was not to tell; though now it's past caring for, I fear! It is no use looking after the seal when the letter's burnt.'

"Blow me," cried Dunnaker, with unaffected vehemence, "I sees as how you know vot's come of he! Many's the good turn I'll do you, if you vill but tell I."

"Why, does he owe you a dozen *bobs*,[1] or what, Dummie?" said Ned.

"Not he—not he," cried Dummie.

"What then, you want to do him some mischief of some sort?"

"Do little Paul a mischief!" ejaculated Dummie; "vy I've known the cull ever since he was *that* high! No, but I vants to do him a great sarvice, Meester Pepper, and myself too,—and you to boot, for aught that I know, Meester Pepper."

"Humph!" said Ned; "humph! what do you mean? I do, it is true, know where Paul is; but you must tell me first why you wish to know, otherwise you may ask your grandfather for me."

A long, sharp, wistful survey did Mr. Dummie Dunnaker cast around him before he rejoined. All seemed safe and convenient for confidential communication. The supine features of Mrs. Lobkins were hushed in a drowsy stupor: even the grey cat that lay by the fire was curled in the embrace of Morpheus. Nevertheless, it was in a close whisper that Dummie spoke.

"I dares be bound, Meester Pepper, that you 'members vell ven Harry Cook, the great highvayman,—poor fellow! he's gone vhere ve must all go,—brought you, then quite a *gossoon*,[2] for the first

---

[1] Shillings.

[2] The reader has probably observed the use made by Dummie and Mrs. Lobkins of Irish phraseology or pronunciation. This is a remarkable trait in the dialect of the lowest orders in London, owing, we suppose, to their constant association with emigrants from "the first flower of the earth." Perhaps it is a modish affectation among the gentry of St Giles's, just as we eke out our mother-tongue with French at Mayfair.

time, to the little back parlour at the Cock and Hen, Devereux Court?"

Ned nodded assent.

"And you 'members as how I met Harry and you there, and I vas all afeard at you—cause vy? I had never seen you afore, and ve vas a going to *crack a swell's crib.*[1] And Harry spoke up for you, and said as ow, though you had just gone on the town, you was already prime up to gammon :—you 'members, eh?"

"Ay, I remember all," said Ned; "it was the first and only house I ever had a hand in breaking into. Harry was a fellow of low habits, so I dropped his acquaintance, and took solely to the road, or a chance ingenuity now and then. I have no idea of a gentleman turning *cracksman*."[2]

"Vell, so you vent vith us, and ve slipped you through a pane in the kitchen-vindow. You vas the least of us, big as you be now; and you vent round and opened the door for us; and ven you had opened the door, you saw a voman had joined us, and you were a funked then, and stayed vithout the *crib*, to keep vatch vhile ve vent in."

"Well, well," cried Ned, "what the devil has all this rigmarole got to do with Paul?"

"Now don't be glimflashey, but let me go on smack right about. Vell, ven ve came out, you minds as ow the voman had a bundle in her arms, and you spake to her; and she answered you roughly, and left us all, and vent straight home; and ve vent and *fenced the swag*[3] that very night, and afterwards *napped the regulars*.[4] And sure you made us laugh artily, Meester Pepper, when you said, says you, 'That 'ere voman is a rum blowen!' So she vas, Meester Pepper!"

"O spare me," said Ned, affectedly, "and make haste; you keep me all in the dark. By the way, I remember that you joked me about the bundle; and when I asked what the woman had wrapped in it, you swore it was a child. Rather more likely that the girl, whoever she was, would have left a child behind her than carried one off!" The face of Dummie waxed big with conscious importance.

"Vell, now, you would not believe us; but it vas all true; that 'ere bundle vas the voman's child, I spose an unnatural von by the gemman: she let us into the ouse on condition we helped her off vith it. And, blow me tight, but ve paid ourselves vel for our trouble. That 'ere voman vas a strange cretur; they say she had been a lord's blowen; but howsomever, she was as ot-eaded and hodd as if she had been. There vas hold Nick's hown row made on the matter, and the revard for our (de)tection vas so great, that as you

---

1 Break into a gentleman's house.   2 Burglar.
3 Sold the booty.   4 Took our shares.

vas not much tried yet. Harry thought it best for to take you vith im down to the country, and told you as ow it vas all a flam about the child in the bundle ! "

" Faith," said Ned, " I believed him readily enough ; and poor Harry was twisted shortly after, and I went into Ireland for safety, where I stayed two years,—and deuced good claret I got there ! "

" So, vhiles you vas there," continued Dummie, " poor Judy, the voman, died,—she died in this weiy ouse, and left the horphan to the (af)fection of Piggy Lob, who was 'nation fond of it, sure*ly* ' Oh ! but I 'members vot a night it vas ven poor Judy died ; the vind vistled like mad, and the rain tumbled about as if it had got a holyday ; and there the poor creature lay raving just over ed of this room we sits in ! Laus-a-me, vot a sight it vas ! "

Here Dummie paused, and seemed to recall in imagination the scene he had witnessed ; but over the mind of Long Ned a ray of light broke slowly.

" Whew ! " said he, lifting up his fore-finger, " whew ! I smell a rat ; this stolen child, then, was no other than Paul. But, pray, to whom did the house belong ? For that fact Harry never communicated to me. I only heard the owner was a lawyer, or parson, or *some such thing*."

" Vy now, I'll tell you, but don't be glimflashey. So, you see, ven Judy died, and Harry was scragged, I vas the only von living who vas up to the secret ; and vhen Mother Lob vas a taking a drop to comfort her vhen Judy vent off, I hopens a great box in which poor Judy kept her duds and rattle-traps, and sure*ly* I finds at the bottom of the box hever so many letters and sich like,—for I knew as ow they vas there ; so I vhips these off and carries 'em ome with me, and soon arter, Mother Lob sold me the box o' duds for two quids—'cause vy ? I vas a rag merchant ! So now, I 'solved, since the secret vas all in my hown keeping, to keep it as tight as vinkey : for first, you sees as ow I vas afeard I should be hanged if I vent for to tell,—'cause vy ? I stole a vatch, and lots more. as vell as the hurchin ; and next I vas afeard as ow the mother might come back and haunt me the same as Sall haunted Villy, for it vas a orrid night ven her soul took ving. And hover and above this, Meester Pepper, I thought summut might turn hup by-and-by, in vhich it vould be best for I to keep my hown counsel and nab the revard, if I hever durst make myself known."

Here Dummie proceeded to narrate how frightened he had been lest Ned should discover all ; when (as it may be remembered, Pepper informed Paul at the beginning of this history) he encountered that worthy at Dame Lobkins's house,—how this fear had induced him to testify to Pepper that coldness and rudeness which had so enraged the haughty highwayman, and how great had been his relief and delight at finding that Ned returned to the Mug no more. He next proceeded to inform his new confidant of his meeting with the father (the sagacious reader knows where and when), and of what took place at that event. He said how, in his first negotiation with the father, prudently resolving to communicate drop by drop such information as he possessed, he merely, besides confessing to a share in the robbery, stated that *he thought* he knew the house, &c. to which the infant had been consigned,—and that, if so, it was still alive ; but that he would inquire. He then related how the sanguine father, who saw that hanging Dummie for the robbery of his house might not be half so likely a method to recover his son as bribery and conciliation, not only forgave him his former outrage, but whetted his appetite to the search by rewarding him for his disclosure. He then proceeded to state how, unable anywhere to find Paul, or any trace of him, he amused the sire from time to time with forged excuses ;—how, at first, the sums he received made him by no means desirous to expedite a discovery that would terminate such satisfactory receipts ;—how at length the magnitude of the proffered reward, joined to the threats of the sire, had made him become seriously anxious to learn the real fate and present " whereabout " of Paul :—how, the last time he had seen the father, he had, by way of propitiation and first fruit, taken to him all the papers left by the unhappy mother and secreted by himself; and how he was now delighted to find that Ned was acquainted with Paul's address. Since he despaired of finding Paul by his own exertions alone, he became less tenacious of his secret, and he now proffered Ned, on discovery of Paul, a third of that reward the whole of which he had once hoped to engross.

Ned's eyes and mouth opened at this proposition. "But the name,—the name of the father? you have not told me that yet !" cried he impatiently.

"Noa, noa ! " said Dummie, archly, " I doesn't tell you all, till you tells I summut. Vhere's little Paul, I say ; and vhere be us to get at him ?"

Ned heaved a sigh.

"As for the oath," said he, musingly, " It would be a sin to keep it, now that to break it can do him no harm, and may do him good ; especially as, in case of imprisonment or death, the oath is not held to be binding : yet I fear it is too late for the reward. The father will scarcely thank you for finding his son !—Know, Dummie, that Paul is in —— gaol, and that he is one and the same person as Captain Lovett !"

Astonishment never wrote in more legible characters than she now

displayed on the rough features of Dummie Dunnaker. So strong
are the sympathies of a profession compared with all others, that
Dummie's first confused thought was *that of pride*. "The great
Captain Lovett!" he faltered.   "Little Paul at the top of the profession !   Lord, Lord !—I always said as how he'd the hambition to
rise !"

"Well, well, but the father's name?"

At this question, the expression of Dummie's face fell,—a sudden
horror struggled to his eyes—

*   *   *   *   *
*   *   *   *   *

CHAPTER XXXV.

" Why is it that, at moments, there creeps over us an awe, a terror, over-
powering but undefined ?   Why is it that we shudder without a cause, and feel
the warm life-blood stand still in its courses?   Are the dead too near ?   —
FALKLAND.

*   *   *   *   *

" Ha ! sayest thou?   Hideous thought, I feel it twine
O'er my iced heart, as curls around his prey
The sure and deadly serpent !

*   *   *   *   *

What ! in the hush and in the solitude
Pass'd that dread soul away ?"—' LOVE AND HATRED '

THE evening prior to that morning in which the above conversation occurred, Brandon passed alone in his lodging
at * * * *. He had felt himself too unwell to attend the
customary wassail, and he sat indolently musing in the
solitude of the old-fashioned chamber to which he was consigned.
There, two wax-candles on the smooth, quaint table, dimly struggled
against the gloom of heavy panels, which were relieved at unfrequent
intervals by portraits in oaken frames, dingy, harsh, and important
with the pomp of laced garments and flowing wigs. The predilec-
tion of the landlady for modern tastes had, indeed, on each side of
the huge fireplace, suspended more novel masterpieces of the fine
arts. In emblematic gorgeousness hung the pictures of the four
Seasons, buxom wenches all, save Winter, who was deformedly
bodied forth in the likeness of an aged carle. These were interspersed by an engraving of Lord Mauleverer, the lieutenant of the
neighbouring county, looking extremely majestical in his peer's

robes ; and by three typifications of Faith, Hope, and Charity—
ladies with whom it may be doubted if the gay earl ever before
cultivated so close an intimacy. Curtains, of that antique chintz in
which fasces of stripes are alternated by rows of flowers, filled the
interstices of three windows ; a heavy sideboard occupied the greater
portion of one side of the room ; and on the opposite side, in the
rear of Brandon, a vast screen stretched its slow length along, and
relieved the unpopulated and, as it were, desolate comfort of the
apartment.

Pale and imperfectly streamed the light upon Brandon's face, as he
sat in his large chair, leaning his cheek on one hand, and gazing
with the unconscious earnestness of abstraction on the clear fire. At
that moment a whole phalanx of gloomy thought was sweeping in
successive array across his mind. His early ambition, his ill-omened
marriage, the causes of his after-rise in the wrong-judging world, the
first dawn of his reputation, his rapid and flattering successes, his
present elevation, his aspiring hope of far higher office, and more
patrician honours—all these phantoms passed before him in
chequered shadow and light : but ever with each stalked one dis-
quieting and dark remembrance—the loss of his only son.

Weaving his ambition with the wish to revive the pride of his
hereditary name, every acquisition of fortune or of fame rendered
him yet more anxious to find the only one who could perpetuate
these hollow distinctions to his race.

"I shall recover him yet !" he broke out suddenly and aloud. As
he spoke, a quick—darting—spasmodic pain ran shivering through
his whole frame, and then fixed for one instant on his heart with a
gripe like the talons of a bird : it passed away, and was followed
by a deadly sickness. Brandon rose, and filling himself a large
tumbler of water, drank with avidity. The sickness passed off like
the preceding pain ; but the sensation had of late been often felt by
Brandon and disregarded,—for few persons were less afflicted with
the self-torture of hypochondria ; but now, that night, whether it
was more keen than usual, or whether his thought had touched on
the string that jars naturally on the most startling of human antici-
pations, we know not, but, as he resumed his seat, the idea of his
approaching dissolution shot like an ice-bolt through his breast.

So intent was this scheming man upon the living objects of the
world, and so little were his thoughts accustomed to turn towards
the ultimate goal of all things, that this idea obtruding itself abruptly
upon him, startled him with a ghastly awe. He *felt* the colour rush
from his cheek, and a tingling and involuntary pain ran wandering
through the channels of his blood, even from the roots of the hair to
the soles of his feet. But the stern soul of Brandon was not one

which shadows could long affright. He nerved himself to meet the grim thought thus forced upon his mental eye, and he gazed on it with a steady and enduring look.

"Well," thought he, "*is* my hour coming, or have I yet the ordinary term of mortal nature to expect? It is true, I have lately suffered these strange revulsions of the frame with somewhat of an alarming frequency: perhaps this medicine, which healed the anguish of one infirmity, has produced another more immediately deadly? Yet why should I think this? My sleep is sound and calm, my habits temperate, my mind active and clear as in its best days. In my youth, I never played the traitor with my constitution; why should it desert me at the very threshold of my age? Nay, nay, these are but passing twitches, chills of the blood that begins to wax thin. Shall I learn to be less rigorous in my diet? Perhaps wine may reward my abstinence in avoiding it for my luxuries, by becoming a cordial to my necessities! Ay, I will consult—I will consult, I must not die yet. I have—let me see, three—four grades to gain before the ladder is scaled. And, above all, I must regain my child! Lucy married to Mauleverer, myself a peer, my son wedded to—whom? Pray God he be not married already! My nephews and my children nobles! the house of Brandon restored, my power high in the upward gaze of men; my fame set on a more lasting basis than a skill in the quirks of law these are *yet* to come, these I will *not* die till I have enjoyed! Men die not till their destinies are fulfilled. The spirit that swells and soars within me says that the destiny of William Brandon is but half begun!"

With this conclusion, Brandon sought his pillow. What were the reflections of the prisoner whom he was to judge? Need we ask? Let us picture to ourselves his shattered health, the languor of sickness heightening the gloom which makes the very air of a gaol,—his certainty of the doom to be passed against him, his knowledge that the uncle of Lucy Brandon was to be his judge, that Mauleverer was to be his accuser; and that in all human probability the only woman he had ever loved must sooner or later learn the criminality of his life and the ignominy of his death: let us but glance at the above blackness of circumstances that surrounded him, and it would seem that there is but little doubt as to the complexion of his thoughts! Perhaps, indeed, even in that terrible and desolate hour, one sweet face shone on him, "and dashed the darkness all away." Perhaps, too, whatever might be the stings of his conscience, one thought, one remembrance of a temptation mastered, and a sin escaped, brought to his eyes tears that were sweet and healing in their source. But the heart of a man, in Clifford's awful situation, is dark and inscrutable ; and often, when the wildest and gloomiest external circumstances surround us, their reflection sleeps like a shadow, calm and still upon the mind.

The next morning, the whole town of * * * * (a town in which, we regret to say, an accident once detained ourself for three wretched days, and which we can, speaking therefore from profound experience, assert to be in ordinary times the most melancholy and peopleless-looking congregation of houses that a sober imagination can conceive) exhibited a scene of such bustle, animation, and jovial anxiety, as the trial for life or death to a fellow-creature can alone excite in the phlegmatic breasts of the English. Around the court the crowd thickened with every moment, until the whole market-place, in which the town-hall was situated, became one living mass. The windows of the houses were filled with women, some of whom had taken that opportunity to make parties to breakfast ; and little round tables, with tea and toast on them, caught the eyes of the grinning mobbists as they gaped impatiently upwards.

"Ben," said a stout yeoman, tossing up a halfpenny, and catching the said coin in his right hand, which he immediately covered with the left,—"Ben, heads or tails that Lovett is hanged ; heads hanged, tails not, for a crown."

"Petticoats, to be sure," quoth Ben, eating an apple ; and it was heads !

"Dammee, you've lost !" cried the yeoman, rubbing his rough hands with glee.

It would have been a fine sight for Asmodeus, could he have perched on one of the housetops of the market-place of * * * *, and looked on the murmuring and heaving sea of mortality below. Oh ! the sight of a crowd round a court of law, or a gibbet, ought to make the devil split himself with laughter.

While the mob was fretting, and pushing, and swearing, and grinning, and betting, and picking pockets, and trampling feet, and tearing gowns, and scrambling nearer and nearer to the doors and windows of the court, Brandon was slowly concluding his abstemious repast preparatory to attendance on his judicial duties. His footman entered with a letter. Sir William glanced rapidly over the seal (one of those immense sacrifices of wax used at that day), adorned with a huge coat of arms, surmounted with an earl's coronet, and decorated on either side with those supporters so dear to heraldic taste. He then tore open the letter, and read as follows :—

"MY DEAR SIR WILLIAM,

"You know that, in the last conversation I had the honour to hold with you, I alluded, though perhaps somewhat distantly, to the esteem which his Majesty had personally expressed for your principles and talents, and his wish to testify it at the earliest opportunity. There will be, as you are doubtless aware, an immediate creation of four peerages. Your name stands second on the list. The choice of title his Majesty graciously leaves to you ; but he has hinted, that the respectable antiquity of your f mily would make him best pleased were you to select the name of your own family-seat, which, if I mistake not, is Warlock. You will instruct me at your leisure as to the manner in which the patent should be made out, touching the succession, &c. Perhaps (excuse the licence of an old friend) this event may induce you to forsake your long cherished celibacy. I need not add that this accession of rank will be accompanied by professional elevation. You will see by the papers that the death of * * * * * * leaves vacant the dignity of Chief Baron : and I am at length empowered to offer you a station proportioned to your character and talents.

"With great consideration,
"Believe me, my dear Sir,
" Very truly yours,
"_____ ____ . _

"(*Private and Confidential.*)"

Brandon's dark eye glanced quickly from the signature of the Premier, affixed to this communication, towards the mirror opposite him. He strode to it, and examined his own countenance with a long and wistful gaze. Never, we think, did youthful gallant about to repair to the trysting spot, in which fair looks make the greatest of earthly advantages, gaze more anxiously on the impartial glass than now did the ascetic and scornful judge ; and never, we ween, did the eye of the said gallant retire with a more satisfied and triumphant expression.

"Yes, yes!" muttered the judge, "no sign of infirmity is yet written *here ;* the blood flows clear and warm enough, the cheek looks firm too, and passing full, for one who was always of the lean kind. Aha ! this letter is a cordial, an *elixir vitæ.* I feel as if a new lease were granted to the reluctant tenant. Lord Warlock, the first Baron of Warlock,—Lord Chief Baron —What next ?"

As he spoke, he strode unconsciously away ; folding his arms with that sort of joyous and complacent gesture which implies the idea of a man hugging himself in a silent delight. Assuredly, had the most skilful physician then looked upon the ardent and all-lighted face, the firm step, the elastic and muscular frame, the vigorous air of Brandon, as he mentally continued his soliloquy, he would have predicted for him as fair a grasp on longevity as the chances of mortal life will allow. He was interrupted by the servant entering.

"It is twenty-five minutes after nine, sir," said he, respectfully.

"Sir,—*sir!*" repeated Brandon. "Ah, well! so late!"

"Yes, sir, and the sheriff's carriage is almost at the door."

"Humph,—Minister,—Peer,—Warlock,—succession.—My son, my son!—would to God that I could find thee!"

Such were Brandon's last thoughts as he left the room. It was with great difficulty, so dense was the crowd, that the judge drove up to the court. As the carriage slowly passed, the spectators pressed to the windows of the vehicle, and stood on tiptoe to catch a view of the celebrated lawyer. Brandon's face, never long indicative of his feelings, had now settled into its usual gravity, and the severe loftiness of his look chilled, while it satisfied, the curiosity of the vulgar. It had been ordered that no person should be admitted until the judge had taken his seat on the bench; and this order occasioned so much delay, owing to the accumulated pressure of the vast and miscellaneous group, that it was more than half an hour before the court was able to obtain that decent order suiting the solemnity of the occasion. At five minutes before ten, an universal and indescribable movement announced that the prisoner was put to the bar. We read in one of the journals of that day, that "on being put to the bar, the prisoner looked round with a long and anxious gaze, which at length settled on the judge, and then dropped, while the prisoner was observed to change countenance slightly. Lovett was dressed in a plain dark suit; he seemed to be about six feet high; and though thin and worn, probably from the effect of his wound and imprisonment, he is remarkably well made, and exhibits the outward appearance of that great personal strength which he is said to possess, and which is not unfrequently the characteristic of daring criminals. His face is handsome and prepossessing, his eyes and hair dark, and his complexion pale, possibly from the effects of his confinement; there was a certain sternness in his countenance during the greater part of the trial. His behaviour was remarkably collected and composed. The prisoner listened with the greatest attention to the indictment, which the reader will find in another part of our paper, charging him with the highway robbery of Lord Mauleverer, on the night of the —— of —— last. He occasionally inclined his body forward, and turned his ear towards the court; and he was observed, as the jury were sworn, to look steadily in the face of each. He breathed thick and hard when the various aliases he had assumed, Howard, Cavendish, Jackson, &c., were read; but smiled, with an unaccountable expression, when the list was completed, as if exulting at the varieties of his ingenuity. At twenty-five minutes past ten, Mr. Dyebright, the counsel for the crown, stated the case to the jury."

Mr. Dyebright was a lawyer of great eminence ; he had been a Whig all his life, but had latterly become remarkable for his insincerity, and subservience to the wishes of the higher powers. His talents were peculiar and effective. If he had little eloquence, he had much power ; and his legal knowledge was sound and extensive. Many of his brethren excelled him in display ; but no one, like him, possessed the secret of addressing a jury. Winningly familiar ; seemingly candid to a degree that scarcely did justice to his cause, as if he were in an agony lest he should persuade you to lean a hairbreadth more on his side of the case than justice would allow ; apparently all made up of good, homely, virtuous feeling, a disinterested regard for truth, a blunt yet tender honesty, seasoned with a few amiable fireside prejudices, which always come home to the hearts of your fathers of families and thorough-bred Britons ; versed in all the niceties of language, and the magic of names ; if he were defending crime, carefully calling it misfortune ; if attacking misfortune, constantly calling it crime ;—Mr. Dyebright was exactly the man born to pervert justice, to tickle jurors, to cozen truth with a friendly smile, and to obtain a vast reputation as an excellent advocate. He began by a long preliminary flourish on the importance of the case. He said that he should, with the most scrupulous delicacy, avoid every remark calculated to raise unnecessary prejudice against the prisoner. He should not allude to his unhappy notoriety, his associations with the lowest dregs.—(Here up jumped the counsel for the prisoner, and Mr. Dyebright was called to order.) "God knows," resumed the learned gentleman, looking wistfully at the jury, "that my learned friend might have spared himself this warning. God knows that I would rather fifty of the wretched inmates of this county gaol were to escape unharmed, than that a hair of the prisoner you behold at the bar should be unjustly touched. The life of a human being is at stake ; we should be guilty ourselves of a crime, which on our deathbeds we should tremble to recall, were we to suffer any consideration, whether of interest or of prejudice, or of undue fear for our own properties and lives, to bias us even to the turning of a straw against the unfortunate prisoner. Gentlemen, if you find me travelling a single inch from my case—if you find me saying a single word calculated to harm the prisoner in your eyes, and unsupported by the evidence I shall call, then I implore you not to depend upon the vigilance of my learned friend, but to treasure these *my* errors in your recollection, and to consider them as so many arguments in favour of the prisoner. If, gentlemen, I *could* by any possibility imagine that your verdict would be favourable to the prisoner, I can, unaffectedly and from the bottom of my heart, declare to you that I should rejoice ; a case might be lost, but a fellow-creature would be saved ! Callous as we of the legal profession are believed, we have feelings like you ; and I ask any one of you, gentlemen of the jury, any one who has ever felt the pleasures of social intercourse, the joy of charity, the heart's reward of benevolence,—I ask any one of you, whether, if he were placed in the arduous situation I now hold, all the persuasions of vanity would not vanish at once from his mind, and whether his defeat as an advocate would not be rendered dear to him, by the common and fleshly sympathies of a man ! But, gentlemen (Mr. Dyebright's voice at once deepened and faltered), there is a duty, a painful duty, we owe to our country ; and never, in the long course of my professional experience, do I remember an instance in which it was more called forth than in the present. Mercy, gentlemen, is dear, very dear to us all ; but it is the deadliest injury we can inflict on mankind, when it is bought at the expense of justice."

The learned gentleman then, after a few farther prefatory observations, proceeded to state how, on the night of —— last, Lord Mauleverer was stopped and robbed by three men masked, of a sum of money amounting to above three hundred and fifty pounds, a diamond snuff-box, rings, watch, and a case of most valuable jewels,—how Lord Mauleverer, in endeavouring to defend himself, had passed a bullet through the clothes of one of the robbers—how, it would be proved, that the garments of the prisoner, found in a cave in Oxfordshire, and positively sworn to by a witness he should produce, exhibited a rent similar to such a one as a bullet would produce,—how, moreover, it would be positively sworn to by the same witness, that the prisoner Lovett had come to the cavern with two accomplices not yet taken up, since their rescue by the prisoner, and boasted of the robbery he had just committed ; that in the clothes and sleeping apartment of the robber the articles stolen from Lord Mauleverer were found, and that the purse containing the notes for three hundred pounds, the only thing the prisoner could probably have obtained time to carry off with him, on the morning in which the cave was entered by the policemen, was found on his person on the day on which he had attempted the rescue of his comrades, and had been apprehended in that attempt. He stated, moreover, that the dress found in the cavern, and sworn to by one witness he should produce, as belonging to the prisoner, answered exactly to the description of the clothes worn by the principal robber, and sworn to by Lord Mauleverer, his servant, and the postilions. In like manner, the colour of one of the horses found in the cavern corresponded with that rode by the highwayman. On these circumstantial proofs, aided by the immediate testimony of the king's evidence (that witness whom he should produce), he rested a case which could, he averred, leave no doubt on the minds of any impartial jury." Such, briefly and plainly alleged, made the substance of the details entered into by the learned counsel, who then proceeded to call his witnesses. The evidence of Lord Maul[e]verer (who was staying at Mauleverer Park, which was within a few miles of * * * *) was short and clear; (it was noticed as a singular circumstance, that at the end of the evidence the prisoner bowed respectfully to his lordship) The witness of the postilions and of the valet was no less concise ; nor could all the ingenuity of Clifford's counsel shake any part of their evidence in his cross-examination. The main witness depended on by the crown was now summoned, and the solemn countenance of Peter Mac Grawler rose on the eyes of the jury One look of cold and blighting contempt fell on him from the eye of the prisoner, who did not again deign to regard him during the whole of his examination.

The witness of Mac Grawler was delivered with a pomposity worthy of the ex-editor of the "Asinæum" Nevertheless, by the skill of Mr. Dyebright, it was rendered sufficiently clear a story to leave an impression on the jury damnatory to the interests of the prisoner The counsel on the opposite side was not slow in perceiving the ground acquired by the adverse party ; so, clearing his throat, he rose with a sneering air to the cross-examination.

"So, so !" began Mr. Botheram, putting on a pair of remarkably large spectacles, wherewith he truculently regarded the witness, —" so, so, Mr. Mac Grawler,—is that your name? eh ! Ah, it is, is it? a very very respectable name it is too, I warrant. Well, sir, look at me. Now, on your oath, remember, were you ever the editor of a certain thing published every Wednesday, and called 'the Attenæum,' or 'the Asinæum,' or some such name ?"

Commencing with this insidious and self-damnatory question, the learned counsel then proceeded, as artfully as he was able, through a series of interrogatories, calculated to injure the character, the respectable character, of Mac Grawler, and weaken his testimony in the eyes of the jury. He succeeded in exciting in the audience that feeling of merriment, wherewith the vulgar are always so delighted to intersperse the dull seriousness of hanging a human being. But though the jury themselves grinned, they were not convinced. The Scotsman retired from the witness-box, "scotched," perhaps, in reputation, but not "killed" as to testimony. It was just before this witness concluded, that Lord Mauleverer caused to be handed to the judge a small slip of paper, containing merely these words in pencil:—

"DEAR BRANDON,—A dinner waits you at Mauleverer Park, only three miles hence. Lord —— and the Bishop of —— meet you. Plenty of news from London, and a letter about you, which I will show to no one till we meet. Make haste and hang this poor fellow, that I may see you the sooner; and it is bad for both of us to wait long for a regular meal like dinner. I can't stay longer, it is so hot, and my nerves were always susceptible.

"Yours,

"MAULEVERER.

"If you will come, give me a nod. You know my hour, it is always the same."

The judge glancing over the note, inclined his head gravely to the earl, who withdrew; and in one minute afterwards, a heavy and breathless silence fell over the whole court. The prisoner was called upon for his defence: it was singular what a different sensation to that existing in their breasts the moment before, crept thrillingly through the audience. Hushed was every whisper—vanished was every smile that the late cross-examination had excited; a sudden and chilling sense of the dread importance of the tribunal made itself abruptly felt in the minds of every one present.

Perhaps, as in the gloomy satire of Hogarth (the moral Mephistopheles of painters), the close neighbourhood of pain to mirth made the former come with the homelier shock to the heart;—be that as it may, a freezing anxiety numbing the pulse, and stirring through the air, made every man in that various crowd feel a sympathy of awe with his neighbour, excepting only the hardened judge and the hackneyed lawyers, and one spectator, an idiot who had thrust himself in with the general press, and stood, within a few paces of the prisoner, grinning unconsciously, and every now and then winking with a glassy eye at some one at a distance, whose vigilance he had probably eluded.

The face and aspect, even the attitude of the prisoner, were well fitted to heighten the effect which would naturally have been created by any man under the same fearful doom. He stood at the very front of the bar, and his tall and noble figure was drawn up to its full height; a glow of excitement spread itself gradually over features at all times striking, and lighted an eye naturally eloquent, and to which various emotions at that time gave a more than commonly deep and impressive expression. He began thus —

"My lord, I have little to say, and I may at once relieve the anxiety of my counsel, who now looks wistfully upon me, and add, that that little will scarcely embrace the object of defence. Why should I defend myself? Why should I endeavour to protract a life that a few days, more or less, will terminate, according to the ordinary calculations of chance? Such as it is, and has been, my life is vowed to the law, and the law will have the offering Could I escape from this indictment, I know that seven others await me, and that by one or the other of these my conviction and my sentence must come. Life may be sweet to all of us, my lord; and were it possible that mine could be spared yet awhile, that continued life might make a better atonement for past actions than a death which, abrupt and premature, calls for repentance while it forbids redress.

"But, when the dark side of things is our only choice, it is useless to regard the bright; idle to fix our eyes upon life, when death is at hand; useless to speak of contrition, when we are denied its proof. It is the usual policy of prisoners in my situation to address the feelings and flatter the prejudices of the jury; to descant on the excellence of our laws, while they endeavour to disarm them; to praise justice, yet demand mercy; to talk of expecting acquittal, yet boast of submitting without a murmur to condemnation. For me, to whom all earthly interests are dead, this policy is idle and superfluous. I hesitate not to tell you, my lord judge—to proclaim to you, gentlemen of the jury, that the laws which I have broken through my life I despise in death! Your laws are but of two classes; the one makes criminals, the other punishes them. I have suffered by the one—I am about to perish by the other.

"My lord, it was the turn of a straw which made me what I am. Seven years ago I was sent to the house of correction for an offence which I did not commit; I went thither, a boy who had never infringed a single law—I came forth, in a few weeks, a man who was prepared to break all laws! Whence was this change?—was it my fault, or that of my condemners? You had first wronged me by a punishment which I did not deserve—you wronged me yet more deeply, when (even had I been guilty of the first offence) I was sentenced to herd with hardened offenders, and graduates in vice and vice's methods of support. The laws themselves caused me to break the laws: first, by implanting within me the goading sense of injustice; secondly, by submitting me to the corruption of example. Thus, I repeat—and I trust my words will sink solemnly into the hearts of all present—your legislation made me what I am! and it now *destroys me, as it has destroyed thousands, for being what it made me!* But for this the first aggression on me, I might have been what the world terms honest,—I might have advanced to old age and a peaceful grave, through the harmless cheateries of trade, or the honoured falsehoods of a profession. Nay, I might have supported the laws which I have now braved; like the counsel opposed to me, I might have grown sleek on the vices of others, and advanced to honour by my ingenuity in hanging my fellow creatures! The canting and prejudging part of the press has affected to set before you the merits of 'honest ability,' or 'laborious trade,' in opposition to my offences. What, I beseech you, are the props of your 'honest' exertion—the profits of 'trade?' Are there no bribes to menials? Is there no adulteration of goods? Are the rich never duped in the price they pay?—are the poor never wronged in the quality they receive? Is there honesty in the bread you eat, in a single necessity which clothes, or feeds, or warms you? Let those whom the law protects consider it a protector: when did it ever protect *me?* When did it ever protect the poor man? The government of a state, the institutions of law, profess to provide for all those who 'obey.' Mark! a man hungers—do you feed him? He is naked—do you clothe him? If not, you break your covenant, you drive him back to the first law of nature, and you hang him, not because he is guilty, but because you have *left* him naked and starving! (A murmur among the mob below, with great difficulty silenced.) One thing only I will add, and that not to move your mercy. No, nor to invest my fate with an idle and momentary interest; but because there are some persons in this world who have not known me as the criminal who stands before you, and whom the tidings of my fate may hereafter reach; and I would not have those persons view me in blacker colours than I deserve. Among all the rumours, gentlemen, that have reached you, through all the tales and fables kindled from my unhappy notoriety and my approaching doom, I put it to you, if you have heard that I have committed one sanguinary action, or one ruinous and deliberate fraud? You have heard that I have lived by the plunder of the rich—I do not deny the charge. From the grinding of the poor, the habitual overreaching, or the systematic pilfering of my neighbours, my conscience is as free as it is from the charge of cruelty and bloodshed. Those *errors* I leave to honest mediocrity or virtuous exertion! You may perhaps find, too, that my life has not passed through a career of outrage without scattering some few benefits on the road. In destroying me, it is true that you will have the consolation to think, that among the benefits you derive from my sentence, will be the salutary encouragement you give to other offenders to offend to the *last degree*, and to divest outrage of no single aggravation ! But if this does not seem to you any very powerful inducement, you may pause before you cut off from all amendment a man who seems neither wholly hardened nor utterly beyond atonement. My lord, my counsel would have wished to summon witnesses,—some to bear testimony to redeeming points in my own character, others to invalidate the oath of the witness against me—a man whom I saved from destruction in order that he might destroy me. I do not think either necessary. The public press has already said of me what little good does not shock the truth ; and had I not possessed something of those qualities which society does not disesteem, you would not have beheld me here at this hour ! If I had saved myself as well as my companions, I should have left this country, perhaps for ever, and commenced a very different career abroad. I committed offences ; I eluded you ; I committed what, in my case, was an act of duty : I am seized, and I perish. But the weakness of my body destroys me, not the strength of your malice. Had I (and as the prisoner spake, the haughty and rapid motion, the *enlarging of the form*, produced by the passion of the moment, made impressively conspicuous to all the remarkable power of his frame,)—had I but my wonted health, my wonted command over these limbs and these veins, I would have asked no friend, no ally, to favour my escape. I tell you, engines and guardians of the law, that I would have mocked your chains, and defied your walls, as ye know that I have mocked and defied them before. But my blood creeps now only in drops through its courses ; and the heart that I had of old stirs feebly and heavily within me." The prisoner paused a moment, and resumed in an altered tone :—"Leaving, then, my own character to the ordeal of report, I cannot perhaps do better than leave to the same criterion that of the witness against me. I will candidly own that, under other circumstances, it might have been otherwise. I will candidly avow that I might have then used such means as your law awards me to procure an acquittal and to prolong my existence,—though in a new scene : as it is, what matters the cause in which I receive my sentence? Nay, it is even better to suffer by the first than to linger to the last. It is some consolation not again to stand where I now stand ; to go through the humbling solemnities which I have this day endured ; to see the smile of some, and retort the frown of others ; to wrestle with the anxiety of the heart, and to depend on the caprice of the excited nerves It is something to feel one part of the drama of disgrace is over, and that I may wait unmolested in my den until, for one time only, I am again the butt of the unthinking and the monster of the crowd. My lord, I have now done ! To you, whom the law deems the prisoner's counsel,—to you, gentlemen of the jury, to whom it has delegated his fate, I leave the chances of my life."

The prisoner ceased; but the same heavy silence which, save when broken by one solitary murmur, had lain over the court during his speech, still continued even for several moments after that deep and firm voice had died on the ear. So different had been the defence of the prisoner from that which had been expected; so assuredly did the more hackneyed part of the audience, even as he had proceeded, imagine that, by some artful turn, he would at length wind into the usual courses of defence, that when his unfaltering and almost stern accents paused, men were not prepared to feel that his speech was finished, and the pause involuntarily jarred on them, as untimeous and abrupt. At length, when each of the audience slowly awoke to the conviction that the prisoner had indeed concluded his harangue, a movement, eloquent of feelings released from a suspense which had been perhaps the more earnest and the more blended with awe, from the boldness and novelty of the words on which it hung, circled round the court. The jurors looked confusedly at each other, but not one of them spoke even by a whisper; their feelings, which had been aroused by the speech of the prisoner, had not, from its shortness, its singularity, and the haughty impolicy of its tone, been so far guided by its course, as to settle into any state of mind clearly favourable to him, or the reverse; so that each man waited for his neighbour to speak first, in order that he might find, as it were, in another, a kind of clue to the indistinct and excited feelings which wanted utterance in himself.

The judge, who had been from the first attracted by the air and aspect of the prisoner, had perhaps, notwithstanding the hardness of his mind, more approvingly than any one present, listened to the defence; for in the scorn of the hollow institutions, and the mock honesty of social life, so defyingly manifested by the prisoner, Brandon recognised elements of mind remarkably congenial to his own; and this sympathy was heightened by the hardihood of physical nerve and moral intrepidity displayed by the prisoner; qualities which, among men of a similar mould, often form the strongest motive of esteem, and sometimes (as we read of in the Imperial Corsican and his chiefs) the *only* point of attraction! Brandon was, however, soon recalled to his cold self by a murmur of vague applause circling throughout the common crowd, among whom the general impulse always manifests itself first, and to whom the opinions of the prisoner, though but imperfectly understood, came more immediately home than they did to the better and richer classes of the audience. Ever alive to the decorums of form, Brandon instantly ordered silence in the court; and when it was again restored, and it was fully understood that the prisoner's defence had closed, the judge proceeded to sum up.

It is worthy of remark, that many of the qualities of mind which seem most unamiable in private life often conduce with a singular felicity to the ends of public ; and thus the stony firmness characteristic of Brandon was a main cause which made him admirable as a judge.   For men in office err no less from their feelings than their interests.

Glancing over his notes, the judge inclined himself to the jury, and began with that silver ringing voice which particularly distinguished Brandon's eloquence, and carries with it in high stations so majestic and candid a tone of persuasion.   He pointed out, with a clear brevity, the various points of the evidence ; he dwelt for a moment on the attempt to cast disrepute upon the testimony of Mac Grawler —but called a proper attention to the fact, that the attempt had been unsupported by witnesses or proof. As he proceeded, the impression made by the prisoner on the minds of the jury slowly melted away ; and perhaps, so much do men soften when they behold clearly the face of a fellow-man dependent on them for life, it acted disadvantageously on the interests of Clifford, that, during the summing up, he leant back in the dock, and prevented his countenance from being seen.   When the evidence had been gone through, the judge concluded thus .—

"The prisoner, who, in his defence (on the principles and opinions of which I now forbear to comment), certainly exhibited the signs of a superior education, and a high though perverted ability, has alluded to the reports circulated by the public press, and leant some little stress on the various anecdotes tending to his advantage, which he supposes have reached your ears.   I am by no means willing that the prisoner should be deprived of whatever benefit may be derivable from such a source ; but it is not in this place, nor at this moment, that it can avail him.   All you have to consider is the evidence before you.   All on which you have to decide is, whether the prisoner be or be not guilty of the robbery of which he is charged.   You must not waste a thought on what redeems or heightens a supposed crime—you must only decide on the crime itself.   Put away from your minds, I beseech you, all that interferes with the main case.   Put away also from your motives of decision all forethought of other possible indictments to which the prisoner has alluded, but with which you are necessarily unacquainted. If you doubt the evidence, whether of one witness or of all, the prisoner must receive from you the benefit of that doubt.   If not, you are sworn to a solemn oath, which ordains you to forego all minor considerations—which compels you to watch narrowly that you be not influenced by the infirmities natural to us all, but criminal in you, to lean towards the side of a mercy that would be rendered by your oath a perjury to God, and by your duty as impartial citizens, a treason to your country. I dismiss you to the grave consideration of the important case you have heard ; and I trust that He to whom all hearts are open and all secrets are known, will grant you the temper and the judgment to form a right decision ! "

There was in the majestic aspect and thrilling voice of Brandon something which made the commonest form of words solemn and impressive ; and the hypocrite, aware of this felicity of manner, generally, as now, added weight to his concluding words by a religious allusion or a Scriptural phraseology. He ceased ; and the jury, recovering the effect of his adjuration, consulted for a moment among themselves ; the foreman then, addressing the court on behalf of his fellow-jurors, requested leave to retire for deliberation. An attendant bailiff being sworn in, we read in the journals of the day, which noted the divisions of time with that customary scrupulosity rendered terrible by the reflection how soon all time and seasons may perish for the hero of the scene, that " it was at twenty-five minutes to two that the jury withdrew."

Perhaps in the whole course of a criminal trial there is no period more awful than that occupied by the deliberation of the jury. In the present case, the prisoner, as if acutely sensible of his situation, remained in the rear of the dock, and buried his face in his hands. They who stood near him observed, however, that his breast did not seem to swell with the convulsive emotions customary to persons in his state, and that not even a sigh or agitated movement escaped him. The jury had been absent about twenty minutes, when a confused noise was heard in the court. The face of the judge turned in commanding severity towards the quarter whence it proceeded. He perceived a man of a coarse garb and mean appearance endeavouring rudely and violently to push his way through the crowd towards the bench, and at the same instant he saw one of the officers of the court approaching the disturber of its tranquillity, with no friendly intent. The man, aware of the purpose of the constable, exclaimed with great vehemence, "I vill give this to my lord the judge, blow me if I von't ! " and as he spoke, he raised high above his head a soiled scrap of paper folded awkwardly in the shape of a letter. The instant Brandon's eye caught the rugged features of the intrusive stranger, he motioned with rather less than his usual slowness of gesture to one of his official satellites. " Bring me that paper instantly ! " he whispered.

The officer bowed and obeyed. The man, who seemed a little intoxicated, gave it with a look of ludicrous triumph and self-importance.

"Stand avay, man!" he added to the constable, who now laid hand on his collar—"you'll see vot the judge says to that 'ere bit of paper ; and so vill the prisoner, poor fellow !"

This scene, so unworthy the dignity of the court, attracted the notice and (immediately around the intruder) the merriment of the crowd, and many an eye was directed towards Brandon, as with calm gravity he opened the note and glanced over the contents. In a large school-boy hand—it was the hand of Long Ned—were written these few words :—

"MY LORD JUDGE,

"I make bold to beg you will do all you can for the prisoner at the barre ; as he is no other than the ' Paul ' I spoke to your Worship about. You know what I mean.

"DUMMIE DUNNAKER."

As he read this note, the judge's head was observed to droop suddenly, as if by a sickness or a spasm ; but he recovered himself instantly, and whispering the officer who brought him the note, said, "See that that madman be immediately removed from the court, and lock him up *alone*. He is so deranged as to be dangerous !"

The officer lost not a moment in seeing the order executed. Three stout constables dragged the astounded Dummie from the court in an instant, yet the more ruthlessly for his ejaculating—

"Eh, sirs, what's this? I tells you I have saved the judge's hown flesh and blood. Vy now, gently there ; you'll smart for this, my fine fellow ! Never you mind, Paul, my arty : I'se done you a pure good——"

"Silence !" proclaimed the voice of the judge, and that voice came forth with so commanding a tone of power that it awed Dummie, despite his intoxication. In a moment more, and, ere he had time to recover, he was without the court. During this strange hubbub, which nevertheless scarcely lasted above two or three minutes, the prisoner had not once lifted his head, nor appeared aroused in any manner from his reverie. And scarcely had the intruder been withdrawn before the jury returned.

The verdict was as all had foreseen,—"Guilty ;" but it was coupled with a strong recommendation to mercy.

The prisoner was then asked, in the usual form, whether he had to say anything why sentence of death should not be passed against him ?

As these dread words struck upon his ear, slowly the prisoner rose. He directed first towards the jury a brief and keen glance, and his eyes then rested full, and with a stern significance, on the face of his judge.

"My lord," he began, "I have but one reason to advance against the sentence of the law. If you have interest to prevent or mitigate it, that reason will, I think, suffice to enlist you on my behalf. I said that the first cause of those offences against the law which bring me to this bar, was the committing me to prison on a charge of which I was wholly innocent! My lord judge, *you* were the man who accused me of that charge, and subjected me to that imprisonment! Look at me well, my lord, and you may trace in the countenance of the hardened felon you are about to adjudge to death the features of a boy whom, some seven years ago, you accused before a London magistrate of the theft of your watch. On the oath of a man who has one step on the threshold of death, the accusation was unjust. And, fit minister of the laws you represent! you, who will now pass my doom,—YOU were the cause of my crimes! My lord, I have done I am ready to add another to the long and dark list of victims who are first polluted, and then sacrificed, by the blindness and the injustice of human codes!"

While Clifford spoke, every eye turned from him to the judge, and every one was appalled by the ghastly and fearful change which had fallen over Brandon's face. Men said afterwards, that they saw written there, in terrible distinctness, the characters of death; and there certainly seemed something awful and preternatural in the bloodless and haggard calmness of his proud features Yet his eye did not quail, nor the muscles of his lip quiver; and with even more than his wonted loftiness, he met the regard of the prisoner. But, as alone conspicuous throughout the motionless and breathless crowd, the judge and criminal gazed upon each other; and as the eyes of the spectators wandered on each, a thrilling and electric impression of a powerful likeness between the doomed and the doomer, for the first time in the trial, struck upon the audience, and increased, though they scarcely knew why, the sensation of pain and dread which the prisoner's last words excited. Perhaps it might have chiefly arisen from a common expression of fierce emotion conquered by an iron and stern character of mind, or perhaps, now that the ashy paleness of exhaustion had succeeded the excited flush on the prisoner's face, the similarity of complexion thus obtained, made the likeness more obvious than before; or, perhaps, the spectators had not hitherto fixed so searching, or, if we may so speak, so alternating a gaze upon the two. However that be, the resemblance between the men, placed as they were in such widely different circumstances—that resemblance which, as we have hinted, had at certain moments occurred startlingly to Lucy—was plain and

N 2

unavoidably striking, the same the dark hue of their complexions, the same the haughty and Roman outline of their faces, the same the height of the forehead, the same even a displeasing and sarcastic rigidity of mouth, which made the most conspicuous feature in Brandon, and which was the only point that deteriorated from the singular beauty of Clifford. But, above all, the same inflexible, defying, stubborn spirit, though in Brandon it assumed the stately cast of majesty, and in Clifford it seemed the desperate sternness of the bravo, stamped itself in both. Though Clifford ceased, he did not resume his seat, but stood in the same attitude as that in which he had reversed the order of things, and merged the petitioner in the accuser. And Brandon himself, without speaking or moving, continued still to survey him. So, with erect fronts, and marble countenances, in which what was defying and resolute did not altogether quell the mortal leaven of pain and dread, they looked as might have looked the two men in the Eastern story, who had the power of gazing each other unto death.

What, at that moment, was raging in Brandon's heart, it is in vain to guess. He doubted not for a moment that he beheld before him his long-lost, his anxiously demanded son! Every fibre, every corner of his complex and gloomy soul, that certainly reached, and blasted with a hideous and irresistible glare. The earliest, perhaps the strongest, though often the least acknowledged principle of his mind, was the desire to rebuild the fallen honours of his house; its last scion he now beheld before him, covered with the darkest ignominies of the law! He had coveted worldly honours; he beheld their legitimate successor in a convicted felon! He had garnered the few affections he had spared from the objects of pride and ambition, in his son. That son he was about to adjudge to the gibbet and the hangman! Of late, he had increased the hopes of regaining his lost treasure, even to an exultant certainty. Lo! the hopes were accomplished! How? With these thoughts warring, in what manner we dare not even by an epithet express, within him, we may cast one hasty glance on the horror of aggravation they endured, when he heard the prisoner accuse HIM, as the cause of his present doom, and felt himself at once the murderer and the judge of his son!

Minutes had elapsed since the voice of the prisoner ceased; and Brandon now drew forth the black cap. As he placed it slowly over his brows, the increasing and corpse-like whiteness of his face became more glaringly visible, by the contrast which this dread headgear presented. Twice as he essayed to speak his voice failed him, and an indistinct murmur came forth from his hueless lips, and died away like a fitful and feeble wind. But with the third effort, the resolution and long self-tyranny of the man conquered, and his voice went clear and unfaltering through the crowd, although the severe sweetness of its wonted tones was gone, and it sounded strange and hollow on the ears that drank it.

"Prisoner at the bar!—It has become my duty to announce to you the close of your mortal career. You have been accused of a daring robbery, and, after an impartial trial, a jury of your countrymen and the laws of your country have decided against you. The recommendation to mercy"—(here, only, throughout his speech, Brandon gasped convulsively for breath)—"so humanely added by the jury, shall be forwarded to the supreme power, but I cannot flatter you with much hope of its success"—(the lawyers looked with some surprise at each other: they had expected a far more unqualified mandate, to abjure *all* hope from the jury's recommendation).—"Prisoner! for the opinions you have expressed, you are now only answerable to your God; I forbear to arraign them. For the charge you have made against me, whether true or false, and for the anguish it has given me, may you find pardon at another tribunal! It remains for me only—under a reserve too slight, as I have said, to afford you a *fair* promise of hope—only to—to—(all eyes were on Brandon: he felt it, exerted himself for a last effort, and proceeded) —to pronounce on you the sharp sentence of the law! It is, that you be taken back to the prison whence you came, and thence (when the supreme authority shall appoint) to the place of execution, to be there hanged by the neck till you are dead; and the Lord God Almighty have mercy on your soul!"

With this address concluded that eventful trial; and while the crowd, in rushing and noisy tumult, bore towards the door, Brandon, concealing to the last, with a Spartan bravery, the anguish which was gnawing at his entrails, retired from the awful pageant. For the next half hour he was locked up with the strange intruder on the proceedings of the court. At the end of that time the stranger was dismissed; and in about double the same period Brandon's servant readmitted him, accompanied by another man, with a slouched hat, and in a carman's frock. The reader need not be told that the newcomer was the friendly Ned, whose testimony was indeed a valuable corroborative to Dummie's, and whose regard for Clifford, aided by an appetite for rewards, had induced him to venture to the town of * * * * , although he tarried concealed in a safe suburb, until reassured by a written promise from Brandon of safety to his person, and a sum for which we might almost doubt whether he would not have consented (so long had he been mistaking means for an end) to be hanged himself. Brandon listened to the details of these confederates, and when they had finished, he addressed them thus:—

"I have heard you, and am convinced you are liars and impostors: there is the money I promised you"—(throwing down a pocket-book)—"take it;—and, hark you, if ever you dare whisper—ay, but a breath of the atrocious lie you have now forged, be sure I will have you dragged from the recess or nook of infamy in which you may hide your heads, and hanged for the crimes you have already committed. I am not the man to break my word—begone!—quit this town instantly: if, in two hours hence, you are found here, your blood be on your own heads!—Begone, I say!"

These words, aided by a countenance well adapted at all times to expressions of a menacing and ruthless character, at once astounded and appalled the accomplices. They left the room in hasty confusion; and Brandon, now alone, walked with uneven steps (the alarming weakness and vacillation of which he did not himself feel) to and fro the apartment. The hell of his breast was stamped upon his features, but he uttered only one thought aloud!

"I may,—yes, yes,—I *may* yet conceal this disgrace to my name!"

His servant tapped at the door to say that the carriage was ready, and that Lord Mauleverer had bid him remind his master that they dined punctually at the hour appointed.

"I am coming!" said Brandon, with a slow and startling emphasis on each word. But he first sat down and wrote a letter to the official quarter, strongly aiding the recommendation of the jury; and we may conceive how pride clung to him to the last, when he urged the substitution for death, of transportation *for life!* As soon as he had sealed this letter, he summoned an express, gave his orders coolly and distinctly, and attempted, with his usual stateliness of step, to walk through a long passage which led to the outer door. He found himself fail. "Come hither," he said to his servant—"give me your arm!"

All Brandon's domestics, save the one left with Lucy, stood in awe of him, and it was with some hesitation that his servant ventured to inquire "if his master felt well."

Brandon looked at him, but made no reply: he entered his carriage with slight difficulty, and, telling the coachman to drive as fast as possible, pulled down (a general custom with him) all the blinds of the windows

Meanwhile, Lord Mauleverer, with six friends, was impatiently awaiting the arrival of the seventh guest.

"Our august friend tarries!" quoth the bishop of ——, with his hands folded across his capacious stomach. "I fear the turbot your lordship spoke of may not be the better for the length of the trial."

"Poor fellow!" said the Earl of ——, slightly yawning.

"Whom do you mean?" asked Lord Mauleverer, with a smile. "The bishop, the judge, or the turbot?"

"Not one of the three, Mauleverer,—I spoke of the prisoner."

"Ah, the fine dog! I forgot him," said Mauleverer. "Really, now you mention him, I must confess that he inspires me with great compassion, but, indeed, it is very wrong in him to keep the judge so long!"

"Those hardened wretches have such a great deal to say," mumbled the bishop sourly.

"True!" said Mauleverer; "a religious rogue would have had some bowels for the state of the church esurient."

"Is it really true, Mauleverer," asked the Earl of ——, "that Brandon *is* to succeed * * * *?"

"So I hear," said Mauleverer. "Heavens! how hungry I am!"

A groan from the bishop echoed the complaint.

"I suppose it would be against all decorum to sit down to dinner without him?" said Lord ——.

"Why, really, I fear so," returned Mauleverer. "But our health —our health is at stake: we will only wait five minutes more. By Jove, there's the carriage! I beg your pardon for my heathen oath, my lord bishop."

"I forgive you!" said the good bishop, smiling.

The party thus engaged in colloquy were stationed at a window opening on the gravel road, along which the judge's carriage was now seen rapidly approaching; this window was but a few yards from the porch, and had been partially opened for the better reconnoitring the approach of the expected guest.

"He keeps the blinds down still! Absence of mind, or shame at unpunctuality—which is the cause, Mauleverer?" said one of the party.

"Not shame, I fear!" answered Mauleverer. "Even the indecent immorality of delaying our dinner could scarcely bring a blush to the parchment skin of my learned friend."

Here the carriage stopped at the porch; the carriage-door was opened

"There seems a strange delay," said Mauleverer, peevishly "Why does not he get out?"

As he spoke, a murmur among the attendants, who appeared somewhat strangely to crowd around the carriage, smote the ears of the party.

"What do they say?—What?" said Mauleverer, putting his hand to his ear.

The bishop answered hastily; and Mauleverer, as he heard the reply, forgot for once his susceptibility to cold, and hurried out to the carriage-door. His guests followed.

They found Brandon leaning against the farther corner of the carriage—a corpse. One hand held the check-string, as if he had endeavoured involuntarily, but ineffectually, to pull it. The right side of his face was partially distorted, as by convulsion or paralysis; but not sufficiently so to destroy that remarkable expression of loftiness and severity which had characterised the features in life. At the same time, the distortion which had drawn up on one side the muscles of the mouth, had deepened into a startling broadness the half sneer of derision, that usually lurked around the lower part of his face. Thus unwitnessed and abrupt had been the disunion of the clay and spirit of a man, who, if he passed through life a bold, scheming, stubborn, unwavering hypocrite, was not without something high even amidst his baseness, his selfishness, and his vices; who seemed less to have loved sin, than by some strange perversion of reason to have disdained virtue, and who, by a solemn and awful suddenness of *fate* (for who shall venture to indicate the judgment of the arch and unseen Providence, even when it appears to mortal eye the least obscured?), won the dreams, the objects, the triumphs of hope, to be blasted by them at the moment of acquisition!

CHAPTER XXXVI.

THE LAST.

"——— Subtle,—Surly,—Mammon, Dol,
Hot Ananias, Dapper, Drugger, all
With whom I traded"—'The Alchemist.'

AS when some rural citizen—retired for a fleeting holyday, far from the cares of the world, "*strepitumque Romæ,*"[1] to the sweet shades of Pentonville, or the remoter plains of Clapham—conduct some delighted visitor over the intricacies of that Dædalian masterpiece which he is pleased to call his labyrinth or maze,—now smiling furtively at his guest's perplexity,—now listening with calm superiority to his futile and erring conjectures,—now maliciously accompanying him through a flattering path, in which the baffled adventurer is suddenly checked by the

[1] "*And the roar of Rome.*"

blank features of a thoroughfareless hedge,—now trembling as he sees the guest stumbling unawares into the right track, and now relieved, as he beholds him, after a pause of deliberation, wind into the wrong, —even so, O pleasant reader! doth the sage novelist conduct thee through the labyrinth of his tale, amusing himself with thy self-deceits, and spinning forth, in prolix pleasure, the quiet yarn of his entertainment from the involutions which occasion thy fretting eagerness and perplexity. But as when—thanks to the host's good-nature or fatigue!—the mystery is once unravelled, and the guest permitted to penetrate even into the concealed end of the leafy maze ; the honest cit, satisfied with the pleasant pains he has already bestowed upon his visitor, puts him not to the labour of retracing the steps he hath so erratically trod, but leads him in three strides, and through a simpler path, at once to the mouth of the maze, and dismisseth him elsewhere for entertainment ; even so will the prudent narrator, when the intricacies of his plot are once unfolded, occasion no stale and profitless delays to his wearied reader, but conduct him, with as much brevity as convenient, without the labyrinth which has ceased to retain the interest of a secret.

We shall, therefore, in pursuance of the cit's policy, relate, as rapidly as possible, that part of our narrative which yet remains untold. On Brandon's person was found the paper which had contained so fatal an intelligence of his son; and when brought to Lord Mauleverer, the words struck that person (who knew Brandon had been in search of his lost son, whom we have seen that he had been taught however to suppose illegitimate, though it is probable that many doubts, whether he had not been deceived, must have occurred to his natural sagacity) as sufficiently important to be worth an inquiry after the writer. Dummie was easily found, for he had not yet turned his back on the town when the news of the judge's sudden death was brought back to it , and, taking advantage of that circumstance, the friendly Dunnaker remained altogether in the town (albeit his long companion deserted it as hastily as might be), and whiled the time by presenting himself at the gaol, and, after some ineffectual efforts, winning his way to Clifford : easily tracked by the name he had given to the governor of the gaol, he was conducted the same day to Lord Mauleverer, and his narrative, confused as it was, and proceeding even from so suspicious a quarter, thrilled those digestive organs, which in Mauleverer stood proxy for a heart, with feelings as much resembling awe and horror as our good peer was capable of experiencing. Already shocked from his worldly philosophy of indifference by the death of Brandon, he was more susceptible to a remorseful and salutary impression at this moment than he might have been at any other : and he could not, without some twinges of conscience, think of the ruin he had brought on the mother of the being he had but just prosecuted to the death, He dismissed Dummie, and, after a little consideration, he ordered his carriage, and, leaving the funeral preparations for his friend to the care of his man of business, he set off for London, and the house, in particular, of the Secretary of the Home Department. We would not willingly wrong the noble penitent ; but we venture a suspicion that he might not have preferred a personal application for mercy to the prisoner to a written one, had he not felt certain unpleasant qualms in remaining in a country house, overshadowed by ceremonies so gloomy as those of death. The letter of Brandon, and the application of Mauleverer, obtained for Clifford a relaxation of his sentence. He was left for perpetual transportation. A ship was already about to sail, and Mauleverer, content with having saved his life, was by no means anxious that his departure from the country should be saddled with any superfluous delay.

Meanwhile, the first rumour that reached London respecting Brandon's fate was, that he had been found in a fit, and was lying dangerously ill at Mauleverer's ; and before the second and more fatally sure report arrived, Lucy had gathered from the visible dismay of Barlow, whom she anxiously cross-questioned, and who, really loving his master, was easily affected into communication, the first and more flattering intelligence. To Barlow's secret delight, she insisted instantly on setting off to the supposed sick man ; and, accompanied by Barlow and her woman, the affectionate girl hastened to Mauleverer's house on the evening after the day the earl left it. Lucy had not proceeded far before Barlow learned, from the gossip of the road, the real state of the case. Indeed, it was at the first stage that, with a mournful countenance, he approached the door of the carriage, and announcing the inutility of proceeding farther, begged of Lucy to turn back. So soon as Miss Brandon had overcome the first shock which this intelligence gave her, she said, with calmness, " Well, Barlow, if it be so, we have still a duty to perform. Tell the postboys to drive on ! "

" Indeed, madam, I cannot see what use it can be fretting yourself,—and you so poorly. If you will let *me* go, I will see every attention paid to the remains of my poor master."

" When my father lay dead," said Lucy, with a grave and sad sternness in her manner, " he who is now no more sent no proxy to perform the last duties of a brother ; neither will I send one to discharge those of a niece, and prove that I have forgotten the gratitude of a daughter. Drive on ! "

We have said that there were times when a spirit was stricken from Lucy little common to her in general, and now the command of her uncle sat upon her brow. On sped the horses, and for several minutes Lucy remained silent. Her woman did not dare to speak. At length Miss Brandon turned, and, covering her face with her hands, burst into tears so violent that they alarmed her attendant even more than her previous stillness, "My poor, poor uncle!" she sobbed, and those were all her words.

We must pass over Lucy's arrival at Lord Mauleverer's house,—we must pass over the weary days which elapsed till that unconscious body was consigned to dust with which, could it have retained yet one spark of its haughty spirit, it would have refused to blend its atoms. She had loved the deceased incomparably beyond his merits, and, resisting all remonstrance to the contrary, and all the forms of ordinary custom, she witnessed herself the dreary ceremony which bequeathed the human remains of William Brandon to repose and to the worm. On that same day Clifford received the mitigation of his sentence, and on that day another trial awaited Lucy. We think, briefly to convey to the reader what that scene was, we need only observe that Dummie Dunnaker, decoyed by his great love for little Paul, whom he delightedly said he found not the least "stuck up by his great fame and helewation," still lingered in the town, and was not only aware of the relationship of the cousins, but had gleaned from Long Ned, as they journeyed down to * * * *, the affection entertained by Clifford for Lucy. Of the manner in which the communication reached Lucy, we need not speak : suffice it to say, that on the day in which she had performed the last duty to her uncle, she learned, for the first time, her lover's situation.

On that evening, in the convict's cell, the cousins met. Their conference was low, for the gaoler stood within hearing ; and it was broken by Lucy's convulsive sobs But the voice of one, whose iron nerves were not unworthy of the offspring of William Brandon, was clear and audible to her ear, even though uttered in a whisper that scarcely stirred his lips. It seemed as if Lucy, smitten to the inmost heart by the generosity with which her lover had torn himself from her, at the time that her wealth might have raised him, in any other country, far above the perils and the crimes of his career in this,—perceiving now, for the first time, and in all their force, the causes of his mysterious conduct, melted by their relationship, and forgetting herself utterly in the desolation and dark situation in which she beheld one who, whatever his crimes, had not been criminal towards her ;—it seemed as if, carried away by these emotions, she had yielded altogether to the fondness and devotion of her nature,—that she had wished to leave home, and friends, and fortune, and share with him his punishment and his shame.

"Why!" she faltered—"why—why not? we are all that is left to each other in the world! Your father and mine were brothers, let me be to you as a sister. What is there left for me here? Not one being whom I love, or who cares for me—not one!"

It was then that Clifford summoned all his courage, as he answered:—perhaps, now that he felt—(though here his knowledge was necessarily confused and imperfect),—his birth was not unequal to hers—now that he read, or believed he read, in her wan cheek and attenuated frame, that desertion to her was death, and that generosity and self-sacrifice had become too late,—perhaps, these thoughts concurring with a love in himself beyond all words, and a love in her which it was above humanity to resist, altogether conquered and subdued him. Yet, as we have said, his voice breathed calmly in her ear, and his eye only, which brightened with a steady and resolute hope, betrayed his mind "Live, then!" said he, as he concluded. "My sister, my mistress, my bride, live! In one year from this day . . . . . I repeat . . . . I promise it thee!"

The interview was over, and Lucy returned home with a firm step. She was on foot; the rain fell in torrents; yet, even in her precarious state, her health suffered not; and when within a week from that time she read that Clifford had departed to the bourne of his punishment, she read the news with a steady eye and a lip that, if it grew paler, did not quiver.

Shortly after that time, Miss Brandon departed to an obscure town by the sea-side; and there, refusing all society, she continued to reside. As the birth of Clifford was known but to few, and his legitimacy was unsuspected by all except, perhaps, by Mauleverer, Lucy succeeded to the great wealth of her uncle, and this circumstance made her more than ever an object of attraction in the eyes of her noble adorer. Finding himself unable to see her, he wrote to her more than one moving epistle; but as Lucy continued inflexible, he at length, disgusted by her want of taste, ceased his pursuit, and resigned himself to the continued sterility of unwedded life. As the months waned, Miss Brandon seemed to grow weary of her retreat; and immediately on attaining her majority, which she did about eight months after Brandon's death, she transferred the bulk of her wealth to France, where it was understood (for it was impossible that rumour should sleep upon an heiress and a beauty) that she intended in future to reside. Even Warlock (that spell to the proud heart of her uncle) she ceased to retain. It was offered to the nearest relation of the family at a sum which he did not hesitate to close with. And, by the common vicissitudes of Fortune, the estate of the ancient Brandons has now, we perceive by a weekly journal, just passed into the hands of a wealthy alderman.

It was nearly a year since Brandon's death, when a letter, bearing a foreign post-mark, came to Lucy. From that time, her spirits— which before, though subject to fits of abstraction, had been even, and subdued, not sad—rose into all the cheerfulness and vivacity of her earliest youth; she busied herself actively in preparations for her departure from this country; and, at length, the day was fixed, and the vessel was engaged. Every day till that one, did Lucy walk to the seaside, and, ascending the highest cliff, spend hours, till the evening closed, in watching, with seemingly idle gaze, the vessels that interspersed the sea; and with every day her health seemed to strengthen, and the soft and lucid colour she had once worn, to rebloom upon her cheek.

Previous to her departure, Miss Brandon dismissed her servants, and only engaged one female, a foreigner, to accompany her: a certain tone of quiet command, formerly unknown to her, character-ised these measures, so daringly independent for one of her sex and age. The day arrived—it was the anniversary of her last interview with Clifford. On entering the vessel, it was observed that she trembled violently, and that her face was as pale as death. A stranger, who had stood aloof wrapped in his cloak, darted forward to assist her;—that was the last which her discarded and weeping servants beheld of her from the pier where they stood to gaze.

Nothing more, in this country, was ever known of the fate of Lucy Brandon; and as her circle of acquaintances was narrow, and interest in her fate existed vividly in none, save a few humble breasts, conjecture was never keenly awakened, and soon cooled into forgetfulness. If it favoured, after the lapse of years, any one notion more than another, it was that she had perished among the victims of the French Revolution.

Meanwhile, let us glance over the destinies of our more subor-dinate acquaintances.

Augustus Tomlinson, on parting from Long Ned, had succeeded in reaching Calais; and, after a rapid tour through the Continent, he ultimately betook himself to a certain literary city in Germany, where he became distinguished for his metaphysical acumen, and opened a school of morals on the Grecian model taught in the French tongue. He managed, by the patronage he received, and the pupils he enlightened, to obtain a very decent income; and as he wrote a folio against Locke, proved that men had innate feel-ings, and affirmed that we should refer everything not to reason, but to the sentiments of the soul, he became greatly respected for his extraordinary virtue. Some little discoveries were made after his death, which, perhaps, would have somewhat diminished the general odour of his sanctity, had not the admirers of his school carefully hushed up the matter, probably out of respect for "the sentiments of the soul!"

Pepper, whom the police did not so anxiously desire to destroy as they did his two companions, might have managed, perhaps many years longer, to graze upon the public commons, had not a letter, written somewhat imprudently, fallen into wrong hands. This, though after creating a certain stir it apparently died away, lived in the memory of the police, and finally conspired, with various peccadilloes, to produce his downfall. He was seized, tried, and sentenced to seven years' transportation. He so advantageously employed his time at Botany Bay, and arranged things there so comfortably to himself, that, at the expiration of his sentence, he refused to return home. He made an excellent match, built himself an excellent house, and remained in "the land of the blest" to the end of his days, noted to the last for the redundance of his hair, and a certain ferocious coxcombry of aspect.

As for Fighting Attie and Gentleman George, for Scarlet Jem and for Old Bags, we confess ourselves destitute of any certain information of their latter ends. We can only add, with regard to Fighting Attie,—"Good luck be with him wherever he goes!" And for mine host of the "Jolly Angler," that, though we have not the physical constitution to quaff "a bumper of blue ruin," we shall be very happy, over any tolerable wine, and in company with any agreeable convivialists, to bear our part in the polished chorus of—

"Here's to Gentleman George, God bless him!"

Mrs. Lobkins departed this life like a lamb; and Dummie Dunnaker obtained a licence to carry on the business at Thames Court. He boasted, to the last, of his acquaintance with the great Captain Lovett, and of the affability with which that distinguished personage treated him. Stories he had, too, about Judge Brandon, but no one believed a syllable of them; and Dummie, indignant at the disbelief, increased, out of vehemence, the marvel of the stories: so that, at length, what was added almost swallowed up what was original, and Dummie himself might have been puzzled to satisfy his own conscience as to what was false and what was true.

The erudite Peter Mac Grawler, returning to Scotland, disappeared by the road: a person, singularly resembling the sage, was afterwards seen at Carlisle, where he discharged the useful and praiseworthy duties of Jack Ketch. But whether or not this respectable functionary *was* our identical Simon Pure, *our* ex-editor of "The Asinæum," we will not take it upon ourselves to assert.

Lord Mauleverer, finally resolving on a single life, passed the remainder of his years in indolent tranquillity. When he died, the newspapers asserted that his Majesty was deeply affected by the loss of so old and valued a friend. His furniture and wines sold remarkably high : and a Great Man, his particular intimate, who purchased his books, startled to find, by pencil marks, that the noble deceased had read some of them, exclaimed, not altogether without truth,—"Ah! Mauleverer might have been a deuced clever fellow,—if he had liked it ! "

The earl was accustomed to show as a curiosity a ring of great value, which he had received in rather a singular manner. One morning, a packet was brought him which he found to contain a sum of money, the ring mentioned, and a letter from the notorious Lovett, in which that person, in begging to return his lordship the sums of which he had *twice* assisted to rob him, thanked him, with earnest warmth, for the consideration testified towards him in not revealing his identity with Captain Clifford ; and ventured, as a slight testimony of respect, to enclose the aforesaid ring with the sum returned.

About the time Mauleverer received this curious packet, several anecdotes of a similar nature appeared in the public journals ; and it seemed that Lovett had acted upon a general principle of restitution,—not always, it must be allowed, the offspring of a robber's repentance. While the idle were marvelling at these anecdotes, came the tardy news, that Lovett, after a single month's sojourn at his place of condemnation, had, in the most daring and singular manner, effected his escape. Whether, in his progress up the country, he had been starved or slain by the natives,—or whether, more fortunate, he had ultimately found the means of crossing the seas, was as yet unknown. There ended the adventures of the gallant robber ; and thus, by a strange coincidence, the same mystery which wrapped the fate of Lucy involved also that of her lover. And here, kind reader, might we drop the curtain on our closing scene, did we not think it might please thee to hold it up yet one moment, and give thee another view of the world behind.

In a certain town of that Great Country, where shoes are imperfectly polished,[1] and opinions are not prosecuted, there resided, twenty years after the date of Lucy Brandon's departure from England, a man held in high and universal respect, not only for the rectitude of his conduct, but for the energies of his mind, and the purposes to which they were directed. If you asked who cultivated that waste? the answer was—"Clifford ! " Who

---

[1] See Captain Hall's late work on America.

procured the establishment of that hospital?—"Clifford!" Who
obtained the redress of such a public grievance?—"Clifford!"
Who struggled for and won such a popular benefit?—"Clifford!"
In the gentler part of his projects and his undertakings,—in that
part, above all, which concerned the sick or the necessitous, this
useful citizen was seconded, or rather excelled, by a being over
whose surpassing loveliness Time seemed to have flown with a
gentle and charming wing. There was something remarkable and
touching in the love which this couple (for the woman we refer
to was Clifford's wife) bore to each other; like the plant on the
plains of Hebron, the time which brought to that love an additional strength, brought to it also a softer and a fresher verdure.
Although their present neighbours were unacquainted with the
events of their earlier life, previous to their settlement at * * * *, it
was known that they had been wealthy at the time they first came
to reside there, and that, by a series of fatalities, they had lost all :
but Clifford had borne up manfully against fortune ; and in a new
country, where men who prefer labour to dependence cannot easily
starve, he had been enabled to toil upward through the severe
stages of poverty and hardship, with an honesty and vigour of
character which won him, perhaps, a more hearty esteem for every
successive effort, than the display of his lost riches might ever have
acquired him. His labours and his abilities obtained gradual but
sure success; and he now enjoyed the blessings of a competence
earned with the most scrupulous integrity, and spent with the
most kindly benevolence. A trace of the trials they had passed
through was discernible in each ; those trials had stolen the rose
from the wife's cheek, and had sown untimely wrinkles in the
broad brow of Clifford. There were moments, too, but they were
only moments, when the latter sank from his wonted elastic and
healthful cheerfulness of mind, into a gloomy and abstracted reverie ;
but these moments the wife watched with a jealous and fond
anxiety, and one sound of her sweet voice had the power to dispel
their influence : and when Clifford raised his eyes, and glanced
from *her* tender smile around his happy home and his growing
children, or beheld through the very windows of his room the
public benefits he had created, something of pride and gladness
glowed on his countenance, and he said, though with glistening
eyes and subdued voice, as his looks returned once more to his
wife,—"I owe these to thee !"

One trait of mind especially characterised Clifford—indulgence to
the faults of others ! "Circumstances make guilt," he was wont to
say : "let us endeavour to *correct the circumstances*, before we rail
against the guilt !" His children promised to tread in the same

useful and honourable path that he trod himself.   Happy was
considered that family which had the hope to ally itself with his.

Such was the after-fate of Clifford and Lucy.   Who will condemn
us for preferring the moral of that fate to the moral which is extorted
from the gibbet and the hulks?—which makes scarecrows, not
beacons; terrifies our weakness, not warms our reason.   Who does
not allow that it is better to repair than to perish,—better, too, to
atone as the citizen than to repent as the hermit?   O John Wilkes!
Alderman of London, and Drawcansir of Liberty, your life was not
an iota too perfect,—your patriotism might have been infinitely
purer,—your morals would have admitted indefinite amendment:
you are no great favourite with us or with the rest of the world; but
you said one excellent thing, for which we look on you with benevolence, nay, almost with respect.   We scarcely know whether to
smile at its wit, or to sigh at its wisdom.   Mark this truth, all ye
gentlemen of England, who would make laws as the Romans made
fasces—a bundle of rods with an axe in the middle; mark it, and
remember! long may it live, allied with hope in ourselves, but with
gratitude in our children;—long after the book which it now
"adorns" and "points" has gone to its dusty slumber;—long, long
after the feverish hand which now writes it down can defend or
enforce it no more.—"THE VERY WORST USE TO WHICH YOU CAN
PUT A MAN IS TO HANG HIM!"

NOTE.

Page 372.

In the second edition of this novel there were here inserted two "characters" of "Fighting Attie" and "Gentleman George," omitted in the subsequent edition published by Mr. Bentley in the *Standard Novels.* At the request of some admirers of those eminent personages, who considered the biographical sketches referred to impartial in themselves, and contributing to the completeness of the design for which men so illustrious were introduced, they are here retained,—though in the more honourable form of a separate and supplementary notice.

FIGHTING ATTIE.

When he dies, the road will have lost a great man, whose foot was rarely out of his stirrup, and whose clear head guided a bold hand. He carried common sense to its perfection—and he made the straight path the sublimest. His words were few, his actions were many. He was the Spartan of Tobymen, and laconism was the short soul of his professional legislation!

Whatever way you view him, you see those properties of mind which command fortune; few thoughts not confusing each other—simple elements, and bold. His character in action may be summed in two phrases, "a fact seized and a stroke made." Had his intellect been more luxurious, his resolution might have been less hardy—and his hardiness made his greatness. He was one of those who shine but in action—chimneys (to adapt the simile of Sir Thomas More) that seem useless till you light your fire. So in calm moments you dreamed not of his utility, and only on the road you were struck dumb with the outbreaking of his genius. Whatever situation he was called to, you found in him what you looked for in vain in others; for his strong sense gave to Attie what long experience ought, but often fails, to give to its possessors: his energy triumphed over the sense of novel circumstance, and he broke in a moment through the cobwebs which entangled lesser natures for years. His eye saw a final result, and disregarded the detail. He robbed his man without chicanery; and took his purse by applying for it, rather than scheming. If his enemies wish to detract from his merit,—a merit great, dazzling, and yet solid,—they may, perhaps, say that his genius fitted him better to continue exploits than to devise them; and thus that, besides the renown which he may justly claim, he often wholly engrossed that fame which should have been shared by others; he took up the enterprise where it ceased at Labour, and carried it onwards, where it was rewarded with Glory. Even this charge proves a new merit of address, and lessens not the merit less complicated we have allowed him before. The fame he has acquired may excite our emulation; the envy he has not appeased may console us for obscurity.

$$\text{——Ἀμφὶ δ' ἀνθρώ-}$$
πων φρεσὶν ἀμπλακίαι
Ἀναρίθματοι κρέμανται

Τοῦτο δ' ἀμάχανον εὑρεῖν
Ὅ τι νῦν, καὶ ἐν τελευ-
τᾷ φέρτατον ἀνδρὶ τυχεῖν,

PIND *Olymp.* vii 1, 43, 48.[1]

GENTLEMAN GEORGE.

For thee, Gentleman George, for thee, what conclusive valediction remains? Alas! since we began the strange and mumming scene wherein first thou wert introduced, the grim foe hath knocked thrice at thy gates; and now, as we write,[2] thou art departed thence—thou art no more! a new lord presides in thine easy chair, a new voice rings from thy merry board—thou art forgotten! thou art already like these pages, a tale that is told to a memory that retaineth not! Where are thy quips and cranks? where thy stately coxcombries and thy regal gauds? Thine house, and thy pagoda, thy Gothic chimney, and thy Chinese sign-post; these yet ask the concluding hand: *thy* hand is cold; their completion, and the enjoyment the completion yields, are for another! Thou sowest, and thy follower reaps; thou buildest, thy successor holds; thou plantest, and thine heir sits beneath the shadow of thy trees;—

"Neque harum, quas colis, arborum
Te, præter invisas cupressos,
Ulla brevem dominum sequetur!"[3]

---

[1] Thus, not too vigorously, translated by Mr. West.—

"But wrapt in error is the human mind,
And human bliss is ever insecure.
Know we what fortune shall remain behind?
Know we how long the present shall endure?"

[2] In 1830

[3] Nor will any of these trees thou didst cultivate follow thee, the short-lived lord,—save the hateful cypress.

At this moment, thy life—for thou wert a Great Man to thine order, and they have added thy biography to that of Abershaw and Sheppard—thy life is before us! What a homily in its events! Gaily didst thou laugh into thy youth, and run through the courses of thy manhood. Wit sat at thy table, and Genius was thy comrade ; Beauty was thy handmaid ; and Frivolity played around thee,—a buffoon that thou didst ridicule, and ridiculing enjoy ! Who among us can look back to thy brilliant era, and not sigh to think that the wonderful men who surrounded thee, and amidst whom thou wert a centre, and a nucleus, are for him but the things of history, and the phantoms of a bodiless tradition? Those brilliant suppers, glittering with beauty, the memory of which makes one spot (yet inherited by Bachelor Bill) a haunted and a fairy ground; all who gathered to that Armida's circle, the Grammonts, and the Beauvilliers, and the Rochefoucaults of England and the Road,—who does not feel that to have seen these, though but as Gil Blas saw the festivities of his actors, from the sideboard and behind the chair, would have been a triumph for the earthlier feelings of his old age to recall ? What, then, must it have been to have seen them as thou didst see—(thou, the deceased and the forgotten !)—seen them from the height of thy youth, and power, and rank (for early went thou keeper to a public), and reckless spirits, and lusty capacities of joy ? What pleasures where sense lavished its uncounted varieties ? What revellings where wine was the least excitement?

Let the scene shift —How stirring is the change ! Triumph, and glitter, and conquest ! For thy public was a public of renown: thither came the Warriors of the Ring—the Heroes of the Cross, —and thou, their patron, wert elevated on their fame : *Principes pro victoriâ pugnant—comites pro principe.*[1] What visions sweep across us ! What glories didst thou witness ! Over what conquests didst thou preside ! The mightiest epoch—the most wonderful events which the world, *thy* world, ever knew—of these was it not indeed, and dazzlingly thine,

"To share the triumph and partake the gale?"

Let the scene shift—Manhood is touched by Age ; but Lust is "heeled" by Luxury, and Pomp is the heir of Pleasure ; gewgaws and gaud, instead of glory, surround, rejoice, and flatter thee to the last There rise thy buildings—there lie, secret but gorgeous, the tabernacles of thine ease, and the earnings of thy friends, and the riches of the people whom they plunder, are waters to thine imperial whirlpool. Thou art lapped in ease as is a silkworm ; and profusion flows

---

[1] Chiefs for the victory fight,—for chiefs the soldiers.

from thy high and unseen asylum as the rain poureth from a cloud.
Much didst thou do to beautify chimney-tops—much to adorn the
snuggeries where thou didst dwell;—thieving with thee took a
substantial shape, and the robberies of the public passed into a
metempsychosis of mortar, and became public-houses. So there and
thus, building and planning, didst thou spin out thy latter yarn, till
Death came upon thee; and when we looked around, lo! thy brother
was on thy hearth. And thy parasites, and thy comrades, and thine
ancient pals, and thy portly blowens, they made a murmur, and they
packed up their goods—but they turned ere they departed, and they
would have worshipped thy brother as they worshipped thee;—but
he would not! And thy sign-post is gone and mouldered already;
and to the "Jolly Angler" has succeeded the "Jolly Tar!" And
thy picture is disappearing fast from the print-shops, and thy name
from the mouths of men! And thy brother, whom no one praised
while thou didst live, is on a steeple of panegyric built above the
churchyard that contains thy grave. Oh! shifting and volatile hearts
of men! Who would be keeper of a Public? Who dispense the
wine and the juices that gladden when, the moment the pulse of the
hand ceases, the wine and the juices are forgotten?

To History—for thy name will be preserved in that record, which,
whether it be the Calendar of Newgate or of Nations, telleth us alike
how men suffer, and sin, and perish—to History we leave the sum
and balance of thy merits and thy faults. The sins that were thine
were those of the man to whom pleasure is all in all: thou wert, from
root to branch, sap and in heart, what moralists term the libertine;
hence the light wooing, the quick desertion, the broken faith, the
organized perfidy, that manifested thy bearing to those gentler
creatures who called thee—'Gentleman George.' Never, to one
solitary woman, until the last dull flame of thy dotage, didst thou so
behave as to give no foundation to complaint, and no voice to wrong.
But who shall say be honest to one, but laugh at perfidy to another?
Who shall wholly confine treachery to one sex, if to that sex he hold
treachery no offence? So in thee, as in all thy tribe, there was a
laxness of principle, an insincerity of faith, even unto men:—thy
friends, when occasion suited, thou couldst forsake; and thy luxuries
were dearer to thee than justice to those who supplied them. Men
who love and live for pleasure as thou are usually good-natured; for
their devotion to pleasure arises from the strength of their constitution,
and the strength of their constitution preserves them from the irritations of weaker nerves; so wert thou good-natured, and often
generous; and often with thy generosity didst thou unite a delicacy
that showed thou hadst an original and a tender sympathy with men.
But as those who pursue pleasure are above all others impatient of

interruption, so to such as interfered with thy main pursuit, thou didst testify a deep, a lasting, and a revengeful anger. Yet let not such vices of temperament be too severely judged! For to thee were given man's two most persuasive tempters, physical and moral —Health and Power! Thy talents, such as they were—and they were the talents of a man of the world—misled rather than guided thee, for they gave thy mind that demi-philosophy, that indifference to exalted motives which is generally found in a clever rake. Thy education was wretched; thou hadst a smattering of Horace, but thou couldst not write English, and thy letters betray that thou wert wofully ignorant of logic. The fineness of thy taste has been exaggerated; thou wert unacquainted with the nobleness of simplicity; thy idea of a whole was grotesque and overloaded, and thy fancy in details was gaudy and meretricious But thou hadst thy hand constantly in the public purse, and thou hadst plans and advisers for ever before thee; more than all, thou didst find the houses in that neighbourhood wherein thou didst build, so præternaturally hideous, that thou didst require but little science to be less frightful in thy creations. If thou didst not improve thy native village and thy various homes with a solid, a lofty, and a noble taste, thou didst nevertheless very singularly improve. And thy posterity, in avoiding the faults of thy masonry, will be grateful for the effects of thy ambition The same demi-philosophy, which influenced thee in private life, exercised a far benigner and happier power over thee in public. Thou wert not idly vexatious in vestries, nor ordinarily tyrannic in thy parish; if thou wert ever abitrary, it was only when thy pleasure was checked, or thy vanity wounded. At other times, thou didst leave events to their legitimate course, so that in thy latter years thou wert justly popular in thy parish; and in thy grave, thy great good fortune will outshine thy few bad qualities, and men will say of thee with a kindly, nor an erring judgment,—"In private life he was not worse than the Rufflers who came to this bar; in public life he was better than those who kept a public before him."— Hark! those huzzas! what is the burthen of that chorus?—Oh, grateful and never time-serving Britons, have ye modified already for another the song ye made so solely in honour of Gentleman George; and must we, lest we lose the custom of the public, and the good things of the taproom, must we roar with throats yet hoarse with our fervour for the old words, our ardour for the new?

> "Here's to *Mariner Bill*, God bless him!
> God bless him!
> God bless him!
> Here's to *Mariner Bill*, God bless him!"

TOMLINSONIANA;

OR

THE POSTHUMOUS WRITINGS

OF THE CELEBRATED

AUGUSTUS TOMLINSON,

PROFESSOR OF MORAL PHILOSOPHY IN THE UNIVERSITY OF ——

ADDRESSED TO HIS PUPILS

AND COMPRISING

I.

MAXIMS ON THE POPULAR ART OF CHEATING, ILLUSTRATED BY TEN
CHARACTERS, BEING AN INTRODUCTION TO THAT NOBLE SCIENCE, BY WHICH
EVERY MAN MAY BECOME HIS OWN ROGUE.

II.

BRACHYLOGIA: OR, ESSAYS, CRITICAL, SENTIMENTAL, MORAL, AND ORIGINAL.

INTRODUCTION.

―――◇―――

. HAVING lately been travelling in Germany, I spent some time at that University in which Augustus Tomlinson presided as Professor of Moral Philosophy. I found that that great man died, after a lingering illness, in the beginning of the year 1822, perfectly resigned to his fate, and conversing, even on his death-bed, on the divine mysteries of Ethical Philosophy. Notwithstanding the little peccadilloes, to which I have alluded in the latter pages of *Paul Clifford*, and which his pupils deemed it advisable to hide from

"The gaudy, babbling, and remorseless day,"

his memory was still held in a tender veneration. Perhaps, as in the case of the illustrious Burns, the faults of a great man endear to you his genius. In his latter days the PROFESSOR was accustomed to wear a light-green silk dressing-gown, and, as he was perfectly bald, a little black velvet cap ; his small-clothes were pepper and salt. These interesting facts I learned from one of his pupils. His old age was consumed in lectures, in conversation, and in the composition of the little *morceaux* of wisdom we present to the public. In these essays and maxims, short as they are, he seems to have concentrated the wisdom of his industrious and honourable life. With great difficulty I procured from his executors the MSS. which were then preparing for the German press. A valuable consideration induced those gentlemen to become philanthropic, and to consider the inestimable blessings they would confer upon this country by suffering me to give the following essays to the light, in their native and English dress, on the same day whereon they appear in Germany in the graces of foreign disguise.

At an age when, while Hypocrisy stalks, simpers, sidles, struts, and hobbles through the country, Truth also begins to watch her adversary in every movement, I cannot but think these lessons of Augustus Tomlinson peculiarly well-timed. I add them as a fitting Appendix to a Novel that may not inappropriately be termed a Treatise on Social Frauds, and if they contain within them that evidence of diligent attention and that principle of good, in which the satire of Vice is only the germ of its detection, they may not, perchance, pass wholly unnoticed ; nor be even condemned to that hasty reading in which the Indifference of to-day is but the prelude to the Forgetfulness of to-morrow.

CONTENTS.

MAXIMS

ON

THE POPULAR ART OF CHEATING,

ILLUSTRATED BY TEN CHARACTERS;

BEING AN INTRODUCTION TO THAT NOBLE SCIENCE, BY WHICH EVERY MAN
MAY BECOME HIS OWN ROGUE.

"Set a thief to catch a thief."—PROVERB

I.

WHENEVER you are about to utter something astonishingly false, always begin with, "It is an acknowledged fact," &c. Sir Robert Filmer was a master of this method of writing. Thus with what a solemn face that great man attempted to cheat! *"It is a truth undeniable* that there cannot be any multitude of men whatsoever, either great or small, &c.—but that in the same multitude there is one man amongst them *that in nature hath a right to be King of all the rest—as being the next heir to Adam!"*

II.

When you want something from the public, throw the blame of the asking on the most sacred principle you can find. A common beggar can read you exquisite lessons on this the most important maxim in the art of popular cheating. *"For the love of God,* sir, a penny!"

III.

Whenever on any matter, moral, sentimental, or political, you find yourself utterly ignorant, talk immediately of "The Laws of Nature." As those laws are written nowhere,[1] they are known by nobody. Should any ask you *how* you happen to know such or such a doctrine as the dictate of Nature, clap your hand to your heart and say, "Here!"

[1] Locke.

O 2

IV.

Yield to a man's tastes, and he will yield to your interest.

v.

When you talk to the half-wise, twaddle; when you talk to the ignorant, brag; when you talk to the sagacious, look very humble, and ask their opinion.

VI.

Always bear in mind, my beloved pupils, that the means of livelihood depend not on the virtues, but the vices of others. The lawyer, the statesman, the hangman, the physician, are paid by our sins; nay, even the commoner professions, the tailor, the coach-maker, the upholsterer, the wine merchant, draw their fortunes, if not their existence, from those smaller vices—our foibles. Vanity is the figure prefixed to the ciphers of Necessity. Wherefore, O, my beloved pupils! never mind what a man's virtues are; waste no time in learning them. Fasten at once on his infirmities. Do to the One as, were you an honest man, you would do to the Many. This is the way to be a rogue individually, as a lawyer is a rogue professionally. Knaves are like critics [1]—"flies that feed on the sore part, and would have nothing to live on were the body in health." [2]

VII.

Every man finds it desirable to have tears in his eyes at times—one has a sympathy with humid lids. Providence hath beneficially provided for this want, and given to every man, in Its divine fore-thought, misfortunes painful to recall. Hence, probably, those human calamities which the atheist rails against! Wherefore, when you are uttering some affecting sentiment to your intended dupe, think of the greatest misfortune you ever had in your life; habit will soon make the association of tears and that melancholy remembrance constantly felicitous. I knew, my dear pupils, a most intelligent Frenchman, who obtained a charming legacy from an old poet by repeating the bard's verses with streaming eyes. "How were you able to weep at will?" asked I (I was young then, my pupils). "*Je pensois*," answered he, "*à mon pauvre père qui est mort*." [3] The union of sentiment with the ability of swindling made that Frenchman a most fascinating creature!

[1] Nullum simile est quod idem.—EDITOR.
[2] Tatler.
[3]

VIII.

Never commit the error of the over-shrewd, and deem human nature worse than it is. Human Nature is so damnably good, that if it were not for human Art we knaves could not live. The primary elements of a man's mind do not sustain us—it is what he owes to "the pains taken with his education," and "the blessings of civilised society!"

IX.

Whenever you doubt, my pupils, whether your man be a quack or not, decide the point by seeing if your man be a positive asserter. Nothing indicates imposture like confidence. Volney[1] saith well, "that the most celebrated of charlatans[2] and the boldest of tyrants begins his extraordinary tissue of lies by these words, "There is no doubt in this book!"

X.

There is one way of cheating people peculiar to the British Isles, and which, my pupils, I earnestly recommend you to import hither —cheating by subscription. People like to be plundered in company; dupery then grows into the spirit of party. Thus one quack very gravely requested persons to fit up a ship for him and send him round the world as its captain to make discoveries, and another patriotically suggested that 10,000*l.* should be subscribed—for what?—to place *him* in Parliament! Neither of these fellows could have screwed an individual out of a shilling had he asked him for it in a corner; but a printed list, "with His Royal Highness" at the top, plays the devil with English guineas. A subscription for individuals may be considered a society for the ostentatious encouragement of idleness, impudence, beggary, imposture,—and other public virtues!

XI.

Whenever you read the life of a great man, I mean a man eminently successful, you will perceive all the qualities given to him are the qualities necessary even to a mediocre rogue. "He possessed," saith the biographer, "the greatest address [viz. the faculty of wheedling]; the most admirable courage [viz. the faculty of bullying]; the most noble fortitude [viz. the faculty of bearing to be bullied]; the most singular versatility [viz. the faculty of saying one thing to one man, and its reverse to another], and the most wonderful command over the mind of his contemporaries [viz. the faculty of victimising their purses or seducing their actions]" Wherefore, if luck cast you in humble life, assiduously study the biographies of the great, in order to accomplish you as a rogue ; if in the more elevated range of society, be thoroughly versed in the lives of the roguish,——so shall you fit yourself to be eminent !

XII.

The hypocrisy of virtue, my beloved pupils, is a little out of fashion now-a-days ; it is sometimes better to affect the hypocrisy of vice. Appear generously profligate, and swear with a hearty face, that you do not pretend to be better than the generality of your neighbours. Sincerity is not less a covering than lying ; a frieze great coat wraps you as well as a Spanish cloak.

XIII.

When you are about to execute some great plan. and to defraud a number of persons, let the first one or two of the allotted number be the cleverest, shrewdest fellows you can find. You have then a reference that will alone dupe the rest of the world. " That Mr. Lynx is satisfied," will amply suffice to satisfy Mr. Mole of the honesty of your intentions ! Nor are shrewd men the hardest to take in ; they rely on their strength ; invulnerable heroes are necessarily the bravest. Talk to them in a business-like manner, and refer your design at once to their lawyer. My friend, John Shamberry, was a model in this grand stroke of art He swindled twelve people to the tune of some thousands, with no other trouble than it first cost him to swindle—whom do you think ? the Secretary to the Society for the Suppression of Swindling !

XIV.

Divide your arts into two classes : those which cost you little labour—those which cost much. The first,—flattery, attention, answering letters by return of post, walking across a street to oblige the man you intend to ruin ; all these you must never neglect. The least man is worth gaining at a small cost. And besides, while you are serving yourself, you are also obtaining the character of civility, diligence, and good-nature. But the arts which cost you much labour—a long subservience to one testy individual ; aping the semblance of a virtue, a quality, or a branch of learning which you do not possess, to a person difficult to blind—all these, never begin except for great ends, worth not only the loss of time, but the chance of detection. Great pains for small gains is the maxim of the miser. The rogue should have more *grandeur d'âme*.[1]

XV

Always forgive.

¹ C........ .f .. ¹

XVI.

If a man owe you a sum of money—(pupils though you be of mine, you *may* once in your lives be so silly as to lend)—and you find it difficult to get it back, appeal, not to his justice, but his charity. The components of justice flatter few men ! Who likes to submit to an inconvenience because he ought to do it?—without praise, without even self-gratulation ? But charity, my dear friends, tickles up human ostentation deliciously. Charity implies superiority ; and the feeling of superiority is most grateful to social nature. Hence the commonness of charity, in proportion to other virtues, all over the world ; and hence you will especially note, that in proportion as people are haughty and arrogant will they laud almsgiving and encourage charitable institutions.

XVII.

Your genteel rogues do not sufficiently observe the shrewdness of the vulgar ones. The actual beggar takes advantage of every sore ; but the moral swindler is unpardonably dull as to the happiness of a physical infirmity. To obtain a favour—neglect no method that may allure compassion. I knew a worthy curate, who obtained two livings by the felicity of a hectic cough ; and a younger brother, who subsisted for ten years on his family by virtue of a slow consumption.

XVIII.

When you want to possess yourself of a small sum, recollect that the small sum be put into juxta-position with a great. I do not express myself clearly—take an example. In London there are sharpers who advertise 70,000*l.* to be advanced at four per cent., principals only conferred with. The gentleman wishing for such a sum on mortgage, goes to see the advertiser ; the advertiser says he must run down and look at the property on which the money is to be advanced ; his journey and expenses will cost him a mere trifle— say twenty guineas. Let him speak confidently—let the gentleman very much want the money at the interest stated, and three to one, but our sharper gets the twenty guineas, so paltry a sum in comparison to 70,000*l.*, though so serious a sum had the matter related to half-pence !

XIX.

Lord Coke has said, " To trace an error to its fountain-head is to refute it." Now, my young pupils, I take it for granted that you are interested in the preservation of error ; you do not wish it, therefore, to be traced to its fountain-head. Whenever, then, you see a sharp fellow tracking it up, you have two ways of settling the matter.

You may say with a smile, "Nay, now, sir, you grow speculative—I admire your ingenuity;" or else look grave, colour up, and say—" I fancy, sir, there is no warrant for this assertion in the most sacred of all authorities!" The Devil can quote Scripture, you know, and a very sensible Devil it is too!

XX.

Rochefoucault has said, "The hate of favourites is nothing else but the love of favour." The idea is a little cramped; the hate we bear to any man is only the result of our love for some good which we imagine *he* possesses, or which, being in our possession, we imagine he has attacked. Thus envy, the most ordinary species of hate, arises from our value for the glory, or the plate, or the content we behold; and revenge is born from our regard for our fame that has been wounded, or our acres molested, or our rights invaded But the most noisy of all hatreds is hatred for the rich, from love for the riches. Look well on the poor devil who is always railing at coaches and four! Book him as a man to be bribed!

XXI.

My beloved pupils, few have yet sufficiently studied the art by which the practice of jokes becomes subservient to the science of swindlers. The heart of an inferior is always fascinated by a jest. Men know this in the knavery of elections. Know it now, my pupils, in the knavery of life! When you slap yon cobbler so affectionately on the back it is your own fault if you do not slap your purpose into him at the same time. Note how Shakspeare (whom study night and day—no man hath better expounded the mysteries of roguery!) causes his grandest and most accomplished villain, Richard III., to address his good friends, the murderers, with a jocular panegyric on that hardness of heart on which, doubtless, those poor fellows most piqued themselves—

> " Your eyes drop millstones, where *fools'* eyes drop tears—
> I like you, lads '"

Can't you fancy the knowing grin with which the dogs received this compliment, and the little sly punch in the stomach with which Richard dropped those loving words, " I like you, lads!"

XXII.

As good-nature is the characteristic of the dupe, so should good-temper be that of the knave; the two fit into each other like joints. Happily, good-nature is a Narcissus, and falls in love with its own likeness. And good-temper is to good-nature what the Florimel of snow was to the Florimel of flesh—an exact likeness made of the coldest materials.

XXIII.

BEING THE PRAISE OF KNAVERY.

A knave is a philosopher, though a philosopher is not necessarily a knave. What hath a knave to do with passions. Every irregular desire he must suppress; every foible he must weed out; his whole life is spent in the acquisition of knowledge : for what is knowledge? —the discovery of human errors! He is the only man always consistent, yet ever examining; he knows but one end, yet explores every means; danger, ill-repute, all that terrify other men, daunt not him; he braves all, but is saved from all : for I hold that a knave ceaseth to be the knave—he hath passed into the fool—the moment mischief befalls him. He professes the art of cheating; but the *art* of cheating is to cheat without peril. He is *teres et rotundus,* strokes fly from the lubricity of his polish, and the shiftings of his circular formation. He who is insensible of the glory of his profession, who is open only to the profit, is no disciple of mine. I hold of knavery, as Plato hath said of virtue—"Could it be seen incarnate, it would beget a personal adoration!" None but those who are inspired by a generous enthusiasm, will benefit by the above maxims; nor (and here I warn you solemnly from the sacred ground, till your head be uncovered, and your feet be bared in the awe of veneration,) enter with profit upon the following descriptions of character—that Temple of the Ten Statues—wherein I have stored and consecrated the most treasured relics of my travelled thoughts and my collected experience.

TEN CHARACTERS.

I.

THE mild, irresolute, good-natured, and indolent man. These qualities are accompanied with good feelings, but no principles. The want of firmness evinces also the want of any peculiar or deeply-rooted system of thought. A man conning a single and favourite subject of meditation, grows wedded to one or the other of the opinions on which he revolves. A man universally irresolute, has generally led a desultory life, and never given his attention long together to one thing; this is a man most easy to cheat, my beloved friends; you cheat him even with his eyes open : indolence is dearer to him than all things, and if you get him alone and put a question to him point blank—he cannot answer. No,

II.

The timid, suspicious, selfish, and cold man. Generally, a character of this description is an excellent man of business, and would, at first sight, seem to baffle the most ingenious swindler. But you have one hope—I have rarely found it deceive me—this man is usually ostentatious. A cold, a fearful, yet a worldly person, has ever an eye upon others ; he notes the effect certain things produce on them ; he is anxious to learn their opinions, that he may not transgress ; he likes to know what the world say of him ; nay, his timidity makes him anxious to repose his selfishness on their good report. Hence he grows ostentatious, likes that effect which is favourably talked of, and that show which wins consideration. At him on this point, my pupils !

III.

The melancholy, retired, sensitive, intellectual character. A very good subject this for your knaveries, my young friends ; though it requires great discrimination and delicacy. This character has a considerable portion of morbid suspicion and irritation belonging to it—against these you must guard—at the same time, its prevailing feature is a powerful, but unacknowledged vanity. It is generally a good opinion of himself, and a feeling that he is not appreciated by others, that make a man reserved · he deems himself unfit for the world because of the delicacy of his temperament, and the want of a correspondent sensibility in those he sees ! This is your handle to work on. He is peculiarly flattered, too, on the score of devotion and affection ; he exacts in love, as from the world—too much. He is a Lara, whose females must be Medoras : and even his male friends should be extremely like Kaleds ! Poor man ! you see how easily he can be duped. Mem.—Among persons of this character are usually found those oddities, humours, and peculiarities, which are each a handle. No man lives out of the world with impunity to the solidity of his own character. Every new outlet to the humour is a new inlet to the heart

IV.

The bold, generous, frank, and affectionate man ;—usually a person of robust health. His constitution keeps him in spirits, and his spirits in courage and in benevolence. He is obviously not a hard character, my good young friends, for you to deceive : for he wants suspicion, and all his good qualities lay him open to you. But beware his anger when he finds you out ! he is a terrible Othello when his nature is once stung. Mem.—A good sort of character to seduce into illegal practices : makes a tolerable traitor, or a capital smuggle· · ·ou· ·· ··········· ·· ·· ····· ······· ··· ·····l offence :

ar'n't there cats-paws for the chesnuts? As all laws are oppressions (only necessary and often sacred oppressions, which you need not explain to him), and his character is especially hostile to oppression, you easily seduce the person we describe into braving the laws of his country Yes! the bold, generous, frank, and affectionate man, has only to be born in humble life to be sure of a halter!

V.

The bold, selfish, close, grasping man, will, in all probability, cheat *you*, my dear friends. For such a character makes the master-rogue, the stuff from which Nature forms a Richard the Third. You had better leave such a man quite alone. He is bad even to serve. He breaks up his tools when he has done with them. No, you can do nothing with him, my good young men!

VI.

The eating, drinking, unthoughtful, sensual, mechanical man—the ordinary animal. Such a creature has cunning, and is either cowardly or ferocious; seldom in these qualities he preserves a medium. He is not by any means easy to dupe. Nature defends her mental brutes by the thickness of their hide. Win his mistress if possible; she is the best person to manage him. Such creatures are the natural prey of artful women; their very stolidity covers all but sensuality. To the Sampson—the Dalilah

VII.

The gay, deceitful, shrewd, polished, able man; the courtier, the man of the world, In public and stirring life, this is the fit antagonist —often the successful and conquering rival of Character V. You perceive a man like this varies so greatly in intellect, from the mere butterfly talent to the rarest genius; from the person you see at cards to the person you see in cabinets—from the —— to the Chesterfield— from the Chesterfield to the Pericles;—that it is difficult to give you an exact notion of the weak points of a character so various. But while he dupes his equals and his superiors, I consider him, my attentive pupils, by no means a very difficult character for an inferior to dupe. And in this manner you must go about it. Do not attempt hypocrisy; he will see through it in an instant. Let him think you at once, and at first sight, a rogue. Be candid on that matter yourself: but let him think you *an useful* rogue. Serve him well and zealously: but own that you do so, because you consider your interest involved in this. This reasoning satisfies him; and as men of this character are usually generous, he will acknowledge its justice by throwing you plenty of sops, and stimulating you with bountiful cordials. Should he not content you herein, appear contented ; and profit in betraying him (*that* is the best way to cheat him), not by his failings, but by opportunity. Watch not his character, but your time.

VIII.

The vain, arrogant, brave, amorous, flashy character. This sort of character we formerly attributed to the French, and it is still more common to the Continent than that beloved island which I shall see no more ! A creature of this description is made up of many false virtues ; above others, it is always profuse where its selfishness is appealed to, not otherwise. You must find, then, what pleases it, and pander to its tastes. So will ye cheat it—or ye will cheat it also by affecting the false virtues which it admires itself—rouge your sentiments highly, and let them strut with a buskined air : thirdly, my good young men, ye will cheat it by profuse flattery, and by calling it in especial, "the mirror of chivalry."

IX.

The plain, sensible, honest man.—A favourable, but not elevated specimen of our race. This character, my beloved pupils, you may take in once, but never twice. Nor can you take in such a man as a stranger ; he must be your friend, or relation, or have known intimately some part of your family A man of this character is always open, though in a moderate and calm degree, to the duties and ties of life. He will always do something to serve his friend, his brother, or the man whose father pulled *his* father out of the Serpentine. Affect with him no varnish ; exert no artifice in attempting to obtain his assistance. Candidly state your wish for such or such a service—sensibly state your pretensions—modestly hint at your gratitude. So may you deceive him once, then leave him alone for ever !

X.

The fond, silly, credulous man ; all impulse, and no reflection !— How my heart swells when I contemplate this excellent character ! What a Canaan for you does it present ! I envy you launching into the world with the sanguine hope of finding all men such ! Delightful enthusiasm of youth—would that the hope could be realised ! Here is the very incarnation of gullibility. You have only to make him love you, and no hedgehog ever sucked egg as you can suck him. Never be afraid of his indignation ; go to him again and again ; only throw yourself on his neck and weep. To gull him once, is to gull him always ; get his first shilling, and then calculate what you will do with the rest of his fortune. Never desert so good a man for new friends · that would be ungrateful in you ! And take

with you, by the way, my good young gentlemen, this concluding
maxim. Men are like lands ; you will get more by lavishing all
your labour again and again upon the easy, than by ploughing up
new ground in the sterile !

Legislators—wise—good—pious men,—the Tom Thumbs of
moral science, who make giants first, and then kill them : [1] you
think the above lessons villanous : I honour your penetration ! they
are not proofs of my villany, but of your folly ! Look over them
again, and you will see that they are designed to show that while ye
are imprisoning, transporting, and hanging thousands every day, a
man with a decent modicum of cunning might practise every one of
those lessons which seem to you so heinous, and not one of your
laws could touch him !

> '' He made the giants first, and then he killed them.''
> *The Tragedy of Tom Thumb.*

BRACHYLOGIA;

OR

ESSAYS,

CRITICAL, SENTIMENTAL, MORAL, AND ORIGINAL.

ADDRESSED TO HIS PUPILS

By AUGUSTUS TOMLINSON.

The irony in the preceding essays is often lost sight of in the present. The illness of this great man, which happened while composing these little gems, made him perhaps more in earnest than when in robust health.—EDITOR'S NOTE.

ON THE MORALITY TAUGHT BY THE RICH TO THE POOR.

As soon as the urchin pauper can totter out of doors, it is taught to pull off its hat, and pull its hair to the quality. "A good little boy," says the squire; "there's a ha'penny for you." The good little boy glows with pride. That ha'penny instils deep the lesson of humility. Now goes our urchin to school. Then comes the Sunday teaching—before church—which enjoins the poor to be lowly, and to honour every man better off than themselves. A pound of honour to the squire, and an ounce to the beadle. Then the boy grows up; and the Lord of the Manor instructs him thus. "Be a good boy, Tom, and I'll befriend you; tread in the steps of your father; he was an excellent man, and a great loss to the parish; he was a very *civil, hard-working,* well-behaved creature, knew his station;—mind, and do like him!" So perpetual hard labour, and plenty of cringing, make the ancestral virtues to be perpetuated to peasants till the day of judgment! Another insidious distillation of morality is conveyed through a general praise of the poor. You hear false friends of the people, who call themselves Liberals, and Tories, who have an idea of morals, half chivalric, half pastoral, agree in lauding the unfortunate creatures whom they keep at work for them. But mark the virtues the poor are always to be praised for;—Industry, Honesty, and Content. The first virtue is extolled to the skies, because Industry gives the rich everything they have ; the second, because Honesty prevents an iota of the said everything being taken away again ; and the third, because Content is to hinder these poor devils from ever objecting to a lot, so comfortable to the persons who profit by it. This, my Pupils, is the morality taught by the Rich to the Poor !

EMULATION.

The great error of emulation is this,—we emulate effects without inquiring into causes ; when we read of the great actions of a man, we are on fire to perform the same exploits, without endeavouring to ascertain the precise qualities which enabled the man we imitate to commit the actions we admire. Could we discover these, how often might we discover that their origin was a certain temper of body, a certain peculiarity of constitution, and that, wish we for the same success, we should be examining the nature of our *bodies*, rather than sharpening the faculties of our minds ; should use dumb-bells, perhaps, instead of books ; nay, on the other hand, contract some grievous complaint, rather than perfect our moral salubrity. Who should say whether Alexander would have been a hero, had his neck been straight ? or Boileau a satirist, had he never been pecked by a turkey ? It would be pleasant to see you, my beloved pupils, after reading "Quintus Curtius," twisting each other's throat ; or, fresh from Boileau, hurrying to the poultry-yard, in the hope of being mutilated into the performance of a second Lutrin.

CAUTION AGAINST THE SCOFFERS OF "HUMBUG."

My beloved pupils, there is a set of persons in the world daily-increasing, against whom you must be greatly on your guard ; there is a fascination about them. They are people who declare them-selves vehemently opposed to humbug ; fine, liberal fellows, clear-sighted, yet frank. When these sentiments arise from reflection, well and good, they are the best sentiments in the world ; but many take them up second-hand ; they are very inviting to the indolence of the mob of gentlemen, who see the romance of a noble principle, not its utility. When a man looks at everything through this dwarfing philosophy, everything has a great modicum of humbug. You laugh with him when he derides the humbug in religion, the humbug in politics, the humbug in love, the humbug in the plausi-bilities of the world : but you may cry, my dear pupils, when he derides what is often the safest of all *practically* to deride,—the humbug in common honesty! Men are honest from religion, wisdom, prejudice, habit, fear, and stupidity; but the few only are wise; and the persons we speak of deride religion, are beyond prejudice, unawed by habit, too indifferent for fear, and too experienced for stupidity.

POPULAR WRATH AT INDIVIDUAL IMPRUDENCE.

You must know, my dear young friends, that while the appearance of magnanimity is very becoming to you, and so forth, it will get you a great deal of ill-will, if you attempt to practise it to your own detriment Your neighbours are so invariably, though perhaps insensibly, actuated by self-interest [1]—self-interest is so entirely, though every twaddler denies it, the axis of the moral world, that they fly into a rage with him who seems to disregard it. When a man ruins himself, just hear the abuse he receives; his neighbours take it as a personal affront !

DUM DEFLUAT AMNIS.

One main reason why men who have been great are disappointed, when they retire to private life, is this : memory makes a chief source of enjoyment to those who cease eagerly to hope ; but the memory of the great recalls only that public life which has disgusted them. Their private life hath slipped insensibly away, leaving faint traces of the sorrow or the joy which found them too busy to heed the simple and quiet impressions of mere domestic vicissitude.

SELF-GLORIFIERS.

Providence seems to have done to a certain set of persons, who always view their own things through a magnifying medium ; deem their house the best in the world, their gun the truest, their very pointer a miracle,—as Colonel Hanger suggested to economists to do, viz. provide their servants each with a pair of large spectacles, so that a lark might appear as big as a fowl, and a two-penny loaf as large as a quartern.

THOUGHT ON FORTUNE.

It is often the easiest move that completes the game. Fortune is like the lady whom a lover carried off from all his rivals by putting an additional lace upon his liveries.

---

[1] Mr. Tomlinson is wrong here But his ethics were too much narrowed to Utilitar— — — — — — — —

WIT AND TRUTH.

People may talk about fiction being the source of fancy; and wit being at variance with truth; now some of the wittiest things in the world are witty solely from their truth. Truth is the soul of a good saying. "You assert," observes the Socrates of modern times, "that we have a *virtual* representation; very well, let us have a virtual taxation too!" Here the wit is in the fidelity of the *sequitur*. When Columbus broke the egg, where was the wit?—In the completeness of conviction in the broken egg.

AUTO-THEOLOGY.

Not only every sect but every individual modifies the general attributes of the Deity towards assimilation with his own character: the just man dwells on the justice, the stern upon the wrath; the attributes that do not please the worshipper he insensibly forgets. Wherefore, oh my pupils, you will not smile when you read in Barnes that the pigmies declared Jove himself was a pigmy. The pious vanity of man makes him adore his own qualities under the pretence of worshipping those of his God.

GLORIOUS CONSTITUTION.

A sentence is sometimes as good as a volume. If a man ask you to give him some idea of the laws of England, the answer is short and easy: in the laws of England there are somewhere about one hundred and fifty laws by which a poor man may be hanged, but not one by which he can obtain justice for nothing!

ANSWER TO THE POPULAR CANT THAT GOODNESS IN A STATES-MAN IS BETTER THAN ABILITY.

As in the world we must look to actions, not motives, so a knave is the man who injures you; and you do not inquire whether the injury be the fruit of malice or necessity. Place then a fool in power, and he becomes unconsciously the knave. Mr. Addington stumbled on the two very worst and most villanous taxes human malice could have invented,—one on medicines, the other on justice. What tyrant's fearful ingenuity could afflict us more than by impeding at once redress for our wrongs and cure for our diseases? Mr. Addington was the fool *in se*, and therefore the knave in office; but, bless you! he never meant it!

COMMON SENSE.

Common sense—common sense. Of all phrases, all catchwords, this is often the most deceitful and the most dangerous. Look, in especial, suspiciously upon common sense whenever it is opposed to discovery. Common sense is the experience of every day. Discovery is something against the experience of every day. No wonder, then, that when Galileo proclaimed a great truth, the universal cry was, "Psha! common sense will tell you the reverse." Talk to a sensible man, for the first time, on the theory of vision, and hear what his common sense will say to it. In a letter in the time of Bacon, the writer, of no mean intellect himself, says, "It is a pity the chancellor should set his opinion against the experience of so many centuries and the dictates of common sense." Common sense, then, so useful in household matters, is less useful in the legislative and in the scientific world than it has been generally deemed. Naturally the advocate for what has been tried, and averse to what is speculative, it opposes the new philosophy that appeals to reason, and clings to the old which is propped by sanction.

LOVE, AND WRITERS ON LOVE.

My warm, hot-headed, ardent young friends, ye are in the flower of your life, and writing verses about love,—let us say a word on the subject. There are two species of love common to all men and to most animals;[1] one springs from the senses, the other glows out of custom. Now neither of these, my dear young friends, is the love that you pretend to feel—the love *of lovers*. Your passion having only its foundation (and that unacknowledged) in the senses, owes everything else to the imagination. Now the imagination of the majority is different in complexion and degree, in every country and in every age; so also, and consequently, is the love of the imagination: as a proof, observe that you sympathise with the romantic love of other times or nations only in proportion as you sympathise with their poetry and imaginative literature. The love which stalks through the Arcadia, or Amadis of Gaul, is to the great bulk of readers coldly insipid, or solemnly ridiculous. Alas! when those works excited enthusiasm, so did the love which they describe. The long speeches, the icy compliments, expressed the feeling of the day. The love madrigals of the time of Shenstone, or the brocade gallantries of the French poets in the last century, any woman now would consider hollow or childish, imbecile or artificial. *Once* the songs were natural and the love seductive. And now, my young friends, in the year 1822, in which I write, and shall probably die, the love which glitters through Moore, and walks so ambitiously ambiguous through the verse of Byron; the love which you consider now so deep and so true; the love which tingles through the hearts

1 .1.

of your young ladies, and sets you young gentlemen gazing on
the evening star; all that love too will become unfamiliar or
ridiculous to an after age; and the young aspirings, and the moon-
light dreams, and the vague fiddle-de-dees, which ye now think so
touching and so sublime, will go, my dear boys, where Cowley's
Mistress and Waller's Sacharissa have gone before; go with the
Sapphos and the Chloes, the elegant "charming fairs," and the
chivalric "most beauteous princesses!" The only love-poetry that
stands through all time and appeals to all hearts, is that which is
founded on either or both the species of love natural to all men; the
love of the senses, and the love of custom. In the latter is included
what middle-aged men call the rational attachment, the charm of
congenial minds, as well as the homely and warmer accumulation of
little memories of simple kindness, or the mere brute habitude of
seeing a face as one would see a chair. These, sometimes singly,
sometimes skilfully blended, make the theme of those who have
perhaps loved the most honestly and the most humanly; these yet
render Tibullus pathetic, and Ovid a master over tender affections;
and these, above all, make that irresistible and all-touching inspiration which subdues the romantic, the calculating, the old, the
young, the courtier, the peasant, the poet, the man of business, in
the glorious love-poetry of Robert Burns.

THE GREAT ENTAILED.

The great inheritance of man is a commonwealth of blunders;
one race spend their lives in botching the errors transmitted to them
by another; and the main cause of all political, *i.e.*, all the worst
and most general, blunders is this,—the same rule we apply to
individual cases we will not apply to public. All men consent that
swindling for a horse is swindling,—they punish the culprit and
condemn the fault. But in a state there is no such unanimity.
Swindling, Lord help you! is called by some fine name, and
cheating grows grandiloquent, and styles itself "Policy." In consequence of this, there is always a battle between those who call
things by their right names, and those who pertinaciously give them
the wrong ones. Hence all sorts of confusion; this confusion
extends very soon to the laws made for individual cases; and thus
in old states, though the world is still agreed that private swindling
is private swindling, there is the devil's own difficulty in punishing
the swindling of the public. The art of swindling now is a different
thing to the art of swindling an hundred years ago; but the laws
remain the same. Adaptation in private cases is innovation in
public; so, without repealing old laws they make new,—sometimes
these are effectual but more often not. Now, my beloved pupils, a

law is a gun, which if it misses a pigeon always kills a crow ;—if it does not strike the guilty it hits some one else. As every crime creates a law, so in turn every law creates a crime ; and hence we go on multiplying sins and evils, and faults and blunders, till society becomes the organised disorder for picking pockets.

THE REGENERATION OF A KNAVE.

A man who begins the world by being a fool, often ends it by becoming a knave ; but he who begins as a knave, if he be a rich man (and so not hanged), may end, my beloved pupils, in being a pious creature. And this is the wherefore : "a knave early" soon gets knowledge of the world. One vice worn out makes us wiser than fifty tutors. But wisdom causes us to love quiet, and in quiet we do not sin. He who is wise and sins not can scarcely fail of doing good ; for let him but *utter* a new truth, and even his imagination cannot conceive the limit of the good he may have done to man !

STYLE.

Do you well understand what a wonderful thing style is ? I think not ; for in the exercises you sent me, your styles betrayed that no very earnest consideration had been lavished upon them. Know, then, that you must pause well before you take up any model of style. On your style often depends your own character,—almost always the character given you by the world. If you adopt the lofty style ;—if you string together noble phrases and swelling sonora, you have expressed, avowed, a flame of mind which you will insensibly desire to act up to : the desire gradually begets the capacity. The life of Dr. Parr is Dr. Parr's style put in action. And Lord Byron makes himself through existence unhappy for having accidentally slipped into a melancholy current of words. But suppose you escape this calamity by a peculiar hardihood of temperament, you escape not the stamp of popular opinion. Addison must ever be held by the vulgar the most amiable of men, because of the social amenity of his diction ; and the admirers of language will always consider Burke a nobler spirit than Fox, because of the grandeur of his sentences. How many wise sayings have been called jests because they were wittily uttered ! How many nothings swelled their author into a sage ; ay, a saint, because they were strung together by the old hypocrite nun—Gravity !

THE END.

R. Clay and Sons London and Bungay